ED

RES

Published in Association with
The Open University

The Open University

P·C·P
Paul Chapman
Publishing Ltd

Paul Chapman Publishing Ltd
144 Liverpool Road
London
N1 1LA

British Library Cataloguing in Publication Data

Improving Educational Management Through
Research and Consultancy
  I. Bennett, Nigel
  371.2

ISBN 1-85396-277-5

Typeset by Dorwyn Ltd, Rowlands Castle, Hants
Printed and bound by Athenaeum Press Ltd, Gateshead, Tyne & Wear.

A B C D E F G H   9 8 7 6 5 4

This reader comprises a collection of papers published in connection with the Open University course *Educational Management in Action* (E828). This course involves carrying out three small-scale investigations of management practice and making recommendations for improved practice.

This reader is one part of an Open University integrated teaching system and the selection is therefore related to other material available. The editors have nevertheless attempted to make it of value to all those concerned with undertaking small-scale investigations of professional practice. Opinions expressed in it are not necessarily those of the course team or of the University.

# Contents

*Acknowledgements* ix

Introduction: Investigating Educational Management 1
NIGEL BENNETT

PART ONE: RESEARCH AND CONSULTANCY FOR
CHANGE AND IMPROVEMENT 9

1 Change and Leadership 11
ANDREW LEIGH

2 An Analysis of Selected School Improvement Practices 27
COLIN MARSH

3 Rethinking Professional Development 46
KAREN OSTERMAN AND ROBERT KOTTKAMP

4 Consultants, Clients and the Consulting Process 58
PETER COCKMAN, BILL EVANS AND PETER REYNOLDS

5 The Philosophy of Research Design 76
MARK EASTERBY-SMITH, RICHARD THORPE AND
ANDY LOWE

6 Research ethics 93
R. M. BERGER AND M. A. PATCHNER

PART TWO: APPROACHES TO INVESTIGATION 99

7 Evaluation in the Management Cycle 101
GLYN ROGERS AND LINDA BADHAM

8 Auditing as Institutional Research: A Qualitative Focus 117
DAVID M. FETTERMAN

9 Surveys 127
L. COHEN AND L. MANION

10 Designing Single- and Multiple-Case Studies 135
ROBERT K. YIN

11 Action Research for Managing Change 156
PAMELA LOMAX

**PART THREE: METHODS OF DATA COLLECTION,
ANALYSIS AND PRESENTATION**   169

12 Planning Small-Scale Research   171
DAPHNE JOHNSON

13 Diagnosis, Data Collection and Feedback in Consultancy   187
PHILIP HOPE

14 Using Success Criteria   209
KATH ASPINWALL, TIM SIMKINS, JOHN F. WILKINSON
AND M. JOHN MCAULEY

15 Literature Searching: Finding, Organizing and Recording
Information   223
SALLY BAKER AND JOAN CARTY

16 Analysing Documents and Records   237
COLIN ROBSON

17 Designing and Using Questionnaires   248
M. B. YOUNGMAN

18 Conducting and Analysing Interviews   267
E. C. WRAGG

19 Telephone Interviewing   283
BRIAN FIDLER

20 Exploring Institutional Images Through Focus Group Interviews   290
TRUDY H. BERS

21 On Diaries and Diary Keeping   300
ROBERT G. BURGESS

22 Observing and Recording Meetings   312
G. L. WILLIAMS

23 Observation Outside Meetings   325
L. COHEN AND L. MANION

24 Analysing and Presenting Quantitative Data   330
JASON HARDMAN

25 Analysing Qualitative Data   344
MARK EASTERBY-SMITH, RICHARD THORPE AND
ANDY LOWE

26 Using a Computer for Personal Efficiency   353
ROSALIND LEVAČIĆ

27 Writing the Report   364
JUDITH BELL

*Index*   375

# Acknowledgements

We thank those listed below for their permission to use the following copyrighted material:

CHAPTER 1 reprinted by permission of The Institute of Personnel Management from Andrew Leigh (1988) *Effective Change: Twenty Ways to Make it Happen*, London, Institute of Personnel Management.

CHAPTER 2 reprinted by permission of the author, from Colin Marsh (1988) *Spotlight on School Improvement*, Sydney, Allen & Unwin. pp. 21–2 and Ch 9.

CHAPTER 3 reprinted by permission of Corwin Press, Inc., from K. Osterman and R. Kottkamp, *Reflective Practice for Educators: Improving Schooling through professional Development*, Ch. 2, Corwin Press, 1993.

CHAPTER 4 reprinted by permission of McGraw-Hill, from P Cockman, B Evans and P Reynolds (1992) *Client-Centred Consulting*, McGraw-Hill Book Company Europe, Ch 1.

CHAPTERS 5 AND 25 reprinted by permission of Sage Publications, from: M. Easterby-Smith, R. Thorpe and A. Lowe (1991) *Management Research – an introduction*, London, Sage, Ch 3 and pp. 104–15.

CHAPTER 6 R. M. Berger and M. A. P chner, Implementing The Research Plan, Sage Human Services Guide no 51, 1988.

CHAPTER 7 reprinted by permission of Routledge, from G Rogers and L Badham (1992) *Evaluation in Schools*, London, Routledge, Chs 1 and 2.

CHAPTER 8 reprinted by permission of Jossey-Bass Inc., from D Fetterman (1991) *Using Qualitative Methods in Institutional Research*, New Directions in Institutional Research no. 72. Copyright © 1991 by Jossey-Bass Inc, Publishers.

CHAPTERS 9 AND 23 reprinted by permission of Routledge, from L Cohen and L Manion (1994) *Research Methods in Education* 3/e, London, Routledge, Ch 4 and pp. 122–9.

CHAPTER 10 reprinted by permission of Sage Publications, Inc., from R. K. Yin, Designing Single- and Multiple-Case Studies, pp. 27–60. *Case Study Research: Design and Methods* (Revised edition) 1989, Sage Publications, Inc.

CHAPTERS 11 AND 12 copyright © 1994 The Open University.

CHAPTER 13 reprinted by permission of Longman Group Ltd., from P Hope (1992) *Making the Best Use of Consultants*, Harlow, Longman, Chs 5 and 6.

CHAPTER 14 reprinted by permission of Routledge, from K Aspinwall, T Simkins, J F Williams and M J McAuley (1992) *Managing Evaluation in Education*, London, Routledge, Ch 7.

CHAPTER 15 copyright © 1994 The Open University.

CHAPTER 16 reprinted by permission of Blackwell Publishers, from C Robson (1993) *Real World Research,* Oxford, Blackwell, pp. 272–85.

CHAPTER 17 this version copyright © 1994 The Open University. Revised by the author, from M B Youngman (1992) Rediguide 12, Guides in Educational Research, Nottingham, Rediguides.

CHAPTER 18 reprinted by permission of the author, from E C Wragg, Rediguide 11, Guides in Educational Research, Nottingham, Rediguides.

CHAPTER 19 reprinted by permission of the author, from Brian Fidler (1992) Telephone Interviewing, a paper presented at the 4th Research Conference of the British Educational Management and Administration Society.

CHAPTER 20 reprinted by permission of Jossey-Bass Inc., from R S Lay and J J Endo (eds.) (1987) *Designing and using Market Research,* New Directions for Institutional Research no 54. Copyright 1991 by Jossey-Bass Inc., Publishers.

CHAPTERS 21 AND 22 © copyright 1994 The Open University.

CHAPTER 24 © copyright 1994 The Open University.

CHAPTER 26 copyright © 1994 The Open University

CHAPTER 27 reprinted by permission of Open University Press, from J Bell (1993) *Doing Your Research Project 2/e,* Buckingham, Open University Press, Ch 12.

*Every effort has been made to trace and acknowledge ownership of copyright. The publishers will be glad to make suitable arrangements with any copyright holders from whom it has not been possible to elicit a response.*

# Investigating Educational Management

## NIGEL BENNETT

## WHAT THIS BOOK IS ABOUT

This collection of articles is designed to help people who need to investigate their own professional practice or that of their colleagues. It is intended to provide practical assistance with the work of designing, carrying out, and presenting the findings of small-scale investigations. Such studies have always been a part of higher degree work, but they are also being carried out increasingly as part of the continuing process of review and reflection on practice which should inform all professional development. We hope that we can help to encourage both better professional review and more reflection on individual and organizational development by equipping educational professionals with the understanding and ability necessary to carry out good investigations sensitively and well.

The focus of the discussion in the book is on educational management. However, investigating management practice raises many of the same questions as investigating classroom practice or other forms of professional activity, and the issues addressed and methods examined in this book are therefore relevant to anyone working in education who wishes to examine and reflect on their professional practice, or who may wish to assist others in that process.

## INVESTIGATING EDUCATIONAL MANAGEMENT

Management in education has become the management of change. National and local policies throughout the world have required educational establishments from nursery schools through to universities to take on board new legislative requirements and obligations and come to terms with new ways of thinking about the delivery of public services. Faced with a plethora of changing demands, managers have to balance the twin demands of implementing changes and providing a bulwark against too much change so as to create a stable working environment for their colleagues and those they teach.

Managers are not concerned just with their own work, because their work involves that of other people. They are expected to motivate their colleagues, to provide leadership and support, and to encourage the professional development of those who work within their area of responsibility. But managers also have another potential role to play, as a support to colleagues outside their immediate area of responsibility. Just as many teachers seek out professional assistance informally from the network of experience and expertise to be found in the staffroom or faculty common room, so competent managers can provide similar assistance in the field of management to their colleagues. Although the term has rarely been used to describe such supportive activity, this kind of informal support is akin to that provided more formally by the internal adviser or internal consultant who is common in some parts of industry and commerce. In England and Wales, where the move to site-based management is being accompanied by a progressive reduction in the role and funding of local authority advisory services, the support schools have traditionally received free from this source is being both reduced and charged for. A school or college which can develop a structured resource of potential internal consultants is better placed to cope with the consequences of the change in the status of the advisory services than one which cannot.

The central parts of any consultancy assignment are investigation and reporting. One is engaged as a consultant because the client has a problem and needs help in solving it. A major function of this book therefore is to assist would-be consultants to develop the skills needed for investigating complex management problems. In many ways, these skills are those of the researcher, and we have designed the book so that it can be used by more traditional researchers undertaking small-scale projects for other reasons, for example as part of a management development programme. However, as well as having the skills of data collection and analysis, it is also important to ensure that the approach taken to studying the problem is appropriate. This requires the investigator to give some thought to the kind of project being undertaken, the kinds of data likely to be sought, and how those data are likely to be affected by the particular research techniques and strategies employed. We felt therefore that it was essential that a book on methods of investigation should give some thought to these questions too.

Investigating educational management problems, however, is not simply an activity which people do on behalf of others. We can also be faced with difficult decisions or apparently intractable problems in our own work which we need to investigate and resolve. Many of the techniques and considerations discussed in this book are relevant to such work, but we also include some discussion of what is increasingly being seen as a central aspect of personal development: reflection on the thinking behind one's practice. We argue that all of us bring to our work a set of 'theories in use' through which we make sense of what is happening and identify what we ought to do in any given situation. They are usually deeply internalized and drawn upon unconsciously. A necessary part of dealing with problems is engaging with such theories, bringing them into our conscious thinking and, if necessary, allowing them to be developed and changed. Such an activity may also be an important part of our consultancy role, if we find that there is a resistance to acknowledging key elements of the problem which we believe we can identify. Then we may have to try and persuade our clients to engage in such reflection, extending the nature of our consultancy relationship.

This book, then, is divided into three parts. The first, covering Chapters 1 to 6, outlines a number of key concepts and perspectives which we believe it is essential the budding researcher or consultant should take on board in order that necessary fundamental questions about the nature of the study and the role of the investigator can be addressed. This part locates our view of management investigations in writing about change, leadership and institutional improvement, and introduces our view of the nature of reflection and consultancy. It discusses the nature of the knowledge we acquire through our inquiries, and outlines some ethical issues. The second part, covering Chapters 7 to 11, examines a number of what we have called major strategies of research appropriate to the kind of small-scale management investigation which is typically done 'in-house' or as part of a management development course. It provides general discussions of the nature and applicability of evaluation studies, surveys, case studies and action research. The last part, which covers Chapters 12 to 27, introduces a range of methods and techniques of planning, data collection, data analysis and presentation which are relevant to the kinds of study we anticipate being taken by readers of this book.

## PART ONE: CONCEPTS AND PERSPECTIVES

This book is designed on the basis that the reason why individuals investigate management problems is to improve management practice. Therefore we begin by reviewing briefly some of the writing on change strategies in education. In Chapter 1, Leigh explores a number of key concepts in the management of change and develops from that a view of the manager as leader in bringing about change. He points out that change can be strategic or operational, and suggests that it has different dimensions – political, cultural and technical. A similar view of change, derived from the writings of House (1979), is used by Marsh in his discussion of what he calls 'school improvement' strategies which forms Chapter 2. He examines critically the self-managing school model of Caldwell and Spinks, which became very popular in the early 1990s, and two other approaches which he sees as less technical and more political/cultural: an approach which he calls 'people-centred action', and action research. These two chapters establish a frame of reference in which to consider the kinds of investigations you might be making, the purposes they might serve, and therefore the kinds of methods and strategies you might employ.

Chapter 3, by Osterman and Kottkamp, introduces the idea of personal reflection as a fundamental requirement of individual change, and examines its assumptions, as well as discussing how the role of the tutor on a management development course is changed by a move from traditional to reflective modes of delivery. This element of the chapter is important, because it recognizes that to some extent when you engage in an investigation, the activity is part of the learning exercise both for you and for those who are involved in helping you. The manager who is investigating management practice with a view to bringing about improvements should see the process as a learning activity for all involved. To do so is to recognize that change only occurs when the people involved are prepared to acknowledge both that it is needed and that what is being proposed is reasonable. This draws most small-scale investigations of management practice away from the traditional model of research towards a form of consultancy. However, much consultancy is seen as the importing of an expert who can tell you what to do and then collect a large fee for leaving you to sort out the consequences. This model has become increasingly discredited as consultants and clients alike have recognized that there is a more complex process at work. Clients have their own view of the problem, and consultants may have to negotiate and renegotiate the nature of the study. They may also need to involve their clients actively not just in providing information but in developing the investigation as it goes along. This view of consultancy is developed by Cockman, Evans and Reynolds in Chapter 4, where they link the view of the consultancy process with the Kolb (1985) model of learning that also underpins Chapter 3.

Chapter 5 extends the discussion to consider the assumptions which we make when deciding on the kind of investigation we are going to undertake. Much of our thinking assumes that there is an objective truth 'out there', which can be identified and tested. This may be a helpful way of thinking about knowledge of the technical world, but can be less useful if we are trying to take account of what people think or feel, and management research often has to be concerned with thoughts and feelings. In Chapter 5, Easterby-Smith, Thorpe and Lowe explore what they call two basic paradigms of research into management: positivist and phenomenological or interpretivist. (The term interpretivist is probably better, since 'phenomenology' is variously used both as a general alternative to positivism and as a specific philosophy within a broader, non-positivist perspective.) In developing this characterization of approaches to management research, Easterby-Smith *et al.* discuss a number of practical questions which any intending investigator needs to consider when trying to identify and design a potential project. The chapter is followed by a short examination by Berger and Patchner of a number of key ethical concerns which also need consideration (Chapter 6).

## PART TWO: APPROACHES TO INVESTIGATION

The next five chapters introduce several different strategies of research, and offer one significant omission. They begin with a discussion of evaluation by Rogers and Badham (Chapter 7). Most management research is likely to have an evaluative element in it, and since the intention of this book is that the investigations its readers carry out are concerned to bring about improvements, evaluation becomes almost inevitable. However, much 'evaluation' is carried out without having made any attempt to clarify what is being evaluated, why and how: Rogers and Badham present a clear and simple approach to considering these basic questions.

With Chapter 8, we look in more detail at one major element of evaluation: the idea of audit. Audit is normally associated with financial regulation and monitoring, and indeed monitoring and audit are often seen as synonymous – simply finding out what is happening without asking the wider evaluative questions of whether it should be taking place. However, Fetterman's discussion of institutional audit widens the possible uses of auditing strategies so that they become a valuable approach to investigation in their own right.

Chapter 9, by Cohen and Manion, discusses doing surveys, the form of investigation probably associated most commonly with the word 'research'. Surveys can be an important part of investigations into management, and might sometimes stand alone as the entire study – a survey of parental attitudes, perhaps.

Chapter 10, by Yin, introduces a detailed examination of another increasingly common form of management investigation: the case study. Case studies are common as teaching materials, and since they are almost by definition concerned with single instances of a particular problem they are a typical form of consultancy investigation. However, Yin identifies different forms of case study, and suggests ways in which it might be possible to generalize from the particular case to other circumstances, and towards the proposal of a specific theory for subsequent testing through other, replicatory case studies. Although some of his arguments are perhaps more relevant to larger studies than the smaller-scale projects we envisage most of our readers undertaking, he is making important points about the strengths of the case study model, and also for case studies, rather than experimental studies of the traditional scientific method, as a major route for the development of new theory in the social sciences. As we agree that experimental research is rarely if ever appropriate for the sort of investigations we anticipate our readers undertaking, we have not included it. Yin's discussion of the process of undertaking case study investigations, the pitfalls open to the investigator, and ways of overcoming them, presents important advice to the author of any case study, whatever its scale and scope.

In the last chapter of this part, Lomax introduces the key concepts of action research. Action research places the investigator in the centre of the process being investigated, and sees change as the purpose of the enterprise. It is therefore important to see how it relates to the discussion of change and school improvement in Chapters 1 and 2, and to the discussion of personal reflection in Chapter 3. It is also worth pointing out that action research is essentially a cyclical process, and so for it to be carried through to a satisfactory conclusion the researcher will need to have a reasonable timescale in which to operate. Consultants and readers undertaking small-scale projects may find action research difficult to use for this reason, but the clarity of Lomax's outline will allow readers to judge when it might be appropriate and whether their circumstances make it possible.

## PART THREE: METHODS OF DATA COLLECTION, ANALYSIS AND PRESENTATION

Part Three, the longest section of the book, presents the reader with a tool-kit of approaches to the basic work of investigation. Chapter 12, by Johnson, outlines the planning and execution process for the traditional small-scale research project. Much of the advice is relevant to any kind of investigation. Chapter 13, by Hope, explores the process of data collection, analysis and presentation in a client-centred consultancy. The differences between research and consultancy are pointed up sharply in this chapter, especially in the discussion of analysis and presentation. Chapter 14, by Aspinwall *et al.*, deals with the basic evaluative task of generating success criteria.

After these three general chapters, we move into a range of data collection chapters. Chapter 15, by Baker and Carty, outlines ways of accessing the literature on the subject of your investigation, while Chapter 16, by Robson, deals with procedures for analysing documents. The approach to content analysis discussed here can also be useful when analysing other data such as diaries or interview data, although it may be too positivist an approach for some, as Chapter 25 demonstrates. Chapter 17, by Youngman, takes you through the process of questionnaire design and analysis, while Chapters 18 to 20 explore different aspects of interviewing. Wragg's Chapter 18 discusses the demands of individual face-to-face interviews, and also makes reference to group interviews, while Fidler examines the procedures necessary for telephone interviewing in Chapter 19. Telephone interviewing is becoming a more common approach to data collection now, but little has been written about it. In Chapter 20, Bers discusses the processes involved in running focus group interviews, an important but often underused approach to collecting data on feelings and ideas which has been extensively used in market research and by some healthcare researchers. Bers also indicates the limitations of the approach.

Chapter 21, by Burgess, examines the use of diary evidence. Much has been written, notably by Burgess himself, about the use of a diary by a researcher; in this chapter, he examines how the diary might be used as a source of data from others. Chapters 22 and 23 are concerned with the use of observation techniques: Chapter 22, by Williams, looks at observing and recording meetings, while in Chapter 23 Cohen and Manion discuss observation in other settings. Observation can be an important means of gathering both background information and more substantive data, central to the study.

The next two chapters are concerned with data analysis. In most cases, the small-scale study is unlikely to generate sufficient data from sufficient sources to make substantial statistical testing worth while, but it is often possible, as Chapter 5 suggested, to exploit and present numerical data effectively in even quite small studies. In Chapter 24, Hardman examines the analysis and presentation of simple quantitative data. We examine the process of preparing and analysing qualitative data through the second extract we have drawn from Easterby-Smith *et al.*, which forms Chapter 25. Although they are assuming comprehensive interview transcripts in their discussion, the procedures they recommend are applicable even to less comprehensive qualitative data, and they make useful warnings about the limits of some approaches to content analysis.

The last two chapters of this part examine more overall concerns. In Chapter 26, Levačić outlines some of the uses to which a personal computer can be put, and demonstrates how much time it can save. The final chapter, by Bell, in a sense takes us back to the opening chapter of this part, in outlining the procedures for writing up and checking the final draft of the research report. Those readers who are undertaking a consultancy report should read this final chapter alongside Hope's discussion of data analysis and presentation in consultancies in Chapter 13.

# A FINAL COMMENT

This book is not designed to be read from cover to cover! Part Three in particular is a quarry to be exploited as needed. However, Parts One and Two, which are concerned with the prior assumptions and expectations you have of a study, would repay careful reading before embarking on any investigation: the questions they pose are important, and failure to address them could all too easily lead to serious problems. Small-scale practical studies should assist us to develop and improve our personal practice and cope with change. We should undertake them with a clear awareness of the assumptions behind our study, and our involvement with the subject being investigated. Without this, it is all too easy to finish with a project which does not deliver what was wanted, or even fails to deliver anything at all!

# REFERENCES

House, E. R. (1979) Technology versus craft: a ten-year perspective on innovation, *Journal of Curriculum Studies*, Vol. 11, no. 1, pp. 1–15.
Kolb, D. (1985) *Learning style inventory*. Boston, MA: McBer.

# PART ONE

## *Research and Consultancy for Change and Improvement*

# CHAPTER 1

## *Change and Leade*

ANDREW LEIGH

Several factors are causing a re-think about how managers should handle change. First, there is the realization that organizational change is here to stay. We must stop opposing it and, like a judo expert, turn it to our advantage.

Stability was once a central management goal. The demand was for organizations in which you could predict and control events, organizations in which it was 'safe' to work. A manager worrying about stability becomes fixated on information and control. [. . .]

Yet stability is only one type of goal. Equally relevant are those shown in Figure 1.1. Organizations wanting to survive and grow must abandon the

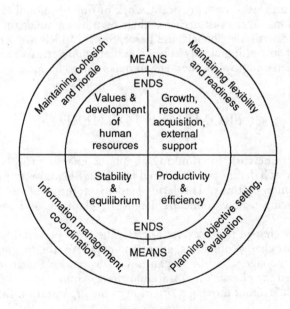

FIGURE 1.1 The goals managers seek

effects of demanding certainty, predictability and minimal risk. Nor they opt solely for growth, productivity or simply developing human sets.

Competing goals force us to accept that moving towards one may take us away from another. Hence we must be willing to accept a certain amount of instability. Taking this view to its logical conclusion the American efficiency specialist Tom Peters argues that 'success will come to those who love chaos – constant change, not those who attempt to eliminate it.'

The second factor that has forced a re-think in handling change is the accelerating pace of change. The impact has become so noticeable that in the 1970s Alvin Toffler dubbed it 'Future Shock' and people have been writing, researching and commenting on it ever since. [. . .]

Many managers, unsure how to respond, become obsessed with structures, centralization versus de-centralization, quality of work programmes, revamping incentive systems, new personnel systems and so on. Once it hardly mattered if change was approached in such a narrow way as there was scope to recover from any major mistakes. But for the foreseeable future the climate is turbulent and stressful, and the high price of large-scale failure has become unacceptably high.

Considering the mass of contradictory advice from often highly credible and respectable sources, it is no wonder that many managers believe that learning to handle change constructively only comes from hard won experience (see Box [1]). Yet it is possible to make some sense of what seems to work. A useful starting point is to have a model of organizational change which you can personally use, a mind map which is not confined to textbooks and management courses.

There is no universal model or framework of organizational change, however, and each manager must arrive at their own by an amalgam of personal values, hunches, attitudes, beliefs and perceptions. Models are a mind set for thinking about something clearly. They stimulate more creative ways of tackling where, when and how to intervene to make things happen.

## FROM HERE TO THERE

The simplest framework for thinking about the change process appears in Figure 1.2 in which diagnosis of the need for change leads on to planning and eventually to interventions. The latter lead to more problems and opportunities producing a new round of diagnosis, planning and interventions. [. . .]

We can view change from several angles. The most personal is how we as individuals must change ourselves, adapt and cope. Another angle, of particular interest to managers, is how organizations as a whole change. Excessive usage has turned the phrase 'organizational change' into a woolly concept, but at its simplest it is about moving a situation in the organization from

HERE to  . . . . . . . . . . . . . . . . . . . . . . . . . . . . . . . .  THERE.

BOX 1

## Conflicting advice about change

| | |
|---|---|
| Analyse the need for change thoroughly | Don't bother! Organizations are too complex to justify the effort |
| Don't rush into action. Be more reflective about the likely impact of change | Have a bias for action; beware of the paralysis of analysis; action precipitates change |
| We know little about the true levers of change | We know quite a lot! Research has uncovered the essential change process and how to make it happen |
| Resistance to change is bad | Resistance is functional and should be welcomed |
| When you have made a big change evaluate before continuing | Maintain the momentum; heap change on change to get real results |
| Go to great lengths to tell people what changes you want | Avoid announcements; make changes quietly so they become established facts of life |
| Reactive management is bad | Reactive management is good |
| Managers should be highly proactive | Managers are too prone to rush into action |
| Good managers do not need to use power relationships to achieve change | Effective managers use power relationships to foster change |
| Stability should follow from a major change effort | Stability is unattainable and undesirable |
| React to the environment to avoid organizational obsolescence | Act on the environment and transform it |
| Treat the organization as a giant system – everything depends on everything else | Treat the organization as merely loosely linked subsystems |
| To manage change manage the interdependencies | To manage change promote individualism and personal autonomy |
| Change is best generated by good teamwork | Real change stems from rampant individualism and product or service champions |
| Go for evolutionary, step-by-step change | Go for radical transformations |
| Participation reduces the power gap between managers and subordinates | Participation leaves the power gap unchanged, it merely links the needs of managers and subordinates |

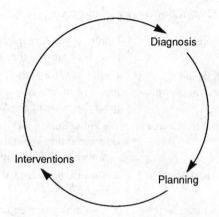

FIGURE 1.2  A simplified view of the change process

[. . .] There are two main types of organizational change:

- strategic;
- operational (day-to-day).

The first is highly distinctive and relates to the future direction of the organization affecting one or more of the goals shown in Figure 1.1. Strategic change involves some major switch in what the organization does and how it does it, and it usually takes place over months or years, rather than days or weeks.

Operational or day-to-day change, on the other hand, happens constantly. Managers are always either causing or responding to events which seldom in themselves amount to strategic change, although a succession of day-to-day events can accumulate into a significant shift. Another angle on operational change is that it is mainly opportunity change in which managers take advantages of situations to alter situations [. . .].

## CHANGING MODELS [OF CHANGE]

Models and theories [. . .] of change are often spurned because they:

- do not accurately reflect the real world;
- are incomplete and can encourage narrow thinking;
- seldom offer detailed, validated guidance for action.

Despite these drawbacks they provide a rough framework, a mind set, within which to consider what results you want, how you might achieve them and the possible consequences of any actions. Apart from models of the change process itself there have been three important ways of viewing organizations that have influenced management thinking this century and hence how to achieve effective change: the traditional or classical model; the human relations model; and the systems model.

## Traditional/classical model

The traditional/classical model sees organizations as machines, with layers of management, concerned mainly with mass production. Specialization is triumphant. What counts are the buzz words of scheduling, planning, organizing, monitoring, motivating [and] counselling.

This model directs attention to spans of control and requires that people's authority matches their responsibilities. It has lost favour because it is rigid, predictable and does not reflect what actually occurs in real organizations.

## Human relations model

Human relations models view organizations as living organisms with mutually connected and interdependent parts. Authority flows from below upwards, not from the top down. Groups have as much influence on change as the manager. This model is a reaction to the stark certainties of the mechanistic approach.

The buzz words for this model are managing groups, understanding the informal parts of the organization, an emphasis on democratic leadership, flat hierarchies and team development.

## Systems model

[. . .] The systems model is a response to growing size and complexity. Confusion is made manageable by treating the organization rather like a giant computer. Jargon from the computer field is used, such as inputs, outputs and various processes in between.

In a giant system everything is related to everything else. For managers the message is:

- To handle change well you must understand the whole, then unravel how the bits fit together.

The buzz words for this model are openness in relationships, need for rationality, teamwork and cohesive groups, interdependence, and so on. The systems model has had a significant impact on how managers handle change, particularly advanced technology. It has focused attention on what results the organization wants and is achieving.

This model is losing its appeal because practical experience shows that mastering the interdependence of a giant, tightly linked system is beyond the skills of the majority of managers, no matter how well equipped they might be with analytical tools.
[. . .]

## The loosely coupled system

From this battleground of models has come a more pragmatic view of the organization. It is a realistic response to the extreme rate of change of our times.

Although the organization is still seen as various subsystems these are almost independent and only loosely linked to create the whole. They are systems of action rather than geographical chunks of the enterprise. The systems model makes managers take a macro look at the organization by expecting them to understand its parts by first understanding the whole. The loosely coupled model, on the other hand, asks managers to take a more micro view, expecting them to grasp the whole through understanding the parts.

This newer model accepts change and turbulence; despite their impact the entire system is bound together by shared values, sentiments and symbols. The manager is still concerned with interdependencies, but between different systems of action, not people. The main actor in this model is often the individual, not a group.

The buzz words for this model are de-centralization, devolution, smaller corporate headquarters, smaller business units, and the autonomy of individuals. For senior managers interested in handling change the loosely coupled model has important implications. One of the main tasks of top management is managing the organization's culture and values. Managers are concerned with developing an overall vision with which to inspire and direct the subsystems.

Teamwork is taken for granted. Individuals are not trapped by the group's boundaries. When the interests of the organization demand it individuals act to transform and if necessary transcend the group. In this model the personal values which individual employees hold are important, not a minor irritation. What counts is how you promote the freedom of the individual to work with others for the benefit of the organization. Thus personal autonomy has a central place in this particular model.

Strengthening the individual's role is a particular challenge for managers. It has been seen to work, for example, in abolishing quality inspectors and putting the responsibility where it belongs, with those actually doing the work. Widening the individual's role means tolerating ambiguity, independence, and an ability to deal with complexity. Consequently the management skills for handling change are different to those previously expected. There is more emphasis on empathy and feelings, on transforming skills such as visualization techniques and on certain types of mental abilities such as seeing the 'big picture'.

Loosely coupled subsystems are an alternative to seeing change as occurring in a giant system which the manager must somehow learn to master. Instead, change is a developmental process in which **growth** and **direction** are the main issues – the model is going somewhere. Everyone is a change agent. The manager can be seen less as an analyst and more like a gardener tending a plant, watching and helping it grow in its own natural direction.

Using this model enables you to identify expectations about the future, both your own and the organization's. 'Where are we going?' becomes a central issue along with 'How are we going to get there?'

## RELEVANCE

[. . .] In the loosely coupled model managers achieve change by influencing the subsystems, not the entire enterprise in one go. Since there are many

subsystems it can be helpful to reduce these to manageable propo[ ]
concept like Tichey's (1983) strategic rope in which the or[ ]
simplified into three woven-together strands: technical, cultural, [ ]

As with a rope these strands are not easily distinguished from a[ ]
achieving strategic change the management role is to unravel the[ ]
then work on one or more in depth; secondly to knit them together again so
that change is implemented and made permanent. Integrating the strands is an
ongoing management activity, not a once only event.

The strategic rope idea is also useful because it draws attention to the
common tendency amongst practising managers to put their trust in a single
way of achieving change. Regardless of the nature of the problem some managers will always re-structure, others will always improve communications,
whilst others will always alter how services or goods are produced.

To affect the three subsystems managers can use the tools of mission or
strategy, structure, administrative and human resource procedures. [. . ]

This picture of change focuses our attention on a usually much neglected
issue, namely 'what happens before we reach the end state?' Managing the
transition state can be a complex task requiring considerable skill. Some managers are much better at initiating change and handling the transition stage
than they are the results of the transformation. Some people prefer developing
and creating while others enjoy consolidating and systematizing.
[. . .]

# WHAT IS LEADERSHIP?

[. . .]
Virtually every research finding about leadership has been challenged
or contradicted by other studies. Leadership is a sophisticated concept with
as many different definitions as people who have attempted to define it (see
Box [2]).

## BOX 2

*Different ways of looking at leadership*

- A focus of group processes
- Personality and its effects
- The art of inducing compliance
- An exercise in influence
- Act or behaviour
- A form of persuasion
- Power relationship
- An instrument of goal achievement
- A way of defining an individual's role

[. . .] What has altered in recent years is first the realization that leadership is not the exclusive preserve of the most senior manager, and secondly that today's leaders who make things happen are transformational, they revitalize entire organizations.

## EVERYBODY DOES IT

Anybody can play a leadership role, depending on the local situation. During a major change effort, leadership may move around the organization and be shared by many different people. In fact situations throw up leaders, and leadership skills can certainly be learned both through work experience as well as carefully targeted training.

In 1985 United Technologies (UT), a major US aerospace company which has diversified into a multinational concern, began trying to define what it meant by leadership. It gradually narrowed the field to:

- a clear sense of direction;
- an ability to involve the whole organization in clarifying that direction;
- a willingness to encourage initiative and risk taking – and tolerance of failure;
- a management style that empowers people to do the job without abdicating accountability;
- an emphasis on teamwork.

To help all its managers achieve these objectives UT managers concluded that they needed to practise a range of skills including: creating and developing a shared vision; taking initiatives; empowering others; and gaining support in the organization. The UT view of leadership stems from a highly practical need to turn a much misused concept into a management tool.
[. . .]

## THE LEADERSHIP TASKS

From a combination of research and the practical experience of companies such as United Technologies, we have a rough idea about what managerial leaders do to make things happen. These are shown in Box [3].

### A clear sense of direction

[. . .] Knowing 'where we are going' is what makes leaders attractive to followers. While managers often become stuck in a morass of objectives, leaders are more concerned with a general direction than detailed targets.
[. . .]

Leaders create new approaches and imagine new areas to explore. They relate to people more intuitively and in empathetic ways, moving to where opportunity and reward are high, and projecting ideas into images which excite people. Since the road to the final goal may be a long one, leaders also have the task of helping people to keep their sights on the end results and not become diverted to less relevant ones. They must be able to see and hold on to 'the big picture'.

## BOX 3

### *How managers offer leadership*

- A CLEAR SENSE OF DIRECTION (OBJECTIVES)
  - define goals
  - involve whole organization in clarifying that direction
  - provide means for goal attainment
  - maintain goal direction

- VALUES
  - engender core values
  - pursue core values with total persistence and meticulous attention to details which help achieve this end
  - constant interaction with employees to promote core values

- EXCITEMENT
  - engender this amongst employees

- TEAMWORK
  - emphasis on teamwork
  - provide and maintain group structure
  - facilitate group interactions
  - maintain member satisfaction
  - facilitate group task performance

- ACCOUNTABILITY
  - empower people to do the job without abdicating accountability
  - encourage initiative and risk taking
  - tolerate failure

## Values

While it is possible that leadership and management may coincide, it is nevertheless true that effective managers are not always good leaders and successful leaders may sometimes be poor managers. What seems to set leaders apart from managers is found in the idea which the Woolworths UK management adopted in their work of changing their organization:

- Managers do it right, leaders do what is right.

[. . .]

Effective leadership pays meticulous attention to details that engender and show in practical ways the importance of core values.

[. . .]

[It] demands that these become a high priority for everyone. For example, the Adult Services Division of the London Borough of Croydon identified a core value as 'improving the quality of our services by actively involving users and their relatives'. To translate this statement into action senior management asked every team in the division to identify ways of doing this as part of setting their own annual objectives. Thus virtually all members of the staff were involved in discussing and planning the pursuit of the core value of involving users. It was further backed up with training support on how to be more helpful to users and their relatives.

Effective management leadership seeks to ensure a constant interaction with employees to promote core values. This goes beyond sending round notices or putting up posters. Management must be out and about communicating or modelling the importance of core values and hearing what obstacles there are to turning these values into a reality.

## Excitement

Change through leadership also means causing excitement. Some years ago a leading computer company booked a football stadium to announce and praise the successes of its sales force. The huge electronic score board flashed up the sales results of each individual salesman as they came running on to the pitch to cheers from the audience of employees, friends and relatives. Outrageous? Perhaps, yet employees of the company still talk about it to this day. Excitement keeps alive those values and goals that leaders want to pursue.

## Teamwork

Most managers will affirm that they believe in teamwork; leaders actually achieve it. Sometimes this is done with team-building skills. Occasionally, however, using teams stems from fear – people are forced to use teams as a defensive way of coping with anxiety or uncertainty. Effective leaders must model good behaviour by paying attention to teamwork in their own working group of senior managers.

## Accountability

[. . .]

In managing change leaders hand over power in numerous ways. They accept that goals can only be achieved if people accept responsiblity for taking initiatives. How far this approach permeates throughout the organization depends on management style. A participating style will expect this accountability to go both wide and deep.

Leaders also refuse to become embroiled in areas of responsibility which rightly belong to their subordinates. By constantly asking 'Why can't you deal with it?' leaders challenge their followers to assert themselves and maximize their own use of authority and accountability.

# LEADERSHIP SKILLS

Learning the various activities associated with the leadership of change [. . .] may often rely on being thoroughly tenacious about finding new ways to undertake key tasks.

[. . .] Loosely coupled system leadership demands rather different skills to those associated with more traditional models of the organization.

[. . .] These include:

- transforming;
- ability to get things done;
- ability to see the big picture;
- ability to think clearly;
- personal maturity.

## Transforming skills

Across the industrial and commercial landscape we are seeing the emergence of a new breed of leader – the transformational leader. These people take on the responsibility for revitalizing an organization, defining the need for change, creating new visions and mobilizing commitment to these visions. Ultimately they intend to transform the organization. This kind of thinking demands new thinking about strategy, structure and people.

The ability to manage and relate to people is now widely seen as a core skill in managing change. There is a stress on combining right-brained activity (thinking which is creative and intuitive) with left-brained thinking (that which is systematic, logical and rational).

[. . .]

Transforming leadership is able to find ways to develop and supervise auto-nomous individuals rather than depend on exercising coercive or hierarchical power in the more traditional way.

Managers will have to develop such skills increasingly if they want to pro-duce results. In practical terms it means that you as a manager may have to:

- DEPEND less on your position in the hierarchy and more on your expertise, leadership and personality;
- PAY more attention to what a wider range of other people in the organiza-tion think and say;
- ADAPT easily to new information and situations;
- ATTEND more to your own and other people's intuition;
- PLACE more value on the creative, experimenting style of making things happen;
- RELY less on rules, systems, procedures and control and hence live with a greater degree of risk and uncertainty;
- RECOGNIZE the needs of followers to satisfy their higher needs of personal development, autonomy and self-realization.

## Ability to get things done

Where the various subsystems are often only connected by fairly tenuous links, effective leadership of change stresses proactive, transforming skills. [. . .]

[It] requires a manager to be more than responsive to people and situations. It demands pragmatic common sense combined with a good knowledge of the organization's principal aims. In practical terms it means that you as a man-ager may have to:

- FORMULATE your own goals;
- EVALUATE your own successes and failures with ruthless and sometimes painful honesty;
- SEEK constantly to clarify and simplify aims so that the tasks to make them happen are clearly identified and allocated;
- GO beyond your own job boundaries and take an interest in events throughout the whole organization;
- TEST constantly whether proposed action is really achievable and desirable;
- KEEP an eye on the 'bottom line' which may be profitability, quality of service, morale and so on.

## Ability to see the big picture

[. . .] Managers constantly have to resist becoming bogged down in activities which, on reflection, are not really central to core values and priority tasks.
[. . ]
In practical terms it means that you as a manager may have to:

- DEVELOP political and networking skills in which you learn to read the political and economic climate;
- LOOK outward beyond your own work area and the organization itself;
- ACQUIRE public relations skills, in particular learning how to handle the media;
- ORGANIZE how you spend your time and limited energy;
- MAXIMIZE delegation;
- BUILD yourself good channels of communication and systems for monitoring what is happening.

## Ability to think clearly

[. . .]
In organizations which are constructed of separate subsystems with links of varying strengths, managers must be extremely clear about goals and responsibilities, and be able to think through what they are trying to achieve. Intuition, right-brain activity and the concept of thinking laterally, all form part of the culture of change. There is less emphasis on managers mastering their environment and more on being able to ask 'what if?' questions.
Hence the leadership task is to demand information about likely outcomes, [. . .] though of course it still considers assessments of risk and coping with uncertainty. In practical terms it means that you as a manager may have to:

- FOCUS attention on defining clear aims;
- SEARCH constantly for new ways of doing things;
- TAKE few plans or proposals for granted;
- DEVELOP scenarios of possible outcomes and evaluate these systematically.

## Personal maturity

Maturity can be defined as how far a person is willing and able to take responsibility for their own behaviour. The effectiveness of your leadership of

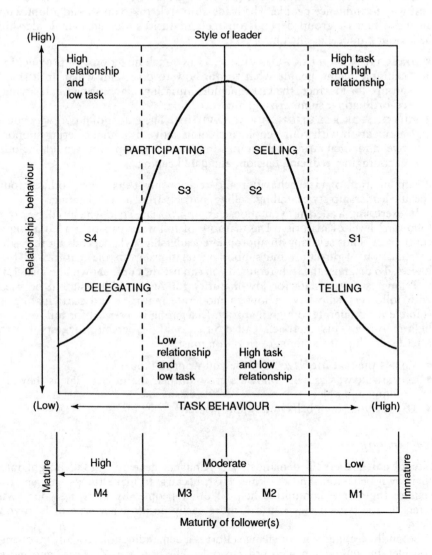

FIGURE 1.3 **Leadership styles**

the change effort will depend on two aspects of maturity: your own and that of your followers.

### Follower maturity

[. . .] People bring different degrees of maturity to the tasks which they perform. Though age brings maturity in one sense, it does not guarantee that a person develops a mature personality.

An important conclusion from this view of maturity is that there is no one best way to influence people. The leadership style that you should adopt with an individual or group depends on their maturity. Management leadership behaviour can be classified into:

- DIRECTION OR TASK BEHAVIOUR. How much direction you provide, for example telling people what to do, how to do it and when. In a small group, for instance, the tasks include: initiating; elaborating or clarifying; co-ordinating; summarizing; and recording.
- SUPPORT OR RELATIONSHIP BEHAVIOUR. The extent of a two-way communication with your people, including active listening; offering supportive and facilitating behaviour. In a small group this would include encouraging; reducing tension; and gate keeping.

A combination of task behaviour and relationship behaviour produces four specific leadership styles: telling, selling, participating and delegating.

In exercising leadership you choose an appropriate style which reflects your followers' level of maturity. The maturity of followers can be graded along a continuum. Thus selecting an appropriate leadership style depends on the right combination of direction and support in relationship to the maturity of followers. To diagnose the style required you can use the curve shown in Figure 1.3.

Telling is appropriate for low-maturity followers, selling should be used with followers who have a low to moderate maturity and participating is suitable for moderate to high maturity. Delegating is reserved for followers of high maturity. This approach, called Situational Leadership, suggests that to offer leadership of the change effort you must:

- ASSESS the maturity level of those you want to influence;
- CONSIDER was to help followers grow in their maturity as far as they are willing and able;
- ADJUST your own behaviour appropriately.

### Your maturity

Situational Leadership demands that managers develop a good insight into their own behaviour and thinking. First, because to make things happen you require the active, committed help of other people. By knowing your own strength and weaknesses you can more easily decide what type of help you need.

Secondly, leading a major change effort is a demanding role, usually involving considerable interaction with other people. This too is made easier and more effective if you have insight into how you perform during such interactions.

Thirdly, self-awareness enables you to respond better during change. If you know that you tend to avoid risk taking, have a tendency to procrastinate or demand too much information before making a decision, then you can find ways to deal with these traits. Continuous self-evaluation is therefore a common feature of effective leaders of major change efforts. They are always mentally reviewing their own performance, seeking new ways to be more effective.

An aspect of maturity which is not tied to chronological age is the ability to cope with stress. Sometimes younger managers are better able to handle stresses than their older colleagues who may see too many angles on a situation or become over-committed to certain people, ideas or ways of working which are being challenged by the change effort. A leader who handles stress well is likely to be more effective than one who does not.

A mature personality in practical terms means that you as a manager may have to:

- SPEND time regularly assessing your own strengths and weaknesses;
- SEEK help willingly to objectively review your personal performance;
- CREATE a personal development programme either within your organization or outside of it;
- ACQUIRE a strong commitment to, or acceptance of, the values of the organization; develop loyalty;
- LEARN how to handle stress well.

The sign of a mature personality is that the manager copes well in a turbulent environment. Things get done despite both real and psychological barriers to change. The manager learns to live with and help others cope with complexity, uncertainty and ambiguity.

Finally, what do the successful leaders in organizations tend to be like? Box [4] shows the sort of qualities such people are likely to possess.

BOX 4

---

### Qualities of successful organizational leaders

- INTELLIGENCE – slightly higher than the average of their followers with an ability to analyse, comprehend situations and communicate effectively
- BREADTH AND MATURITY – generally possess broader interests than their followers; more shock proof, more mature emotionally and not over-elated by success or crushed by failure
- MOTIVATION AND DRIVE FOR ACHIEVEMENT – a strong personal need to keep achieving something; constantly seeking self-realization and creativity and works hard for satisfactions of inner drives rather than material rewards
- ATTITUDE TO PEOPLE – understands that they can only get their job done through others; develops a healthy respect for people and a skill in relating to them; employee oriented, approaches problems in terms of people rather than technical aspects
- SPECIALIST KNOWLEDGE AND SKILLS – tends to have greater specialist knowledge and skill than followers in the particular specialization of the group

---

[. . .]

# REFERENCE

Tichey, N. (1983) Essentials of Stategic Management, *Journal of Business Strategy*, Spring.

CHAPTER 2

# An Analysis of Selected School Improvement Practices

COLIN MARSH

*This material has been abridged*

[To focus this analysis of school improvement models, we start by summarizing three major perspectives on change. Following House (1979), we shall call
them the technological, political, and cultural perspectives.]

## TECHNOLOGICAL PERSPECTIVE

This perspective has been dominant and continues to be supported by many
individuals and groups. Teaching is conceived as a technology, and therefore it
can be improved simply by applying new techniques. The emphasis is not so
much on improving the methods and materials used. There seems to be an
implicit assumption that the teacher will want to implement the new techniques and that he or she will be able to do so in an effective way. As noted by
House (1979), technological thinking involves selecting the most efficient
means to a given end. Such rational planning appears and reappears in the
educational literature as a desirable way of bringing about change.

This perspective may be of value for innovations that are well developed in
terms of materials, activities and strategies. [. . .]

## POLITICAL PERSPECTIVE

The political perspective focuses on the conflicts and compromises that occur
among factional groups. Co-operation on school improvement projects, according to this perspective, can occur only through various processes of negotiation and compromise.

House (1979) describes in detail the subgroups that can develop in a school
community, such as various teacher factions, student factions and parent
groups. [. . .] Often school communities are affected by political activities
occurring in the wider community. [. . .]

The term *mutual adaptation* is often used to describe what happens to school improvement projects subjected to various political forces. The original plans are almost inevitably adapted or reshaped by different groups so that the final set of practices or products becomes more congruent with their own values.

## CULTURAL PERSPECTIVES

This perspective reflects the different cultures or subcultures that operate in a school community. Each subgroup has its own values and norms which may be very different from those of other groups. [. . .] Conflicts between subgroups can be traced to fundamental differences in values. This perspective seems to indicate that changes are very difficult to achieve; conservative, traditional approaches will be sustained by teachers as long as possible.

[. . .]

We shall look at three school improvement models, namely: Collaborative School Management, People-Centred Action and Action Research. To a certain extent they have been chosen because they illustrate each of the three perspectives. However, it is simplistic to believe that any one model fits exclusively into only one dimension. The Collaborative School Management Model is strongly oriented towards the technological perspective, but not entirely. The Action Research Model is closely aligned to the political perspective but also is associated with the cultural. The Person-Centred Action Model seems to straddle the political and the technological perspectives.

[. . .]

## COLLABORATIVE SCHOOL MANAGEMENT MODEL

The Collaborative School Management (CSM) approach was developed by Caldwell and Spinks (1986b). [. . .] The emphasis is on planning, budgeting, defining roles for participants, collaborative management and systematic monitoring and evaluation.

[. . .]

CSM consists of six phases which are intended to operate as a management cycle (see Figure 2.1):

(1) goal-setting and identification of needs;
(2) policy-making;
(3) planning of programs;
(4) preparation and approval of program budgets;
(5) implementing;
(6) evaluating.

(Caldwell and Spinks, 1986b, p. 8)

What makes the CSM so appealing to school decision-makers is not just the six phases [. . .] but the highly practical guidelines that the authors provide. As indicated in Table 2.1 the guidelines provide [. . .] a set of no-nonsense routines which should (and do) appeal to participants in school-level decision-

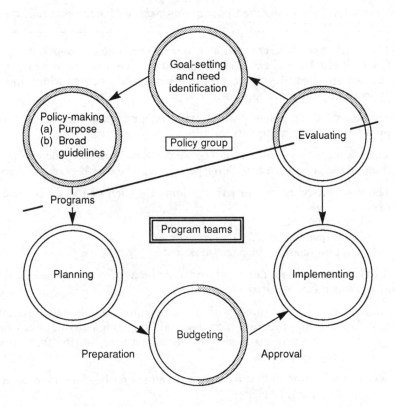

FIGURE 2.1 Phases in the Collaborative School Management (CSM) cycle (Reproduced with permission from B. J. Caldwell and J. Spinks (1986b) *Policy-making and planning for school effectiveness*, Hobart: Education Department, Tasmania, p. 21)

making. Furthermore, the guidelines and six phases are directly linked to day-to-day school routines.

The separation of tasks (and rules) for a *policy group* and for *project teams* is a vital aspect of the CSM approach. It is an attempt to provide a task-oriented focus with a set of checks and balances to provide some degree of accountability. The *policy group* need not be narrow and prescriptive, but might be a school council with a wide representation of parents and students as well as teachers. The policy group is required to make decisions about goals, identification of needs and policy-making guidelines and to share responsibility for evaluation activities. Its task is to shape the direction and range of activities for their school community. By contrast, the task of the *project teams* (largely comprised of teachers) is to undertake evaluation. One of the checks is that their program plans and budgets have to be approved by the policy group.

Let us now examine the six phases in more detail.

## TABLE 2.1
*Guidelines for establishing the Collaborative School Management (CSM) cycle*

---

(1) There are two different action groups. The *policy group* (e.g. School Council) sets the policies and the priorities. The *program teams* (e.g. the Mathematics team) prepare program plans and budgets which must be approved by the policy group.

(2) The use of these teams enables teachers, principal, students and community to all be participants.

(3) There is inevitably some overlap between the tasks of the policy group and those of the program teams. Some persons may be members of both groups.

(4) There are strict maximum writing limits for each of the six phases. For example,
    Policy statement:    1 page (maximum)
    Program plan:        2 pages (maximum)
    Evaluation report:   1 page (maximum)

(5) All planning and evaluation reports must be written in non-technical language which can be easily understood.

(6) School communities should work on completing a small number (e.g. 3–5) of policy-making, program planning and budgeting activities each *calendar year,* with a systematic plan in subsequent years for the evaluation of existing programs.

(7) Each school community should plan for a period of 3–5 years to complete most of their planned changes.

---

SOURCE: *Caldwell and Spinks (1986b) pp. 20–3.*

## Goal-setting and identification of needs

Goal-setting and needs identification is the typical starting-off point for the process, but it need not be, and any of the other five phases could be used as the entry point. However, it is evident that Caldwell and Spinks (1986b) do prefer a rational, relatively linear approach to decision-making, and so it is probably important to describe the phases in the anticlockwise sequence as depicted in Figure 2.1.

*Goals,* according to Caldwell and Spinks, should [. . .] be a statement of broad direction. [. . .] Formulating these goals will involve contestation by different individuals Not all will agree upon particular goals about specific student outcomes or the provision of resources or the management of the school.

A related activity is *identifying needs*. The authors [. . .] view it simply as the difference between 'what is' and 'what should be'. They tend to use quantitative examples (for example, teaching workloads) to illustrate needs and do not delve into discussions about why and how needs might vary between individuals and groups. They prefer to be practical, businesslike and target-oriented by suggesting that important questions to ask include:

- Is the discrepancy between 'what is' and 'what ought to be' large enough to warrant action?
- What harm will be done if the gap is not closed?
- How important is this need compared with others that may exist?

(Caldwell and Spinks, 1986a, p. 11)

## Policy-making

[. . .] Caldwell and Spinks (1986b, p. 62) define a policy 'as a set of guidelines which provide a framework for action in achieving some purpose on a substantive issue'.

Policies need to be prepared for all issues that are viewed by participants as being more than routine procedures. For example, a policy is usually needed for school homework but not for supervision of school bus pick-ups. [. . .]

Each policy should be written down but be no more than *one page* in length. They suggest that the process of policy-making involves:

- Giving attention to the various desires which occur in various ways in a school community. These are the issues that must be shaped into a definite school policy.
- The first step is to search for policy alternatives – gathering information about legal, economic and political aspects of each issue.
- The next step is to communicate with all stake-holders (teachers, parents, students) about possible alternatives. Criteria to use are *desirability, workability and acceptability*.
- Issues should be classified as either contentious or non-contentious. Different strategies are recommended for each.
- A timetable for policy-making must be established. Contentious issues: three to five policies per year. Non-contentious issues: up to four policies each month. A total of one to two years is needed for a school community to establish all policies required.

The task for *non-contentious issues* is to have the writing of one-page written policies shared between various teachers and others with special expertise. Previously developed examples can provide a useful model and can save time for the persons involved. Draft policies should be pinned up on staff noticeboards (to avoid paper wars). Refined policies, in due course, must be submitted for approval to the policy group. Once adopted, policies must be made known to all the school community, preferably in a policy handbook.

For a *contentious issue* it is suggested that a working party of six to eight people should be formed (presumably nominated by the policy group or the school council). Information should be gathered from a wide range of indiviudals and groups, by informal conversations and by the use of surveys. Caldwell and Spinks insist that at least three options for each issue should be prepared (to incorporate and reflect the range of views) and submitted in due course to the policy group. How priorities are devised between the three options is not discussed in detail by the authors, but elsewhere Caldwell and Spinks (1986b, pp. 141–53) discuss strategies for managing conflict and building consensus. They hint that the school principal has a major role to play in initiating and orchestrating the various processes listed above.

## Planning and budgeting

After written policy statements have been produced it is possible for the program teams to develop plans for implementation. Caldwell and Spinks stress the need to make direct links between policies and programs.

The programs can be concerned with simply the traditional subject divisions, but there might also be cross-subject programs (for example, Pastoral Care). It may be necessary in each school to have a few all-encompassing programs and a number of specific ones [. . .].

Again, the authors stress that an economical use of time is a major consideration in writing up details of the program plan and budget. This document should be no longer than two pages, and useful headings are:

- purpose;
- broad guidelines;
- plan for implementation;
- resources required (budget);
- evaluation;
- details of program team members.

The first two headings provide a link with the policy document, in that they will have been taken directly from this source.

The plan for implementation establishes specific information about which groups of students will be involved, the staff involved, materials and equipment to be used, and other related matters. [. . .] Caldwell and Spinks (1986b) argue that being precise about this information, using standardized headings, and completing the document at the same time each year, enables a much better integration of school management activities.

[. . .]

The program budget summary should identify expenditure required for each program in terms of teaching staff, travel, book materials and services. A total expenditure figure is then calculated, which has to be reconciled with resources available. The authors point out that 'deficits' are usually the order of the day, and so lower-priority programs may have to be deleted. These decisions are typically made by the policy group or a finance committee. Regardless of who is involved in the reconciliation decisions, the policy group must give final approval to the budget.

## Implementing

The implementing phase belongs squarely with the program teams, because it is concerned with:

- learning;
- teaching;

- use of resources;
- supervision and day-to-day facilitation of each program.

Caldwell and Spinks (1986b) provide little specific information about the learning–teaching aspect except to assume that this belongs to the teachers, who have the appropriate professional training to do the task. The authors pay more attention to the need for the principal or a member of each program team nominated by the principal to *supervise* the implementation process. The supervisor in each team should take responsibility to ensure that policy guidelines are followed; materials and services are made available when needed; and to have control over the selection and ordering of materials and services. [. . .]

## Evaluating

Caldwell and Spinks [. . .] make three assumptions which guide all the evaluative activities:

(1) The policy statements and programs are used to judge whether or not a program has achieved its objectives.
(2) The details of programs are used to judge how achievement levels were intended to occur, and if not, why not.
(3) The details can pinpoint which resources are being used and whether redistribution of certain resources should occur.

Caldwell and Spinks (1986b) maintain that their CSM cycle facilitates and provides the direction for evaluative activities. It can also save teachers and administrators valuable time because a wealth of data is readily available via the various policy statements. Nevertheless, the authors suggest that other practical measures are needed, such as:

- Choose to evaluate only a few programs in depth each year.
- Each in-depth evaluation should be written up in a maximum of two pages and should use standard headings (success indicators, areas of concern, comments and recommendations).
- Each major evaluation should be carried out by a group including parents, program team and others as appropriate.
- Other programs in any one year should have minor evaluations; the report on each should be completed in a maximum of one page.
- Both major and minor evaluation reports must be presented to the policy group for review and possible future action.

## Commentary on the CSM approach

The Collaborative School Management approach to school improvement is an eminently practical one, which does seem to work. It is possible to schedule the tasks over the school year to suit the routines of administrators, teachers and others. The six phases that comprise the CSM cycle are logical and easy to follow. The practical guidelines, which tend to channel the activities of participants within reasonable time limits, are a very important feature of CSM. [. . .]

However, it is necessary to balance these positive features with [. . .] deficits [. . .].

Although the CSM cycle emphasizes collaborative and open discussion, the separation of the policy group from the project teams appears to encourage [. . .] hierarchical distinctions. [. . .] It might be argued that the CSM cycle covertly supports and reinforces the principal's role while subjugating teachers to a limited, subservient role. Although some attention is given to the participation of parents as members of the policy group, [. . .] there is minimal treatment given to the inclusion of students.

Another criticism relates to the orientation of the CSM approach towards rational/logical/ordered processes. By default, the CSM approach seems to dismiss the spontaneities, wide-ranging discussions, outbursts and arguments that so often occur in schools. The contestations and conflicts, although mentioned in terms of how they might be effectively managed, seem to be categorized according to how they might be contained and if possible avoided.

There also appears to be overemphasis on the financial aspects of school planning. All inputs into policy and program planning are expressed quantitatively and, in some cases, in money terms. [. . .] Phases of the CSM cycle that can be couched in financial terms are given detailed treatment by the authors, whereas other aspects such as implementation and evaluation are treated very briefly indeed. Attention to the specifics of implementation are crucial if planning goals are to be realized. It also seems to be particularly narrow to focus only on the specified policy objectives for evaluation and to ignore unintended outcomes and wider contextual issues.

Finally, CSM [. . .] does appear to be very demanding on the energies of school staff. [. . .] The range and frequency of activities required over the school year would be draining. The model also assumes that staff will co-operate effectively with each other, will always be efficient, goal-directed, prompt and thorough, in undertaking the various tasks associated with CSM. This does appear over-optimistic [. . .].

## A PEOPLE-CENTRED ACTION MODEL

'People-Centred Action' (PCA) is an attempt to summarize into one category a number of related approaches to school improvement. [. . .] It is very different from the CSM approach, both in emphasis and in scope, even though the actual phases or processes may not appear to be dissimilar.

The PCA approach has no normal hierarchy of policy-makers, although it is assumed that support and/or leadership from the principal is vital, and that support from parent and community groups can be desirable. As noted in Table 2.2, it assumes that *external* and *internal* change agents are often vitally important to school improvement activities.

Various individuals on a school staff might take on the role of internal catalyst (change facilitator) in certain ways. Research in the USA [. . .] concluded that there are other change facilitators (CF) apart from the principal, whom they called 'second CFs'.

They are likely to be curriculum specialists, deputy principals, resource teachers. . . . They work more interactively with teachers involved in the change providing training, consultation and problem solving on an individual basis. They monitor the process for the purpose of corrective feedback and planning rather than for summative evaluation.

(Stiegelbauer *et al.*, 1986)

TABLE 2.2

*Major emphases of the People-Centred Action (PCA) approach*

(1) Planning of school improvement is important, but it is the interactions with participants that are crucial.
(2) A person doesn't have to have formal status to carry out school improvement. A lot of school improvement activities are generated informally by individuals with no formal status positions.
(3) Most school improvement activities require the support of internal and external consultants and field officers from time to time.
(4) Curriculum changes are a major focus for most school improvement activities.
(5) Teachers undergo developmental stages in implementing new curricula. This is an important understanding for all school improvement efforts.
(6) Teacher participation in school improvement activities is essential.
(7) Various support initiatives (material, human, peers) are needed to ensure that school improvement activities are successful.

SOURCES: *Loucks and Lieberman, 1983; Loucks-Horsley and Hergert, 1985.*

*External consultants* can be very significant in assisting with school improvement activities. They may be teachers from neighbouring schools [or] [. . .] full-time consultants who have process skills and subject-area skills. Change agents from outside the school, can often provide a balance of power in school improvement activities – a neutral force to balance conflicting interests. Above all, they can provide a dynamism needed to ensure that the school improvement actions don't lose their momentum (Cox, 1983).

Another major feature of the PCA approach is the focus upon teachers' developmental needs and concerns. If there is a good understanding of how teachers change in their feelings about a new curriculum and go through various stages in acquiring new skills, then school improvement ventures are likely to be far more successful. [. . .] Change is accomplished first by individuals and then by institutions. This is an important principle because it highlights the need for school improvement efforts to focus on the individuals involved, especially the teachers.

Hall *et al.* (1973) devised a theory to explain how teachers react to a new curriculum in a series of stages, termed 'Stages of Concern'. The concerns typically felt by teachers as they experience a new curriculum go from *informational*, to *personal*, to *management*, and then to *student concerns* (see Figure 2.2).

The 'Stages of Concern' highlight another important feature: the time factor. Change is a process, and it will take a considerable period of time for teachers to be fully comfortable and competent with a new curriculum [– perhaps] three

6 *Refocusing*   The focus is on exploration of more universal benefits from the innovation, including the possibility of major changes or replacement with a more powerful alternative. Individual has definite ideas about alternatives to the proposed or existing form of the innovation.

↑

5 *Collaboration*   The focus is on co-ordination and co-operation with others regarding use of the innovation.

↑

4 *Consequence*   Attention focuses on impact of the innovation on students in his/her immediate sphere of influence. The focus is on relevance of the innovation for students, evaluation of student outcomes, including performance and competencies, and changes needed to increase student outcomes.

↑

3 *Management*   Attention is focused on the processes and tasks of using the innovation and the best use of information and resources. Issues related to efficiency, organizing, managing, scheduling, and time demands are uppermost.

↑

2 *Personal*   Individual is uncertain about the demands of the innovation, his/her inadequacy to meet those demands, and his/her role with the innovation. This includes analysis of his/her role in relation to the reward structure of the organization, decision-making and consideration of potential conflicts with existing structures or personal commitment. Financial or status implications of the program for self and colleagues may also be reflected.

↑

1 *Informational*   A general awareness of the innovation and interest in learning more detail about it is indicated. The person seems to be unworried about himself/herself in relation to the innovation. She/he is interested in substantive aspects of the innovation in a selfless manner such as general characteristics, effects, and requirements for use.

↑

0 *Awareness*   Little concern about or involvement with the innovation is indicated.

FIGURE 2.2 The teacher's 'Stages of Concern' about an innovation (after Hall *et al.*, 1973).

VI  *Renewal*   The user is seeking more effective alternatives to the established use of the innovation.

↑

V  *Integration*   The user is making deliberate efforts to co-ordinate with others in using the innovation.

↑

IVb *Refinement*   The user is making changes to increase outcomes.

↑

IVa *Routine*   The user is making few or no changes and has an established pattern of use.

↑

III  *Mechanical use*   The user is making changes to better organize the use of the innovation.

↑

II  *Preparation*   The individual is preparing to use the innovation.

↑

I  *Orientation*   The individual is seeking out information about the innovation.

↑

0  *Non-use*   No action is being taken with respect to the innovation.

FIGURE 2.3 'Levels of Use' of the innovation: typical teacher behaviour at each level (after Hall *et al.*, 1973)

to five years. Once a stable period of competence has been reached, teachers will want to explore other alternatives and *refocus* their efforts (the sixth stage in Figure 2.2), so a new cycle begins.

Hall *et al.* (1973) also developed a series of 'Levels of Use', to indicate how the behaviour of teachers using a new curriculum also changes developmentally over time (see Figure 2.3). Whereas the 'Stages of Concern' concept deals with teachers' feelings and concerns, the 'Levels of Use' concept tries to pinpoint how teachers are actually implementing a new curriculum. It is suggested that teachers progress through various levels, from a *preparatory* level to a *mechanical* level of just coping, through a competent *routine* level and then several levels of sophistication to achieve better student outcomes (for example, *refinement* and *integration*).

Again, it assumes that teachers take a considerable period of time before they reach a level of proficiency whereby they can demonstrate competence with the new curriculum. Adaptations and variations come only after teachers have gone beyond basic mastery and routine levels.

The phases for the People-Centred Action (PCA) approach might at first glance appear to be similar to Collaborative School Management (CSM), but the emphasis is quite different. The PCA approach typically includes the following phases:

(1) establishing the project;
(2) assessment and goal-setting;
(3) identifying a solution;
(4) preparing for implementation;
(5) implementing the project;
(6) reviewing progress and problems;
(7) maintenance and institutionalization.

## Establishing the project

Unlike CSM which prescribes that the policy team at a school initiates and drives all school improvement efforts, PCA focuses on *any individual in the school* who might want to initiate a project and offers guidelines about how he or she might get support. [. . .]

In every case it is suggested that the person concerned must spend a lot of time negotiating for resources and for acceptance of the project. Some activities suggested include:

- seeking out resources (money, time, services) from the principal and other sources (regional offices, professional associations, funding bodies);
- trying to build up allies for the project [. . .];
- getting assistance from external consultants to help reinforce your arguments and strategies;
- forming a school improvement team of 5–15 people as soon as practicable to ensure a broad base of support, and making sure it includes administrators, teachers and parents (and perhaps students).

PCA assumes that every school context is different and changing over time and that it is unwise to establish standardized practices for school improvement. Each time another project is initiated it requires a new set of negotiations between individuals and groups.

## Assessment and goal-setting

PCA emphasizes the importance of assessing the present situation in a school [. . .] to target the problem areas that might become a focus for improvement [. . .]. Summary forms to collect this kind of information should include such headings as:

- kind of problem;
- who is affected;
- how they are affected;

- evidence;
- causes;
- goals for improvement.

School improvement teams, with their broad representation, are admirably suited to contributing to this data-collecting and subsequent formulating of goals. PCA does not specify details about goal-setting, apart from warning that often too much data are collected and too much time spent on this phase. It is recommended that a brief report is fed back to all personnel in a school community and reactions sought from different groups. The goals that are finally decided upon must be both specific and attainable within the limits set down for the project.

## Identifying a solution

[. . .] Each [possible] solution has certain costs and benefits, which need to be considered before a choice is finally made. Criteria have to be agreed upon before a decision can be made. Examples of criteria and related questions include:

- *Cost*
  What will be the start-up and ongoing expenses?
  Will the solution involve new materials, new personnel?
  If training for staff is needed, how long will it take?
- *Philosophy and norms of the school*
  What are the preferred methods of instruction?
  What are the accepted methods of evaluating students?
  [. . .]
- *Congruency with other activities at the school*
  Will the proposal affect other programs at the school?
  Are there any likely long-term effects which need to be considered?

During this phase, the preferred solutions should be analysed so that we have specific details of what might be expected to occur. For example, if the solution is a new curriculum, it is suggested that specific details need to be provided about:

- what the teacher will be doing when using the new curriculum;
- what students will be doing when using the new curriculum;
- how the students and teachers will interact with the materials.

Various checklists have been developed [. . .] [which] seek specific information which will indicate how a curriculum might be taught in practice. [. . .] For teachers who are about to implement the innovation, this would enable them to realize, at a glance, what key aspects to include in their day-to-day teaching.

## Preparing for implementation

The implementation phase is a critical element of any school improvement project.
    [. . .]

Research studies indicate that definite *game plans* can and should be used (Hall *et al.*, 1984). That is, specific interventions are used by change facilitators as part of an overall plan to produce the desired level of implementation. In the American schools examined by these researchers, they found four components of the game plans; and if all components were used, implementation successes were very common.

Component 1    *Developing supportive organization arrangements*
● covers logistical and scheduling activities (for example, seeking additional funds for part-time resource persons).
Component 2    *Training*
● to develop positive attitudes, knowledge and skills in relation to using the new curriculum;
● is normally scheduled and announced in advance.
Component 3    *Providing consultation and reinforcement*
● actions taken to encourage and to assist individuals;
● involves consulting and coaching users and non-users.
Component 4    *Monitoring and evaluation*
● actions taken to gather, analyse or report data about the rise of the new curriculum.

## Implementing the project

[. . .] Drawing on the 'Stages of Concern' and 'Levels of Use' methodologies (see Figures 2.2 and 2.3) it might be expected that teachers will experience a number of difficulties such as poor co-ordination, lack of confidence in using the materials, and inability to anticipate problems. Furthermore, each teacher will have different problems, and so specially tailored, supportive strategies and training will be needed.

The person (or persons) selected to assist with implementation therefore needs to be very flexible, non-judgemental and supportive. Various kinds of personalized training may be needed. Few of the desired improvements may actually occur during the first six months or even the first year. Sessions need to be established at regular intervals for teacher-implementers to reflect upon their practices, current problems and planned solutions.

## Reviewing progress and problems

This is really a later stage of implementation after the initial flurry of implementation activities. It might typically occur one to two years into the implementation phase. Obtaining data on 'Stages of Concern' and 'Levels of Use' of individual teachers [. . .] is a valuable way of monitoring success levels. Checklists of teacher and student use are another way. An analysis of data from these sources will indicate whether individual teachers are making reasonable progress or not in implementing the curriculum, [and] reveal problem areas which can then become the focus for the future training sessions and workshops.

It is only after a curriculum has been in place in a school for several years, and the teachers are relatively comfortable in using it, that any attempt should be made to evaluate student outcomes. [. . .] When it is deemed appropriate to measure student progress, a variety of evaluative techniques should be used. Such evaluative actions may in turn provide valuable information about how the curriculum should be modified to suit the needs of particular classes.

## Maintenance and institutionalization

This final phase is needed to ensure that the new practices [. . .] are maintained and become a regular part of the school's norms (institutionalization). [. . .] Definite plans need to be made to ensure that there will be administrative support for the continuance of a new curriculum. [. . .] Strenuous efforts may be needed by advocates to ensure institutionalization.

## Commentary on the PCA approach

People-Centred Action places emphasis on the implementation aspects of a school improvement project and ways to ensure that progress can be made [. . .]. Considerable emphasis is given to face-to-face strategies for supporting, encouraging and training teachers to cope with new curricula. Informal meetings and flexible, open channels of communication are preferred, rather than formal organization structures and procedures.

[. . .] PCA incorporates numerous techniques for evaluating curriculum packages and relating these findings to individual school goals and improvement plans.

However, there are aspects of PCA that can be criticized. A major problem is that it may be very appropriate for curriculum-related school improvement but not for other projects. For example, [. . .] pastoral care might take many forms, such as spontaneous meetings between a teacher and students as well as scheduled tutorial groups, house meetings, etc. Not all the seven phases would be appropriate for trying to monitor changes to a pastoral care program.

Furthermore, PCA places very heavy reliance upon internal and/or external consultants ('change agents') [. . .] [which schools may not have sufficient resources to employ].

PCA relies on linkages between people and the development of positive relationships between them. Little attention is given to the formal structures of a school such as the school board and senior staff positions. Although PCA acknowledges the power of the school principal and the need for planning groups to include parents and students if possible, minimal emphasis is given to the ways in which formal structures and policies can direct or inhibit school improvement projects. It might be argued that this emphasis upon personal relationships is over-stressed and that insufficient attention is given to harnessing the power of formal groups within the school.

## ACTION RESEARCH MODEL

[. . .]

It is important to distinguish between several different types of action research.

Tripp (1985) cites four types [. . .]:

(1) Technical action research – participants work on tasks initiated by others. They are highly skilled and efficient professionals.
(2) Practical action research – this is self-directed. Participants are involved in designing and improving, even inventing.
(3) Critical action research – individual participants develop a critical consciousness and as a result change their values and circumstances.
(4) Emancipatory action research – a critical mass of participants work together and help each other to raise their levels of consciousness and resulting actions.

[. . .]

## 'Moments' of Action Research

[. . .] Writers in this area avoid using the term 'stages' and use instead such terms as 'moments' and 'spirals'. Proponents of action research are emphatic that the processes should diffuse imperceptibly together, although whether the participants see it this way is far from certain. The four moments of action research are typically described as:

(1) developing a plan of action to improve what is already happening;
(2) acting to implement the plan;
(3) observing the effects of action in the context in which it occurs;
(4) reflecting on these effects as a basis for further planning, subsequent action and so on, through a succession of cycles.

(Kemmis and McTaggart, 1984, p. 7)

The 'moments' involve focusing on *prospective aspects* through to *present actions*, and monitoring and then through to *retrospective aspects* of analysis and evaluation. This cyclical series of actions is the hub of action research. So too are the emphases of *collaboration* and *improvement* and *involvement*.

## Plan of action

Developing a plan of action includes several aspects:

- general idea;
- reconnaissance;
- field of action;
- first action step;
- monitoring;
- timetable.

(Kemmis and McTaggart, 1984, p. 21)

*Framing the general idea* is a crucial step and involves a teacher or teachers in trying to sort out and select the problem(s) they want to focus on. Participants should give attention to questions such as:

- What is happening now?
- In what sense is this problematic?
- What can I do about it?

The problems chosen [should be] manageable within the time constraints, and not wide-ranging issues – problems need to be selected for which something can be tried out as a solution.

*Reconnaissance* involves putting a general idea into perspective. The social and political context of the school setting has to be considered. There may be other constraints. All kinds of questions need to be [thought] through, including:

• What is the rationale for what is happening already?
• What are the opportunities to implement action that reflects the general idea?
• Exactly what aspects of present practice am I trying to change?
• What are the constraints of content, time, resources, manpower?
• What constraints are 'absolute', and which might be negotiable?
• With whom must I negotiate?
• How am I to protect the rights of those involved or affected in privacy? confidentiality? discretion?

Determining the *field of action* means finalizing the plan, and this usually entails writing down the details. Here, attention has to be paid to what is intended to change and why; what aspects will remain unchanged; and what strategic action will be taken.

The *first action step* should be outlined in even more detail to ensure that there will be a reasonable degree of success.

Kemmis and McTaggart (1984) suggest that when the plan of action is written, details are needed for all the above headings, especially those referring to intended changes. If these details are recorded under standard headings, then at each cycle a complete description can be written of the improvements that occurred and how these related to specific actions.

For the plan of action the *monitoring step* involves devising techniques that will enable details to be recorded about what happened during the first action step. It will be necessary to record the circumstances in which the action took place as well as the consequences of the action. Kemmis and McTaggart (1984) recommend keeping a diary [. . .]. Also valuable is the use of other participants to give their interpretations of what occurred.

Having a *timetable* which sets out a schedule for the planned activities is also essential, especially if other people are involved in the action research activity.

## Implementing

The implementation of the plan is the *action* 'moment'. If the planning has been well designed, the activity will be a success, but there are always unexpected happenings. Instant decisions may have to be made which could affect the intended plan. The implementation stage should attempt to bring about improvement of practice, of understanding (individually and collaboratively) and of the situation in which the action took place.

## Observing

Observing is also an important 'moment'. Careful observation is needed, as this will later form the basis for reflection. The observational methods used must be comprehensive and flexible, so that they can record the unexpected. It is important that the observational details are accurate and record the specific happenings. It is too easy to believe that what was intended to occur did, in fact, happen.

## Reflecting

The final 'moment' of the cycle is to reflect upon what has occurred. In recalling action, participants try to make meaning out of the various activities and events. Discourse between participants is very helpful in trying to reconstruct meaning of the actions. Tripp (1985) suggests that a journal account by the participants is a very useful way of reflecting upon what has occurred. Writing these case study accounts helps the individuals concerned to crystallize thoughts about their actions, the circumstances and the consequences, and the problems and the successes. Another reason for writing an account of the completed cycle is to provide a general background of preparation before entering the next cycle. Once the four 'moments' have been completed it is time to consider revisions and then go through the same stages in a revised cycle.

[. . .]

Many research studies cited in the literature have been about consultants assisting an individual teacher or group of teachers. [. . .] Many specialists argue that the role of consultant/facilitator is crucial to success. [. . .] Consultants certainly have a major part to play in being a reactor – a critical friend – and thus providing opportunities, especially for individual teachers to enter into discussion about their efforts.

## Commentary

The published accounts of action research reveal that it is an extremely valuable model for bringing about school improvement; [. . .] teachers involved in action research can and do examine and reflect upon what is actually happening in their classrooms.

There are a number of problems. An organizational and managerial one for school communities is that action research projects are typically undertaken by individual teachers or small groups of teachers, [and] leave little scope for other members of the school community to be involved. [. . .]

Other problems are the enormous requirements of time and the energy needed by participants in action research projects. The planning steps are comprehensive and require considerable periods of time. The writing up of reports on cycles, and the discussions needed with participants, also consume large amounts of time. In addition to time and energy inputs, action research programs could be extremely expensive if extensive use was made of a consultant.

There is also the problem of confidentiality of data. Presumably this would not be a problem for individual teachers involved in their own class research, but if the project was expanded to include other teachers, classes and even parents, then the question of who controls the materials gathered (and therefore has access to the data) would require careful negotiation between the parties concerned.

# SUMMARY

Each of the models described in this chapter has strengths and weaknesses. A preference for any particular model will probably be related to the overriding values one has about school improvement. Values can be classified as technological, political or cultural.

For those who prefer an approach that is *technological* in orientation, the Collaborative School Management (CSM) Model is extremely practical and has proved to be highly successful.

The People-Centred Action (PCA) Model has proved to be a very successful approach where the emphasis has been on implementing practices and products developed by external agencies. This model highlights *political* and *technological* aspects of school improvement and the various tactics that can be used to enlist the support of administrators and to assist teachers.

The Action Research Model can provide new levels of critical consciousness for teachers as they explore and reflect on their current practices. In these circumstances, action research can provide valuable *cultural* insights about the role of teachers and the avenues available to them for wider levels of empowerment and emancipation.

[. . .]

# REFERENCES

Caldwell, B. J. (1985) Collaborative school management: a framework for curriculum change. Paper presented at the 7th Western Australian Curriculum Conference, Perth.

Caldwell, B. J. and Spinks, J. (1986a) *Policy formation and resource allocation.* Geelong: Deakin University.

Caldwell, B. J. and Spinks, J. (1986b) *Policy-making and planning for school effectiveness.* Hobart: Education Department, Tasmania.

Cox, P. L. (1983) Complementary roles and successful change, *Educational Leadership,* Vol. 41, no. 3.

Hall, G. E., Rutherford, W. L., Hord, S. M. and Huling, L. L. (1984) The effects of three principals' styles on school improvement, *Educational Leadership,* Vol. 41, no. 5, pp. 22–31.

Hall, G. E., Wallace, R. and Dossett, W. (1973) *A developmental conceptualization of the adoption process within educational institutions.* Austin: Research and Development Center for Teacher Education, University of Texas.

House, E. R. (1979) Technology versus craft: a ten-year perspective on innovation, *Journal of Curriculum Studies,* Vol. 11, no. 1.

Kemmis, S. and McTaggart, R. (1984) *The action research planner* (2nd edn) Geelong: Deakin University.

Loucks, S. F. and Lieberman, A. (1983) Curriculum implementation, in F. W. English (ed.) *Fundamental curriculum decisions.* Alexandria, Virginia: ASCD.

Loucks-Horsley, S. and Hergert, L. F. (1985) *An action guide to school improvement.* Alexandria, Virginia: ASCD.

Stiegelbauer, S. M., Muscella, D. B. and Rutherford, W. L. (1986) The facilitation of change in elementary and secondary schools: similarities, differences and interactions about the process. Paper presented at the annual conference of the American Educational Research Association, San Francisco.

Tripp, D. H. (1985) *Action research and professional development.* Professional Development Project Melbourne: Australian College of Education.

# CHAPTER 3

# *Rethinking Professional Development*

KAREN OSTERMAN AND ROBERT KOTTKAMP

*This material has been abridged*

[. . .] The first part of this chapter describes reflective practice as a professional development process: What does it look like? How does it begin? The second part contrasts this mode of professional development with more traditional approaches focusing on differences in assumptions, content, and processes.

## DEFINING REFLECTIVE PRACTICE

Reflective practice, while often confused with reflection, is neither a solitary nor a relaxed meditative process. To the contrary, reflective practice is a challenging, demanding, and often trying process that is most successful as a collaborative effort.

[. . .] Within our discussion, reflective practice is viewed as a means by which practitioners can develop a greater level of self-awareness about the nature and impact of their performance, an awareness that creates opportunities for professional growth and development.

Awareness is essential for behavioural change. To gain a new level of insight into personal behaviour, the reflective practitioner assumes a dual stance, being, on the one hand, the actor in a drama and, on the other hand, the critic who sits in the audience watching and analysing the entire performance. To achieve this perspective, individuals must come to an understanding of their own behaviour; they must develop a conscious awareness of their own actions and effects and the ideas or theories-in-use that shape their action strategies.

Achieving this level of conscious awareness, however, is not an easy task. Theories-in-use are not easily articulated. Schon (1983) has described this process in the context of professional practice. As he explained, professional knowledge is grounded in professional experience: 'Competent practitioners usually know more than they can say. They exhibit a kind of knowing-in-practice, most of which is tacit' (p. viii). Consequently, when asked, master teachers or master administrators are often unable to identify the components of their work that lead to successful outcomes. Similarly, practitioners who want to improve their performance are often unclear about how their own actions prevent them from being more successful. So, if the purpose of reflective practice is to enhance awareness of our own thoughts and action, as a means of professional growth, how do we begin this process of reflection? How do we begin to develop a critical awareness about our own professional practice? Where do we start?

## REFLECTIVE PRACTICE AS EXPERIENTIAL LEARNING

Reflective practice is located within the older tradition of experiential learning and also the more recently defined perspective of situated cognition. Experiental learning theorists, including Dewey, Lewin and Piaget, maintain that learning is most effective, most likely to lead to behavioural change, when it begins with experience, and specifically problematic experience. From experience and research, we know that learning is most effective when people become personally engaged in the learning process, and engagement is most likely to take place when there is a need to learn. [. . .] Situated cognition focuses on both the process and the context of learning [. . .] [which] is most effective when the learner is actively involved in the learning process, when it takes place in a context relevant to the learner (Brown, Collins and Duguid, 1989a, 1989b; Prestine and LeGrand, 1991).

Experiential learning theory maintains further that learning is a dialectic and cyclical process consisting of four stages: experience, observation and reflection, abstract reconceptualization, and experimentation (Kolb, 1984). While experience is the basis for learning, learning cannot take place without reflection. Conversely, while reflection is essential to the process, reflection must be integrally linked with action (Figure 3.1). Reflective practice, then, integrating theory and practice, thought and action, is, as Schon described, a 'dialogue of thinking and doing through which I become more skillful' (1987, p. 31).

In this cyclical process, learning or the process of inquiry begins with what Dewey (1938) described as a problematic or an indeterminate situation: a troublesome event or experience, an unsettling situation that cannot be resolved using standard operating procedures. Prompted by a sense of uncertainty

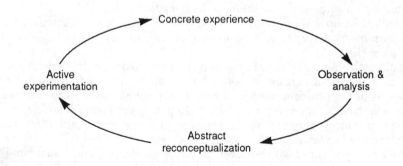

FIGURE 3.1 Experiential learning cycle

or unease, the reflective practitioner steps back to examine this experience: What was the nature of the problem? What were my intentions? What did I do? What happened? In the process of observing and analysing this experience, problems emerge. The problem – a discrepancy between the real and the ideal, between intention and action, or between action and effects – further stimulates the inquiry and motivates the learner to absorb new information as part of an active search for better answers and more effective strategies. The final stages of the process involve reconceptualization and experimentation. Having examined and analysed the experience, the learner moves again into the realm of theory. Now motivated by an awareness of a problem, the learner uses new information to develop alternate theories that are more useful in explaining the relationship between actions and outcomes and to begin the search for strategies that are more consistent with espoused theories and more effective in achieving intended outcomes. This changed perspective becomes a stimulus for experimentation: new theories suggest different strategies that can then be tested through action. In short, raising questions about practice begins a learning process that leads to behavioural change. The section that follows illustrates each of these stages in more detail.

## Concrete experience

The first step of the learning process is to identify problematic situations. Because the intent of reflective practice is to improve the quality of professional performance, we begin our inquiry by focusing on problems of practice.

There are many different types of problems (Getzels, 1979). In some situations, the problem, with readily available solutions, is presented to the problem solver. In other situations, the problem emerges from one's own experience. In whatever form, the problems arise out of a sense of discomfort or a desire to change. There is a discrepancy between what we perceive to be and what we consider desirable; in some way, the situation falls short of the ideal.

These discrepancies come to our attention in different ways. In some cases, information from another source – an individual or group or a report – helps us to see a problem. [. . .]

In other cases, our own experience helps us to identify problems. [. . .]

Dilemmas can also lead to problem identification, [. . .] [and it] may also come through a surprise or attention to the unexpected. [. . .]

Regardless of how we develop awareness of the problem, its discovery or recognition motivates us to gather information and moves us further into the reflection cycle. [. . .]

Not all problems are of equal dimensions. Some involve only a few people; others may involve an entire school. What is important is not the scope or dimensions of the problem but the significance of the problem to the individual. In reflective practice, we are seeking deep engagement in learning, and relevance produces engagement: a relevant problem rivets attention and arouses the need to learn.

Identification of problems, however, is not easy. People, and educators in particular, desire to view things positively and to be optimistic. In response to organizational problems, discussion turns quickly to solutions while problem identification and analysis are cut short (Bolman and Deal, 1991). Identification of personal problems is even more difficult. Think of the child who comes to the parent with a problem but cannot bring herself to disclose it. Once the problem is spoken, what seemed overwhelming becomes manageable, but the resistance initially was great. Adults are not very different: problems are often seen as an indicator of incompetence and failure. As a result, most of us have effective defences for preventing problem recognition.

With practice in reflection, we learn to take a conscious orientation toward problem finding; but, initially, this step of the process may seem difficult or feel 'unnatural'. Although this skill develops quickly, because the learning cycle begins with problematic experience, one of the initial tasks of the facilitator in a formal reflective practice setting is to enable individuals to uncover or discover problematic situations within the context of their practice.

## Observation and analysis

In the first stage of the process, the inquiry is focused on a particular aspect of practice. Finding the problem motivates the practitioner; there is a genuine need for new information. In the second stage of the process, the practitioner assumes the role of a researcher and begins to gather information. Because reflective practice focuses on personal behaviour within the professional context, we begin to gather and analyse rich information about the experience and particularly about our own behaviour. We become the critic watching our own actions on stage. We stand back from the experience itself, assume a more detached stance, and step outside the action to observe it critically and to describe it fully.

A full description incorporates cognitive and emotional aspects of behaviour. [. . .] To understand experience requires that we explore feelings that were aroused in the situation. Actions are influenced not only by ideas but by feelings as well; only by understanding the personal reactions of ourselves and others can we come to a full understanding of the problem and develop appropriate solutions. Consequently, when we gather information about experience, we mean the full range of human experience including beliefs, values, intentions, attitudes, feelings, ideas, and action (Osterman, 1990).

The means of obtaining observational data are broad and limited only by our own creativity: [. . .] self-reports and recollections, observations of our practice or simulated practice by others reported to us in various ways, completely objective data recorded on audio- or videotapes, documents such as memos, journals, minutes of meetings, or supervisory conference reports, feedback from survey research and action research projects, and sometimes information from debriefing of deliberately generated behaviors such as role plays. Much, if not most, of the data we collect in the observational phase will be qualitative rather than quantitative. The basic issues remain – usefulness, richness, and comprehensiveness.

Once information is at hand, we analyse the experience; we reflect upon it. [. . .] Through reflection and analysis, we strive to understand the experience. We examine experience – both actions and outcomes – as a means to articulate and understand espoused theories and theories-in-use. Why did events take place as they did? What ideas or feelings prompted my actions? Did my actions correspond with my intentions? Did my actions lead to the outcomes I intended?

The term *reflection* is often thought of as a solitary and meditative process; and, in fact, analysis may be done alone – while listening to a tape recording of a committee meeting, watching ourself teach on a videotape, or analysing the contents and attitudes contained in our memos. None the less, because of the deeply ingrained nature of our behavioural patterns, it is sometimes difficult to develop a critical perspective on our own behaviour. For that reason alone, analysis occurring in a collaborative and co-operative environment is likely to lead to greater learning. The whole committee might analyse the tape recording; you and a supervisor might probe into the teaching episode together; a colleague who has 'shadowed' you all day might help to analyse what he or she saw.

The process of inquiry began with a problematic or indeterminate situation. In the initial stages, understanding of the problem may have been little more than an intuitive sense or a gut feeling that something was wrong or could be better. Through these integrally linked processes of observation and analysis, we come to see clearly the discrepancies, incongruities, and failures to reach intentions. The problem begins to emerge more clearly, and we begin to see our own role in the problem more clearly.

[. . .]

Argyris and Schon (1974) made a distinction between single-loop learning and double-loop learning. The 'fix-it' model is a form of single-loop learning: a solution is developed to correct the presenting problem, but the underlying causes of the problem are neither recognized nor addressed. Single-loop learning is largely ineffective in contributing to long-term solutions to problems because the underlying assumptions that reinforce the ineffective behaviours are never examined. Double-loop learning, on the other hand, holds the potential for real change because it examines these underlying assumptions, or theories-in-use, as part of the problem-solving process. Analysis within the framework of reflective practice is designed to lead to double-loop learning. At the completion of this phase, the practitioner has come to an understanding – incomplete though it may be – of espoused theories and theories-in-use. With this knowledge in hand, the practitioner begins the next stage of inquiry: reconceptualization.

## Abstract reconceptualization

In the third stage of the learning cycle, we consider alternate ways of thinking and acting, new action theories that encompass the relationship between actions and outcomes. At this point the practitioner has identified a problem or problem area and, through observation and reflection, has come to understand what was done and why. This theory-in-use, now articulated, has been examined relative to the espoused theory and assessed for effectiveness. With this complete behavioural description in place, the practitioner is now ready to reconsider old ideas and to search for new ones that will lead to a greater alignment between ideas, actions, and outcomes.

This point in the cycle involves an active search for new ideas and new strategies. We are highly motivated to find new information, theories, techniques, or processes to address *our* problem. At this point, we know what we did in the prior situation, and we have an idea of why we did it. We are also well aware of why it didn't work. The objective now is to develop alternate hypotheses or action research strategies that may address the problem. To do that, we gather information that will help us to develop a more effective conceptual and strategic approach.

At every stage of the cycle, the nature of the learning has been personal and engaging. The problem is self-defined and relevant, and the process of observation and analysis in focusing on the individual role in the problem context generates a felt need to improve, change, or reinforce effective behaviours. At this stage of reconceptualization, then, the professional is strongly motivated to seek out and consider new ideas.

We are prompted to try things that before we rejected. We see relevance in ideas that formerly seemed irrelevant. We are now able to make connections between theory and practice, to integrate new information and ideas into our practice. We are now beginning to reshape theories-in-use.

Unlike traditional models of professional development, in the reflective practice approach, the practitioner can use information from a wide variety of sources from the worlds of research and practice. The important issue again is not the source but its utility. Practitioners may find relevant information in research studies or other publications and workshops or formal study. Observations or discussions with colleagues may serve a similar purpose. Confronted with the problem and now with a clearer understanding of the problem and our own role in that problem, the search for knowledge becomes more directed and focused, and – an important distinction – the search is self-directed.

There are many ways to approach the reconceptualization stage. We may do it alone through reading or finding already existing 'answers'. We may take a more creative self-definitional approach. And we may find great value in working collaboratively with others also attempting to work through solutions to the same or similar problems (Miller, 1990). In working with colleagues, we greatly increase the pool of available ideas and resources. [. . .]

## Active experimentation

The final stage in experiential learning is testing our reconceptualized behaviour and assumptions. In the reconceptualization phase, we developed new action theories and framed them as hypotheses. [. . .] We have articulated an action theory that maintains that, if we act in a particular way, we can expect a particular type of response. In this stage, we begin to test this assumption. We make a conscious decision to act in a particular way to test this new conceptualization: we engage in behavioural experiments. These may be trials of our new ideas in actual workplaces or they may be role plays in the relative safety of a reflection group.

This stage completes one cycle and begins another. The experiment produces new concrete experience and the learning process begins anew, but with one important difference. By now, our reflective skills have developed and self-awareness is acute and focused. Although, in the early experiences with reflective practice, it was difficult to distance ourselves from our performance, at this stage of experimentation we go into the action better able to handle the dual role of actor and drama critic. We ourselves are more skilled at gathering information: we are more aware of our own actions, more sensitive to the feelings and reactions of others, and more adept at using a variety of techniques to gather information. At this point, the circular nature of the process is obvious. With the data in hand, we analyse the sequence of events to confirm or disconfirm the new hypothesis. Confirmation reinforces the new theory and provides an incentive for repeating what initially may have been awkward behaviours. Those instances where the experiment doesn't work as expected lead to a renewed search to refine the theory and/or to develop strategies that are more appropriate tests of the theory. Whether the next cycle focuses in a more detailed way on the same problem or addresses another issue, it builds upon and profits from the earlier cycle: learning and professional development become a progressive and continuing process.

## EXPERIENTIAL LEARNING IN ACTION

We have described reflective practice as a form of experiential learning and have done so in a linear and segmented fashion. This was done for conceptual clarity but does not adequately describe the process itself, which is far more fluid and holistic. When we engage in reflective practice, we move back and forth among the stages. For example, some new idea in the reconceptualizatoin stage may momentarily take us back to the analysis phase to check out something we did not think about earlier. Often we will not be aware of particular 'stages' in our reflection. In other instances, dialogue might show evidence that several stages were brought into play almost simultaneously. This will occur even more often when we become very adept at reflection, for reflection like other activities becomes habitual. For newcomers to the reflective process, however, it is probably good counsel to keep the four stages of the experiential cycle clearly in mind as road signs to guide learning and progress through the process.

## CONTRASTING TRADITIONAL AND REFLECTIVE APPROACHES TO PROFESSIONAL DEVELOPMENT

[. . .] Reflective practice and its underlying assumptions are in sharp contrast with the traditional practice of professional development. [. . .]

The following section compares their purposes, assumptions, and practices. [. . .]

### Purpose

The ultimate purpose in the traditional model may be improved performance, but the directly observable purpose – and the purpose embedded in the theory-in-use guiding the behaviours of both instructor and participants – clearly is knowledge acquisition. The instructor spends most of the available time transferring information to generally passive recipients and testing the acquisition of that information.

The immediate as well as ultimate purpose of reflective professional development is behavioural change and improved performance. Attention is focused directly on behaviour, either behaviour enacted before the session and re-collected and analysed during the meeting or behaviour generated during the session itself. While at various times the facilitator may provide information or theories, such presentations are focused directly on behaviour change and improvement of performance.

## Assumptions

The two models differ greatly in their assumptions about behavioural change. [. . .] The traditional approach to professional development, then, reflects an underlying assumption that information is a stimulus for behavioural change, that individuals receiving knowledge will use it to improve performance. Knowing a better way to behave, individuals will simply act on the knowledge. This approach places total faith in rational processes as the source of be-haviour. [. . .]

In reality, there is little evidence that this approach works well and more reason to believe that it seldom leads to noticeable improvement or change in professional practice. [. . .] The administrator introduced to more effective methods of supervision and evaluation finds that day-to-day pressures and demands make it impossible to try the suggested alternatives. [. . .] The new information or programme doesn't produce the desired results. But the as-sumption remains: if the change doesn't occur, the fault is with the specific idea or with the professional to whom the idea has been presented.

The assumptions made about behavioural change in the reflective practice model are more complex [. . .]. [It] comes through self-awareness of formerly unrecognized assumptions in the theory-in-use, unrecognized habitual be-haviours, and unrecognized negative outcomes of these behaviours. Change is a process begun by recognition that something is not exactly 'right' in one's own professional practice. It is initiated [. . .] through careful attention to individual practice. The motivating force behind change is [. . .] the desire to function well in a professional capacity coupled with the awareness that cur-rent behaviour is not fully reaching this goal.

In reflective practice, change includes an emotional as well as a rational dimension. [. . .] Emotions attach to the ways we view ourselves, our actions, and their results. When we inquire into our own unrecognized assumptions and behaviours and find them wanting, there is an emotional load associated with self-confrontation and with personal wrestling about how to respond to the awareness. On the other hand, when we inquire into our own unrecognized assumptions and find them to be positive and effective, there is a strong posi-tive emotional response. Reflective practice assumes the centrality of emotion along with cognition. It strives to recognize, work with, and support the emo-tional aspect of behavioural change.

That personal behavioural change always intersects with culture is another assumption undergirding reflective practice. Unrecognized, habitual be-haviours result from deep acculturation. Behavioural change, then, entails changing the relationship between culture and behaviour. Often, behavioural changes resulting from successful reflection are at odds with the ongoing larger and organizational culture. [. . .] Thus reflective practice assumes that achiev-ing and maintaining desired personal changes also means working for cultural changes, ones that will then buttress the new behaviours. Understanding the cultural dimension of change helps us see why the 'fix-it' approach of the traditional model so frequently fails. The 'fix-it' orientation replaces a part or piece assumed to be broken, but it pays no heed to the culture in which the part is embedded or to the relationship between the cultural values and assumptions and those residing in the part. When the 'fix' is not supported by the surrounding culture, it is quickly rejected. This is especially true when the relationship between behaviour and culture remains unrecognized.

These assumptions about learning, and specifically professional development, directly shape the method of instruction that is adopted: both content and process.

## Content

[. . .] The traditional approach emphasizes knowledge transmission as the means toward improved practice. This knowledge may be described as public knowledge, knowledge as given, and knowledge as content. Public knowledge is [. . .] 'traditions of knowledge that have stood the test of time' (Berlak and Berlak, 1981, p. 145). Knowledge is given when it is assumed to be 'a truth "out there"' (p. 148), that has been discovered and verified. It can then be 'given' or transmitted to others. Knowledge as content is a form of public knowledge that has been organized as 'bodies of information, codified facts, theories, [and] generalizations' (p. 147).

The kind of knowledge transmitted in traditional approaches, especially graduate courses, is often called 'theory' [. . .]. Those who assume such knowledge will improve practice also assume that what is 'wrong' with practice or 'needs improvement' is relatively generalized or standard across individuals and that it is best assessed and prescribed from an external, objective position by experts possessing theoretical knowledge.

In the traditional model, practice assumes a secondary, subordinate relationship to public, given, or theoretical knowledge. [. . .] Even so-called practice courses, taught by practitioners – often retired administrators – containing mostly 'war stories', are really based on the same assumptions as 'theory' courses. In these cases, an individual takes his or her own experience and 'elevates' it to the status of given, public knowledge and generalizes it to the needs of others without the support of the verifying mechanisms used in developing theoretical knowledge. What remains the same is an external agent who decides what the participants need and transmits it to them. In [. . .] neither case is direct attention paid to the individual practice of the learner.

[. . .] Whereas in the traditional model of professional development, public, content, and given knowledge are both the beginning and the end of the process, in the reflective model, this kind of knowledge is used in more limited ways. Transmission of such knowledge is useful in consciousness- or awareness-raising as a stimulus to thinking about discrepancies between intentions and actions or espoused theories and theories-in-use. It is also useful as a source of possibilities for new ways of behaving *after* discrepancies are acknowledged and the individual is motivated to change.

In reflective practice, other varieties of knowledge are central. [. . .]

The predominant, but not sole, emphasis is on knowledge about personal professional practice. Underlying the reflective process is the assumption that useful knowledge addresses specific needs of the individual or constituency; it is experiential knowledge, practitioner knowledge, knowledge of craft, knowledge of personal action theories, and what Schon (1983) called knowing-in-action. Professional growth is envisioned as an odyssey whose purpose is not knowledge in an abstract sense but knowledge of a very personal and purposeful nature. [. . .] The typical relationship between theory and practice is inverted. In the traditional model, theory or public knowledge is the means to improve practice; in the reflective model, attention to practice is the means toward the development and refinement of theory – specifically, personal action theory. Within the reflective process, study of formal theory functions as an important resource in the developmental process, but it is not an end in itself.

In the reflective practice model, the link between theory and practice is explicit – not implicit as in the traditional approach – and the developmental process begins with practice. If we wish to develop new and better methods of practice, we begin by examining the behaviour we want to improve. [. . .] Theory *and* practice are integral and central considerations, and theory includes ideas derived both from formal research and from personal experience. Attention to public knowledge and formal theory is not lost or diminished, but practice – specifically, personal practice – assumes a far greater importance.

## Process

[. . .] Because of the assumption that knowledge transmission leads to behavioural change and the corresponding belief that knowledge is developed and interpreted by researchers or academicians rather than by practitioners, didacticism is the central and legitimate means in the traditional model [. . .] to convey knowledge and to develop cognitive skills. Reflective practice, in contrast, relies to a greater extent on dialectic learning and is rooted in the experience – and particularly the problematic experience – of the learners.

Given the emphasis on public, given, and content knowledge, the instructor assumes the dominant role in the process while the learner functions in a subordinate, largely passive role. In reflective practice, the shift in focus and purpose of learning alters the nature of the learner–instructor relationship and shifts the balance of power and control. In the traditional model, power – to define problems, develop knowledge, prescribe answers, determine processes – and hence control over the nature, direction, and outcomes, rests with university professors, consultants, or other external experts. Participants in the professional development are essentially controlled by others. In juxtaposition, power and control in the reflective process are shared.

In the traditional model, the practitioner adopts a passive role as a consumer of knowledge. In the reflective practice model, the learner's role is far more active. 'The practitioner becomes a researcher . . . and engages in a continuing process of self-education' (Schon, 1983, p. 299). In doing so, the learner assumes a central position, and the model of instructor as expert gives way to that of the instructor as facilitator. The role of the leader is no longer to deliver but to guide – to provide information and resources to facilitate the individual's personal inquiry and professional growth. The facilitator enters into what

Schon (1983) called a *reflective conversation*. In this relationship, the instructor is not an expert responsible for conveying standardized and scientifically determined knowledge to guide the actions of the practitioner but a communication specialist engaged in a discussion of personal meaning.

[. . .] The learner is active and directive in the learning process, and the facilitator and learner – each of whom brings knowledge and expertise to the situation – become collaborators working on a shared task.

Three other aspects of the learning process [should be contrasted]. In the traditional approach, learning is molecular, while, in the reflective approach, it is holistic. The 'fix-it' orientation of traditional development often focuses on discrete skills or segments of behaviour and organizational life. Reflective practice assumes a holistic approach to learning. Beginning with individual behaviour, anything related to it becomes part of the process. At the very least, this includes the individual's background and cultural context. In the traditional situation, with its emphasis on knowledge transmission, the primary emphasis is on cognition in a very narrowly defined sense. The learner is expected to gather and retain information that can be applied to problems of practice; there is little need to involve the indiviudal as a person. In reflective practice, however, the intent is to enable the individual to develop competence.

TABLE 3.1
*Contrasting approaches to professional development*

|  | TRADITIONAL MODEL | REFLECTIVE PRACTICE MODEL |
| --- | --- | --- |
| PURPOSE | Knowledge acquisition | Behavioural change |
| ASSUMPTIONS | Change via standardized knowledge | Change via self-awareness |
|  | Change: Rational | Change: Rational, emotional, social, cultural |
| CONTENT | Knowledge: | Knowledge: |
|  | Public | Public and personal |
|  | Given | Given and problematic |
|  | Content | Content and process |
|  | Theory: | Theory *and* practice |
|  | Espoused theory | Behaviour: Espoused and theories-in-use, actions and outcomes |
|  | Theory/practice: Implicit/discrete | Theory/practice: Explicit/integral |
| PROCESS | Didactic/abstract | Dialectic/experimental |
|  | Individual, molecular, cognitive | Collaborative, holistic, personal |
|  | Instructor as expert | Instructor as facilitator |
|  | Learner as subordinate | Learner as agent |
|  | Practitioner as passive consumer | Practitioner as action researcher |

Accordingly, the focus expands to incorporate the individual as person. Individuals are assumed to have cognitive, emotional, and social dimensions. Learning to behave in different ways involves all of these. The concept of cognition also expands from a narrow emphasis on information gathering or recall to the development of analytic and conceptual skills that enable the individual to create knowledge needed to respond to the diverse demands of practice. Finally, in the reflective mode, learning is a social process, whereas in the traditional mode, it is individual. In the usual process, learners are addressed as isolated individuals learning in parallel but not interrelated ways. In reflective practice, learning is co-operatively based. Collaboration extends beyond the learner–facilitator relationship to include all of the individuals in an interdependent learning process.

Table 3.1 presents a condensed summary of the various contrasting assumptional and belief differences for the traditional and reflective practice models of professional development.

[. . .]

# REFERENCES

Argyris, C. and Schon, D. A. (1974) *Theory in practice: increasing professional effectiveness*. San Francisco: Jossey-Bass.

Berlak, A. and Berlak, H. (1981) *Dilemmas of schooling*. New York: Methuen.

Bolman, L. G. and Deal, T. E. (1991) *Reframing organizations: artistry, choice, and leadership*. San Francisco: Jossey-Bass.

Brown, J. S., Collins, A. and Duguid, P. (1989a) Debating the situation: a rejoinder to Palincsar and Wineburg, *Educational Researcher*, Vol. 19, no. 4, pp. 10–12.

Brown, J. S., Collins, A. and Duguid, P. (1989b) Situated cognition and the culture of learning, *Educational Researcher*, Vol. 18, no. 1, pp. 32–42.

Dewey, J. (1938) *Logic: the theory of inquiry*. New York: Holt.

Getzels, J. W. (1979) Problem-finding and research in educational administration, in G. L. Immegart and W. L. Boyd (eds) *Problem-finding in educational administration* (pp. 5–22). Lexington, MA: Lexington.

Kolb, D. A. (1984) *Experiential learning: experience as the source of learning and development*. Englewood Cliffs, NJ: Prentice-Hall.

Miller, J. L. (1990) *Creating spaces and finding voices: teachers collaborating for empowerment*. Albany: State University of New York Press.

Osterman, K. F. (1990) Reflective practice: a new agenda for education, *Education and Urban Society*, Vol. 22, no. 2, pp. 133–52.

Prestine, N. A. and LeGrand, B. F. (1991) Cognitive learning theory and the preparation of educational administrators: implications for practice and policy, *Educational Administration Quarterly*, Vol. 27, no. 1, pp. 61–89.

Schon, D. A. (1983) *The reflective practitioner: how professionals think in action*. New York: Basic Books.

Schon, D. A. (1987) *Educating the reflective practitioner*. San Francisco: Jossey-Bass.

# CHAPTER 4

# Consultants, Clients and the Consulting Process

PETER COCKMAN, BILL EVANS AND PETER REYNOLDS

*This material has been abridged*

## WHAT IS CONSULTING?

[. . .] You have been hired to facilitate change in your organization. It is your job to influence and advise people, to help them and persuade them to do things differently. You are likely to be asked to help people adapt to new technology, changes in the market-place or changes in the organizational structure. If you are successful, people's lives will be different when you have moved on. Making this sort of impact on an organization is difficult even if you are the chief executive with all the power incumbent in that position. But somebody has asked you to make your imprint on the organization and given you no formal authority over anyone. Indeed, you may well be in a comparatively lowly position. No one would blame you if you are feeling frustrated and powerless.
   [. . .]
   We believe that consulting should be what happens when someone with a problem or difficulty seeks help to solve that problem or resolve that difficulty from someone who has special skill.

## HOW IS CONSULTING DIFFERENT FROM COUNSELLING?

From our point of view a counsellor is someone who specializes in working with a single client or maybe a couple to help them with personal difficulties which they are experiencing in their lives. [. . .]
   Counselling is a specialized form of consultancy which tends to be used with people who have personal problems which they find difficult or impossible to solve on their own. Consultants, especially client-centred consultants, sometimes find themselves in the role of counsellor during the course of their work in organizations. Indeed, we would argue that counselling skills should be part of the stock in trade of every effective client-centred consultant.

# WHO NEEDS CONSULTING SKILLS?

[. . .]

Anyone who is in a role where the main emphasis is on helping individuals, departments or organizations to be more effective in whatever they do can be fairly considered to be a consultant. [. . .]

Furthermore, with the move towards collaboration and involvement at work and the need to gain commitment to change, managers themselves are beginning to act as consultants to their own staff whenever possible. When they interact with staff about their performance or development, talk to customers about their needs, or deal with the hundreds of consumer associations and community groups, they need the same skills as those who have more formal consultant roles. So for our purposes consultants are:

> People who find themselves having to influence other people, or advise them about possible courses of action to improve the effectiveness of any aspect of their operations, without any formal authority over them or choosing not to use what authority they have.

This can be described as a *consultant/client* relationship. It is present whether you find yourself helping managers to be more effective; helping teachers relate better to their pupils, to one another or to the headteacher; helping teams work better together; providing career guidance to pupils leaving school, graduates leaving university or women returning to work; or launching a major initiative to improve quality throughout an organization be it commercial, industrial or educational. Whether you are someone stopped in the corridor by a colleague saying 'Can I have a word with you?' or the Secretary General of the United Nations jetting across the world in an effort to avert global war – *you* are a consultant.

From our point of view, if you are involved for even part of your time in providing help to someone else, in whatever manner you do it you need consulting skills. [. . .]

# WHAT IS CLIENT-CENTRED CONSULTING?

[. . .]

While many consultants seem to be in the business of dispensing small amounts of professional advice for very large fees (and in the process ensuring dependency) that is not our view of a healthy relationship with a client. That is not to say that there aren't times when the client wants and needs professional advice to solve a problem. If a piece of machinery breaks down what most people want is an expert to fix it so that it stays fixed. But, and we believe it is a big but, for each one of those there are hundreds of situations and problems which the client could solve with a little judicious help from a client-centred consultant who is not interested in fostering dependency but wants the client to be able to solve similar problems in future without recourse to the consultant.

[This book] is about consultants who are client-centred. They are presumed to have sufficient expertise in their own technical discipline. [. . .] What they have in addition is an extra competence in the process of consultation. They are also likely to have:

- a high level of self-awareness;
- a thorough understanding of the ways in which clients are likely to behave as individuals and in groups;
- a wide range of professional and interpersonal skills;
- sufficient flexibility of style to deal with a variety of clients and situations;
- a real understanding of the helping process within the context of their professional discipline.

We believe that all consultants are more effective if they have a feeling of self-confidence which stems from adequate knowledge, skill and ability and consequently a positive self-image. [. . .] However, the effective use of that technical knowledge depends to a large extent upon the personal style of the consultant. The most effective consultants seem to be those who have worked on their personal styles to make them appropriate to the circumstances, particularly in the way they build relationships, identify problems and arrange implementation of solutions.

The ways of influencing and generally being sensitive and responsive to the needs and feelings of clients are at least as important and probably more important than technical expertise. It is our experience that when consultants and clients treat each other with mutual respect then the outcome is usually successful.

In summary, client-centred consulting is about:

- starting where the clients are, not where you think they are;
- helping clients decide what data or information to collect;
- allowing clients to diagnose their problem for themselves;
- helping clients make sense of the data rather than doing it yourself;
- providing theory to help clients make sense of the data or make decisions about courses of action;
- helping clients gain commitment to the plan of action;
- assisting clients to implement the decisions and arranging follow-up if appropriate;
- disengaging responsibly as soon as possible;
- ensuring that clients retain ownership of the problem and don't become dependent on you.

## HOW DO I STAY CLIENT-CENTRED?

[. . .] While many consultants take it upon themselves to decide what is right for the client and therefore get involved in influencing, persuading or directing the client into changed behaviour, the client-centred consultant does not operate this way. It is always possible for the client to terminate the consultation; the consultant, while having an opinion, leaves the client with the option to change or not. Thus the client-centred consultant is less likely to be manipulative in helping the client come to a decision about how to solve the problem. The client always has freedom of choice. This is not to say that the consultant shouldn't work very hard to ensure the client assesses the implications of not changing and considers the advantages and disadvantages of all the options for solving the problem. But the final decision about action or inaction should remain with the client.

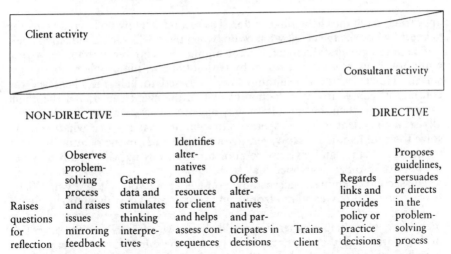

FIGURE 4.1 Levels of client/consultant activity (adapted from Lippitt and Lippitt, *The consulting process in action*, Pfeiffer & Company, San Diego, CA, 1978. Reproduced with permission of the publisher.)

Most behaviour, whether of an individual, members of a team or people in a larger organization or social system, follows standard patterns and is repetitive or cyclical in nature. [. . .] Much of the time such standard patterns are useful: [. . .] but sometimes such behavioural patterns are not functional. [. . .] Often ineffective behaviour patterns do not get challenged by the people working in the department or company. How many times have you heard the answer 'We've always done it that way' to the naive question 'Why do you do that?'.

The consultant's function is to challenge ineffective patterns of behaviour which are seen to be inhibiting effectiveness or change. When you see a management group constantly ending meetings in uproar, it is up to you, the consultant, to point out the incidence and implications of such cyclical behaviour and help the client replace it with more effective behaviour. The consultant's function is to help the client identify and break out of such damaging cycles of behaviour.

One way of looking at the levels of activity between client and consultant in the problem-solving process is illustrated by Lippitt and Lippitt (1978) in Figure 4.1. All these styles of operating are valid and legitimate. The real difficulty facing the consultant is deciding how to use them appropriately.

At the directive end of the continuum we find the consultant who has technical knowledge and expertise that the client lacks. It may be appropriate, therefore, to give the client advice or information to solve the immediate problem. This may be what you want when your car, television or computer has broken down. However, [. . .] having fixed the immediate problem it may be more appropriate to move towards the non-directive end and help the client learn how to avoid getting into similar difficulties in future, or how to rectify the malfunction without recourse to a consultant.

There seem to be two important dilemmas for the client-centred consultant. The first is 'How do I use my technical expertise and know-how without appearing to tell the client what to do?' The second is 'How do I avoid being the "expert" who tells the client what to do, when the role is such a seductive one?'

To address the first dilemma, the consultant should never withhold expertise and know-how from the client if, by withholding it, the problem doesn't get solved. However, the consultant is well advised to help the client see the consultant as a source of information which the client can use. If the client cannot see this then the consultant may have to be prescriptive. This is especially so if the client is in a desperate situation and has no idea what to do to solve the problem. [. . .] However, giving advice early in the relationship may set up dependency and give rise to poor problem solving. Giving advice when the relationship has developed may be acceptable.

The second dilemma concerns how you feel about yourself and your client. If your personal power comes from being seen as an expert then you are likely to be very attracted to giving advice. Likewise, if you view your client as incompetent and helpless then you are likely to give advice. From the other side of the relationship the client may wish to be in the safe hands of an expert and therefore could ask for advice. Some of the following questions attempt to spring the trap:

- What would you do in my position?
- You must have experience of such problems; what did you do?
- How do other people solve similar problems?
- I have no experience. I can't possibly solve this problem, can I?
- I'm new to this, can you just give me a few ideas?

[. . .]

The training role can offer opportunities for powerful client-centred work. However, it is possible to train and educate entirely prescriptively. [. . .] But in the training and educating role the client-centred consultant helps the client to diagnose the difficulty, may offer theories, models or frameworks to help the client understand the difficulty and what to do about it and may then help the client implement the new methods or ways of working. However, the client always retains the ability to reject the particular theory or model or to adapt it to the particular situation. [. . .]

Moving further towards the non-directive end of the Lippitts' continuum, we can start to identify a problem-solving approach that gives the client more involvement. This requires the consultant to work hard to stay out of the content of the problem, and help the client get some clarity about the problem and the options available. Such a role is entirely about being and staying client-centred. You are there to enable the client to see how many different problems make up the presenting problem, how many strands there are to the same problem and maybe how the presenting problem relates to the real problem. Once that has been done you can help the client to think about alternative courses of action to solve the problem, evaluate these alternatives and the implications and decide which one to choose. The client may need help to decide on a plan of action but the final plan should belong to the client rather than the consultant. It is important to note that this role is not about accepting all that the client says without question. There may be inconsistencies between what the client says and what the client does and this may need confronting. Overall, however, the consultant is there to help the client:

- perceive the situation more clearly;
- devise alternative strategies for solving the problem;
- evaluate the alternatives;
- decide on a course of action (including doing nothing);
- plan the implementation and take action.

At the extreme of the non-directive end the consultant stays entirely within the client's frame of reference and helps the client get a clearer understanding of the problem. This includes identifying any feelings which may be forming a block to logical problem solving. The client is therefore ultimately responsible for doing something about the problem or not. This is also the extreme of client-centred consulting. The consultant doesn't get involved in the problem, accepts the client as he or she is, works hard to establish a trusting and open relationship but does not give advice. Unless, of course, the client is absolutely floundering, when a prescriptive solution may be all that is left. What the consultant can and must do is to reflect back key words, summarize and paraphrase the client's thoughts and feelings.

While it will be obvious that a consultant can fulfil many roles during any one intervention (and may change from moment to moment) it is important to maintain client-centredness throughout if you wish to enhance your client's problem-solving ability and do not wish to be seen as an expert. In order to stay client-centred you need to address the following types of questions:

- Do I get defensive when challenged or confronted?
- Does my self-esteem depend upon being seen as an expert?
- Do I like giving advice to people to influence their behaviour?

## WHO ARE THE CLIENTS?

[. . .] When people seek help to deal with some difficulty or to solve a problem by approaching someone they believe can provide help, they become clients. [. . .] Clients are often individuals seeking assistance for themselves. However, the client can also be a group, a department or an organization. We find it more useful to think of a 'client system'. [. . .] Also, in organizations it is seldom the case that an individual can bring about any necessary change alone.

It is important not to define your client system too narrowly. You need to ask yourself which people are likely to be significantly affected by the changes. The answer may lead you to identify individuals or groups from other sections, other departments, or even other companies in different geographical locations. All these people are potentially part of your client system.

In summary then a client is:

- any individual, or group of people who need some kind of help from outside (the consultant) to work on a problem;
- probably someone with whom the relationship is temporary – although some assignments can last for months or even years;
- someone who enters into the relationship with the consultant on a voluntary basis.

# DO I HAVE THE REAL CLIENT?

Even when you have identified that there is more than one client or that there is a whole client system it is often quite difficult to know that you have reached the point where you are dealing with the real or total client system. Revans (1980) talks about the artfulness of effective negotiation to find 'Who knows? Who cares? Who can?' If we apply these three questions to finding out who our real client or client system is, we can ensure that we involve all three if they happen to be different.

**Who knows** – about the problem or has most of the information that we need to be able to diagnose and help solve the problem is often the person doing the job. [. . .] Unless we accept that they are part of the system we shall not get very far.

**Who cares** – that something is done about the problem might well be the manager with the problem. It is likely to be the manager who identified the problem or who is bearing the pain due to the ineffectiveness of the department. However, there may be other people who care about the problem who also have to be considered.

**Who can** – do something about the solution? If those with the problem have to ask for authority or approval to implement the solution, if they need more resources in terms of money or time or people and someone else controls those resources, then you had better involve that person as part of the client system at the beginning. [. . .]

Great care is therefore needed to ensure that before you get very far into your intervention you have identified (as far as you can) all the parts of the client system. Also, as far as possible, you will need to work with all these various parts of the system so that you don't get to the end and find that the implementation doesn't go ahead because you didn't identify who had to authorize the necessary finance.

# THE INTERNAL CONSULTANT

[. . .] External consultants are usually there by invitation, but this may not be so for the internal consultant. As an internal consultant you may be imposed by the client's boss or by someone who recognizes that there is a problem and has the authority to order a consultation to take place. This is likely to give rise to all manner of difficulties when you are trying to establish a relationship or find out what the client's needs are. The following appear to us to be some of the advantages and disadvantages we experienced when working as internal consultants:

| Advantages | Disadvantages |
| --- | --- |
| You may be able to take longer gaining entry | You are part of the culture you are seeking to change |
| You will probably know the client | Your department may have a poor image |
| You may know something about the client's problems | You may have a poor image |

| | |
|---|---|
| You know the history of the company | You may be imposed by the organization |
| You may share the same values | You may know things about the client that you can't disclose |
| You may spot non-genuine reasons for calling you in | You may have problems over confidentiality |
| You will probably know where to go for more information | You may be part of the problem |
| You will be able to find the real client more easily | You may have difficulty consulting either above you or below you in grade or status |
| You may already have established a good reputation for helping | You may have to confront people who might take offence |
| You may be able to ask for help from other internal consultants | You may be discounted as a prophet in your own land |
| You may find it easier to get involved in implementation and follow-up | You may fear that giving bad news could adversely affect your career prospects |

We have found that many of these disadvantages exist solely in the mind of the internal consultant and are not borne out in practice. However, it is our view that if any of them appear to be potential disadvantages they are best high-lighted as early in the consultation as possible.

## THE CONSULTING CYCLE

Whenever you decide to work with someone to help solve a problem you are beginning a process which is similar to starting a journey together. The journey starts with an initial meeting and hopefully ends with the implementation of a different and more effective way of operating. The phases that make up this consulting cycle are:

(1) Starting the consultation – making initial contact and establishing a work-ing relationship (or, as we call it, gaining entry).
(2) Contracting – finding out what the client wants.
(3) Collecting data – finding out what happens now.
(4) Making sense of the data – diagnosing the problem.
(5) Generating options, making decisions and planning.
(6) Implementing the plans and taking action.
(7) Disengaging – arranging any necessary follow-up action.

This presents you with your first dilemma as a consultant. More often than not your client will want to tell you all about the problem and what needs to be done about it at the very first meeting. You, on the other hand, will know the folly of rushing into data collection and problem solving without getting to know your client, letting the client get to know you and reaching clear agree-ment on what he or she wants you to do, i.e. contracting.

This is likely to be even more difficult for the internal consultant. The temptation to gloss over these early phases is likely to be very strong as you will often be expected to know quite a lot about your potential clients and their problems. [. . .]

## Starting the consultation

This consists of making initial contact with the client and starting to build a relationship – we call it gaining entry. Initial contact means the first meeting with a person you assume to be the client. [. . .] To prepare for this meeting you will need to have given some thought to how you feel. Are you ready for the meeting? Are you as well prepared as you might be? What sort of first impression do you want to make? Are you in the right frame of mind to meet your client and deal with any difficulties that might arise?

Gaining entry means you and the client coming together to start to build a relationship of mutual trust and respect. You will want to find out a little about the client and the situation the client is in, as well as getting to know something about the problem you are there to help solve. You will also want the client to find out something about you so that confidence in you can begin to build up.

## Contracting

Contracting is about making explicit as many of the client's needs as you can. It is also the opportunity to let the client know, as explicitly as possible, what you are prepared to do and what part you want the client to play in the problem-solving process. It is important for both of you to understand in detail your mutual expectations of the relationship – who will do what and any boundaries that may exist. Contracting is therefore about ownership. One of the main difficulties in contracting is deciding when you have done enough to begin working on the problem. Delay too long and your client is likely to get frustrated with your apparent inactivity. Cut it short and you may find that your mutual expectations have not been specific enough and that too much is left to the imagination. In the context of client-centred consulting, contracting is not an exact science and there are bound to be grey areas. Fortunately, you can usually renegotiate as you progress through the assignment.

## Collecting data

This means collecting data about what is happening now. Provided you have completed gaining entry and contracting satisfactorily you should have a clear idea of where the client's difficulty lies. You will then be able to help the client collect data relevant to the problem. There are many sources for this data: factual data from staff or records; feelings and opinions of everyone involved or comments and attitudes of both internal and external customers. Most professions have their own methods of collecting the data they need. [. . .] However, you will also be collecting data that gives you an impression of how the problem is managed, what organizational constraints are in place, what policies and procedures help or hinder how the department operates. And even as you collect this sort of organizational data you will have feelings about the staff, the managers and the environment which come to you through your intuition. All this data can be useful and can be fed back to the client.

Up to now the phases in the consulting cycle have been linear, following each other in a sequence. While it is often necessary to go back and forth from one to another it is generally possible to complete one before going on to the next. But by the time you reach the point where you begin to help the client collect data, the cyclical part of consulting has begun.

## Making sense of the data and diagnosing the problem

This phase of the cycle involves helping the client to spend time reflecting, questioning and discussing the data in order to make sense of it in terms of the difficulty being faced. Where there is insufficient data you may have to return to the previous phase and collect some more; where there is sufficient data or too much data, you may have to help the client determine what is important and relevant. In this case the data may need sorting or presenting in a clearer, more understandable way. It may be possible for you to offer the client data-presentation frameworks to help the client decide what extra data is needed. Alternatively, you could help by designing a questionnaire or actually collecting the data yourself. But whatever way you choose to help, the decision about which data or information to collect must come from the client.

This phase presents another significant dilemma for the client-centred consultant. On the one hand, you want to stay with the client's diagnosis so that you don't take ownership of the problem. But on the other hand you will often realize that the client is dealing with symptoms rather than the real problem. Often the client will stay firmly in the content or task aspects of the problem when the real difficulties are embedded in issues about how the problem is managed and how people feel about it. This issue about the real problem may have to be confronted before the client enters the next phase.

## Generating options, making decisions and planning

Once the problem has been diagnosed you should be in a position to help your client generate the maximum number of options or possible solutions. In client-centred consulting it sometimes happens that you can see more options than the client can. Great care has to be taken about introducing these options, or the client may adopt one without really thinking and then blame you when it doesn't solve the problem. So in many situations it is better to stick with the client's chosen option even though you can think of a 'better' one. Your job is to challenge and confront so that your client doesn't just take the easy option. You may also have to help your client think through the implications of the decisions he or she makes so that there is as little doubt as possible that the right decision has been made.

Having made the decision the next step involves planning. Without a detailed plan of action very little is likely to happen to solve the problem. It is your job to encourage the client to question every aspect of the plan, to try to foresee what might go wrong and to anticipate the resources required (including time and financial costs). You are also there to help the client get commitment from the whole client system before implementation.

Helping the client in Phases 4 and 5 might involve introducing some theory to the client. Such theory might help to make sense of the data, or diagnose the problem, or make decisions or plans. The kind of theory that might be of use could be just those theories you use to help yourself. This brings in yet another dilemma for the client-centred consultant. Do you merely use the theory to help the client, or do you spend time *teaching* the theory so that the client will be able to use it to solve similar problems in the future without assistance?

## Implementing the plan and taking action

Many consultants leave before the plans are implemented and action taken. They will often write a report recommending certain action and present it to the client either by post or at a feedback meeting. [. . .] The only way you can be sure that the plan is implemented is to be there while it happens. You may agree to be part of the implementation team but not to be in charge. Your job is to be there monitoring, mentoring, encouraging, supporting, confronting, opening doors or counselling and training, but not to take ownership. It may be very tempting to take a leading role during implementation especially if you think there is a danger of all your hard work being wasted. We always try to remember that the problem belongs to the client and so does the solution. If clients wish to exercise the option to do nothing, that is their privilege.

In our experience most barriers to implementation are about four key issues: capability, organization, ownership and leadership. Briefly, this means that people do not have the skills and knowledge needed, or believe that they don't. They may not be really committed to the plan either because they were not involved or because their attitude to the problem and its solution is one of apathy or mistrust, and therefore there is no ownership. Alternatively, the leadership may be such that people do not believe that the organization or its managers are committed and fear they will not provide the support necessary for the solution to work. Equally, where people involved in the implementation come from different disciplines, how they are organized can become a problem. Unless these issues are addressed during the planning stage, successful implementation is highly problematic.

## Disengaging

Once the plans have been implemented and action taken it is necessary to check that the new way of working is what is required and has replaced the old way which was causing the problem. If it has then you can probably disengage with some certainty that the new way of operating will stay in place. If it hasn't then you may have to go around the consulting cycle again until it does. You may have to help the clients examine the options or generate more. You may have to help them make different decisions or amend their plans. You may have to go further back into the process to examine the data, make different inferences from it and amend the diagnosis. You may even have to go back to collect more data or revisit the contract to check whether or not it contributed to inadequate implementation. Figure 4.2 shows the [entire] process.

However, and whenever, you disengage it is vitally important that you do it well. Your aim should be to bring the consultation to a satisfactory end for both the client and yourself. It is especially important for the internal consultant to leave on good terms with the client, however successful or unsuccessful the outcome of the consultation. Your reputation and that of your colleagues in your department may well depend on how well you disengage. [. . .]

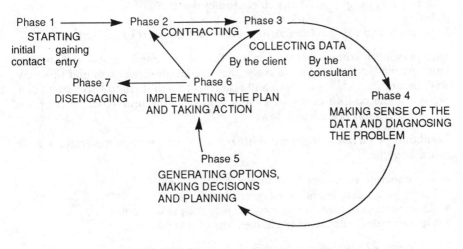

FIGURE 4.2 The consulting process

## Follow-up

Follow-up may often be needed to help the client maintain the implementation to the required standard. It may be that you have to arrange monitoring and support for the client either in the short term or on a continuous or occasional basis. However, it is very easy to get seduced into being available long after you should have left the client alone. Client dependence is easy to develop but very hard to stop. If your follow-up action happens some time after the implementation you may well find yourself having to start a new consultation from initial contact and gaining entry.

## LEARNING STYLES AND THE CONSULTING PROCESS

[. . .]

We have, for many years, helped our clients to see the relevance of their learning styles and their applicability to their problem-solving and consulting ability. In this respect we have been greatly influenced by Kolb (1985) [who . . .] argues that there are four distinct stages in the learning cycle:

*Learning from feeling*
[('Concrete
Experience')]

Learning from specific experiences
Relating to people
Sensitivity to feelings and people

*Learning by watching*
[('Reflective
Observation')]

Careful observation before making a judgement
Viewing things from different perspectives
Looking for the meaning of things

*Learning by thinking*
[('Abstract
Conceptualization')]

Logical analysis of ideas
Systematic planning
Acting on intellectual understanding of a situation

| *Learning by doing* | Ability to get things done |
|---|---|
| [('Active | Risk taking |
| Experimentation')] | Influencing people and events through action |

Each person's learning style is a combination of the four basic styles. However, most people have one or more styles they are comfortable with and this may well distort their ability to learn and also tend to pull them towards particular phases of the consulting cycle. Combinations of the four basic descriptions provide the styles described below.

Combining *concrete experience* with *reflective observation* generates a style called *diverger*:

• Sees concrete situations from many points of view.
• Understands people and is sensitive to feelings.
• Recognizes problems but observes rather than takes action.
• Open-minded, adaptable to change, lots of imagination.

Combining *reflective observation* with *abstract conceptualization* generates a style called *assimilator*:

• Collects and understands a wide range of information.
• Puts information into concise, logical form.
• Focuses on abstract ideas and concepts rather than people.
• Logical soundness more important than practicality.
• Creates models and plans and develops theories.

Combining *abstract conceptualization* with *active experimentation* generates a style called *converger*:

• Finds practical uses for theories and ideas.
• Able to solve problems and make decisions based on finding solutions.
• Better with technical problems than interpersonal issues.
• Deductive reasoning.

Combining *active experimentation* with *concrete experience* generates a style called *accommodator*:

• Implements plans involving new challenges.
• Acts more on intuition than logical analysis.
• Relies on people rather than technical analysis for information.
• Risk taking.

Figure 4.3 illustrates how these styles fit into the basic model.
  [. . .]
When the learning styles model is integrated with the consulting cycle it can be seen that some learning styles have particular strengths which are useful in particular phases of the consulting cycle (see Figure 4.4).

When collecting data about what is happening now the *accommodators* and *divergers* will be particularly useful. As you move into making sense of the data and diagnosing the problem you will want to make use of the *divergers* and *assimilators*. As you progress towards exploring options, making decisions and

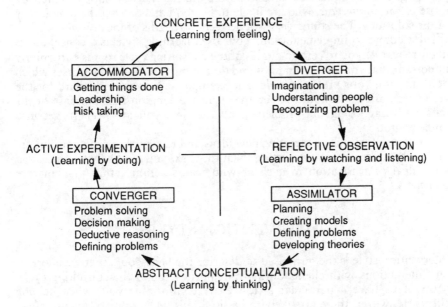

FIGURE 4.3 Kolb learning styles

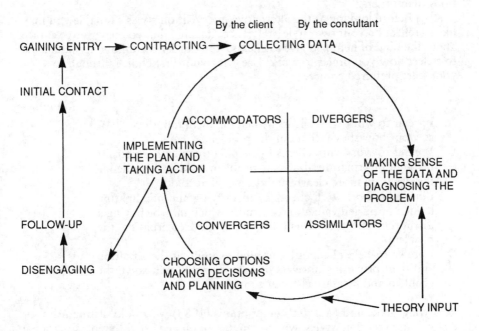

FIGURE 4.4 Learning styles and the consulting process

planning, the strengths of the *assimilators* are likely to be supplemented by those of the *convergers*, who are likely to be good at assessing the practicality of the solutions. The *convergers* will need the strengths of the *accommodators* when it comes to implementation. Your own learning style as a consultant is likely to attract you to certain phases of the consulting cycle so it is particularly important that you know what it is and do not hurry through the phases which don't fit with your preferred style. For example, it is likely to be hard for the very pragmatic consultant to keep the client working on making sense of the data and diagnosing the problem if all the time you are keen to get into implementation.

Similarly, if you like generating new ideas and recognizing problems but are not really concerned about putting them to work, you are likely to generate a great deal of frustration in a client who wants action rather than mature reflection.

## INTERVENTION STYLES

Intervention style is the term used to describe the behaviours that we adopt in our interactions with clients during our journey round the consulting cycle. Most of us have a particular style we are comfortable with when helping clients. However, there are likely to be situations when that style is not effective enough. [. . .] There is no part of the consulting process where one or more styles are not appropriate. Whatever style you choose, there are consequences and implications. Furthermore, some styles are more important in some situations than others.

[. . .] Before looking at the alternative intervention styles available you may like to reflect on your own style preference. Imagine that you have a free choice about the kind of help you give to clients. Rank order the following statements to reflect how you prefer to work. Use 1 for your first choice through to 4 for your least preferred choice.

*Ranking*

A   I prefer to work with clients by helping them talk through or
    sort out how they feel about the problem.                              . . . . . . . . .
B   I prefer to work with clients by helping them gather and sift
    through information about the problem to help them define
    the situation more clearly and decide what to do.                      . . . . . . . . .
C   I prefer to work with clients by identifying and highlighting
    hidden or buried values and attitudes which may be having a
    disruptive effect on client behaviour or exacerbating the
    problem.                                                               . . . . . . . . .
D   I prefer to help clients by carefully examining the situation
    and then providing answers or solutions that will solve the
    problem and increase client effectiveness.                            . . . . . . . . .

Following Blake and Mouton's descriptions (1983) we would distinguish four distinct intervention styles which can be employed in different situations: *acceptant, catalytic, confrontational* and *prescriptive.*

## Acceptant style

A consultant working in an acceptant style helps clients by empathic listening and by providing emotional support. This style of neutral, non-judgemental support can help clients to relax their defences, confront disabling emotional reactions and find their own way forward. It allows and encourages clients to clear what is blocking their ability to deal logically and rationally with their problem. In many respects it is typical of the early stages of counselling. However, [. . .] it can also be useful in many other situations with individuals and groups.

## Catalytic style

A consultant working in a catalytic style helps clients gather more data about the problem, sift through it to decide the relative importance of aspects of the data, or reflect upon it to make a diagnosis of the problem. Not all clients are short of information – some have so much that they can't see the wood for the trees. The intention behind the style is that once the clients have obtained and made sense of the data or information they will be able to choose options and move forward to solving the problem. Although the catalytic style can involve many types of data-gathering methodologies, it is perhaps typified at the interpersonal level by questions which begin with who, what, why, when, where and how. In this sense it is a diagnostic style. However, the important point is that, although catalytic interventions may help clients at the data-gathering stage, the solution is always generated by the clients themselves.

## Confrontational style

A consultant working in a confrontational style helps the clients by calling attention to discrepancies between the values and beliefs they hold and how they put these values and beliefs into practice, i.e. their behaviour. Most of us have theories in our head (espoused theories) and yet we behave in ways which are quite contrary (theories in use). The confrontational style points out these differences to clients so that they are able to recognize the discrepancies and have an opportunity to decide if they wish to change.

## Prescriptive style

Consultants working in a prescriptive style with clients generally listen to the clients' problem, collect the data they require, make sense of it from their own experience and present the clients with a solution or recommendations. It is probably the most common style used by specialists although it may not be the most effective. Typically, it is the style used by experts or those who think they are experts, e.g. doctors with their patients. The assumption is that the clients do not have the skill, knowledge or objectivity to make an accurate diagnosis or prescription of their own. Unfortunately, this is seldom the case; clients seldom know absolutely nothing about their problem and may have had the particular problem for some time. However, consultants can still use their expertise and experience by becoming a source of data to enable clients to provide their own solution or satisfactory way forward, without removing all freedom of action from the clients. There are situations in which the prescriptive style is entirely appropriate.

We suggest that these four styles constitute a practical and comprehensive description of most legitimate consultant behaviour. However, despite the fact that all the styles can be of value, you will probably feel more comfortable with one or two (as the ranking exercise may have shown). You may also tend to use your preferred style more often than the others. This could be detrimental to the consultant/client relationship as all styles have their uses in different situations and phases of the consulting cycle. The key is being able to recognize when a particular style is needed and then to use it appropriately. [. . .]

You may like to turn back and have a second look at your ranking now that you have read about each style. Assuming you have a good understanding of how you operate with clients it could provide insight into your favourite styles and highlight areas where you may need to do some additional work to become more client-centred.

## SUMMARY

- Consulting is what happens when one person has a problem or difficulty and seeks help from someone with special skills.
- Typically, counselling is a specialized type of consultancy and may form part of consulting.
- Consulting skills are needed by many specialists, advisers and helpers in organizations. Many managers are also beginning to find they need consulting skills.
- Consultants can be defined as those who find themselves having to influence or advise others without any formal authority or choosing not to use what authority they have.
- Client-centred consultants recognize that being sensitive and responsive to the needs of clients is as important as technical competence.
- The training role, used appropriately, can offer many opportunities for client-centred work.
- Clients can be single individuals, a disparate group or a whole organization. In organizations, it is often more practical to conceive of 'client systems'.
- The real client is defined by:
  — Who knows?
  — Who cares?
  — Who can?
- The consulting cycle follows the path:
  — initial contact and gaining entry;
  — contracting;
  — collecting data;
  — making sense of the data – diagnosing the problem;
  — generating options, making decisions, planning;
  — implementing plans and taking action;
  — disengaging and follow-up.

- The phases of consulting, from collecting data to implementation, form a cyclic path and are consistent with current thinking on experiential learning. Indeed, consulting and experiential learning are identical.
- The process of consulting requires a variety of personal styles. These are:
  — acceptant;
  — catalytic;
  — confrontational;
  — prescriptive.
- Being able to recognize and use all styles is an important element of consultant competence.

[. . .]

# REFERENCES

Blake, R. R. and Mouton, J. S. (1983) *Consultation: a handbook for individual and organization development*. Wokingham: Addison-Wesley.

Kolb, D. A. (1985) *Learning style inventory*. Boston: McBer & Co.

Lippitt, G. and Lippitt, R. (1978) *The consulting process in action*. University Associates, US.

Revans, R. W. (1980) *Action learning – new techniques for managers*. London: Blond & Briggs.

# CHAPTER 5

# The Philosophy of Research Design

MARK EASTERBY-SMITH, RICHARD THORPE AND ANDY LOWE

*This material has been abridged*

[. . .]

There are at least three reasons why an understanding of philosophical issues is useful. Firstly, it can help to clarify research designs, and by 'research design' we mean more than simply the methods by which data is collected and analysed. It is the overall configuration of a piece of research: what kind of evidence is gathered from where, and how such evidence is interpreted in order to provide good answers to the basic research question. Secondly, a knowledge of philosophy can help the researcher to recognize which designs will work and which will not. It should enable the researcher to avoid going up too many blind alleys and indicate the limitations of particular approaches. Thirdly, a knowledge of philosophy can help the researcher identify, and even create, designs that may be outside his or her past experience. It may also help the researcher to adapt research designs according to the constraints of different subject or knowledge structures.

[. . .] We shall try to provide here a balanced view of the philosophical positions underlying different research methods. The chapter starts by re-viewing a central debate amongst social science philosophers. We then go on to look at the implications of this debate for a number of fundamental choices in research design, and conclude with a look at the way different research contexts and disciplinary structures may affect research methods.

## TWO MAIN TRADITIONS

### The philosophies

There is a long-standing debate in the social sciences about the most appropriate philosophical position from which methods should be derived. In the red corner is phenomenology; in the blue corner is positivism. Each has to some extent been elevated into a stereotype, often by the opposing side. Although it is now possible to draw up comprehensive lists of assumptions and meth-odological implications associated with each position, it is not possible to identify any one philosopher who ascribes to all aspects of one particular view.

Indeed, occasionally an author from one corner produces ideas which belong more neatly to those of the other corner.

Also, when one looks at the practice of research, even self-confessed extremists do not hold consistently to one position or the other. Although there has been a trend away from positivism towards phenomenology over the last few years, there are many researchers, especially in the management field, who adopt a pragmatic view by deliberately combining methods drawn from both traditions.

So what are these traditions? Let us start with *positivism*. The key idea of positivism is that the social world exists externally, and that its properties should be measured through objective methods, rather than being inferred subjectively through sensation, reflection or intuition. [. . .]

Knowledge is only of significance if it is based on observations of this external reality. There follow from this a number of implications [. . .]:

(1) *Independence:* the observer is independent of what is being observed.
(2) *Value-freedom:* the choice of what to study, and how to study it, can be determined by objective criteria rather than by human beliefs and interests.
(3) *Causality:* the aim of social sciences should be to identify causal explanations and fundamental laws that explain regularities in human social behaviour.
(4) *Hypothetico-deductive:* science proceeds through a process of hypothesizing fundamental laws and then deducing what kinds of observations will demonstrate the truth or falsity of these hypotheses.
(5) *Operationalization:* concepts need to be operationalized in a way which enables facts to be measured quantitatively.
(6) *Reductionism:* problems as a whole are better understood if they are reduced into the simplest possible elements.
(7) *Generalization:* in order to be able to generalize about regularities in human and social behaviour it is necessary to select samples of sufficient size.
(8) *Cross-sectional analysis:* such regularities can most easily be identified by making comparisons of variations across samples.

These propositions are [. . .] a collection of points that have come to be associated with the positivist viewpoint. Some 'positivists' would disagree with some of these statements. [. . .] Philosophers within the same school not only disagree with each other; they may also change their own views significantly over time.

[. . .] This philosophy has developed into a distinctive paradigm over the last one and a half centuries. The term 'paradigm' has come into vogue among social scientists recently, particularly through the work of Thomas Kuhn. Kuhn (1962) used it to describe the progress of scientific discoveries in practice, rather than how they are subsequently reconstructed [. . .]. Most of the time, according to Kuhn, science progresses in tiny steps, which refine and extend what is already 'known'. But occasionally experiments start to produce results that do not fit into existing theories and patterns. Then, perhaps many years later, a Galileo or Einstein proposes a new way of looking at things which can account for both the old and the new observations.

It is evident from these examples that major scientific advances are not produced by a logical and rational application of scientific method. They result from independent and creative thinking which goes outside the boundaries of existing ideas. The result of this is a 'scientific revolution' which not only provides new theories, but which may also alter radically the way people see the world, and the kind of questions that scientists consider important to investigate. This combination of new theories and questions is referred to as a new paradigm.

The new paradigm that has arisen during the last half century, largely in reaction to the application of positivism to the social sciences, stems from the view that the world and 'reality' are not objective and exterior, but that they are socially constructed and given meaning by people. As one might expect, this 'phenomenology' is not logically derived from positivism in any way.

Many different variants are associated with phenomenology. These include interpretive sociology (Habermas, 1970), naturalistic inquiry (Lincoln and Guba, 1986), social constructionism (Berger and Luckman, 1966), qualitative methodology (Taylor and Bogdan, 1984) and 'new paradigm' inquiry (Reason and Rowan, 1981). Each takes a slightly different stance in the application of phenomenology and in the features of positivism that it finds most distasteful.

The starting point, as we have said, is the idea that reality is socially constructed rather than objectively determined. Hence the task of the social scientist should not be to gather facts and measure how often certain patterns occur, but to appreciate the different constructions and meanings that people place upon their experience. One should therefore try to understand and explain why people have different experiences, rather than search for external causes and fundamental laws to explain their behaviour. Human action arises from the sense that people make of different situations, rather than as a direct response from external stimuli.

The implications of holding these different views may be seen, for example, in the way researchers might study managerial stress. The social constructionist would be interested in the aspects of work that managers consider to be 'stressful', and perhaps in the strategies that they develop for managing these aspects. She would therefore arrange to talk with a few managers about their jobs, about the aspects they find more, or less, difficult, and so on. The positivist, on the other hand, would start with the assumption that occupational stress exists and might then try to measure the levels of stress experienced by managers and how these relate to a number of external stressors such as organizational changes, interpersonal conflicts, negative appraisals, and so on. Measures of stress could be based on standardized verbal reports from the managers, or on physiological factors such as blood pressure or glandular secretions.

[. . .]

Within the phenomenological or social constructionist viewpoint there are several direct attacks on the assumptions of positivism. [. . .] One of the strongest attacks has been on its assumptions of value-freedom. This is argued most strongly by Habermas (1970), who points out that [. . .] human interests not only guide the way we think, and the structures of work and authority, but they also condition the way we enquire into, and construct our knowledge of, the world. One of the big problems with positivist methods is that they are claimed to be independent of values and interests, yet by and large they support, in practice, the interests of the more powerful members of society.

Habermas thus attempts to demonstrate the true relationship between know-ledge and interest which is otherwise concealed by the objectivist views of positivism.

As we have mentioned above, the term 'paradigm' has become popularized over recent years, and it therefore tends to be used in many different ways. [. . .] Gareth Morgan [. . .] proposed a way of tidying up its usage. He dis-tinguished between three levels of use: the philosophical level, which reflects basic beliefs about the world; the social level, which provides guidelines about how the researcher should conduct his or her endeavour; and the technical level, which involves specifying the methods and techniques which should ideally be adopted in conducting research (Morgan, 1979).

It is this basic classification that we have used in Table 5.1, where we attempt to summarize the main differences between the positivist and the phenomenological viewpoints.

These two positions are, of course, the 'pure' versions of each paradigm. Although the basic beliefs may be quite incompatible, when one comes down to the actual research methods and techniques used by researchers the dif-ferences are by no means so clear cut and distinct. Increasingly, there is a move amongst management researchers to develop methods and approaches which provide a middle ground, and some bridging between the two extreme view-points. These we shall come back to later, but in the meantime we shall look at some classic examples of management and organizational research which are widely acknowledged as representing one or other of these points of view. As we shall see, neither of these are completely pure applications of their respec-tive paradigms.

## Examples of practice

First we shall summarize the main features of two major pieces of research that have been conducted largely from the positivist paradigm. These are the stud-ies of Pugh and his colleagues at Aston into organizational structure, and the work of Geert Hofstede (1984) on culture.

From 1961 onwards, Pugh and his colleagues [. . .] used a highly structured interview schedule in order to gather data on a total of 132 measures which characterized the structure and context of each organization. From an analysis of the data across their sample they were able to come up with a number of general conclusions, for example, that size is the most important determinant of organizational structure, and that organizations which are closely depend-ent on other organizations tend to centralize as many decisions as possible [. . .] (Pugh and Hickson, 1976). Possibly their main significance is the way they highlight the authority structures within organizations as key factors to consider when attempting to change, or understand, organizational behaviour. Pugh (1988) feels that this provides a useful counterbalance to the prevailing emphasis on individual and group-related factors.

Pugh (1983) describes himself as an 'unreconstructed positivist'. The key principles that he applies to his work include: focusing on hard data rather than opinions; looking for regularities in the data obtained; and attempting to produce propositions that can generalize from the specific example to the wider population of organizations. He states his view that facts and values can

TABLE 5.1
*Key features of positivist and phenomenological paradigms*

|  | POSITIVIST PARADIGM | PHENOMENOLOGICAL PARADIGM |
|---|---|---|
| *Basic beliefs:* | The world is external and objective | The world is socially constructed and subjective |
|  | Observer is independent | Observer is part of what is observed |
|  | Science is value-free | Science is driven by human interests |
| *Researcher should:* | focus on facts | focus on meanings |
|  | look for causality and fundamental laws | try to understand what is happening |
|  | reduce phenomena to simplest elements | look at the totality of each situation |
|  | formulate hypotheses and then test them | develop ideas through induction from data |
| *Preferred methods include:* | operationalizing concepts so that they can be measured | using multiple methods to establish different views of phenomena |
|  | taking large samples | small samples investigated in depth or over time |

be clearly separated, but he also adopts a 'systems' view which attempts to examine the full complexity of the data, rather than simply reducing it to its simplest elements. This latter point is perhaps a modification of the positivist view which has arisen partly as a result of developments in the biological sciences (Von Bertalanffy, 1962), and partly as a result of the ability of modern computers to conduct very sophisticated multi-variate analysis of data, provided it is expressed in quantitative terms. Thus, Pugh, by his own admission, sticks fairly closely to the positivist paradigm described above, although in his own research programme he also found it necessary to conduct more detailed case studies of individual organizations in the later stages of his research in order to give a fuller understanding of what was taking place inside (Pugh, 1988).

The second example of positivist research is the classic study of Hofstede (1980) into the effect of national cultures on social and work behaviour. This was based on 116,000 questionnaires completed between 1967 and 1972 by employees of a large American multi-national. Hofstede's data was totally quantitative and its analysis was conducted purely by computer. This analysis indicated four dimensions of national culture:

(1) *Individualism:* whether a society emphasizes individual autonomy as opposed to responsibility to the group.
(2) *Masculinity:* how far roles in society are differentiated between men and women.
(3) *Power distance:* the extent to which inequality is accepted by the less powerful people in society.
(4) *Uncertainty avoidance:* the level of concern about law and order in a society.

Each of these dimensions was statistically independent in the sense that a high score on one would imply neither a high nor a low score on any of the other dimensions. Hofstede, as the researcher, was also distanced and independent from the respondents of the questionnaires. Thus far, Hofstede's highly quantitative research appears to conform closely to the positivist paradigm.

Beyond that, based on his account of the research process (Hofstede, 1980), much of his work simply does not fit the positivist paradigm. For example, he accepts that he is dealing with mental constructs rather than hard objective facts. The four main dimensions of national culture were not formulated as initial hypotheses but only after considerable *post hoc* analysis of the data, and through much reading and discussion with other academic colleagues. Thirdly, he is fully aware of the importance of avoiding assumptions about culture which imply that any one culture is superior to another; and therefore he accepts that his results are not necessarily value-free. Fourthly, he recognizes that different methods will provide different perspectives on what is being studied, and therefore it is worth 'triangulating' where possible by using a combination of both quantitative and qualitative methods. Thus, in practice, Hofstede's work contains elements of both paradigms.

On the side of phenomenology or social constructionism is the work of Melville Dalton (1959), who carried out one of the pioneering studies of what managers do in practice. In a later paper (Dalton, 1964) he describes the ideas and philosophies that guided his work, plus some of the ethical dilemmas that were encountered. For a start Dalton rejects the classical 'scientific method' as inappropriate to his work (this is the sequence of hypothesis, observation, testing, and confirmation or disconfirmation of hypothesis). He points out that not only is this method rather idealistic in the sense that natural scientists do not usually follow it themselves (except in the school laboratory), but it was also not feasible to use it in the situation he had chosen. He is opposed to the tendency to quantify and to reduce variables to their smallest components, on the grounds that this loses most of the real meaning of the situation.

Dalton studied the behaviour of managers while working himself within an organization as a manager. Curiously enough, although he is quite open about his methods and some of the dilemmas this caused, he does not actually say what his role was in the group, but it allowed him 'much unquestioned movement about the firm'. While working in the company he gathered data from his own observations and from those of a number of informants. The informants were clearly aware to some extent of Dalton's purposes, but the rest of the people in the company were largely ignorant of what he was doing – his role was therefore partly overt and partly covert. This clearly meant that he was not in a position to establish any formal experiments to test his ideas, although curiously enough he comments that some of his informants who were aware of his general purpose occasionally deliberately set up situations for him to observe. Thus in no way was Dalton an independent observer of what was taking place; his presence certainly had some impact on the company, even though the nature of that impact is one of the things about which Dalton does not speculate greatly.

Although much of his data was qualitative, in the form of observations by him and comments from his informants, he was not averse to collecting a certain amount of quantitative data such as details of the salaries of managers in the company. This he obtained informally from a secretary in the personnel department in exchange for counselling about whether or not she should marry her boyfriend.

It is clear that Dalton did not start the research with any clearly preconceived set of hypotheses and theories to test; his research grew out of his own 'confusions and irritations'. Rather than trying to formulate explicit hypotheses and guides for his work, he contented himself with framing simple questions about things that were taking place which he did not clearly understand. After looking at a number of specific topics such as the reasons for conflict between different groups of people or the way people accounted for the success of some managers, he finally settled on the overall scheme of attempting to understand the distinction and relationships between official and unofficial action within the organization.

Dalton was also aware that looking at only one organization in depth could limit the generalizability of his conclusions. So he supplemented his work with studies through other contacts of several other organizations in the same area. That at least gave him the confidence that the things he had observed in his own company, Milo, were quite likely to be taking place in most other organizations, at least in that part of the United States. As Lawrence (1988) shows, the assumption that there is both a formal and an informal organization in any institution does not necessarily hold outside the North American culture.

The above studies are often cited as relatively pure examples of either positivist or phenomenological approaches. But, as we have shown, in practice the researchers involved do not hold scrupulously to one or the other approach. [. . .] Increasingly, authors and researchers who work in organizations and with managers argue that one should attempt to mix methods to some extent, because it provides more perspectives on the phenomena being investigated. Fielding and Fielding (1986) advocate the use of both quantitative and qualitative methods, and provide examples of how they have been able to combine these different forms of data to good effect.

The examples they give show how to combine the two kinds of data where the overall direction and significance of the two sources are fairly similar. A problem they do not confront is what to do when quantitative and qualitative forms of data about the same phenomena are in direct opposition. This problem was encountered by Easterby-Smith and a colleague, Morgan Tanton, in a comparative evaluation study of two executive management programmes, each conducted in a different institution. Qualitative data from interviews and observations showed quite clearly that Course A was superior to Course B, but the quantitative data in the form of student ratings about the two courses showed to a high level of significance that Course B was preferred to Course A. Was this discrepancy caused by the methods used, or could it highlight some unusual features of the two courses being examined? It seemed that the best way to tackle the dilemma was to show the discrepancy to some later course participants and ask whether they had any explanations.

Two reasons emerged as most probable. Firstly, participants commented that they tended to be rather cautious when filling in multiple choice rating forms, because they could never be sure what the data would be used for; therefore, they usually avoided extreme responses in either direction. Secondly, it seemed that the course designs and institutional settings affected the criteria that participants used for evaluating the two courses.

In Institution A the emphasis was on the longer-term application of what had been learnt; in Institution B the emphasis was on the immediate quality of sessions conducted within the classroom. Thus it was not surprising that the rating forms which were completed at the end of the course showed one pattern, whereas follow-up interviews conducted some months later showed another.

There are two morals from this story: firstly to be wary of glibly mixing methods simply for the sake of getting a slightly richer picture; and secondly to remember that the reality of what is being investigated may be considerably more complex than the data collection methods are capable of demonstrating.

It is worth summarizing from a pragmatic view what are seen as some of the strengths and weaknesses of each side. This should help the researcher to choose which methods and aspects are most likely to be of help in a given situation. In the case of quantitative methods and the positivist paradigm, the main strengths are that: they can provide wide coverage of the range of situations; they can be fast and economical; and, particularly when statistics are aggregated from large samples, they may be of considerable relevance to policy decisions. On the debit side, these methods tend to be rather inflexible and artificial; they are not very effective in understanding processes or the significance that people attach to actions; they are not very helpful in generating theories; and because they focus on what is, or what has been recently, they make it hard for the policy-maker to infer what changes and actions should take place in the *future*. As Legge (1984) points out, they may only provide illusions of the 'true' impact of social policies. Most of the data gathered will not be relevant to real decisions although it may be used to support the covert goals of decision-makers.

The strengths and weaknesses of the phenomenological paradigm and associated qualitative methods are fairly complementary. Thus they have strengths in their ability to look at change processes over time, to understand people's meanings, to adjust to the evolution of new theories. They also provide a way of gathering data which is seen as natural rather than artificial. There are, of course, weaknesses. Data collection can take up a great deal of time and resources, and the analysis and interpretation of data may be very difficult. Qualitative studies often feel very untidy because it is harder to control their pace, progress and end-points. There is also the problem that many people, especially policy-makers, may give low credibility to studies based on a phenomenological approach.

## RESEARCH DESIGN: SOME CHOICES AND ISSUES

Research designs are about organizing research activity, including the collection of data, in ways that are most likely to achieve the research aims. There are many potential choices to make when developing a research design, and [. . .] many of these choices are allied quite closely to different philosophical positions, [so] an awareness of this can at least ensure that the different elements of a research design are consistent with each other.

In this section we shall describe five choices of particular significance. The first four relate fairly closely to the basic dichotomy between the use of positivist and social constructionist approaches, and the last is a debate located mainly within the positivist paradigm. These five choices are summarized in Table 5.2.

TABLE 5.2
*Key choices of research design*

| | | |
|---|---|---|
| Researcher is independent | *vs* | Researcher is involved |
| Large samples | *vs* | Small numbers |
| Testing theories | *vs* | Generating theories |
| Experimental design | *vs* | Fieldwork methods |
| Verification | *vs* | Falsification |

### Involvement of researcher

The first choice is whether the researcher should remain distanced from, or get involved with, the material that is being researched. Clearly this choice stems from one's philosophical view about whether or not it is possible for the observer to remain independent from the phenomena being observed. The traditional assumption in science is that the researcher must maintain complete independence if there is to be any validity in the results produced, although more recently it has become evident in areas such as nuclear physics that this ideal is not always possible. For example, the very act of measuring the position of a sub-atomic particle is likely to affect its velocity.

In social sciences, where claims of researchers' independence are harder to sustain, there are those who have tried to turn this apparent 'problem' into a virtue. This is the tradition of *action research*. It assumes that any social phenomena are continually changing rather than static. Action research and the researcher are then seen as part of this change process itself. The following two features are normally part of action research projects:

(1) a belief that the best way of learning about an organization or social system is through attempting to change it, and this therefore should to some extent be the objective of the action researcher;
(2) the belief that those people most likely to be affected by, or involved in implementing, these changes should as far as possible become involved in the research process itself.

Although it is possible to conduct action research in a positivist way, for example by attempting to change the organization from the outside and then measuring the results, in most respects it derives from ideas that are alien to positivism. Many people schooled in positivist research methods are sceptical about the value of action research but, as Susman and Evered (1978) point out, action research is *bound* to be found wanting if it is measured against the criteria of positivist science; whereas it is perfectly justifiable from the viewpoint of phenomenology.

The involvement of the researcher is taken a stage further in what has come to be known as *co-operative inquiry* (Reason, 1988). This has been developed for researching human action more at an individual, rather than at organizational levels. It adopts as a starting point the idea that all people have (at least latently) the ability to be self-directing, to choose how they will act and to give meaning to their own experiences. It rejects traditional positivist methods where people are studied as if they were objects under the influence of external forces. Co-operative inquiry not only focuses on the experiences and explanations of the individuals concerned, it also involves them in deciding in the first place what questions and issues are worth researching. Thus the subjects become partners in the research process.

## Sampling

A second design choice is whether to attempt to sample across a large number of organizations or situations, or whether to focus on a small number of situations and attempt to investigate them over a period of time. This is essentially a choice between *cross-sectional* and *longitudinal design.*

Cross-sectional designs usually involve selecting different organizations, or units in different contexts, and investigating how other factors vary across these units. Thus to investigate the relationship between expenditure on management training and corporate performance one needs to select a sample of organizations that are known to represent either a range of levels in training investment *or* a range of levels of corporate performance. One then checks to see whether there is any correlation between the variables. A key problem here is in deciding how large the sample of organizations needs to be in order to be adequately representative.

Cross-sectional designs, particularly where they use questionnaires and survey techniques, have the ability to describe economically features of large numbers of people or organizations. But two limitations are frequently evident. Firstly, they do not explain *why* correlations exist; and secondly, they have difficulty eliminating all the external factors which could possibly have caused the observed correlation.

Pettigrew (1985) suggests that longitudinal research, which focuses on a small number of organizations over long periods of time, can remedy these disadvantages. He recommends that research should focus on change processes within the broader social, economic and political context surrounding each organization, and that it should gather 'time series data' over periods of time significantly longer than the immediate focus. In this way explanations should emerge from examining patterns in the process of change. The main practical advantage to this approach is that it can produce significant results from a very small number of cases and this can reduce the problems of gaining access if the research is to be carried out in organizations. The disadvantages are that it is extremely time consuming and the complexity of data requires very high skills from all researchers involved.

## Theory and data

The third choice is about which should come first: the theory or the data. Again this represents the split between the positivist and phenomenological paradigms in relation to how the researcher should go about his or her work. In the latter case there is the approach known as *grounded theory*, which was first formulated in a classic book by Glaser and Strauss (1967).

Glaser and Strauss see the key task of the researcher as being to develop theory through 'comparative method'. This means looking at the same event or process in different settings or situations. For example, the researcher might be interested in the workings of appraisal interviews and would therefore study a number of appraisal interviews handled by different managers, in different departments, or in different organizations. As a result of the studies it might be noticed that most appraisal interviews either focus on reviewing performance and whether or not last year's objectives have been achieved, or focus on future goals and how the subordinate may be helped to achieve them. They might then be labelled as 'judgemental' or 'developmental' interviews, and the distinction would represent a *substantive theory* about appraisal interviews.

However, the theorizing could be taken further. It might be observed that neither form of interview has much effect on the individual's performance or on the relationships between the managers and their subordinates. Thus one might conclude that both forms of interview are simply organizational rituals which have the function of demonstrating and reinforcing hierarchical power relations. This would be the beginning of a more generalized *formal theory* about power and organizational rituals. Glaser and Strauss consider both kinds of theory to be valuable, and they propose two main criteria for evaluating the quality of a theory. Firstly it should be sufficiently *analytic* to enable some generalisation to take place, but at the same time it should be possible for people to relate the theory to their own experiences, thus *sensitising* their own perceptions.

The contrasting view is that one should start with a theory, or hypothesis, about the nature of the world, and then seek data that will confirm or disconfirm that theory. Thus, continuing with the above example, one might hypothesize that the prevalence of 'judgemental' or 'developmental' appraisal interviews depends on the personality of the boss, and that 'authoritarian' bosses will be more likely to conduct interviews in a judgemental manner. To test this hypothesis one needs to classify the bosses according to their authoritarian tendencies and to classify the appraisal interviews by type. If the data shows that most of the authoritarian bosses do indeed hold judgemental interviews then this will support the initial hypothesis.

The main practical advantage of the 'hypothesis testing' approach described above is that there is initial clarity about what is to be investigated, and hence information can be collected speedily and efficiently. Clarity of method means that it is easier for another researcher to replicate the study, and hence any claims arising from the research can be subjected to public scrutiny. The disadvantages are that its contribution may be quite trivial, confirming what is already known. And if the results are inconclusive or negative, the approach can give little guidance on why this is so. By contrast, the grounded approach is flexible and is good at providing both explanations and new insights. However it may take more time, and researchers often have to live with the fear that nothing of interest will emerge from the work. Some people regard grounded theory as suspect because of the lack of clarity and standardization of methods, but that concern stems largely from a positivist perspective on the importance of 'finding the truth'.

## Experimental designs or fieldwork

Experiments are one of the key elements of scientific method, although they are not necessarily essential to positivist methods. Classic experimental method involves assigning subjects *at random* to either an experimental or a control group. Conditions for the experimental group are then manipulated by the experimenter in order to assess their effect in comparison with members of the control group who are subjected to no unusual conditions. In studies of social and human life, such experiments still remain quite popular amongst psychologists [. . .]. They are very much harder to conduct within real organizations, or where there is no captive population from which to draw volunteers. Occasionally, if she is as lucky as Melville Dalton (1964) was, the researcher might find people who are prepared to set up small artificial experiments for her when she is studying within organizations, but this is obviously a rarity.

Some researchers still working from within the positivist paradigm recognized the practical difficulties of producing pure experimental designs, and thus the idea of 'quasi-experimental' designs was developed. [. . .] One of the most common methods is the 'pre-test/post-test comparison design'. For example, the effects of a course on a group of managers might be evaluated by measuring the managers' knowledge or attitudes before and after the course, and by comparing the differences with those from a similar group of managers who did not attend the course but who completed identical tests at the same times. The problems of using it in real organizations are substantial. For example, the design assumes that 'nothing' happens to the control group during the period that the treatment (course attendance) is being given to the experimental group. This is a naive assumption, as Easterby-Smith found when attempting to evaluate a project-based management development programme held at Durham University Business School (Easterby-Smith and Ashton, 1975). While the 'chosen few' were away on the course several members of the control group seized the opportunity to improve relationships with their bosses and strengthen their political standing in the company, thus effectively shutting out a number of managers who had attended the course.

The alternative to experimental and quasi-experimental designs is *fieldwork*, which is the study of real organizations or social settings. This may involve the use of positivist methods which use quantitative techniques, or it can be much more open-ended and phenomenological. One of the distinctive research styles in the latter case is *ethnography*. Here the researcher tries to immerse himself or herself in a setting and to become part of the group under study in order to understand the meanings and significances that people put upon their own behaviour and that of others.

Most outsiders who are new to an organization or group will encounter things that they do not understand. These are what Agar (1986) calls 'breakdowns': events or situations where the researcher's past experience gives him no help in understanding what is going on. This breakdown therefore represents something unique about that organization, and previously unknown to the researcher. For example, most groups have 'in-jokes', based on experiences shared only by members of the group. In order for an outsider to make sense of the breakdown provided by an 'in-joke' it will be necessary to track back to the original experiences. The breakdown provides a kind of window into exploring aspects of the experiences and meaning systems of groups and organizations. It will only be possible to resolve the breakdown when the researcher has understood these meaning systems. In this way the ethnographer is able to extend conventional wisdom, and to generate new insights into human behaviour.

## Verification or falsification

The distinction between *verification* and *falsification* was made by Karl Popper (1959) as a way of dealing with what has become known as 'the problem of induction'. This is that, however much data one obtains in support of a scientific theory or law, it is not possible to reach a conclusive proof of the truth of that law. Popper's way out of this problem is to suggest that instead of looking for confirmatory evidence one should always look for evidence that will *disconfirm* one's hypothesis or existing view. This means that theories should be formulated in a way that will make them most easily exposed to possible refutation. The advantage then is that only one instance of refutation is needed to falsify a theory, whereas however many confirmations of the theory there are it will still not be conclusively proven.

The example often given to illustrate this approach takes as a start the assertion that all swans are white. If following the verification route, the researcher would start travelling around the country accumulating sightings of swans and, provided that he or she did not go near a zoo, a very high number of white sightings would eventually be obtained, and presumably no black sightings. This gives a lot of confidence to the assertion that all swans are white, but still does not conclusively prove the statement. If on the other hand, the researcher takes a falsification view, he or she would start to search for swans that are *not* white, deliberately looking for contexts and locations where non-white swans might be encountered. Thus, our intrepid researcher would head straight for a zoo, or perhaps book a flight to Australia, where most swans happen to be black. This discovery made, the initial hypothesis would be falsified, and it might then have to be modified to include the idea that all swans are either white or black. This statement has still what Popper calls high 'informative' content because it is expressed in a way that can easily be disproved; whereas a statement like 'all swans are large birds' would not be sufficiently precise to allow easy refutation.

Much of the debate about verification and falsification fits within the positivist view because ideas of 'truth' and 'proof' are associated mainly with that paradigm. But the phenomenologist might also take important lessons from this discussion. For example, Reason (1988) advocates 'critical subjectivity', which involves recognizing one's own views and experiences, but not allowing oneself to be overwhelmed and swept along by them. If the idea of falsification is to be applied more fully to phenomenological research then one should look for evidence that might confirm or contradict what one currently believes to be true. This advice applies not only to researchers but also to managers who are concerned to investigate and understand what is taking place within their own organizations. According to this view it is important for them to resist the strong temptation to look for data that confirms whatever position they are currently holding. By deliberately searching for *disconfirmatory* evidence they may come up with answers much more quickly. If they find themselves unable to find such evidence this will make their current positions far stronger.

## Criteria for choice

These five choices of research design are of course not absolute. People do use designs that incorporate both sides of the picture, and very often the choices that they make are not altogether 'pure'. However, given that time and resources are usually very limited in research, we feel that it is important that researchers are prepared to make choices and thereby provide a clear focus to their efforts. We have indicated some strengths and weaknesses of different design choices as we have progressed through the last section, and we assume that it will also be possible to detect our preference for the social constructionist view. However, we all have initial research training within more positivist traditions, and no doubt will find it necessary occasionally in the future to adopt methods informed by the positivist position. This suggests two possible criteria for choice of research design: the personal preference of the researchers themselves, and the aims or context of the research to be carried out.

A third criterion comes from a very common fear amongst researchers of all persuasions. The question asked is: will the research stand up to outside scrutiny and will anyone believe what I am saying about it? The technical language for examining this problem includes terms such as validity, reliability and generalizability. It should be no surprise by this stage to realise that the meaning of these terms varies considerably with the philosophical viewpoint adopted. Table 5.3 summarizes some of the differences from positivist and phenomenological viewpoints.

As Kirk and Miller (1986) point out, the language of validity and reliability was originally developed for use in quantitative social science, and many procedures have been devised for assessing different facets of each. There has been some reluctance to apply these ideas to phenomenological, and social constructionist, research because they might imply acceptance of one absolute (positivist) reality. However, provided the researcher is committed to providing a faithful description of others' understandings and perceptions, then ideas such as validity and reliability can provide a very useful discipline.

TABLE 5.3
*Questions of reliability, validity and generalizability*

| | POSITIVIST VIEWPOINT | PHENOMENOLOGICAL VIEWPOINT |
|---|---|---|
| *Validity* | Does an instrument measure what is is supposed to measure? | Has the researcher gained full access to the knowledge and meanings of informants? |
| *Reliability* | Will the measure yield the same results on different occasions (assuming no real change in what is to be measured)? | Will similar observations be made by different researchers on different occasions? |
| *Generalizability* | What is the probability that patterns observed in a sample will also be present in the wider population from which the sample is drawn? | How likely is it that ideas and theories generated in one setting will also apply in other settings? |

# RESEARCH DESIGNS WITHIN DIFFERENT MANAGEMENT SUBJECTS

In this final section of the chapter we will look briefly at the extent to which research methods are different in some of the key 'management' subject areas, such as finance and accounting, marketing, operational research, and organizational behaviour. As Morgan and Smircich (1980) observe, the appropriateness of a research approach 'derives from the nature of the social phenomena to be explored' (p. 491). Thus the extent to which the basic subject material in a discipline is quantified exerts a considerable influence on the preference of researchers for more positivist or phenomenological methods. Thus, within finance and accounting and operational research, it is inevitable that a lot of research will focus on measureable and quantifiable factors, and that the researcher remains as distanced as possible from the data or problems being tackled. It is also important to be aware of assumptions about what 'matters' when trying to understand or explain aspects of management and organization. Is it the things themselves, or people's views about them, that are important? Researchers who incline towards the former view will tend to adopt a positivist framework, and those favouring the latter view will be happier with a social constructionist perspective.

One would expect the areas of operational research and management to be dominated by a concern with numbers and 'things'. But a number of well-known people have deviated markedly from the straight and narrow, including

Beer (1975), Revans (1982) and Checkland (1981). The latter has achieved fame for developing a 'soft systems' methodology which adopts a holistic approach – using concepts rather than numbers – to understand the complexity of organizational problems. The methodology provides a systematic way of inquiring into the nature of the world, but in no way assumes that the world itself is, or can be described by a system. Thus the methodology has far more in common with phenomenology than with positivism.

Similar examples of non-positivist research exist in the field of finance and accounting. For example, [. . .] there has been significant growth over the last decade in the area of 'behavioural accounting' which essentially tries to understand the effect of different accounting and control systems on people, and vice versa. In a recent review of research methods in this field, Brownell and Trotman (1988) comment that different kinds of research questions should be investigated with different methodologies. They observe, however, that most research in this area has used either experimental methods or survey techniques. In their view the greater use of methods such as quasi-experiments and participant observation would lead to much richer understanding.

Hirschman (1986) argues that the key factors in marketing are essentially socially constructed: human beliefs, behaviours, perceptions and values. Hence it is important to employ research methods drawn from this perspective, such as observation and qualitative interviews. But academics within the marketing field still show a strong preference for survey research methods, which are aimed at predicting, often statistically, behaviour amongst consumers or clients. [. . .] On the other hand commercial market research agencies rely heavily on qualitative methods. [. . .]

Finally, there is the field of organizational behaviour. Here, again, the traditional methods in the subject have been closer to the quantitative and positivist paradigm [. . .]. Despite some disillusionment about the value of positivist methods in this field, many researchers simply respond by redoubling their efforts. [. . .] But many others advocate the use of qualitative methods which originate from a non-positivist perspective (Silverman, 1979; Pettigrew, 1985; Walker, 1985), and it seems that this trend will continue.

## CONCLUSIONS

In this chapter we have discussed some of the key philosophical debates underlying research methods in the social sciences, and we have looked at the implications these have for the design of management research. Although there is a clear dichotomy between the positivist and social constructionist world views, and sharp differences of opinion exist between researchers about the desirability of methods, the reality of research also involves a lot of compromises between these pure positions.

## REFERENCES

Agar, M. H. (1986) *Speaking of ethnography*. Beverly Hills: Sage.
Beer, S. (1975) *Platform for change*. Chichester: Wiley.
Berger, P. L. and Luckman, T. (1966) *The social construction of reality*. London: Penguin.

Brownell, P. and Trotman, K. (1988) Research methods in behavioural accounting, in K. R. Ferris (ed.) *Behavioral accounting research: a critical analysis*. Columbus, Ohio: Century VII.

Checkland, P. (1981) *Systems thinking, systems practice*. Chichester: Wiley.

Dalton, M. (1959) *Men who manage: fusion of feeling and theory in administration*. New York: Wiley.

Dalton, M. (1964) Preconceptions and methods in *Men who manage*, in P. Hammond (ed.) *Sociologists at Work*. New York: Basic Books.

Easterby-Smith, M. and Ashton, D. (1975) Using repertory grid technique to evaluate management training, *Personnel Review*, Vol. 4, no. 4, pp. 15–21.

Fielding, N. G. and Fielding, J. L. (1986) *Linking data*. Beverly Hills: Sage.

Glaser, D. G. and Strauss, A. L. (1967) *The discovery of grounded theory: strategies for qualitative research*. New York: Aldine.

Habermas, J. (1970) Knowledge and interest, in D. Emmet and A. MacIntyre (eds) *Sociological theory and philosophical analysis*. London: Macmillan.

Hirschman, E. (1986) Humanistic inquiry in marketing research: philosophy, method and criteria, *Journal of Marketing Research*, vol. 23 (August), pp. 237–49.

Hofstede, G. (1980; abridged edition, 1984) *Culture's consequences: international differences in work-related values*. Beverly Hills, Sage.

Kirk, J. and Miller, M. L. (1986) *Reliability and validity in qualitative research*. Beverly Hills: Sage.

Kuhn, T. S. (1962) *The structure of scientific revolutions*. Chicago: University of Chicago Press.

Lawrence, P. (1988) In another country, in A. Bryman (ed.) *Doing research in organisations*, London: Routledge.

Legge, K. (1984) *Evaluating planned organisational change*. London: Academic Press.

Lincoln, Y. S. and Guba, G. (1986) *Naturalistic Inquiry*. London: Sage.

Morgan, G. (1979) Response to Mintzberg, *Administrative Science Quarterly*, Vol. 24, no. 1, pp. 137–9.

Morgan, G. and Smircich, L. (1980) The case for qualitative research, *Academy of Management Review*, Vol. 5, pp. 491–500.

Pettigrew, A. M. (1985) Contextualist research: a natural way to link theory and practice' in E. E. Lawler (ed.) *Doing research that is useful in theory and practice*. San Francisco: Jossey Bass.

Popper, K. (1959) *The logic of scientific discovery*. London: Hutchinson.

Pugh, D. S and Hickson, D. J. (1976) *Organisation structure in its context: the Aston Programme*. Farnborough: Saxon House.

Pugh D. S. (1983) Studying organisational structure and process, in G. Morgan (ed.) *Beyond method*. Beverly Hills: Sage.

Pugh, D. S. (1988) The Aston Research Programme, in A. Bryman (ed.) *Doing research in organisations*. London: Routledge.

Reason, P. (1988) *Human inquiry in action*. London: Sage.

Reason, P. and Rowan, J. (1981) *Human inquiry: a sourcebook of new paradigm research*. London: Wiley.

Revans, R. W. (1982) *The origins and growth of action learning*. Bromley: Chartwell-Bratt.

Silverman, D. (1970) *The theory of organisations: a sociological framework*. London: Heinemann.

Susman, G. I. and Evered, R. D. (1978) An assessment of the scientific merits of action research, *Administrative Science Quarterly*, vol. 23, pp. 582–603.

Taylor, S. J. and Bogdan, R. (1984) *Introduction to qualitative research methods*. New York: Wiley-Interscience.

Von Bertalanffy, L. (1962) General systems theory – a critical review. *General Systems*, vol. VII, pp. 1–20.

Walker, R. (1985) *Applied qualitative research*. Aldershot: Gowner.

# CHAPTER 6

# Research Ethics

## R. M. BERGER AND M. A. PATCHNER

*This material has been abridged*

[. . .]

Principles of ethical research embody a set of norms and guidelines that researchers are obligated to follow. This chapter is designed to present the major ethical considerations involved in conducting research. Before you evaluate a research study or conduct your own research, you should be aware of commonly accepted ethical research principles.

## INFORMED CONSENT

The ethical codes governing research involving human subjects all require that the participation of individuals be completely voluntary. For individuals to be able to voluntarily participate they must be given an explicit choice about whether or not they wish to participate in the study. This occurs prior to their actual participation in the research and only after they have been completely informed of any possible harmful effects of the research and are explicitly made aware that they can discontinue their involvement in the research at any time.

This process in which subjects choose whether to participate in a research study is known as informed consent. The core elements of informed consent are (1) a disclosure of the nature and purpose of the research procedures and an identification of any procedures that are experimental; (2) a disclosure of any risks and the anticipated benefits of the research, either to the subject or to society; (3) where therapy is involved, a description of alternative procedures or courses of treatment, if any, that might be advantageous to the subject; and (4) a provision for assuring that subjects understand they may ask questions and/or withdraw at any time from the research.

Requirements for meeting the provisions of informed consent are that (1) subjects are competent to give their consent, (2) subjects be given adequate information about the proposed study, and (3) consent is voluntary. All three of these guidelines must be met for consent to be effective. Let's now examine each of these in more detail.

In order for persons to be competent to give their consent to participate in a study, they must be legally responsible for themselves and they must be mentally capable of making such a decision. Minors and persons with legal guardians, such as some handicapped and elderly persons, are not legally responsible for themselves and thus cannot give their 'own' permissions to participate in a research study. In these cases parents or guardians must provide consent. Human service research sometimes involves persons who are competent to make decisions for themselves, but who are vulnerable to exploitation, such as nursing home residents or the chronically mentally ill. In such cases a responsible researcher will also obtain consent from a significant other in the prospective subject's life – a spouse, family member, or parent.

The next guideline that needs to be met for informed consent to fully occur is that prospective subjects be given adequate information about the proposed study. In addition, this information must be fully understood. Giving adequate information means that the researcher must communicate the purpose of the study, expectations about the amount of time and types of activities that subjects may be expected to engage in, and potential risks and benefits to subjects and to society. If private information about subjects may be disclosed, subjects must be fully informed about the nature and extent of such disclosure, and they must be told that they may refuse to participate in the study and that they may withdraw at any time.

The final requirement for informed consent – that consent to participate be voluntary – is more complex than it appears. The idea that consent is voluntary implies that persons agree to participate in a study of their own free will. This means that subjects must be free from any implicit or explicit coercion. However, potential subjects may agree to participate in a study because they feel that if they refuse something negative will happen to them (e.g. their services might be cut, or their social worker will think less of them). On the other hand, they may feel that something positive will happen to them (e.g. they will get more services, or their social worker will like them more).

These subtle influences may be even greater for low-income populations and persons who are in institutions. The timing of the request to participate may also influence a person to volunteer to participate. A family about to admit its elderly grandmother to a nursing home may feel that participating in the research project sponsored by the facility might get their grandmother a bed sooner; students in a class who have borderline grades may participate in a study conducted by their professor because they feel that this may earn them a higher grade; prisoners may volunteer because their participation could positively affect the outcome of their upcoming parole hearing.

There is no single method to ensure that subjects' consent to participate in research is fully voluntary. The amount of risk involved to the subjects usually determines how consent will be obtained. Consent may be written or oral, or it may be implicit by virtue of voluntary participation, such as in the completion of a survey instrument. When there is no risk to subjects, when they fill out anonymous questionnaires, for example, informed consent is not required and normally not obtained.

If a written consent form is used it should include at least the core requirements for informed consent given above. It should also include the telephone number of an individual who will be available to answer inquiries from subjects. A copy of this form should be given to the subject.

# HARM

The most basic concern in all research ethics is that people not be harmed by participating in research studies. The notion of harm includes more than physical harm. Subjects can also be psychologically harmed in the course of a study if they are embarrassed, humiliated, placed under stress, or prompted to act in ways that violate their usual standards of conduct. It is the researcher's responsibility to be aware of the physical and psychological dangers that are present in a study and to guard against them.

Certain types of research are potentially more harmful to subjects than others. [. . .]

Sometimes research subjects are harmed in less obvious ways. Surveys that ask respondents to reveal their attitudes, behaviour, and beliefs, and personal information such as income, education, religion, and political affiliation may be harmful in that they cause some respondents to feel uncomfortable or anxious. Some studies may also cause participants to deal with unpleasant thoughts that they do not normally consider. For example, a study of attitudes toward minorities, or a study on interactions between couples, could cause respondents to become introspective and to examine their attitudes and behaviours. This could result in personal conflict for some respondents.

[. . .]

Conducting research in a manner that does not harm subjects is easy to accept in principle, but it is often difficult to ensure in practice. The manner in which research is planned and conducted is very important, and at times great caution must be exercised by the investigator. Sensitivity to subjects and to the details of the research should result in more protection for participants.

[. . .]

# CONFIDENTIALITY

Confidentiality means that information about individual subjects is kept private. In all research involving human subjects, confidentiality of identifiable information is presumed and must be maintained unless the investigator has obtained the explicit permission of the subject to do otherwise. Subjects must be protected from injury that could result from the disclosure of sensitive and personal information obtained in a research study. There are two ways of assuring confidentiality and thus protecting the privacy of individuals who participate in research studies – keeping subjects anonymous and safeguarding information once it is collected.

Participants in research studies are anonymous when the investigator cannot associate collected information with particular subjects. An example is a mailed survey in which no identification numbers are used to identify the persons who completed the instrument. In most studies, however, the investigator is able to identify individual participants, but precautions are taken to conceal their identity to others who might come in contact with the information, such as research assistants, janitors, staff and students using research offices and computer facilities, and others. The most common precaution is to assign code numbers to individual subjects. Of course, the researcher at times may want to know the identity of the subject (e.g. for a follow-up to a mailed survey); therefore a list showing which code number was used for each subject is kept. This list is highly confidential and once data collection is completed [it] should be destroyed.

Other ways to protect the anonymity of research participants are to use fabricated names, to obliterate names on instruments when they are volunteered by subjects, and to design data-gathering instruments that request only identifying information that is absolutely essential to the study.

In addition to protecting the anonymity of subjects, research data must be secured so that information about individual subjects is not made known to anyone who has no legitimate reason for having it. The more sensitive and personal the information, the greater the care that must be exercised in obtaining, handling, and storing it. Interviewers, research assistants, and others collecting information must be trained and made sensitive to their ethical responsibilities. As early as possible, the data should be handled in coded form, while data that include information that would reveal a subject's identity should be kept in files that are accessible only to the researcher and authorized staff. Plans for the ultimate disposition of the data need to be made, and if the data are to be retained indefinitely, plans must be made for their continued security.

## DECEPTION

Faced with the possibility that potential subjects might refuse to participate in a study, or that subjects knowing the purpose of a study might bias its outcome, some researchers have occasionally resorted to the use of deception. Deception involves misleading or not informing subjects about the purpose or nature of a research study, or not informing subjects that they are part of a study.

Studies involving unobtrusive measures may observe individuals or groups without their knowledge. For example, a study of a classroom behavioural management programme may monitor the classroom behaviour of children without their awareness. This may be the only reliable form of monitoring, since the children's behaviour is likely to be atypical if they are aware they are being observed.

In some studies subjects may be given incorrect information. This was the case in Schachter's (1959) study of the effects of fear on people's tendency to affiliate with others. In order to test the hypothesis that more fearful subjects are more likely to affiliate, he administered mild electric shocks to two groups. A 'low-fear' group was correctly informed that the shocks would not be painful or uncomfortable. However, a 'high-fear' group was told incorrectly that the same level of shock would be 'intense' and 'quite painful'. Prior to administration of the shocks, subjects were asked whether they preferred to wait alone, with a group of others, or if they didn't care where they waited. A preference for waiting with others was taken as a tendency to affiliate. Schachter's hypothesis was confirmed: The greater the subjects' fear, the greater their tendency to affiliate.

Many human service researchers feel strongly about lying to subjects, since it is considered immoral, it causes subjects to have improper assumptions about a study, and it violates the trust that should exist between a researcher and the subjects. On the other hand, some researchers feel that withholding information from subjects may be justifiable if a study is useful in advancing scientific knowledge, if the outcomes would be jeopardized if subjects knew the purpose and nature of the study beforehand, and if no other methods for conducting the study were available. The ideal, of course, is to conduct studies in which no deception is involved.

Two practical methods exist as alternatives to the use of deception. One such method is not to give subjects any information about the purpose of a study or what will happen to them during the study. However, when the study is over subjects are given complete information about the purpose of the research. Another method to avoid deception is to simulate 'real-world' situations through the use of role playing. For example, if a researcher wanted to investigate clients' reactions to being asked numerous personal questions when applying for welfare, rather than observing the interviews in a welfare office, the researcher could observe volunteers role playing workers and clients in a 'laboratory' setting.

[. . .]

## OTHER ETHICAL CONSIDERATIONS

We will now examine a few ethical issues that do not involve subjects, but rather focus on the researcher. There are some practices, other than those discussed above, which constitute unethical behaviour. Moreover, there are additional obligations that researchers have in doing responsible research. We will comment on these to alert you to other responsibilities that researchers have when conducting their studies and reporting their findings.

There are strong commitments to honesty in all of the sciences. Outright fabrication of data and more subtle forms of cheating, such as concealing negative evidence, 'covering up data', and incorrectly analysing data, have been regarded with disdain by the professional community. The pressures for accountability and for contributing to the scientific knowledge base are ever increasing and the temptation to cheat may be great. However, the costs to researchers who falsify their research is also great. Their dishonesty in one study will cast doubt on all past studies and causes professionals as well as the general public to suspect all research conducted by the organization where the investigator was based. Further, such researchers risk ostracism by their professional peers and jeopardize their careers.

In doing research it is necessary to review the existing literature to examine knowledge that already exists about a particular topic. Researchers will usually cite this literature when they publish. This practice is very ethical. However, it is unethical to plagiarize the work of another. Plagiarism is the stealing of another's writing or data and passing them off as one's own. When writing about the works of other authors or using the data from other researchers, these individuals must be cited.

Copyright law permits the fair use of copyrighted work [in published reports of research] but does not precisely define 'fair use' in actual number of words. Therefore, when extensive pieces of another's work are to be referenced, permission from the author and/or the publisher must be obtained to do so. A guideline followed by [many publishers], is that up to 300 cumulative words from a journal article or chapter in an edited book and 500 cumulative words from an authored book may be borrowed without securing permission. However, if any table, figure, or illustration is used, permission must be obtained.

There is a general misconception among many researchers that only positive research results – that is, those that confirm the researcher's hypotheses – are worthwhile. This is unfortunate because it is important to know which of our predictions were not supported by our findings. Therefore, if negative findings are at all related to the central focus of the study, investigators are obligated to report them as well as the positive findings. Unfortunately, there may be a bias among professional journals against accepting research papers that report negative results.

Similarly, it is important to be honest in reporting how important results were discovered. Often researchers will examine the relationships between many of the variables in a study and will discover some interesting results. If this happens, report it as such. Do not formulate hypotheses to fit the results that you found by accident in a fabricated attempt to show that these results were the consequence of a carefully planned research strategy.

## SUMMARY

Adherence to ethical standards is essential to the research process. Researchers have an ethical obligation to protect their subjects and to act responsibly and morally. Ethical codes governing research involving human subjects require that subjects give informed consent for their participation, that subjects are not physically or psychologically harmed, that all information about subjects is kept confidential, and that researchers do not deceive study participants. Moreover, the researcher is ethically required to be honest and accurate in conducting and presenting research findings.

## REFERENCE

Schachter, S. (1959) *The psychology of affiliation: experimental studies of the sources of gregariousness*. Stanford, CA: Standford University Press.

# PART TWO

*Approaches to Investigation*

# CHAPTER 7

# Evaluation in the Manageme

## GLYN ROGERS AND LINDA BADH

*This material has been abridged*

*Evaluation is the process of systematically collecting and analysing information in order to form value judgements based on firm evidence.* These judgements are concerned with the extent to which particular targets are being achieved. They should therefore guide decision-making for development.

The term 'evaluation' is sometimes used to refer specifically to the judgemental part of this process only. We have found the broader definition given above more useful, because the validity of the value judgements which can be made is greatly dependent on the nature and provenance of the data collected. In this context, the need is for practicable data collection and handling systems which provide sound evidence on which to base judgements. [. . .]

Evaluation is often set in the context of a monitoring, evaluation and review cycle (Tipple, 1989).

- *Monitoring* is the process of collecting and presenting information in relation to specific objectives on a systematic basis. It should always be undertaken for specific purposes if the effort is to be justified.
- *Evaluation* takes this process a stage further in that the information is analysed and value judgements are made.
- *Review* is a considered reflection on progress, using evaluation data to inform decisions for strategic planning.

A simple model showing the interrelationship between these three activities is shown in Figure 7.1.

## WHY EVALUATE AT ALL?

There are two main purposes for evaluation of performance:

- ACCOUNTABILITY to *prove* quality, for example, to demonstrate that funding is being properly deployed to maintain and improve standards;
- DEVELOPMENT to *improve* quality, for example, to assist in the process of improving curriculum development and delivery.

Accountability is a central thread running through most of the changes enshrined in the 1988 Education Reform Act. It has been suggested that the

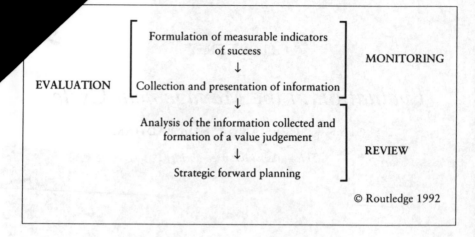

FIGURE 7.1 The interrelationship between monitoring, evaluation and review

various school-based evaluation initiatives of the late 1970s and 1980s were, in general, disappointing because they seldom functioned as appropriate instruments of accountability (Clift, Nuttall and McCormick, 1987). However, in the present climate, school-based evaluation is more likely to take root because schools now have to provide information about their performance over a wide range of issues, and in some detail, to parents, governors and the LEA, particularly, under Local Management of Schools (LMS). With the coming of the Parents' Charter, this accountability is being brought very much to the fore and places an even greater responsibility on schools and their governing bodies, while reducing the role of the LEA.

The primary function of all this accountability is to raise standards. [. . .] However, a major task facing any school's senior management is that of establishing a climate in which staff view evaluation positively. This is more readily achieved when teachers have been fully consulted about the development plan and have had a major say both in determining the evaluation criteria and in agreeing how the information collected is to be used. In this way, schools can ensure that they have the data they need to aid development, and staff will be less likely to feel under threat from the evaluation. Moreover, where the parameters of the evaluation are not explicit within an agreed development plan, teachers may be uncertain about what precisely are the targets at which their school is aiming. It is less than helpful for them to be told *post factum* that they failed to reach these targets – the shifting goal-post syndrome. In sum, evaluation is more effective in raising standards when staff view it as having a developmental as well as an accountability focus. Figure 7.2 summarizes these points.

## WHY ADOPT A PLANNED APPROACH?

School managers have always had to take important and far-reaching decisions. Traditionally, they could often rely on experience to make these

# Evaluation in the Management Cycle

## GLYN ROGERS AND LINDA BADHAM

ACCOUNTABILITY TO PROVE
QUALITY

DEVELOPMENT TO IMPROVE
QUALITY

**THE CHALLENGE**

To establish a climate in which staff:

- view evaluation positively
- do not feel under threat

↓

**THE WAY FORWARD**

Teachers to have a major say in:

- determining the evaluation criteria
- agreeing how the information is to be used

© Routledge 1992

FIGURE 7.2 Purposes of evaluation

decisions against a familiar and relatively stable backcloth. Nowadays, however, change is the norm and crucial decisions are often required very quickly. Managers need reliable information systems to make sound decisions under changing circumstances.

The principal benefit of using a planned approach to evaluation is that it is designed to provide relevant and reliable information on an ongoing basis to inform strategic forward planning. The planned evaluation is characterized by:

- agreed target areas for evaluation;
- explicitness about criteria for the evaluation of success;
- an evaluation plan which outlines who will collect the data, when, and what will be the source of the information;
- a systematic approach to the collection and recording of information where all involved use appropriate, agreed evaluation instruments.

Features of the traditional and planned approaches to evaluation are contrasted in Figure 7.3.

# CONSTRAINTS

School-based evaluation can only succeed if it does not take up disproportionate amounts of time, effort and resources. Constraints on schools include shortage of time, lack of expertise in evaluation, and reluctance of staff to embrace evaluation as an integral part of normal practice. The following list of suggestions is offered to help ameliorate these problems:

| | TRADITIONAL FEATURES | PLANNED FEATURES |
|---|---|---|
| CRITERIA | IDIOSYNCRATIC<br><br>• Tenuous relationship between evaluation criteria and the policy being evaluated<br><br>• Performance indicators non-explicit, not shared between parties involved in the activities | EXPLICIT AND AGREED<br>prior to implementation<br>• Specific target areas for evaluation agreed as priorities; evaluation criteria based on objectives as set out in school development plan<br>• Performance indicators formulated and agreed at the planning stage |
| EVALUATION PLAN | AD HOC<br>• No explicit time-scale<br>• Who does what: unclear<br>• Fitted in when possible<br><br>• Link with policy not clear<br><br>• Undemanding in terms of preparation | STRUCTURES<br>• Agreed time-scale<br>• Who does what: documented<br>• Part of the development planning cycle<br>• Explicit links with aims and objectives<br>• Requires detailed planning |
| METHODS | IMPRESSIONISTIC<br>• Source determined by what/who is available<br>• 'Lucky dip' sample used<br>• Evaluation questions and methods rarely thought out systematically<br>• Lack of consistency in approach<br>• Analysis of data an afterthought | SYSTEMATIC<br>• Source of information detailed<br>• Representative sample used<br>• Evaluation instruments appropriate for the methods used for data collection<br>• Consistency in criteria and methodology<br>• Systems for recording and analysing information<br><br>© Routledge 1992 |

FIGURE 7.3 Traditional and planned evaluation contrasted (*Source:* Based on an original formulation by Dr Colin Morgan, Open University.)

• *Limit the evaluation to a few specific focuses.* Target on some specific, priority objectives which are achievable in the short term and are readily measured, rather than go for the grand plan in a single leap. For example, to increase staff and student use of IT in the National Curriculum core subjects in Years 7 and 8 is a focus for short-term development which is achievable and measurable. By contrast, to improve the quality of IT experiences for all pupils is a laudable aim but one which requires a longer time-span to achieve. Moreover, it would be difficult to measure, needing a level of sophistication in evaluation techniques which few schools would wish to contemplate.

- *Collect essential information only.* Be clear about what information is really necessary for the purposes of evaluation. It is all too easy to be carried away by enthusiasm and to try to collect everything under the sun about the chosen topic when a much more limited exercise would suffice.
- *Make the maximum use of information already available.* Before rushing into designing questionnaires, interview schedules and classroom observation checklists, scan existing sources of information such as attendance registers, room/equipment usage logs, published statistics and other data collected recently by the school. Also make maximum use of any evaluation data about the school, for example, HMI or LEA reports, and TVEI evaluation exercises.
- *Keep it short and simple (KISS).* If you are obliged to gather information from staff or pupils, make your questionnaire/interview brief and unambiguous. Ask only for the information you really need. Avoid questionnaire/interview design requiring complex and time-consuming analysis techniques. Before you collect the data, decide how you will analyse the responses.
- *Make it worthwhile and credible for staff.* Involve staff at an early stage in agreeing the priorities for both development and evaluation in advance. The purposes of the evaluation should then be clear and its potential value to staff in their work and concerns be explicit. The use of the data – who has access to the information and why – also need to be agreed. Finally, the credibility of the evaluation system within a school has to be established by ensuring that:
  — the outcomes are VALUABLE to all the parties concerned;
  — the judgements made must be VALID, that is they must be supported by evidence;
  — the process should be VERIFIABLE, that is, reasons for the judgements should be specific with the supporting evidence presented;
  — the process should be VIABLE, that is, cost-effective in terms of time and resources and therefore sustainable.

Figure 7.4 summarizes these ways of trying to ameliorate the constraints.

---

- Limit the evaluation to a few specific focuses
- Collect essential information only
- Make the maximum use of information already available
- Keep it short and simple (KISS)
- Make it worthwhile and credible for staff

© Routledge 1992

---

FIGURE 7.4 **Possible ways of overcoming the evaluation constraints**

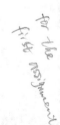

[. . .]

Because a number of technical terms are used in evaluation, we have provided a list of definitions. You may at this stage wish to scan through these definitions and refer back to them as and when you need.

# DEFINITIONS

## Aim

An aim is a general statement of intention that outlines the ultimate goal without specifying the stages by which it could be achieved. It is important to distinguish between aims and the objectives. The latter term defines the stages through which the aims can be achieved. For example, your aim might be to encourage children to make wise and informed curriculum and career choices. One objective which contributes towards meeting this aim might be to provide a planned careers programme in Years 10 and 11 which integrates the work of teachers and careers officers.

## Objective

An objective is a statement of intention that outlines in precise terms a short-term goal which is relevant to achieving the aim. While aims are fairly broad, objectives need to be quite specific. Each should be a clear, concise statement of what is to be achieved.

The development of objectives should, whenever possible, involve agreement by all those concerned, whether they are governors, staff or outside agencies. Such consultation will also help to ensure that the targets set by the objectives are at a level which is achievable. If not, there will be disenchantment because those who have formulated the objectives will be viewed as being out of touch with reality. Worse still, the targets may not be met because the people who are supposed to implement the objectives do not fully appreciate what the school expects from them. Objectives should be measurable so that the school can tell whether or not they are being achieved.

The other important factor to consider is the time-scale over which the objectives are to be achieved. This should be explicit and agreed so that those involved will be clear about when implementation is to take place.

To use an acronym which will be familiar to some readers, objectives should be:

| | |
|---|---|
| S | pecific |
| M | easurable |
| A | greed and achievable |
| R | elevant |
| T | imed |

# Strategy

A strategy is a plan outlining how a specific objective or a series of objectives will be achieved. It indicates what is to be done – how, by whom and when. For example, a school might have the specific objective: within the next academic year to increase from 10% to 25% the number of teachers who have experienced a work placement. The strategy would specify how teachers would be identified, when the placements could occur and with which employers, who would undertake all the necessary organization, how the financial and resource implications would be met.

In the context of evaluation, the strategy will outline what information is to be collected; how, by whom, and when.

# Development plan

The development plan is a statement of priorities to be addressed within a specific period of time. Such plans can be prepared at various levels – LEA, school, department, individual – and should set out common and consistent aims, objectives and strategies. Ideally they should also include evaluation plans.

# Performance indicators (PIs)

Performance indicators are the signals of success which will be used to indicate whether the objectives have been achieved. A performance indicator:

- is an indication of the extent of progress made in one area and is not an absolute or general measure of performance;
- should be viewed alongside other evaluation evidence in order to identify and understand the overall progress achieved;
- should not be used in isolation but as part of an overall system of planning, evaluation and review;
- should be capable of collection over a period of time on a constant basis;
- should be relevant to the objective;
- may be quantitative or qualitative. A quantitative PI is generally used to manufacture fact rather than opinion, for example, the percentage of Year 2 pupils attaining level 2 or better in their National Curriculum subjects at the end of key stage 1. A qualitative PI attempts to obtain a measure of an attitude or perception, for example, the degree of parental satisfaction with the arrangements for pupil transition between primary and secondary school. Obtaining credible and reliable measures for this second type of PI is much more complex and difficult.

# Evaluation instrument

An evaluation instrument is a tool which specifies:

- what information needs to be collected including, where appropriate, lists of questions to be asked;
- what is the source of the information;

- the format for recording the information.

For standardized usage, for example, by a team of evaluators, it may also include guidelines on the analysis of the information. [. . .]

## Review

The review involves considered reflection on the progress of the past year's development plan. The consideration of the evaluation information collected should lead to informed value judgements. These will be concerned both with the success of the strategies in delivering these objectives, and also with whether the objectives are indeed contributing to the achievement of the long-term aims. This review will inevitably lead into the following year's strategic forward planning.

## THE EVALUATION PLANNING TRIANGLE

In planning evaluation, three interrelated aspects have to be specified, namely objectives, performance indicators and evaluation instruments.

### PIs and objectives

Performance indicators are signals of success. They are not general questions or statements in a checklist or audit. Consider the following example:

> Incidence of special educational need/learning difficulties including any provision made for pupils with statements
>
> (DES, 1989, no. 17)

This is not a PI because it gives no indication of how successful a school is in supporting pupils with learning difficulties. It certainly highlights a broad issue which concerns most schools, but it begs the question of what might give a specific signal either that a school's provision for pupils with special educational needs was worthwhile or that there was improvement from the previous state. This question is very difficult to answer without reference to some specific target or objective.

Suppose that a secondary school had decided to focus on its special educational needs provision. At an early stage in implementing a new or revised policy the school might concentrate on encouraging all departments to look afresh at their planning. One possible objective would be: to produce schemes of work for Year 10 in all subjects through consultation between subject staff and members of the special education needs support team. A suitable PI to measure the success of this objective would be: the number of subject areas which have revised their schemes of work for Year 10 in consultation with the special needs support team. Clearly, the limited objective and its associated PI do not deal with the quality of the pupils' learning experiences. The focus is targeted on the planning process for developing suitable schemes of work. Later in the implementation of the new or revised policy, the school might wish to have some measure of the effectiveness of that policy. One possible outcome indicator would be: the percentage of pupils with special educational needs who gain external accreditation during Year 11, since an increase in this percentage would be one – but not the only – possible signal that the policy was indeed improving pupils' learning experiences. It must be remembered that one signal should be considered in conjunction with other information before a value judgement can be made with some degree of confidence.

The examples above are intended to show that PIs are meaningful when they are derived from specific targets or objectives, whether set by the school, the LEA or nationally.

## PIs and evaluation instruments

Even when PIs are linked with aims and specific objectives, they can be open to a variety of interpretations. The evaluation instrument provides opportunities for detailing specific questions which elicit meaningful responses.

Suppose one objective for a secondary or primary school was: to strengthen and increase the number of links between the school's curriculum and the world of work. A possible PI would be: number of deparmtents/year teams making use of links with the world of work in their teaching. The evaluation instrument would need to ask questions in such a way as to clarify what counted as a link with the world of work. Thus heads of department/year teams might be asked:

| Which of the following links with the world of work has your department/year team established? Please tick the relevant boxes. | |
|---|---|
| Pupil projects involving local business/industries/ organizations | |
| Pupil visits to business/industry/other workplace | |
| Use of pupils' work placement experience in lessons (*secondary schools only*) | |
| External speakers/consultants whose contributions are relevant to National Curriculum programmes of study | |
| Teacher-placement involving departmental/year team member(s) | |
| Other: please specify | |
| © Routledge 1992 | |

For a small primary school, these questions could be modified so as to apply to each class teacher.

Sometimes, attempting to design an evaluation instrument throws up so many problems that there may be need to reconsider the PI. Within the constraints that schools face, a PI which is extremely difficult to measure is not

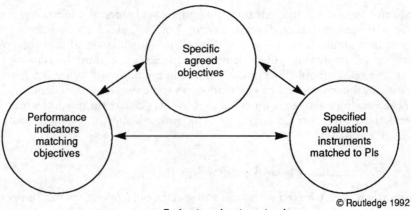

FIGURE 7.5 Evaluation planning triangle

well suited to self-evaluation. For example, a school might wish to measure the incidence of pupils' exercise of initiative and acceptance of responsibility (DES, 1989, no. 40). However, a high level of expertise and experience is required to design an instrument suitable for obtaining a reliable measure of such a qualitative PI. A school might therefore feel the need to employ a professional evaluator. Alternatively, the school might consider modifying the PI to measure one or two specific examples of pupils' behaviour. For example, the percentage of pupils in a particular year group who submit homework and coursework regularly and on time is measureable; it gives one indication of pupils' acceptance of responsibility and requires only a relatively simple evaluation instrument.

## Evaluation instruments and objectives

Similarly, designing the evaluation instruments may throw up problems, not just with PIs, but with the objectives themselves. Sometimes it becomes clear that a given objective is too wide-ranging and ambitious to be achievable in the short term. Also, a group of people working together to design an evaluation instrument may realize that the objective will be open to different interpretations by the staff involved in its implementation. In both cases, the process of evaluation instrument design will have highlighted the need to refine the objective.

In sum, planning evaluation starts with objectives, from which PIs can be formulated; but the planning is not complete until the evaluation instruments to collect the information have been designed. This process is not a simple progression, since designing the evaluation instrument often highlights the need to refine the objective, to make it more specific or less ambiguous. The PI would then be modified accordingly. The three elements are closely interrelated, as illustrated in Figure 7.5.

## LINKING DEVELOPMENT PLANS AND EVALUATION

[. . .] The management cycle of planning, implementation and review is familiar to most schools. The next logical step is to integrate evaluation into this

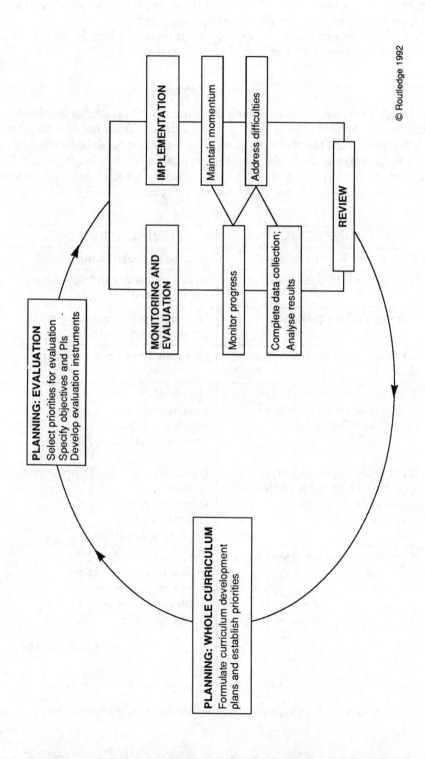

© Routledge 1992

**PLANNING: EVALUATION**
Select priorities for evaluation
Specify objectives and PIs
Develop evaluation instruments

**IMPLEMENTATION**
Maintain momentum
Address difficulties

**MONITORING AND EVALUATION**
Monitor progress
Complete data collection;
Analyse results

**REVIEW**

**PLANNING: WHOLE CURRICULUM**
Formulate curriculum development
plans and establish priorities

FIGURE 7.6  The planning, implementation and review cycle

cycle. Evaluation should be seen as a coherent element of the established management cycle and not as an isolated or intermittent option. Figure 7.6 sets out the sequence of the overall cycle and shows evaluation as an integral and ongoing feature of the curriculum development process.

In order to ensure that evaluation does not become a bolt-on activity, it is important to consider its implication at each stage of the cycle.

## Planning stage

Planning should not stop at deciding what the school's priorities for development are and how to achieve them. It is important to think out how to recognize whether or not the plan is working. The evaluation needs to be planned as early as possible. Indeed, planning the evaluation often helps to clarify the thinking as to what action is required to achieve a given target. The various steps in the planning process are presented in Figure 7.7.

| QUESTIONS | PLANNING RESPONSE |
|---|---|
| What do we wish to achieve? | Determine overall aims |
| How will this be achieved? | Define objectives and determine the associated strategies |
| What should we evaluate? | Decide on priorities/target areas for evaluation |
| What would count as evidence of success? | Establish performance indicators |
| What are the sources of the information and how will we collect the information? | Decide where the information can be obtained and how to acquire it ⎫ Design evaluation instruments |
| What specific information is required to help form a value judgement? | Decide on the specific information to be collected and the format for recording ⎭ |
| How will we use the information collected? | Determine:<br>• how to analyse the data<br>• how to present the data<br>• who will have access to the findings<br><br>© Routledge 1992 |

FIGURE 7.7 Steps in planning which include the planning of evaluation

## Implementation and the formative evaluation stage

There is a tendency for guidelines on school development plans to describe implementation and evaluation as separate phases. In some ways this is understandable, since checking on progress logically follows implementation. However, there is a risk that schools will consider the requirements of evaluation only late in the cycle and therefore lose some of the benefits.

It is desirable to treat the processes of implementation and evaluation as interwoven, not as a period of implementation followed by a separate intense period of evaluation at the end. When implementation and evaluation are integrated and ongoing, evaluation can help to shape and guide the strategies employed. Suppose, for example, that a school had decided to integrate children with special needs into mainstream classes. It would be very necessary to monitor – throughout the year, and not just at the end – the children's progress and the effectiveness of the support strategies for them. This would provide opportunities for addressing difficulties early enough to benefit these particular children.

One way to support integration of implementation and evaluation is to develop the evaluation instruments prior to implementation and to agree an appropriate timetable for data collection. Clearly, the constraints of time will allow for only limited monitoring during the implementation phase. But, as the example above illustrates, dipstick exercises during the year can be beneficial, even though the major collection of data will occur once, prior to the review.

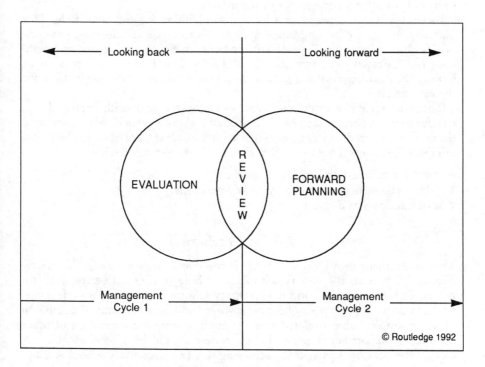

FIGURE 7.8 Evaluation, review and forward planning

## REVIEW

## The relationship between evaluation, review and strategic planning

We have defined 'review' as a considered reflection on the progress of the previous year's development plan. This considered reflection should be such as to provide structured opportunities for all the relevant personnel to meet, discuss and reach agreement. The discussion should use all the available evaluation data to arrive at shared value judgements on:

• whether the objectives set out in the strategic plan have been met;
• the extent to which those objectives are contributing to achieving the broad aims;
• the action required in the light of this.

It is important to remember that the purpose of the review is not simply to point up failures. Recognition of success is essential both to maintain and improve staff morale and to disseminate proven examples of good practice. A wider knowledge of such practice is needed if the positive lessons which have been learned are to be extended to other aspects of school life. Nevertheless, there will be instances where the school has not achieved all it would have wished. Review gives an opportunity for constructive analysis of the difficulties so as to formulate a strategy for future action.

Inevitably, the review process leads into planning for the next cycle. This planning will range beyond ongoing activities to a consideration of new priorities for development. The relationship between evaluation, review and planning is illustrated diagrammatically in Figure 7.8. Review can be seen as linking the evaluation of the present situation with the strategic planning for the next phase.

The term 'review' is often used much more loosely than as illustrated above, to refer to the general notion of looking back and taking stock. We recommend the more structured concept associated with a summative review, as illustrated in Figure 7.9, since the process of review is of greatest value where:

• reflection is based on sound evidence;
• value judgements are agreed by all key personnel;
• action follows as a result.

## Review in school

The involvement of all key personnel is the cornerstone to using the review effectively. In a small primary school, the whole staff could be involved together. In larger primary and in secondary schools, this may not be feasible, both in terms of the number of people involved and because detailed discussion of, for example, subject-related issues is not appropriate to members of other faculties or departments. Nevertheless, review should be a whole-school activity. One possible scenario for achieving this in a secondary school is given below.

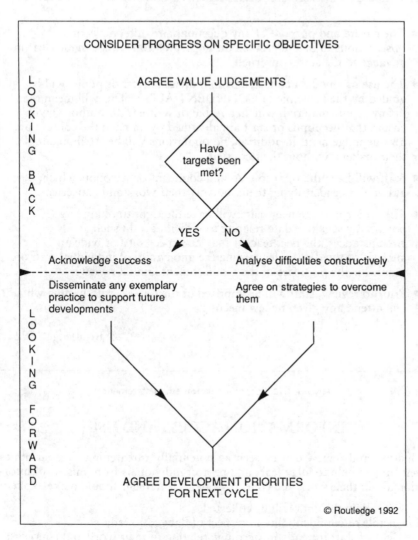

CONSIDER PROGRESS ON SPECIFIC OBJECTIVES

AGREE VALUE JUDGEMENTS

L O O K I N G B A C K

Have targets been met?

YES    NO

Acknowledge success    Analyse difficulties constructively

Disseminate any exemplary practice to support future developments

Agree on strategies to overcome them

L O O K I N G F O R W A R D

AGREE DEVELOPMENT PRIORITIES FOR NEXT CYCLE

© Routledge 1992

FIGURE 7.9 Tasks undertaken in the review

- Senior managers meet to agree on the priorities which the whole-school review should address and, in broad terms, to decide what the school wants out of the review.
- Faculty/department/curricular area reviews consider, with guidance from a senior manager, issues relevant to their work. The outcomes of these reviews will feed into the whole-school formal review.
- Senior and middle managers meet to undertake the formal whole-school review. This may involve LEA personnel in a partnership approach.
- The outcomes of the whole-school review are communicated to all staff and presented and discussed with governors.

- The nature and purpose of any questionnaire, interviews or observations to be undertaken during evaluation will be made clear in advance to the staff concerned.

- The use of any data collected from individual staff or pupils will be guided by the principle of CONFIDENTIALITY. This will mean that, in any report material, whether verbal or written, the author(s) will ensure that no pupils or staff are identified by name in the context of a value judgement. In addition, no quotations will be attributed to their makers, without their consent.

- Staff will have the right to read and comment on accounts which, although not identifying them, portray their work and concerns.

- The senior management team will have the right to retain any potentially sensitive data relating to individuals. In such circumstances, the headteacher may be expected to provide an analysis of the data, safeguarding the anonymity of individual staff or pupils for the purposes of the establishment annual review.

- Prior to review, staff will be apprised of the criteria determining who will attend any given review meeting.

© Routledge 1992

FIGURE 7.10 School evaluation ethics statement

## INFORMATION ACCESS AND USE

Evaluation and review can be seen as potentially threatening. A clear ethics statement can help to allay fears and protect individuals from misuse of information about their work and concerns. Such a statement should make explicit:

- why and how the data will be collected;
- a principle of confidentiality in respect of data collected;
- the right of staff to read any accounts relating to their work and concerns;
- who has access to the raw data, particularly where these may be sensitive, and how the rights of individuals will be safeguarded, including their rights under the Data Protection Act of 1984;
- criteria for including various personnel at the review meeting(s).

Figure 7.10 is an example of an ethics statement designed to be used in a school.

## REFERENCES

Clift, P. S., Nuttall, D. L. and McCormick, R. (1987) *Studies in school self-evaluation.* London: Falmer.
DES (1989) *School indicators for internal management: an aide mémoire.* Publications Despatch Centre, London: Department of Education and Science.
Tipple, C. (1989) Measuring achievement, *Education,* 29 September.

CHAPTER 8

# Auditing as Institutional Research: A Qualitative Focus

DAVID M. FETTERMAN

*This material has been abridged*

Internal auditing is the art and science of describing and testing checks and balances in institutional management. It requires detailed study of departments and functions to improve effectiveness and efficiency and to protect the institution's assets. Many of the techniques used to analyse institutions of higher education are qualitative in nature – notably, participant observation, informal interviews, triangulation, and solicitation of the insider's point of view. Properly conducted, internal auditing in higher education facilitates the academic mission.

This discussion presents the many types of internal audits, including fiscal, operational, electronic data processing, investigative (dealing with fraud or embezzlement), and management consulting. In addition, a new form of auditing is on the horizon: ethnographic auditing. Each approach tests internal controls or mechanisms. Some approaches are broad in focus, others are narrow. However, each relies on both qualitative and quantitative techniques to achieve its goals. This chapter focuses on the qualitative techniques that internal auditors routinely employ.

## FISCAL AUDIT

The foundation of most auditing is a fiscal review. Does the deparmtent or function have a budget? Do the figures add up? Does the system ensure a separation of duties between employees who accept funds and those who record and balance funds? Fiscal auditing is primarily concerned with the books and is conducted to ensure that the department accurately represents its stated self-worth. On the simplest level, a review of petty cash constitutes a basic part of a fiscal audit. A count of the funds and a review of the receipts provide an excellent baseline for determining the financial integrity of the petty cash fund and its custodian. In addition, an informal interview with the custodian of the fund and his or her supervisor sheds some light on actual practice. Does the supervisor periodically check on the custodian? Does the custodian approve the supervisor's reimbursement receipts? If so, are the custodian and supervisor aware of the conflict of interest involved? Has the supervisor considered having the reimbursement receipts approved by his or her own supervisor? These kinds of questions constitute the common-sense, qualitative approach required to protect petty cash funds effectively. A qualitative approach is holistic and contextual. It attempts to look at the whole picture and to place it in a broader social context. Examination of the petty cash fund from a holistic and contextual orientation reveals the cyclical nature of the department's funds as they are routinely used and replenished. In fact, from this perspective there is nothing petty about petty cash. Over time, hundreds of thousands of dollars can pass through a single custodian's hands.

# OPERATIONAL AUDIT

An operational audit subsumes a fiscal audit and builds on it by focusing on an operation's effectiveness and efficiency. Operational audits focus on such topics as supervision, communication, planning, and analysis, as well as such mundane topics as equipment inventories and petty cash.

An operational audit differs from a fiscal audit in both scope and interpretation. For example, an operational audit of a department requires the same kind of review of petty cash as conducted in a fiscal audit. However, an operational review brings the determination about the status of the petty cash fund to a higher level of analysis. A finding about petty cash would be combined with other findings to determine if a pattern existed, such as sloppy management practices. In other words, a problem with the handling of a department's petty cash would be viewed as a potential manifestation of a larger management problem.

Operational audits take more time than do fiscal audits, but they provide a much richer picture of an organization's management. Such audits use both qualitative and quantitative data but require a qualitative review of all quantitative data. A classic audit reviews a department's management information systems. The first questions to ask in this case are traditional audit questions that happen to be qualitative in nature: Do you have a management information system? If so, can I look at it? The auditor must analyse the quality of the quantitative data in the management information system to determine whether management is relying on valid, reliable, and hopefully useful information to make its decisions. Poor-quality data results in poor decisions in even the most sophisticated management information or decision-making systems.

During one audit of a university hospital pharmacy, participant observation was a useful qualitative technique. It involved informally interviewing and observing pharmacists, attempting to solicit their perspectives about their jobs. The technique revealed the pharmacists' belief that the workload statistics used in the pharmacy were a joke because the system of recording productivity data did not accurately reflect the pharmacists' behaviour. The workload system merely counted the number of prescriptions to measure productivity – a misleading measure because one prescription might take two minutes to prepare, whereas another prescription might require half an hour or an hour. Supervisors set schedules and established unrealistic productivity standards based on this information. The system was a clear case of garbage in, garbage out.

In another operational audit, the department under review used a computer spreadsheet to track its income and expenses, a major improvement over the back-of-the-envelope system too many departments rely on. However, an analysis of the formulae in the spreadsheet revealed an error. Masked by the appearance of a computer's technical accuracy, the error was compounded in being repeated week after week, month after month, year after year. An unobtrusive review of the quality of the quantitative data in the spreadsheet saved the institution real money.

A third operational audit revealed that although a department was conscientiously and accurately placing data in the management information system, no one ever looked at the data in aggregate or attempted to sort them in any fashion. This audit finding suggested poor planning and analysis, because decision-makers did not use a valuable source of information. The findings of these three examples largely derived from qualitative forms of inquiry: observing and participating in the lives of employees, conducting informal interviews, soliciting the insider's viewpoint, and analysing the quality of quantitative data.

The operational auditor communicates with clients throughout the audit. Clients have numerous opportunities to comment on preliminary perceptions and findings. The auditor asks the client questions verbally, through memoranda and electronic mail, and in draft reports. This process enables the client to provide input and the auditor to revise continually his or her understanding and assessment of the system. This interactive approach is typical of qualitative research. It brings the auditor close to the client's perceptions of their programme. It also increases the accuracy and usefulness of the findings, making the information directly relevant to programme personnel. The clients are thus more likely to implement the auditor's recommendations to improve the programme.

## ELECTRONIC DATA-PROCESSING AUDIT

An electronic data-processing audit focuses on mainframe and personal computer security controls. The auditor asks questions such as the following: Are users required to use and update passwords? Is access to sensitive records such as payroll information limited? Does the department have written and updated documentation about a given system? Do employees back up their data and programs in case of system failure? Most of these questions can be answered simply by asking individual employees, conducting tests, and reviewing existing documentation. An employee may claim to back up the data but be unable to provide any backup disks. Or another employee may be able to produce a string of cases in which data were lost. A classic qualitative approach – triangulation – involves comparing what people say with what they do, or, more broadly, comparing many sources to determine the accuracy of a given piece of information. Behaviour is an excellent source of evidence in any triangulation effort.

## INVESTIGATIVE AUDIT

The investigative audit focuses on suspicions or allegations of fraud and abuse. Allegations cover a wide range of activities: An employee may routinely receive a payroll check for a non-existent or ghost employee. A faculty member may be consulting in excess of the amount allowable under university policy and procedure. An employee may allege intimidation by management. Investigations in each of these areas rely heavily on qualitative approaches, including informal interviews, use of key informants, and unobtrusive reviews of archival material such as calendars, travel reimbursements, and electronic mail.

In the case of an alleged ghost employee, for example, informal interviews with the complainant co-worker may provide a wealth of information, although interview information alone is rarely sufficient. However, it is invaluable in building a model of the event. Informal interviews may provide sufficient detail about the situation to document it and to confront the individual and ameliorate the problem, or, if necessary, set up a 'sting operation' to catch the individual.

[. . .]

A controversial case about an employee who charged management with intimidation required a series of sensitive exchanges. Informal and formal interviews provided insight into the employee's perspective about the incident. The employee's perception was as important as so-called objective reality: individuals act on their perceptions, and their actions have real consequences. Moreover, in this particular case, a detailed review of the actions of the vice-president above the employee's supervisor provided documentation to support the employee's allegation. Informal interviews with the vice-president also supported the allegations – but provided an explanation as well. The vice-president was concerned that the employee was a zealot and was abusing his position, and she believed that she was entitled to come down hard on someone whom she perceived as insubordinate and misguided. The case study description of this somewhat convoluted event was in itself a valuable finding. This information provided management with a basis for dealing with a highly charged, political problem. The practices of verifying and confirming the information enabled management to rectify the situation.

## MANAGEMENT CONSULTING AUDIT

Management consulting is typically performed at the request of senior management. The audit provides management with information and advice on the institutional vision and goals and conceptualizes or reconceptualizes the particular problem or programme under review. The audit is concerned with internal controls, checks, and balances on a metalevel, rather than on a day-to-day programme level. Management consulting may be broad or highly specific, requiring expertise in a narrow field of specialization. A management consultant/auditor can respond to global policy or programmatic concerns, such as the reorganization of a university, school, or department. Or, the management consultant might be brought in to solve a highly technical problem.

A consistently successful auditor in a management consulting role is highly dependent on qualitative concepts and techniques. A conflict-ridden department provides a useful illustration. I was asked to provide insight and advice about a university research administration in a department fraught with turmoil and internal conflict. I interviewed faculty members to determine their level of satisfaction with the research administrators, who provided proposal support and monitored faculty research budgets. I found that some faculty members were happy with the services that they received from the research administration, while other faculty members were disgusted with the complexity of dealing with research administrators and the lack of any meaningful service. Faculty had a strong, vested interest in this problem because their grants supported the research administration infrastructure. I traced compliments and complaints to specific individuals, and a pattern emerged. There were two separate units within the research administration. They were artifacts of historical development, emerging as the faculty departments evolved.

The compliments were consistently associated with the client-service-oriented section of the research administration. This unit served as the faculty members' contact for all problems and concerns in the proposal/grant process. A faculty member with a problem would call the client representative (the research administrator), who would respond promptly to any request. If the research administrator did not know the answer to a question, he or she would research the problem and get back to the faculty member.

The complaints all traced back to the functionally oriented unit. In essence, a separate person was responsible for each of the major elements of a grant or grant proposal. Researchers had to learn whom to work with at each stage of the proposal/grant administration. Many faculty found this process frustrating. Periodically, the entire system would come to a grinding halt when a single research administrator was absent because no one else in the unit could perform that administrator's function. The research administrators had been functioning in this fashion for decades and could not understand why the faculty were not happy with the service that they provided.

My analysis of this complex set of relationships relied heavily on interviews, observation, and participation in the research administrators' lives on a daily basis in order to draw an accurate portrait of their predicament. I knew that senior administrators were considering a merger of the two research administration units. I recommended against it. True, some economies of scale and overall efficiencies could have been accomplished by the merger. But, clearly, the units' cultures in the administrative organization clashed, and a merger would have resulted in even greater turmoil. (The organizational differences had led, historically, to conflicts, turf wars, personal jealousies, and other dysfunctional relationships.) I also recommended that consideration be given to training the functionally oriented unit in client-service-oriented pilot groups to respond to faculty complaints. The functionally oriented unit was concerned about its autonomy, independence, and dignity, and this training enabled its administrators to test the other approach without having it forced down their throats.

[. . .]

# ETHNOGRAPHIC AUDIT

Ethnographic auditing – the systematic application of ethnographic techniques and concepts to auditing – is a relatively new development in the field. Ethnographic auditing highlights the roles of culture, subculture, values, rituals, and physical environment in higher education and views the institution as a living, breathing organism with its own life cycle. In addition, this approach demonstrates the economic consequences of adopting various philosophical orientations or worldviews and clarifies the role of information systems, the value of data bases for decision making, and the roles of judgement and honesty in management. Ethnographic auditing relies on the application of a host of qualitative approaches such as participant observation, key-informant interviews, informal interviews, triangulation, solicitation of the insider's perspective, and conceptualization of a unit as a sociocultural system.

One of the most effective tools in ethnographic auditing is the case study. Case studies describe a department as a community, subculture, or human organism. A department has its own rules of behaviour, norms, economic systems, power structures, and status symbols and its own identifiable character or ethos. Case studies provide a detailed picture of the human organization, communication, and value system of a department or school. This type of description places individual interactions into a larger context of historical circumstances and illuminates the politics of daily interaction in a department. One of the simplest ways of illustrating the ethnographic auditing approach is to present a case study of a department found on almost every campus: the library.

## LIBRARY AUDIT

I was asked to study and evaluate a university research library by one of the library directors. The overall assessment was not positive. A number of problems warranted attention, ranging from a poor conception of the institutional mission to conflicting worldviews and value systems among the staff.

The core of the problem was that the library had a weak and fragmented cultural system. Employees had no central conception of purpose. The librarians had lost their mission in a maze of departments and of processing and cataloguing rules and regulations. The ethnographic audit findings helped to revitalize the library's cultural system by reminding management and staff members of their mission. The auditors provided a simple mechanical model of library operations to assist library staff in defining their purpose. In essence, the ethnographic audit attempted to make explicit the library's implicit cultural rules and values.

The technical services part of a library, for example, is actually a complex production system. A volume passes through a series of conversion processes, and the processing is complete when the volume is placed on the library shelves for use. The output is a properly bound, catalogued volume, physically accessible to a user. Of course, many subroutines exist within each component of the system's flow pattern. However, the section's basic mission – putting that volume on the shelf for the user – was the cultural thread that held them together.

In this fragmented cultural system, each department and subunit represented a subculture. The library's poorly defined cultural system was confounded by subcultural conflict. 'All companies have subcultures, because functional differences . . . single out special aspects of the business environment. . . . Each has its own relevant environment and world view, special heroes, rituals, ceremonies, language, and symbols communicate particular values. Subcultures can shape beliefs and determine behaviors in much the same way that culture can' (Deal and Kennedy, 1982, p. 151).

From an audit or evaluation perspective, the library management paid insufficient attention to the efficient co-ordination of production operation details and the summative effect of a unit's or department's processes and procedures on the whole system. Translated into cultural language, the subcultures clashed and produced maladaptive behaviour patterns; low morale and low productivity. This problem was discovered by using such techniques as key-informant interviews, informal interviews, semi-autobiographical interviews, archival materials, and listening to the library 'folktales' that various librarians told.

The original cataloguer librarians represented the most vocal and anti-mainstream subculture. They provided detailed accounts of what they perceived as personal injustices inflicted on them by management. They had their own heroes who had won grievances against the library administration. The folktales generated from these events highlighted the employees' individual complaints. Heroic figures in the subculture proved to be extremely articulate key informants, providing vivid and often extensively documented accounts of their lives in the library. Their autobiographical accounts focused on their professional clashes with management. Archival data, such as newspaper articles, were also useful in documenting the problem. Many librarians had repeatedly voiced their displeasure with management in the campus newspaper over the years. They described the working climate as oppressive and hostile. In addition, an overwhelming number of grievances stemmed from this subculture. The grievance documents represented another useful archival data source with which to triangulate individual reports. Interviews with management were valuable in placing the clash of subcultures in an institutional context. Management was attuned to this problem because they had for several years perceived the cataloguer subculture as ripe for unionization.

'Subcultures can be very destructive in weak cultural environments. When the corporation's values are impossible to understand, a subculture can dictate behavior, and eventually cause a sort of cultural drift in the company' (Deal and Kennedy, 1982, p. 152). Library staff members and management shared few values. In fact, value conflict was epidemic and manifest in myriad dysfunctional behaviours. For example, from a management perspective, data for decision-making were fundamental. In the library, each department and subunit had its own separate information system, but there was not an overall information system to collect, aggregate, and monitor productivity data systematically and comprehensively. Many diverse professional forms and data sheets circulated throughout the library. A cursory review suggested that the elaborate data collection system was effective. After a few informal interviews with the librarians, however, I learned of their frustrations with the data collection system. Because they worked in discrete units or departments, they were unable to identify the source of the problem. I viewed the system holistically and attempted to track books through the entire system. I observed immediately that the forms used to collect statistics did not reflect management's information needs. One section of the library aggregated copy, original, and variant-edition categories into a single category: titles. This practice hid the variation within each category – information that is necessary to identify where a production problem exists. This type of problem was endemic to the entire system.

I recommended a management information system, including well-defined goals and objectives (including numerical goals), input and output data to measure work flow, consistent output standards, a measuring device to determine how staff members allocated their time to complete tasks, a feedback signal or monitoring component to evaluate their progress toward specific goals, and a protocol for corrective action. I also recommended that management attempt to support the various subcultures rather than waste time attempting to crush specific ones. I believed that it was important to

> encourage each subculture to enrich its own cultural life. Rather than be afraid of subcultures pulling apart, a symbolic manager will seek to strengthen each subculture as an effective cabal within the overall culture. Thus, he or she will often attend functions called to celebrate a particular subculture; participate in special awards for the heroes of the subculture; and generally endorse the subculture's existence and meaning within the larger culture.
>
> (Deal and Kennedy, 1982, p. 153)

Committees formed of members from various subcultures joined to address common problems. This meeting served to sensitize them to each other's concerns and problems. The emphasis was on using subcultures to enrich the larger culture. The effectiveness of this recommendation was limited by the weakness of the existing cultural system. However, it successfully reduced the existing tension for a majority of the library subcultures.

The supervision system also needed improvement in the library. The most significant areas of weakness involved standards of performance and evaluation and span of supervisory control over staff. The standards of performance and evaluation criteria were not explicit or commonly understood, leading to inconsistent appraisals and misevaluations and resulting in what appeared to be inappropriate terminations. 'If people tend to see the firing as arbitrary and unfair, they become confused and upset. In one fell swoop, the culture is called into question' (Deal and Kennedy, 1982, p. 73).

The lack of clearly established and mutually agreed upon goals and standards unnecessarily exposes management to charges of perceived inequities or capricious decision-making. Once consistency and the foundation of due process are established, rituals are useful tools to ameliorate the untoward effects of appropriate but uncomfortable transitions. These rituals can range from annual performance appraisals to retirement banquets.

> To bring these disturbing events under control, sophisticated companies provide elaborate rites. The rituals not only provide security during an unwanted transition but also put the culture on display and dramatize and reinforce its values and beliefs. Those managers who don't consider the dramatic aspects of a transition ritual will miss an opportunity to use it to extend the culture's influence.
>
> (Deal and Kennedy, 1982, p. 73)

The problem of supervision was clearly linked to poor leadership. A brief historical review, based on archival data such as employment records and informal interviews, revealed a high degree of turnover in management positions. According to one of the library directors, the circumstances included four changes in one department in less than five years, a change in a senior management position four years prior to my audit, and three changes within the same time period in one of the most sensitive or volatile subdepartments. In addition, two other senior managers were new to the library. The high rate of turnover resulted in a lack of continuity in leadership and in management expectations of staff member performance. This lack of continuity in turn led to staff concerns and an unclear understanding of their roles.

An ethnographic auditor views the physical environment as part of the cultural system. In the production part of the library, workspace was not conducive to an efficient production work flow. The limited space available was poorly organized. Equipment was located in areas that were either difficult to access or inappropriate. In addition, the lack of privacy, the noise, and the poor lighting and air circulation were not conducive to efficient operations. This atmosphere contrasted with the plush new offices of the public service librarians, who worked with students and professors at the reference desk, at the computer terminals, and in the stacks. 'Differences in the way physical sites are arranged for different classes of employees is one sure sign of a weak or fragmented culture' (Deal and Kennedy, 1982, pp. 130–1).

Participant observation was instrumental in sensitizing me to these problems in the physical environment. I studied the library culture for more than six months. I was involved in the daily lives of staff members, interviewing them every day, eating lunch with them, and periodically helping them with an acquisition or cataloguing task. The validity of their complaints about workspace inadequacies was easy to verify during daily observation and participation in their work lives. Overall, the inequitable (and disorganized) work station arrangement compounded the cultural disarray in the organization. All these maladaptive patterns impeded productivity.

In addition, I took time to interview librarians at various comparable research libraries throughout the United States and learned that the conflict between librarians who work in the production sections and those who work with faculty, including the physical manifestations in workspace conditions, is typical within the larger research library culture. Nevertheless, because an ethnographic auditor attempts to move the organization beyond the status quo, the findings in my case study led me to recommend extensive renovations of the workspace (now completed) to eliminate the vast discrepancy between the plush surroundings of one group of librarians and the 'sweatshop' conditions of another group. In this particular case, the results of ethnographic auditing vividly captured senior management's attention.

## CONCLUSION

Audits have many forms and faces. However, they are an instrumental but often neglected source of institutional research in education. The various auditing approaches presented in this chapter typically combine both quantitative and qualitative techniques. The discussion here focused on the qualitative concepts and techniques that are indispensable in internal audit work. All forms of auditing use qualitative approaches in one fashion or another. However, some approaches, such as management consulting and ethnographic auditing, rely on qualitative approaches more than do financial or electronic data-processing audits. Qualitative approaches are not a panacea in the pursuit of institutional research. However, they are invaluable tools in the institutional researcher's arsenal and help the researcher to make sense of often chaotic and conflict-ridden environments.

# REFERENCE

Deal, T. E. and Kennedy, A. A. (1982) *Corporate cultures: the rites and rituals of corporate life.* Reading, Mass.: Addison-Wesley.

# CHAPTER 9

# *Surveys*

L. COHEN AND L. MANION

*This material has been abridged*

## INTRODUCTION

In this chapter we discuss what is perhaps the most commonly used descriptive method in educational research – the survey. Typically, surveys gather data at a particular point in time with the intention of describing the nature of existing conditions, or identifying standards against which existing conditions can be compared, or determining the relationships that exist between specific events. Thus, surveys may vary in their levels of complexity from those which provide simple frequency counts to those which present relational analysis.

Surveys may be further differentiated in terms of their scope. A study of contemporary developments in post-secondary education, for example, might encompass the whole of Western Europe; a study of subject choice, on the other hand, might be confined to one secondary school. [. . .]

Whether the survey is large-scale and undertaken by some governmental bureau or small-scale and carried out by the lone researcher, the collection of information typically involves one or more of the following data-gathering techniques: structured or semi-structured interviews, self-completion or postal questionnaires, standardized tests of attainment or performance, and attitude scales. Typically, too, surveys proceed through well-defined stages, though not every stage outlined in Figure 9.1 is required for the successful completion of a survey.

We begin with a consideration of some necessary preliminaries to survey planning before going on to outline a variety of sampling strategies that are used in survey research. We then discuss the construction and sequencing of questions in both interviews and questionnaire, prior to detailed examination of the postal questionnaires as a survey technique. Finally, we identify some of the procedures involved in processing and analysing the results of survey research. Our discussion follows the sequential stages in survey design set out in Figure 9.1.

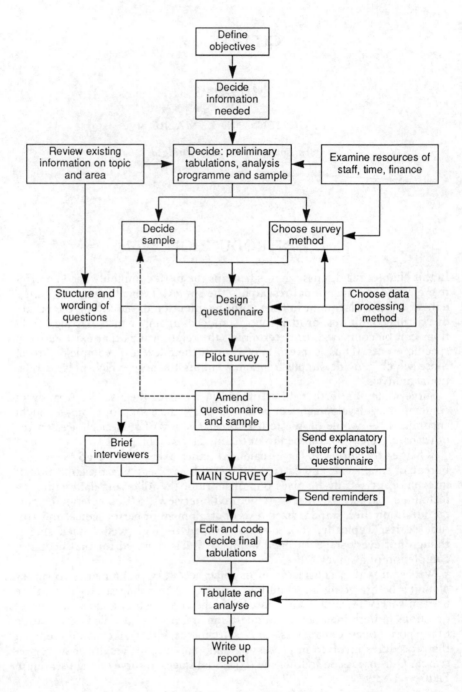

FIGURE 9.1 Stages in the planning of a survey (*Source*: Adapted from Davidson, 1970)

# SOME PRELIMINARY CONSIDERATIONS

Three prerequisites to the design of any survey are the specification of the exact purpose of the enquiry; the population on which it is to focus; and the resources that are available. [. . .]

## The purpose of the enquiry

First, a survey's general purpose must be translated into a specific central aim. Thus, 'to explore teachers' views about in-service work' is somewhat nebulous, whereas 'to obtain a detailed description of primary and secondary teachers' priorities in the provision of in-service education courses' is reasonably specific.

Having decided upon and specified the primary objective of the survey, the second phase of the planning involves the identification and itemizing of subsidiary topics that relate to its central purpose. In our example, subsidiary issues might well include: the types of courses required; the content of courses; the location of courses; the timing of the courses; the design of courses; and the financing of courses.

The third phase follows the identification and itemization of subsidiary topics and involves formulating specific information requirements relating to each of these issues. For example, with respect to the type of courses required, detailed information would be needed about the duration of courses (one meeting, several meetings, a week, a month, a term or a year), the status of courses (non-award bearing, award bearing, with certificate, diploma, degree granted by college or university), the orientation of courses (theoretically oriented involving lectures, readings, etc., or practically oriented involving workshops and the production of curriculum materials).

As these details unfold, consideration would have to be given to the most appropriate ways of collecting items of information (interviews with selected teachers, postal questionnaires to selected schools, etc.).

## The population upon which the survey is focused

The second prerequisite to survey design, the specification of the population to which the enquiry is addressed, affects decisions that researchers must make both about sampling and resources. In our hypothetical survey of in-service requirements, for example, we might specify the population as 'those primary and secondary teachers employed in schools within a 30-mile radius of Loughborough University of Technology'. In this case, the population is readily identifiable and, given sufficient resources to contact every member of the designated group, sampling decisions do not arise. Things are rarely so straightforward, however. Often the criteria by which populations are specified ('severely handicapped', 'under-achievers', 'intending teachers' or 'highly anxious') are difficult to operationalize. Populations, moreover, vary considerably in their accessibility; pupils and student teachers are relatively easy to survey, gypsy children and headteachers are more elusive. More importantly, in a large survey researchers usually draw a sample from the population to be studied; rarely do they attempt to contact every member. We deal with the question of sampling shortly.

## The resources available

The third important factor in the designing and planning a survey is the financial cost. Sample surveys are labour-intensive, the largest single expenditure being the fieldwork where costs arise out of the interviewing time, travel time and transport claims of the interviewers themselves. There are additional demands on the survey budget. Training and supervizing the panel of interviewers can often be as expensive as the costs incurred during the time that they actually spend in the field. Questionnaire construction, piloting, printing, posting, coding, together with computer programming – all eat into financial resources.

# SURVEY SAMPLING

Because questions to do with sampling arise directly from the second of our preliminary considerations, that is, defining the population upon which the survey is to focus, researchers must take sampling decisions early in the overall planning of a survey (see Figure 9.1). We have already seen that due to factors of expense, time and accessibility, it is not always possible or practical to obtain measures from a population. Researchers endeavour therefore to collect information from a smaller group or subset of the population in such a way that the knowledge gained is representative of the total population under study. This smaller group or subset is a 'sample'. Notice how competent researchers start with the total population and work down to the sample. By contrast, novices work from the bottom up, that is, they determine the miniminum number of respondents needed to conduct a successful survey. However, unless they identify the total population in advance, it is virtually impossible for them to assess how representative the sample is that they have drawn. There are two methods of sampling. One yields probability samples in which, as the term implies, the probability of selection of each respondent is known. The other yields non-probabilty samples, in which the probability of selection is unknown. We deal first with various methods of probability sampling (Cohen and Holliday, 1979).

## Probability samples

*Simple random sampling*

In simple random sampling, each member of the population under study has an equal chance of being selected. The method involves selecting at random from a list of the population (a sampling frame) the required number of subjects for the sample. Because of probability and chance, the sample should contain subjects with characteristics similar to the population as a whole; some old, some young, some tall, some short, some fit, some unfit, some rich, some poor, etc. One problem associated with this particular sampling method is that a complete list of the population is needed and this is not always readily available.

## Systematic sampling

This method is a modified form of simple random sampling. It involves selecting subjects from a population list in a systematic rather than a random fashion. For example, if from a population of, say, 2,000, a sample of 100 is required, then every twentieth person can be selected. The starting point for selection is chosen at random.

## Stratified sampling

Stratified sampling involves dividing the population into homogeneous groups, each group containing subjects with similar characteristics. For example, group A might contain males and group B females. In order to obtain a sample representative of the whole population in terms of sex, a random selection of subjects from group A and group B must be taken. If needed, the exact proportion of males to females in the whole population can be reflected in the sample.

## Cluster sampling

When the population is large and widely dispersed, gathering a simple random sample poses administrative problems. Suppose we want to survey children's fitness levels in a particularly large community. It would be quite impractical randomly to select children and spend an inordinate amount of time travelling about in order to test them. By cluster sampling, we can randomly select a specific number of schools and test all the children in those selected schools.

## Stage sampling

Stage sampling is an extension of cluster sampling. It involves selecting the sample in stages, that is, taking samples from samples. Using the large community example referred to earlier, one type of stage sampling might be to select a number of schools at random, and from within each of these schools select a number of classes at random, and from within these classes select a number of pupils.

# Non-probability samples

Small-scale surveys often resort to the use of non-probability samples because, despite the disadvantages that arise from their non-representativeness, they are far less complicated to set up, they are considerably less expensive, and can prove perfectly adequate where researchers do not intend to generalize their findings beyond the sample in question or where they are simply piloting a survey questionnaire as a prelude to their main study. The chief kinds of non-probability sampling are as follows.

## Convenience sampling

Convenience sampling – or as it is sometimes called, accidental sampling – involves choosing the nearest individuals to serve as respondents and continuing that process until the required sample size has been obtained. Captive audiences such as pupils or student teachers often serve as respondents in surveys based upon convenience sampling.

### Quota sampling

Quota sampling has been described as the non-probability equivalent of stratified sampling. It attempts to obtain representatives of the various elements of the total population in the proportions in which they occur there. Thus, researchers interested in race relations in a particular community might set a quota for each ethnic group that is proportionate to its representation in the total population in the area under survey.

### Purposive sampling

In purposive sampling, researchers handpick the cases to be included in the sample on the basis of their judgement of their typicality. In this way, they build up a sample that is satisfactory to their specific needs.

### Dimensional sampling

Dimensional sampling is simply a further refinement of quota sampling. It involves identifying various factors of interest in a population and obtaining at least one respondent of every combination of those factors. Thus, in the study of race relations to which we referred earlier, within each ethnic group, researchers may wish to distinguish between the attitudes of recent immigrants, those who have been in the country for some period of time, and those members of the ethnic group who were born in Great Britain. Their sampling plan might take the form of a multi-dimensional table with 'ethnic group' across the top and 'length of stay' down the side.

### Snowball sampling

Reserachers identify a small number of individuals who have the characteristics that they require. These people are then used as informants to identify others who qualify for inclusion and these, in turn, identify yet others – hence the term snowball sampling.

## SAMPLE SIZE: AN OVERVIEW

A question that often plagues novice researchers is just how large their samples should be in order to conduct an adequate survey. There is, of course, no clearcut answer, for the correct sample size depends upon the purpose of the study and the nature of the population under scrutiny. However, it is possible to give some advice on this matter. Thus, a sample size of 30 is held by many to be the minimum number of cases if researchers plan to use some form of statisitcal analysis on their data, though techniques are available for the analysis of samples below 30. Of more importance to researchers is the need to think out in advance of any data collection the sorts of relationships that they wish to explore within subgroups of their eventual sample. The number of variables researchers set out to control in their analyses and the types of statistical tests they wish to make must inform their decisions about sample size prior to the actual research undertaking.

## Sample size: some statistical considerations

As well as the requirement of a minimum number of cases in order to examine relationships within subgroups, researchers must obtain the minimum sample size that will accurately represent the population under survey. Where simple random sampling is used, the sample size needed to reflect the population value of a particular variable depends both upon the size of the population and the amount of heterogeneity of the variable in the population. Generally, for populations of equal heterogeneity, the larger the population, the larger the sample that must be drawn. For populations of equal size, the greater the heterogeneity on a particular variable, the larger the sample that is needed. To the extent that a sample fails to represent accurately the population under survey, there is sampling error.

## SAMPLING ERROR

If many samples are taken from the same population, it is unlikely that they will all have characteristics identical either with each other or with the population. In brief, there will be sampling error (see Cohen and Holliday, 1979). Sampling error is not necessarily the result of mistakes made in sampling procedures. Rather, variations may occur due to the chance selection of different individuals. For example, if we take a large number of samples from the population and measure the mean value of each sample, then the sample means will not be identical. Some will be relatively high, some relatively low, and many will cluster around an average or mean value of the samples. Why should this occur? We can explain the phenomenon by reference to the Central Limit Theorem which is derived from the laws of probability. This states that if random, large samples of equal size are repeatedly drawn from any population, then the means of those samples will be approximately normally distributed. Moreover, the average or mean of the sample means will be approximately the same as the population mean. We show this diagrammatically in Figure 9.2.

By drawing a large number of samples of equal size from a population, we create a sampling distribution. We can calculate the error involved in such sampling. The standard deviation of the theoretical distribution of sample means is a measure of sampling error and is called the standard error of the mean ($SE_M$). Thus,

$$SE_M = \frac{SD_S}{N}$$

where $SD_S$ = the standard deviation of the sample and
$N$ = the number in the sample

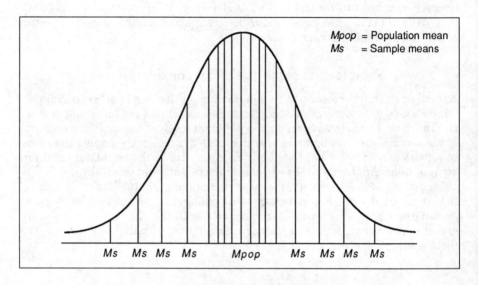

FIGURE 9.2 Distribution of sample means showing the spread of a selection of sample means around the population mean (*Source:* Cohen and Holliday, 1979)

Strictly speaking, the formula for the standard error of the mean is:

$$SE_M = \frac{SD_{pop}}{N}$$

where $SD_{pop}$ = the standard deviation of the population

However, as we are usually unable to ascertain the SD of the total population, the standard deviation of the sample is used instead. The standard error of the mean provides the best estimate of the sampling error. Clearly, the sampling error depends upon the variability (i.e. the heterogeneity) in the population as measured by $SD_{pop}$ as well as the sample size (N). The smaller $SD_{pop}$, the smaller the sampling error; the larger the N, the smaller the sampling error. Where the $SD_{pop}$ is very large, then N needs to be very large to counteract it. Where $SD_{pop}$ is very small, then N, too, can be small and still give a reasonably small sampling error.

[. . .]

## REFERENCES

Cohen, L. and Holliday, M. (1979) *Statistics for education and physical education.* London: Paul Chapman.

Davidson, J. (1970) *Outdoor recreation surveys: the design and use of questionnaires for site surveys.* London: Countryside Commission.

# CHAPTER 10

# Designing Single- and Multiple-Case Studies

### ROBERT K. YIN

*This material has been abridged*

[. . .]

## GENERAL APPROACH TO DESIGNING CASE STUDIES

[. . .]

### Definition of research designs

Every type of empirical research has an implicit, if not explicit, research design. In the most elementary sense, the design is the logical sequence that connects the empirical data to a study's initial research questions and, ultimately, to its conclusions. Colloquially, a research design is *an action plan for getting from here to there*, where 'here' may be defined as the initial set of questions to be answered, and 'there' is some set of conclusions (answers) about these questions. Between 'here' and 'there' may be found a number of major steps, including the collection and analysis of relevant data.

[. . .]

Another way of thinking about a research design is as a 'blueprint' of research, dealing with at least four problems: what questions to study, what data are relevant, what data to collect, and how to analyse the results (see Philliber, Schwab and Samsloss, 1980).

Note that a research design is much more than a workplan. The main purpose of the design is to help to avoid the situation in which the evidence does not address the initial research questions. In this sense, a research design deals with a *logical* problem and not a *logistical* problem. As a simple example, suppose you want to study a single organization. Your research questions, however, have to do with the organization's relationships with other organizations – their competitive or collaborative nature, for example. Such questions can be answered only if you collect information directly from the other organizations and not merely from the one you started with. If you complete your study by examining only one organization, you cannot draw accurate conclusions about interorganizational relationships. This is a flaw in your research design, not in your workplan. The outcome could have been avoided if you had developed an appropriate research design in the first place.

## Components of research designs

For case studies, five components of a research design are especially important:

(1)  a study's questions;
(2)  its propositions, if any;
(3)  its unit(s) of analysis;
(4)  the logic linking the data to the propositions; and
(5)  the criteria for interpreting the findings.

### Study questions

[. . .] Although the substance of your questions will vary, the *form* of the question – in terms of 'who', 'what', 'where', 'how', and 'why' – provides an important clue regarding the most relevant research strategy to be used. The case study strategy is most likely to be appropriate for 'how' and 'why' questions, so your initial task is to clarify precisely the nature of your study questions in this regard.

### Study propositions

As for the second component, each proposition directs attention to something that should be examined within the scope of study. Thus, assume that your research, on the topic of interorganizational relationships, began with the question: How and why do organizations collaborate with one another to provide joint services (for example, a manufacturer and a retail store collaborating to sell certain computer products)? These 'how' and 'why' questions, capturing what you are really interested in answering, led you to the case study as the appropriate strategy in the first place. Nevertheless, these 'how' and 'why' questions do not point to what you should study. Only if you are forced to state some propositions are you beginning to move in the right direction. For instance, you might think that organizations collaborate because they derive mutual benefits. This proposition, besides reflecting an important theoretical issue (that other incentives for collaboration do not exist or are unimportant), also begins to tell you where to look for relevant evidence (to define and ascertain the extent of specific benefits).

At the same time, some studies may have a legitimate reason for not having any propositions. This is the condition – which exists in experiments, surveys, and the other research strategies alike – in which a topic is the subject of 'exploration'. Every exploration, however, should still have some purpose. Instead of propositions, the design for an exploratory study should state this purpose, as well as the criteria by which an exploration will be judged successful.
  [. . .]

## Unit of analysis

This third component is related to the fundamental problem of defining what the 'case' is [. . .].

In the classic case study, a 'case' may be an individual. Thus, you can imagine case studies of clinical patients, of exemplary students, or of certain types of leaders. In each situation, an individual person is the case being studied, and the individual is the primary unit of analysis. Information about each relevant individual would be collected, and several such individuals or 'cases' might be included in a multiple-case study. Propositions would still be needed to help identify the relevant information about this individual or individuals. Without such propositions, an investigator might be tempted to collect 'everything', which is impossible to do. For example, the propositions in studying these individuals might involve the influence of early childhood or the role of peer relationships. Such topics already represent a vast narrowing of the relevant data. The more a study contains specific propositions, the more it will stay within feasible limits.

Of course, the 'case' also can be some event or entity that is less well defined than a single individual. Case studies have been done about decisions, about programmes, about the implementation process, and about organizational change. Beware of these types of topics – none is easily defined in terms of the beginning or end points of the 'case'. For example, a case study of a specific programme may reveal (a) variations in programme definition, depending upon the perspective of different actors, and (b) programme components that pre-existed the formal designation of the programme. Any case study of such a programme would therefore have to confront these conditions in delineating the unit of analysis.

As a general guide, the definition of the unit of analysis (and therefore of the case) is related to the way the initial research questions have been defined. Suppose, for example, you want to study how organizations become more productive when taxes are reduced [. . .]. The primary unit of analysis is the type of organization you want to study, and your study would develop propositions about why organizations would or would not be expected to change under different circumstances. If your real intention, however, was to study how specific tax cutbacks produced changes, the unit of analysis could be very different. In the latter situation, specific tax legislation and laws might be the unit of analysis, and different laws (rather than organizations) would be considered as the subjects of case studies.

Sometimes, the case may have been defined in one manner, even though the phenomenon being studied calls for a different definition. Most frequently, investigators have confused case studies of neighbourhoods with case studies of small groups [. . .]. How a general *area* such as a neighbourhood copes with racial transition, commercialization, and other phenomena can be quite different from how a small *group* copes with these same phenomena. *Street corner society* (Whyte, 1943) and *Tally's corner* (Liebow, 1967), for instance, have often been mistaken for being case studies of neighbourhoods when in fact they are case studies of small groups (note that in neither book is the neighbourhood geography described, even though the small groups lived in a small area with clear neighbourhood implications).

Most investigators will encounter this type of confusion in defining the unit of analysis. To reduce the confusion, one good practice is to discuss the potential case with a colleague. Try to explain to that person what questions you are trying to answer and why you have chosen a specific case as a way of answering those questions. This may help you to avoid incorrectly identifying the unit of analysis.

[. . .]

Once the general definition of the case has been established, other clarifications in the unit of analysis become important. If the unit of analysis is a small group, for instance, the persons to be included within the group (and thus the immediate topic of the case study) must be distinguished from those who are outside it (and thus the context for the case study). [. . .] Finally, for almost any topic that might be chosen, specific time boundaries are needed to define the beginning and end of the case. All of these types of questions need to be considered and answered to define the unit of analysis and thereby to determine the limits of the data collection and analysis.

One final point needs to be made about defining the case and the unit of analysis, pertaining to the role of the available research literature. Most researchers will want to compare their findings with previous research; for this reason, the key definitions should not be idiosyncratic. Rather, each case study and unit of analysis either should be similar to those previously studied by others or should deviate in clear, operationally defined ways. In this manner, the previous literature therefore also can become a guide for defining the case and unit of analysis.

### Linking data to propositions; and criteria for interpreting the findings

The fourth and fifth components have been the least well developed in case studies. These components represent the data analysis steps in case study research, and a research design should lay the foundations for this analysis.

Linking data to propositions can be done any number of ways [. . .]. One promising approach is the idea of 'pattern-matching' described by Donald Campbell (1975), whereby several pieces of information from the same case may be related to some theoretical proposition. In a related article Campbell (1969) illustrated this approach but without labelling it as such.

In this article, Campbell first showed how the annual number of traffic fatalities in Connecticut had seemed to decline after the passage of a new state law, limiting the speed to 55 miles per hour. However, further examination of the fatality rate, over a number of years before and after the legal change, showed unsystematic fluctuation rather than any marked reduction. A simple eyeball test was all that was needed to show that the actual pattern *looked* unsystematic rather than following a down-trend (see Figure 10.1), and thus Campbell concluded that the speed limit had had no effect on the number of traffic fatalities.

What Campbell did was to describe two potential patterns and then to show that the data matched one better than the other. If the two potential patterns are considered rival propositions (an 'effects' proposition and a 'no effects' proposition, regarding the impact of the new speed limit law), the pattern-matching technique is a way of relating the data to the propositions, even though the entire study consists of only a single case (the state of Connecticut).

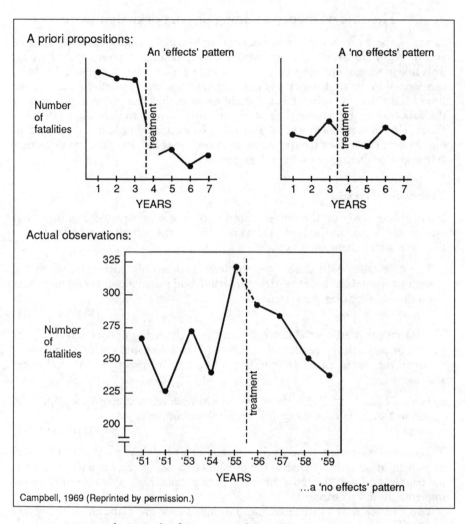

FIGURE 10.1 An example of pattern-matching

This article also illustrates the problems in dealing with the fifth component, the criteria for interpreting a study's findings. Campbell's data matched one pattern much better than they matched the other. But how close does a match have to be in order to be considered a match? Note that Campbell did not do any statistical test to make the comparison. Nor would a statistical test have been possible, because each data point in the pattern was a single number – the number of fatalities for that year – for which one could not calculate a variance and could not conduct any statistical test. Currently, there is no precise way of setting the criteria for interpreting these types of findings. One hopes that the different patterns are sufficiently contrasting that (as in Campbell's case) the findings can be interpreted in terms of comparing at least two rival propositions.

[. . .]

## The role of theory-building as part of design work

Covering these preceding five components of research designs will in effect force you to begin constructing a preliminary theory related to your topic of study. This role of theory-building, prior to the conduct of any data collection, has been overlooked in the traditional way of doing case studies. Typically, students have been taught that, by using the case study method, they can proceed quickly into the data collection phase of their work, and they have been encouraged to make their 'field contacts' as quickly as possible. No guidance could be more misleading. Among other considerations, the relevant 'contacts' depend upon an understanding – or theory – of what is being studied.

### Theory development

Using a case study on the implementation of a new management information system (MIS) as an example (Markus, 1983), the simplest ingredient of a theory is a statement such as the following:

> The case study will show why implementation only succeeded when the organization was able to re-structure itself, and not just overlay the new MIS on the old organizational structure.
>
> (Markus, 1983)

The statement presents the nutshell of a theory of MIS implementation – that is, that organizational restructuring is needed to make implementation work.

Using the same case, an additional ingredient might be the following statement:

> The case study will also show why the simple replacement of key persons was not sufficient for successful implementation.
>
> (Markus, 1983)

This second statement presents the nutshell of a *rival* theory – that is, that MIS implementation fails because of the resistance to change on the part of individual people, and that the replacement of such people is the only requirement for implementation to succeed.

You can see that as these two initial ingredients are elaborated, the stated ideas will increasingly cover the questions, propositions, units of analysis, logic connecting data to propositions, and criteria for interpreting the findings – that is, the five components of the needed research design. In this sense, the complete research design embodies a 'theory' of what is being studied. This theory should by no means be considered with the formality of grand theory in social science, nor are you being asked to be a masterful theoretician. Rather, the simple goal is to have a sufficient blueprint for your study, and this requires theoretical propositions. Then, the complete research design will provide surprisingly strong guidance in determining what data to collect and the strategies for analysing the data. For this reason, theory development prior to the collection of any case study data is an essential step in doing case studies.

However, theory development takes time and can be difficult. Moreover, for some topics, the existing knowledge base does not lend itself to the development of good theoretical statements, and only an 'exploratory' study is likely to result. Nevertheless, even an exploratory case study should be preceded by statements about: (a) what is to be explored, (b) the purpose of the exploration, and (c) the criteria by which the exploration will be judged successful. In other situations, the appropriate theory may be a descriptive theory and your concern should focus on such issues as: (a) the purpose of the descriptive effort, (b) the full but realistic range of topics that might be considered a 'complete' description of what is to be studied, and (c) the likely topic(s) that will be the essence of the description. Good answers to these questions, including the rationales underlying the answers, will help you go a long way toward developing the needed theoretical base – and research design – for your study.

In general, to overcome some of the barriers to theory development, you should try to prepare for your case study by doing such things as reviewing the literature related to what you would like to study (also see Cooper, 1984), discussing your topic and ideas with colleagues or teachers, and asking yourself challenging questions about what you are studying, why you are proposing to do the study, and what you hope to learn as a result of the study.

### Illustrative types of theories

As a further reminder, you should be aware of the full range of theories that might be relevant to your study. For instance, note that the MIS example illustrates 'implementation' theory, and that this is but one type of theory that can be the subject of study. Other types of theories for you to consider include:

- individual theories – for example, theories of individual development, cognitive behaviour, personality, learning and disability, and interpersonal interactions;
- organizational theories – for example, theories of bureaucracies, organizational structure and functions, or excellence in organizational performance (e.g. Harrison, 1987); and
- social theories – for example, theories of urban development, group behaviour, cultural institutions, and marketplace functions.

Other examples cut across some of these illustrative types. Decision-making theory, for instance, is like implementation theory, in that it can involve individuals, organizations, or social groups. As another example, a common topic of case studies is the evaluation of publicly supported programmes, such as federal, state, or local programmes. In this situation, the development of a theory of how a programme is supposed to work is essential to the design of the evaluation, but has been commonly underemphasized in the past (Bickman, 1987).

### Generalizing from case study to theory

Theory development does not facilitate the data collection phase of the ensuing case study. The appropriately developed theory also is the level at which the generalization of the case study results will occur. This role of theory has been characterized [here] as 'analytic generalization' and contrasted with another way of generalizing results, known as 'statistical generalization'. Understanding the distinction between these two types of generalization may be your most important challenge in doing case studies.

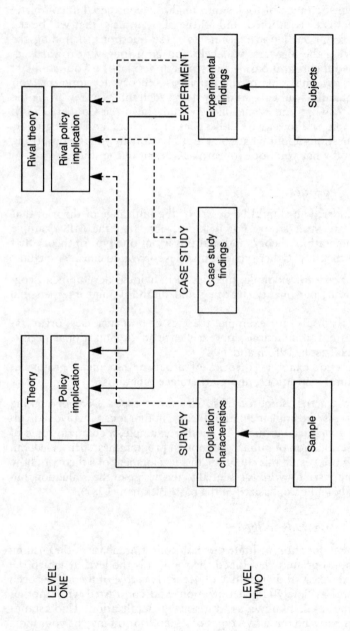

FIGURE 10.2 Making inferences: two levels

Let us take the more commonly recognized way of generalizing – 'statistical generalization' – first, although it is the less relevant one for doing case studies. In statistical generalization, an inference is made about a population (or universe) on the basis of empirical data collected about a sample. This is shown as a *Level Two Inference* in Figure 10.2.[1] [. . .]

A fatal flaw in doing case studies is to conceive of statistical generalization as the method of generalizing the results of the case. This is because cases are not 'sampling units' and should not be chosen for this reason. Rather, individual case studies are to be selected as a laboratory investigator selects the topic of a new experiment. Multiple cases, in this sense, should be considered like multiple experiments (or multiple surveys). Under these circumstances, the method of generalization is 'analytic generalization', in which a previously developed theory is used as a template with which to compare the empirical results of the case study. If two or more cases are shown to support the same theory, replication may be claimed. The empirical results may be considered yet more potent if two or more cases support the same theory but do not support an equally plausible, *rival* theory. Graphically, this type of generalization is shown as a *Level One Inference* in Figure 10.2.

Analytic generalization can be used whether your case study involves one or several cases [. . .]. Further, the logic of replication and the distinction between statistical and analytic generalization will be covered in greater detail in the discussion of multiple-case study designs. The main point at this juncture is that you should try to aim toward analytic generalization in doing case studies, and you should avoid thinking in such confusing terms as 'the sample of cases', or the 'small sample size of cases', as if a single case study were like a single respondent in a survey or a single subject in an experiment. In other words, in terms of Figure 10.2, you should aim for *Level One Inferences* when doing case studies.

Because of the importance of this distinction between the two ways of generalizing, you will find repeated examples and discussion throughout the remainder of this chapter.

[. . .]

## CRITERIA FOR JUDGING THE QUALITY OF RESEARCH DESIGNS

Because a research design is supposed to represent a logical set of statements, we also can judge the quality of any given design according to certain logical tests. Whether one is doing case studies or any other type of social science, four tests are relevant.

[These] have been summarized in numerous social science textbooks (see Kidder, 1981, pp. 7–8):

- *construct validity*: establishing correct operational measures for the concepts being studied;
- *internal validity* (for explanatory or causal studies only, and not for descriptive or exploratory studies): establishing a causal relationship, whereby certain conditions are shown to lead to other conditions, as distinguished from spurious relationships;

- *external validity:* establishing the domain to which a study's findings can be generalized; and
- *reliability:* demonstrating that the operations of a study – such as the data collection procedures – can be repeated, with the same results.

This list is much more complex than the standard 'validity' and 'reliability' notions [. . .], yet each item deserves explicit attention. For case studies, an important revelation is that the several tactics to be used in dealing with these tests should be applied throughout the subsequent conduct of the case study. In this sense, 'design work' actually continues beyond the initial design plans.

## Construct validity

This first test is especially problematic in case-study research. People who have been critical of case studies often point to the fact that a case study investigator fails to develop a sufficiently operational set of measures and that 'subjective' judgements are used to collect the data. Take an example such as studying 'neighbourhood change' – a common case study topic.

Over the years, concerns have arisen over how certain urban neighbourhoods have changed their character. Any number of case studies have examined the types of changes and their consequences. However, without any prior specification of the significant, operational events that constitute 'change', a reader cannot tell whether the recorded changes in a case study genuinely reflect critical events in a neighbourhood or whether they happen to be based on an investigator's impressions only.

[. . .] To meet the test of construct validity, an investigator must be sure to cover two steps:

(1) select the specific types of changes that are to be studied (in relation to the original objectives of the study) and
(2) demonstrate that the selected measures of these changes do indeed reflect the specific types of change that have been selected.

Thus, for example, suppose you satisfy the first step by stating that you plan to study the rise in neighbourhood crime. The second step now demands that you also justify why you might be using police-reported crime (which happens to be the standard measure used in the FBI Uniform Crime Reports) as your measure of crime. Perhaps this is not a valid measure, given that large proportions of crimes are not reported to the police.

Three tactics are available to increase construct validity. The first is the use of *multiple sources of evidence*, in a manner encouraging convergent lines of inquiry, and this tactic is relevant during data collection. A second tactic is to establish a *chain of evidence*, also relevant during data collection. The third tactic is to have the draft case study report reviewed by key informants.

## Internal validity

This second test has been given the greatest attention in experimental and quasi-experimental research (see Campbell and Stanley, 1966; and Cook and Campbell, 1979). Numerous 'threats' to validity have been identified, mainly dealing with spurious effects. However, because so many textbooks already cover this topic, only two points need to be made here.

First, internal validity is a concern only for causal or explanatory studies, where an investigator is trying to determine whether event x led to event y. If the investigator incorrectly concludes that there is a causal relationship between x and y without knowing that some third factor – z – may actually have caused y, the research design has failed to deal with some threat to internal validity. Note that this logic is inapplicable to descriptive or exploratory studies [. . .] which are not concerned with making causal statements.

Second, the concern over internal validity, for case study research, may be extended to the broader problem of making inferences. Basically, a case study involves an inference every time an event cannot be directly observed. Thus, an investigator will 'infer' that a particular event resulted from some earlier occurrence, based on interview and documentary evidence collected as part of the case study. Is the inference correct? Have all the rival explanations and possibilities been considered? Is the evidence convergent? Does it appear to be airtight? A research design that has anticipated these questions has begun to deal with the overall problem of making inferences and therefore the specific problem of internal validity.

However, the specific tactics for achieving this result are difficult to identify. This is especially true in doing case studies. As one set of suggestions, the analytic tactic of *pattern-matching* is one way of addressing internal validity. Two related analytic tactics [are] *explanation-building* and *time-series analysis*.

## External validity

The third test deals with the problem of knowing whether a study's findings are generalizable beyond the immediate case study. [. . .]

The external validity problem has been a major barrier in doing case studies. Critics typically state that single cases offer a poor basis for generalizing. However, such critics are implicitly contrasting the situation to survey research, where a 'sample' (if selected correctly) readily generalizes to a larger universe. *This analogy to samples and universes is incorrect when dealing with case studies.* This is because survey research relies on *statistical* generalization, whereas case studies (as with experiments) rely on *analytical* generalization.

In analytical generalization, the investigator is striving to generalize a particular set of results to some broader theory. For example, the theory of neighbourhood change that led to a case study in the first place is the same theory that will help to identify the other cases to which the results are generalizable. If a study had focused on 'gentrification' (see Auger, 1979), the procedure for selecting a neighbourhood for study also will have identified those types of neighbourhoods within which gentrification was occurring. In principle, theories about changes in all of these neighbourhoods would be the target to which the results could later be generalized.

However, the generalization is not automatic. A theory must be tested through replications of the findings in a second or even a third neighbourhood, where the theory has specified that the same results should occur. Once such replication has been made, the results might be accepted for a much larger number of similar neighbourhoods, even though further replications have not been performed.

This *replication logic* is the same that underlies the use of experiments (and allows scientists to generalize from one experiment to another) and will be discussed further in this chapter in the section on multiple-case designs [. . .].

# RELIABILITY

Most people are probably already familiar with this final test. The objective is to be sure that, if a later investigator followed exactly the same procedures as described by an earlier investigator and conducted the same case study all over again, the later investigator should arrive at the same findings and conclusions. (Note that the emphasis is on doing the *same* case over again, not on 'replicating' the results of one case by doing *another* case study.) The goal of reliability is to minimize the errors and biases in a study.

One prerequisite [. . .] is the need to document the procedures followed in the earlier case. [. . .] In the past, case study research procedures have been poorly documented, making external reviewers suspicious of the reliability of the case study. Thus, as specific tactics for case studies [you could] use a *case study protocol* to deal with the documentation problem in detail [along with] the development of a *case study data base*.

The general way of approaching the reliability problem is to conduct research as if someone were always looking over your shoulder. In accounting and book-keeping, one is always aware that any calculations must be capable of being audited. In this sense, an auditor is also performing a reliability check and must be able to produce the same results if the same procedures are followed. A good guideline for doing case studies is therefore to conduct the research so that an auditor could repeat the procedures and arrive at the same results.

[. . .]

# CASE STUDY DESIGNS

These general characteristics of research designs serve as a background for considering the specific designs for case studies. Four types of designs will be discussed, deriving from a $2 \times 2$ matrix (see Figure 10.3). The matrix is based on the assumption that single- and multiple-case studies reflect different design considerations and that within these two types, there also can be a unitary or multiple units of analysis. Thus, for the case study strategy, the four types of designs are (1) single-case (holistic) designs, (2) single-case (embedded) designs, (3) multiple-case (holistic) designs, and (4) multiple-case (embedded) designs. The rationale for these four types of designs is as follows.

## What are the potential single-case designs?

### Rationale for single-case designs

A primary distinction in designing case studies is between *single-* and *multiple-* case designs. This means the need for a decision, prior to any data collection, on whether a single-case study or multiple cases are going to be used to address the research questions.

| | Single-case Designs | Multiple-case Designs |
|---|---|---|
| Holistic (single unit of analysis) | TYPE 1 | TYPE 3 |
| Embedded (multiple units of analysis) | TYPE 2 | TYPE 4 |

FIGURE 10.3 Basic types of designs for case studies

The single-case study is an appropriate design under several circumstances. [. . .] One rationale for a single case is when it represents the *critical case* in testing a well-formulated theory. The theory has specified a clear set of propositions as well as the circumstances within which the propositions are believed to be true. To confirm, challenge, or extend the theory, there may exist a single case, meeting all of the conditions for testing the theory. The single case can then be used to determine whether a theory's propositions are correct, or whether some alternative set of explanations might be more relevant. [. . .] Such a study can even help to refocus future investigations in an entire field. (See Box 1 for an example in the field of organizational innovation.)

A second rationale is where the case represents an *extreme or unique case*. This has commonly been the situation in clinical psychology, where a specific injury or disorder may be so rare that any single case is worth documenting and analysing, [. . . both to . . .] document the person's abilities and disabilities, and to ascertain whether related disorders exist.

A third rationale for a single-case study is the *revelatory case*. This situation exists when an investigator has an opportunity to observe and analyse a phenomenon previously inaccessible to scientific investigation, such as Whyte's *Street corner society*. A latter-day example is Elliot Liebow's famous case study of unemployed blacks, *Tally's corner*. [. . .] Liebow had the opportunity to meet the men in one neighbourhood in Washington, D.C., and to learn about their everyday lives. His observations of and insights into the problems of unemployment formed a significant case study, because few social scientists had previously had the opportunity to investigate these problems, even though the problems were common across the country (as distinguished from the rare or unique case). When other investigators have similar types of opportunities and can uncover some prevalent phenomenon previously inaccessible to scientists, such conditions justify the use of a single-case study on the grounds of its revelatory nature.

## BOX 1

*The single-case study as the critical case*

[. . .] Neal Gross *et al.* used such a design by focusing on a single school in their book, *Implementing organizational innovations* (1971).

The school was selected because it had a prior history of innovation and could not be claimed to suffer from 'barriers to innovation'. In the prevailing theories, such barriers had been prominently cited as the major reason that innovations failed. Gross *et al.* showed that, in this school, an innovation also failed but that the failure could not be attributed to any barriers. Implementation processes, rather than barriers, appeared to account for the outcomes.

In this manner, the book, though limited to a single case, represents a watershed in innovation theory. Prior to the study, analysts had focused on the identification of barriers; since the study, the literature has been much more dominated by studies of the implementation process.

These three rationales serve as the major reasons for conducting a single-case study. There are other situations in which the single case may be conducted as a prelude to further study, such as the use of case studies as exploratory devices or such as the conduct of a pilot case that is the first of a multiple-case study. [. . .]

Whatever the rationale for doing single cases (and there may be more than the three mentioned here), a potential vulnerability of the single-case design is that a case may later turn out not to be the case it was thought to be at the outset. Thus, single-case designs require careful investigation of the potential case to minimize the chances of misrepresentation and to maximize the access needed to collect the case study evidence. A fair warning is not to commit oneself to the single case until all of these major concerns have been covered.

### Holistic versus embedded case studies

The same case study may involve *more than one unit of analysis*. This occurs when, within a single case, attention is also given to a subunit or subunits [. . .]. For instance, even though a case study might be about a single public programme, the analysis might include outcomes from individual projects within the programme (and possibly even some quantitative analyses of large numbers of projects). Such a design would be called an *embedded case study design* (see Figure 10.3, Type 2). In contrast, if the case study examined only the global nature of the programme, a *holistic design* would have been used (see Figure 10.3, Type 1).

Both variations of single-case studies have different strengths and weaknesses. The holistic design is advantageous when no logical subunits can be identified and when the relevant theory underlying the case study is itself of a holistic nature. Potential problems arise, however, when a global approach allows an investigator to avoid examining any specific phenomenon in operational detail. Thus, a typical problem with the holistic design is that the entire case study may be conducted at an abstract level, lacking any clear measures or data.

A further problem with the holistic design is that the entire nature of the case study may shift, unbeknownst to the researcher, during the course of study. The initial study questions may have reflected one orientation, but as the case study proceeds, a different orientation may emerge, and the evidence begins to address different questions. Although some people have claimed such flexibility to be a strength of the case study approach, in fact the largest criticism of case studies is based on this type of shift – in which the original research design is no longer appropriate for the research questions being asked (see Yin, Bateman and Moore, 1983). Because of this problem, such unsuspected slippage needs to be avoided; if the relevant research questions really do change, the investigator should simply start over again, with a new research design. One way to increase the sensitivity to such slippage is to have a set of subunits. Thus, an embedded design can serve as an important device for focusing a case study inquiry.

An embedded design, however, also has some pitfalls. A major one occurs when the case study focuses only on the subunit level and fails to return to the larger unit of analysis. A programme evaluation that includes project characteristics as a subunit of analysis, for instance, becomes a project study if no investigating is done at the larger unit – that is, the 'programme'. Similarly, a study of organizational climate may involve individual employees as a subunit of study. However, if the data focus only on individual employees, the study will in fact become an employment and not an organizational study. What has happened is that the original phenomenon of interest (organization climate) has become the context and not the target of study.

[. . .]

## What are the potential multiple-case designs?

The same study may contain more than a single case. When this occurs, the study has to use a multiple-case design, and such designs have increased in frequency in recent years. A common example is a study of school innovations (such as open classrooms, teacher aides, or new technology), in which independent innovations occur at different sites. Thus each site might be the subject of an individual case study, and the study as a whole would have used a multiple-case design.

### Multiple- versus single-case designs

[. . .]

Multiple-case designs have distinct advantages and disadvantages in comparison to single-case designs. The evidence from multiple cases is often considered more compelling, and the overall study is therefore regarded as being more robust. At the same time, the rationale for single-case designs cannot usually be satisfied by multiple cases. The unusual or rare case, the critical case, and the revelatory case are all likely to involve only single cases, by definition. Moreover, the conduct of a múltiple-case study can require extensive resources and time beyond the means of a single student or independent research investigator.

Therefore, the decision to undertake multiple-case studies cannot be taken lightly. Every case should serve a specific purpose within the overall scope of inquiry. Here, *a major insight is to consider multiple cases as one would consider multiple experiments* – that is, to follow a 'replication' logic. This is far different from a mistaken analogy in the past, which incorrectly considered multiple cases to be similar to the multiple respondents in a survey (or to the multiple subjects *within* an experiment) – that is, to follow a 'sampling' logic. The methodological differences between these two views are revealed by the different rationales underlying the replication as opposed to sampling logics.

### Replication, not sampling logic, for multiple-case studies

[. . .]

Each case must be carefully selected so that it either (a) predicts similar results (a *literal replication*) or (b) produces contrary results but for predictable reasons (a *theoretical replication*). Thus, the ability to conduct six or ten case studies, arranged effectively within a multiple-case design, is analogous to the ability to conduct six to ten experiments on related topics; a few cases (two or three) would be literal replications, whereas a few other cases (four to six) might be designed to pursue two different patterns of theoretical replications. If all the cases turn out as predicted, these six to ten cases, in the aggregate, would have provided compelling support for the initial set of propositions. If the cases are in some way contradictory, the initial propositions must be revised and retested with another set of cases. Again, this logic is similar to the way scientists deal with contradictory experimental findings.

An important step in all of these replication procedures is the development of a rich, theoretical framework. The framework needs to state the conditions under which a particular phenomenon is likely to be found (a literal replication) as well as the conditions when it is not likely to be found (a theoretical replication). The theoretical framework later becomes the vehicle for generalizing to new cases, again similar to the role played in cross-experiment designs. Furthermore, just as with experimental science, if some of the empirical cases do not work as predicted, modification must be made to the theory.

To take but one example, one might consider the initial proposition that an increase in microcomputer use in school districts will occur when such technologies are used for both administrative and instructional applications, but not either alone. To pursue this proposition in a multiple-case study design, three or four cases might be selected in which both types of applications are present, to determine whether, in fact, microcomputer use did increase over a period of time (the investigation would be predicting a literal replication in these three or four cases). Three or four additional cases might be selected in which only administrative applications are present, with the prediction being little increase in use (predicting a theoretical replication). Finally, three or four other cases would be selected in which only instructional applications are present, with the same prediction of little increase in use, but for different reasons than the administrative-only cases (another theoretical replication). If this entire pattern of results across these multiple cases is indeed found, the nine to twelve cases, in the aggregate, would provide substantial support for the initial proposition. [. . .]

This replication logic, whether applied to experiments or to case studies, must be distinguished from the sampling logic commonly used in surveys. According to the sampling logic, a number of respondents (or subjects) is assumed to 'represent' a larger pool of respondents (or subjects), so that data from a smaller number of persons are assumed to represent the data that might have been collected from the entire pool.

The sampling logic demands an operational enumeration of the entire universe or pool of potential respondents, and then a statistical procedure for selecting the specific subset of respondents to be surveyed. This logic is applicable whenever an investigator is interested in determining the prevalence or frequency of a particular phenomenon and when it is too expensive or impractical to survey the entire universe or pool. The resulting data from the sample that is actually surveyed are assumed to reflect the entire universe or pool, with inferential statistics used to establish the confidence intervals for which this representation is actually accurate.

Any application of this sampling logic to case studies would be misplaced. First, case studies should not generally be used to assess the incidence of phenomena. Second, a case study would have to cover both the phenomenon of interest and its context, yielding a large number of potentially relevant variables. In turn, this would require an impossibly large number of cases – too large to allow any statistical consideration of the relevant variables.

Third, if a sampling logic had to be applied to all types of research, many important topics could not be empirically investigated, such as the following problem: Your investigation deals with the role of the presidency of the United States, and you are interested in studying the behaviour of the incumbent from some leadership perspective. The leadership perspective, to be at all faithful to the complexity of reality, must incorporate dozens if not hundreds of relevant variables. Any sampling logic simply would be misplaced under such circumstances, as there have been only 40 presidents since the beginning of the Republic. Moreover, you would probably not have the resources to conduct a full study of all 40 incumbents (and even if you did, you would still have too many variables in relation to the 40 data points available). This type of study just could not be done, following the sampling logic; if the replication logic is followed, however, the study is eminently feasible.

The replication approach to multiple-case studies is illustrated in Figure 10.4. (This figure is derived from research on the case study method; see Yin, Bateman and Moore, 1983). The figure indicates that the initial step in designing the study must consist of theory development, and then shows that case selection and the definition of specific measures are important steps in the design and data collection process. Each individual case study consists of a 'whole' study, in which convergent evidence is sought regarding the facts and conclusions for the case; each case's conclusions are then considered to be the information needing replication by other individual cases. Both the individual cases and the multiple-case results can and should be the focus of a summary

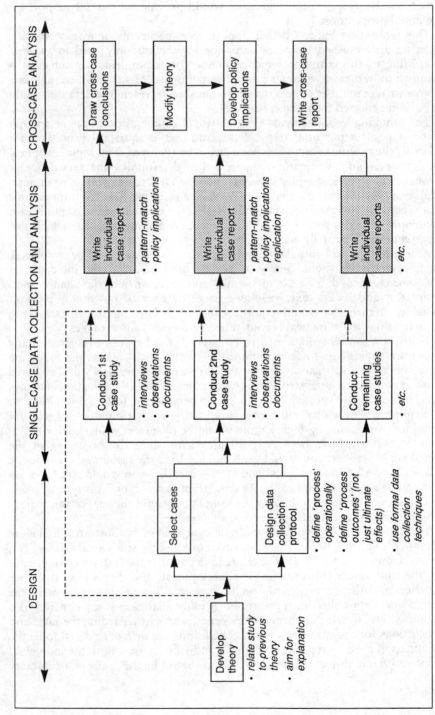

FIGURE 10.4 Case study method

report. For each individual case, the report should indicate how and why a particular proposition was demonstrated (or not demonstrated). Across cases, the report should indicate the extent of the replication logic and why certain cases were predicted to have certain results, whereas other cases were predicted to have contrary results.

Again, Figure 10.4 depicts a very different logic from that of sampling design. This is a difficult step to perceive and is worth extensive discussion with colleagues before proceeding with any case study design.

When using a multiple-case design, a further question you will encounter has to do with the *number* of cases deemed necessary or sufficient for your study. However, because a sampling logic should not be used, the typical criteria regarding sample size also are irrelevant. Instead, you should think of this decision as a reflection of the number of case replications – both literal and theoretical – that you would like to have in your study.

For literal replications, [. . .] the number depends upon the certainty you want to have about your multiple-case results [. . .]. For example, you may want to settle for two or three literal replications when the rival theories are grossly different and the issue at hand does not demand an excessive degree of certainty. However, if your rivals have subtle differences or if you want a high degree of certainty, you may press for five, six, or more replications.

For the number of theoretical replications, the important consideration is related to your sense of the complexity of the realm of external validity. When you are uncertain whether external conditions will produce different case study results, you may want to articulate these relevant conditions more explicitly at the outset of your study and identify a larger number of cases to be included. For example, in the neighbourhood example used previously in discussing external validity (see pp. 145–6), a common concern from the standpoint of policy research (e.g. Majchrzak, 1984) is that ethnically and racially different neighbourhoods do not usually follow similar courses of change. A study of gentrification would therefore want to include at least some number of cases that varied along ethnic or racial lines (and *within* each type of case, one would still want a minimum of two or three literal replications). In contrast, when external conditions are not thought to produce much variation in the phenomenon being studied a smaller number of theoretical replications is needed.

## Multiple-case studies: holistic or embedded

The fact that a design calls for multiple-case studies does not eliminate the variation identified earlier with single cases: Each individual case may still be holistic or embedded. In other words, a multiple-case study may consist of multiple holistic cases (see Figure 10.3, Type 3) or of multiple embedded cases (see Figure 10.3, Type 4).

The difference between these two designs depends upon the type of phenomenon being studied. In an embedded design, a study even may call for the conduct of a survey at each case study site. For instance, supposing a study is concerned with mental health centres and the delivery of services by different projects within the same mental health programme (see Larsen, 1982). Each centre, or project, may rightfully be the topic of a case study; the theoretical framework may dictate that nine such centres be included as case studies, three to replicate a direct result and six others to deal with two other negative propositions.

In all nine centres, an embedded design is used, because surveys of the centres' clients will be conducted. However, the results of each survey will *not* be pooled across centres. Rather, the survey data will be part of the findings for each individual centre, or case. These data may be highly quantitative, focusing on the attitudes and behaviour of individual clients, but the data will be used only to interpret the success and operations at a given centre. If, in contrast, the survey data are pooled across centres, a multiple-centre study design is no longer being used, and the investigation is likely to be using a survey rather than case study design.

[. . .]

## How case study designs can be kept flexible

A final reminder is that a case study design is not something completed at the outset of a study only. The design can be altered and revised after the initial stages of a study, but only under stringent circumstances.

In particular, *pilot* case studies may reveal inadequacies in the initial design. In the event of a single-case design, what was thought to be a revelatory or unique case may not turn out to be so after all. In the event of a multiple-case design, the selection of cases may have to be modified because of new information about the cases. In other words, after some early data collection and analysis, an investigator has every right to conclude that the initial design was faulty and to modify the design. This is an appropriate and desirable use of pilot studies.

At the same time, an investigator must be careful not to shift the theoretical concerns or objectives. If these, rather than the cases themselves, are changed, the investigator can correctly be accused of exercising a bias in conducting the research and interpreting the findings. The point is, the flexibility of case study designs is *in selecting cases different from those initially identified* (with appropriate documentation of this shift) but not in changing the purpose or objectives of the study to suit the case(s) that were found. The former situation is much like changing experiments when it is obvious that an experimental procedure is infeasible; the latter is a more subtle but still illegitimate change.

[. . .]

## NOTE

1. Figure 10.2 focuses only on the formal research design process, not on data collection activities. For all three types of research, data collection techniques might be depicted as a third level and also can involve inferences [. . .]. Similar data collection techniques can be described for surveys or experiments – for example, questionnaire design or stimulus presentation strategies.

# REFERENCES

Auger, D. A. (1979) The politics of revitalization in gentrifying neighborhoods: the case of Boston's South End, *Journal of the American Planning Association*, Vol. 45 (October), pp. 515–22.

Bickman, L. (1987) The functions of programme theory, in L. Bickman (ed.) *Using program theory in evaluation* (pp. 5–18). San Francisco: Jossey-Bass.

Campbell, D. T. (1969) Reforms as experiments, *American Psychologist*, Vol. 24 (April), pp. 409–29.

Campbell, D. T. (1975) Degrees of freedom and the case study, *Comparative Political Studies*, Vol. 8 (July), pp. 178–93.

Campbell, D. T. and Stanley, J. (1966) *Experimental and quasi-experimental designs for research*. Chicago: Rand McNally.

Cook, T. D. and Campbell, D. T. (1979) *Quasi-experimentation: design and analysis issues for field settings*. Chicago: Rand McNally.

Cooper, H. M. (1984) *The integrative research review*. Beverly Hills, CA: Sage.

Gross, N. *et al.* (1971) *Implementing organizational innovations*. New York: Basic Books.

Harrison, M. I. (1987) *Diagnosing organizations*. Newbury Park, CA: Sage.

Kidder, L. (1981) *Research methods in social relations* (4th edn). New York: Holt, Rhinehart & Winston.

Larsen, J. (1982) *Use of knowledge in mental health services*. Palo Alto, CA: American Institutes for Research.

Liebow, E. (1967) *Tally's corner*. Boston: Little, Brown.

Majchrzak, A. (1984) *Methods for policy research*. Beverly Hills, CA: Sage.

Markus, M. L. (1983) Power, politics, and MIS implementation, *Communications of the ACM*, Vol. 26 (June), pp. 430–44.

Philliber, S. G., Schwab, M. R. and Samsloss, G. (1980) *Social research: guides to a decision-making process*. Itasca, IL: Peacock.

Whyte, W. F. (1955, 1943) *Street corner society: the social structure of an Italian slum*. Chicago: University of Chicago Press.

Yin, R. K., Bateman, P. G. and Moore, G. B. (1983, September) *Case studies and organizational innovation: strengthening the connection*. Washington, DC: COSMOS Corporation.

# CHAPTER 11

# Action Research for Managing Change

### PAMELA LOMAX

In this chapter I explore what action research means in the context of managers managing change and share five principles that illuminate my own work as an action researcher.

## WHAT IS ACTION RESEARCH?

When introduced to action research for the first time many people, including managers, see it as a way of working that they already use. They mean they have always reflected on their practice and changed it in the light of new insight. Although I have some sympathy with this view, such informal, personal enquiry undertaken by good management practitioners is only a basis for the more rigorous and reflective ways in which action researchers work. Most importantly, it does not demand that practitioners make public the results of their enquiries, which is a requirement of formal action research.

A simple characterization of action research, that stresses its importance for managing change, is that *action research is an intervention in practice to bring about improvement*. The improvement sought could be a technical issue such as where a manager wants to increase the participation of colleagues in a meeting. This might involve investigating two or three meetings where imagined solutions are tried and evaluated. For example, the manager could try and minimize her own contribution and maximize that of others by asking more questions and giving fewer answers. She could give others more ownership of the meeting by working to their agenda rather than her own. She could share control of the meeting by having a rotating chairperson. Careful evaluation of different solutions should enable the manager to implement an appropriate change.

But in what sense could she claim to have improved practice? To address this question, it would be necessary to examine, critically, values and beliefs about the practice in question, including one's own assumptions about good practice. It is not just what one does that is important, but why one does it. The action researcher puts the values guiding her choice of action 'up front'. These are addressed in a special kind of research question, a 'How can I improve?' question, which fundamentally affects the relationship between the researcher and her data, and the choice of levels of data appropriate for analysis. For example in a study of total quality management in a junior school, Stevens (1993) showed how, through listening to tapes of his conversations with others, he changed his focus from asking 'What is quality?' to 'How can I deliver quality?'

In my example of the manager trying to improve a meeting, a critical enquiry would explore the purpose and process of the meeting within its particular professional context, with others' views being sought. If the context were educational, questions could be raised about issues like the educational consequences of meetings. Such an enquiry would go beyond merely finding a technical solution to a concern and would involve the manager in achieving a deeper understanding of the values that underpin her own and others' practice and how these relate to the chosen outcomes. These examples suggest ways in which change can be accomplished by making technical innovations and achieving increased insight into the values underpinning personal and institutional practice. Trying new ways of working and striving to live one's values in one's practice by closing the gap between the ideal and what actually happens is crucial.

But what about changing the context in which we work? Action research is usually a cycle rather than a single intervention, with each intervention evaluated in order to inform the next stage of planning, so that technical change and increased understanding go hand in hand. An important strategy is to involve others as co-researchers. Where this succeeds, the action research can snowball, and an initial intention to make meetings more participatory could lead to a change in departmental culture. The point is that action research may be self-contained and small scale or it may represent a single cycle in a series of cycles that make up a grand design. It may be mundane and focused on small technical improvements in individual practice or it may be intended to influence whole institutions and ultimately public policies. Most professionals who engage in action research are concerned with small-scale, local enquiries, often linked to award-bearing courses and limited by the duration of their course of study. Despite this, they are able to engage in a critical form of action research that can take them well beyond mere technical concerns.

## ACTION RESEARCH AS EDUCATIONAL RESEARCH

Whatever the scale of action research, it is important that action research should be viewed as an educational practice for those involved in it. This means that it is very different from social science research. Research within the social sciences is subject to the conceptual frameworks of specific disciplines like psychology and sociology. Sociologists and psychologists often apply their techniques to education and carry out 'research on education'. For example, Halsey, Heath and Ridge (1980) used a statistical method to expose the relationship between the origins and destinations of working-class children. Halsey was working within a scientific or positivistic tradition which relies on a belief that concrete facts underpin social events and the work of research is to establish these facts. A different approach was used by Atkinson, Shone and Rees (1981) who used an ethnographic approach to investigate the meaning of industrial training for slow learners. They were working within an interpretive approach which relies on a belief that people create social meanings and therefore research must establish these meanings and how they emerge. But both these examples are different from educational research. Action research, as a form of educational research, incorporates a commitment to act to bring about improved practices, as part of the research process. Thus my own work as a course director is concerned with making changes in the light of a critique of practice in order that the course is more effective, but also so that it becomes a better, more educational experience for those involved.

Educational research, as an educational practice, should lead to the development of mental powers and character for all involved in the research, particularly the researcher herself. Stephen Kemmis recognized this in his definition of action research by making a commitment to *rationality and justice* as an imperative of action research.

> Action research is a form of self-reflective enquiry undertaken by participants in social (including educational) situations in order to improve the rationality and justice of (a) their social or educational practices, (b) their understanding of these practices, and (c) the situations in which the practices are carried out.
>
> (Kemmis, 1988, reprinted in Hammersley, 1993, pp. 177–90)

The Kemmis definition presents action research as an ethical rather than a technical enquiry. Whitehead (1993) picks up this focus in arguing that action enquiry is educational because it enables practitioners to see their practice as part of a living educational theory that is generated from their own critical enquiries. This educational theory codifies the professional judgements that practitioners make as they seek answers to questions like 'How can I improve this practice here?' This potential of action research to generate a living educational theory separates it from social science research. The scientific intention of social science research differs from the professional intention of action research. The former, in line with conceptions of science generally, is to add to a body of knowledge about the social world. The latter is to act to bring about change in line with educational values that are rational and just. For the action researcher, the objective–subjective dimension of social science is reinterpreted, so that the researcher becomes both the subject and the object of the research, driving the action which provides the data of the enquiry. This distinctive feature derives from an intention to work within a framework of professional values that determines acceptable outcomes. These values will need clarifying and sharpening, they will need to be the subject of continuing reaffirmation and critique as part of the research process. This is very different from social science, with its expectation that the researcher's values are kept separate from the data and do not influence its collection or interpretation. The social science disciplines may provide useful concepts and research techniques for the action researcher, but the questions they pose, the research approach favoured and the criteria they apply for judging their research are not useful for action research (Lomax, 1994).

In the second part of this paper I would like to explain how my own work, both as an action researcher and as a facilitator of others' research is illuminated by five main principles.

(1) Action research is about seeking improvement by intervention.
(2) Action research involves the researcher as the main focus of the research.
(3) Action research is participatory and involves others as co-researchers rather than informants.
(4) Action research is a rigorous form of enquiry that leads to the generation of theory from practice.
(5) Action research needs continuous validation by 'educated' witnesses from the context it serves.

## ACTION RESEARCH IS ABOUT SEEKING IMPROVEMENT BY INTERVENTION

In their book *Total quality management and the school,* Murgatroyd and Morgan (1993) propose a way of managing school improvement which is collegiate and enquiry based. However, they limit their concern about improvement to helping teachers understand and respond to the new contexts that governments have legislated. This is not what is meant by improvement within an action research perspective. Action research shares the emphasis on collegiality and enquiry found in total quality management, but action research also incorporates a practical ethic, which Adelman (1989) argues takes precedence over methodology. This practical ethic refers to the professional decisions that practitioners like teachers make as part of their everyday jobs. These professional decisions involve more than choosing the most efficient means to a specific end. When teachers write on blackboards it is part of the methodology of the job and needs technical skill but this skill is the *means to more important ends.* Deciding how to improve professional practices such as teaching is much more difficult than implementing technical improvement because *what counts as improvement* will be influenced by the informed professional judgements that are made within particular professional contexts. It is not only what is done but why it is done that matters. Changing the details of what is done should be influenced by why it is done and is therefore related to professional values. The improvement that professionals seek to make through action research involves recognizing professional goals and committing themselves to achieving them. They seek to transform their routine everyday practice into praxis, which is *morally committed action* (Carr, 1987).

In research aimed to improve playground amenities McGougan (1993) illustrates a self-conscious commitment to educational improvement. The research involved canvassing the views of children, parents and colleagues to identify what needed to be done; and creating a broader 'ownership' of the problem and its solution. By involving children in analysing playground interaction, she helped them use the playground in a more purposeful way. Her explanation illustrates the link between values and the desire to improve educational practice.

The project was founded on my value judgements and I set out to 'live' these, in order to secure a wider commitment to them. I was surprised to the extent these required to be affirmed during the project and felt they came out of it strengthened . . . I valued the confirmation of others about the appropriateness and integrity of the processes used and the results claimed . . . The project needed to be particularly democratic because it involved children's free and traditionally unstructured time . . . As the project progressed it became more collaborative and this mobilized a dynamic force for change which I did find empowering, if a little daunting at first. Discussion and reflection have helped me to explore the relationship between theory and practice, such as links between self-esteem and behaviour, between 'ownership' and successful change-management strategies, and between 'ownership' of changes and prevention of vandalism.

(McGougan, 1993, pp. 154–6)

## ACTION RESEARCH INVOLVES THE RESEARCHER AS THE MAIN FOCUS OF THE INVESTIGATION

When McGougan says that she set out *to live her values* in order to secure a wider commitment from others to improving the play area in her school, she illustrates the way in which an action researcher puts herself at the centre of her work. Action researchers need to be insiders, researching practices integral to their work. The imperative to intervene distinguishes action research and the researcher's professional values should be central to the investigation. This applies to enquiries into management practice or teaching. For *managers* to use action research they must commit themselves to examining the motives and the method of their management practice. If they do not there is the danger that they will use action research techniques to manipulate rather than empower others (Griffiths, 1990). Their potential to empower others is one of the strengths of manager action research. Some good case studies of this in practice may be found in the collection of papers concerned with headteacher reflections on assessment at Key Stage 1 (Lomax and Jones, 1993; Lomax, 1993).

Although action research is value based rather than neutral, the process of research should render this value position problematic. The enquiry is not meant to be comfortable. Taken-for-granted values need to be explored. The action researcher is committed to interrogating her own values and examining any discrepancy between her values and her practice. She should question her own assumptions and be prepared to change the way she conceptualizes issues. The form that the intervention takes, using an action research cycle of plan, act and evaluate, means that the work of exploring values is a continuing process informing the evaluation of action throughout the research. In this sense the research is truly formative, facilitating change as part of the process itself, not as a result.

A good example of action researchers questioning their own effectiveness is provided by Griffiths and Tann. They wanted to help student teachers become reflective teachers. The questions they asked moved between focusing on themselves and focusing on their students. 'What were these reflections? What had we really expected reflections to look like? How had we, as reflective tutors functioned? What had we learned from the experience? What had our students learned? Was any of it worthwhile?' (Griffiths and Tann, 1991, p. 82). Another good example of an attempt to achieve praxis in secondary school teaching comes from an account by Smith (1993) about gender and access to

National Curriculum history. She began by investigating her own classroom practice, looking at how she was delivering the history curriculum herself and asking why it might be that the boys were underachieving in comparison with the girls. She writes:

> I have made an attempt to improve the justice of my own educational practice. . . . I discovered ways in which I was treating boys and girls differently and that this did lead to disadvantage. I identified the link between my positive pupil relationships and pupil performance. So I moved to remove my bias. . . . This has led to a better classroom climate and better results. . . . Action research is a systematically evolving lived process of changing both the researcher and the situations in which he or she acts. . . . the living dialectic of the researcher and the researched.
>
> (Smith, 1993, pp. 107–9)

## ACTION RESEARCH IS PARTICIPATORY AND OTHERS ARE TREATED AS CO-RESEARCHERS RATHER THAN INFORMANTS

Smith investigated her own practice, and as such was a participant in the action not an outside researcher observing the action. Working within the particular professional context of the secondary school, she had to work within the parameters set by the school, her department and the National Curriculum. Parameters like these define professionality. Action researchers must respond to the tensions and constraints of these contexts and actively seek to relate their own value stance to that of other professionals and wider institutional policies and practices. For this reason action research is a collaborative activity rather than one in which people engage in isolation and the action researcher should be proactively aiming for collective action.

McKen's (1993) work to introduce a college-wide monitoring and evaluation system in a further education college linked the collaborative intent of action research with a college requirement for quality control. As a manager she became responsible for introducing a college-wide innovation; and as a teacher trying to live her educational values, she wanted it to be collaborative. The action research and the management task came together in her view that 'at a time of change the college is dependent on self-monitoring innovative teams who see the process of evaluation as a positive tool to improve the quality of their programmes'. She aimed to capitalize on colleagues' strengths; but did this by adopting a style of leadership which she believed reflected the new climate of collaboration she sought to promote. At the core of her work was a strong focus on her own values and practice.

> The concept of ourselves as 'living contradictions' is particularly pertinent in the current further education context and it is vital that all those involved are continually challenged to examine their values. . . . There is clearly a danger in having a system which appears impressive on the surface but which is not owned by those most involved . . . it is easy to collect theory and documentation relating to review and evaluation . . . [but] unlikely that any of these could fulfil the requirements for a system that

would encourage critical reflection and active participation by all those involved in the process.

(McKen, 1993, pp. 15, 19)

In asserting the importance of establishing colleagues as real participants in self-monitoring, innovative teams, McKen sought to encourage them to be co-researchers, achieving their own praxis. This is very different from involving others as informants or respondents which may be useful to the researcher but is dehumanizing for the respondent. Asking others for information is problematic in action research, and needs to be approached with care. It might be feedback about one's own practice, or information about outcomes associated with one's practice, like the accounts produced by self-monitoring innovative teams. There is a fine line between getting feedback to inform one's own practice and making judgements about the practice of others. This is best dealt with openly in groups who debate the issues and formulate and apply ethical guidelines for themselves. In this way critical communities can be created that can work together to help members bring about agreed improvements.

Persuading others to become co-action researchers is the great art of action research, demanding high-level interpersonal skill and strong personal commitment to shared practice on the part of the action researcher. It is not an easy task and is best viewed as a long-term goal rather than something that can be established easily from the start. Many action researchers show how their own practice has improved, using this as an incentive to get others to join them. Unfortunately there is evidence of many an intransigent 'other' in the pages of action research accounts. Using the cyclical discipline of action research, with its built-in mechanism for review and change of direction, should enable a researcher to make contingency plans where their initial plan is thwarted by an uncooperative other.

The example cited at the start of this text concerning the management of meetings is a good example of a situation in which collaborative action is essential. The chairperson of a meeting must convince others to engage in improving their own practice if she is to affect the dynamics of the meeting. She has more opportunity than other members to alter the formal structure of the meeting to accommodate change and in this sense the power of her position is useful, but unless she can influence others to adopt the critically reflective stance that she intends to take herself, her aim to change the dynamics of the meeting may not be achieved. Lack of success in convincing others to change may be because she has not developed the professional skills necessary to communicate her newly developed ideas; it may be because she is not convincing others that she has improved her practice, that it is not self-evident to other professionals that action research is an approach which works. However, the strength of action research is that initial setbacks in implementing a plan can be reconsidered in successive cycles of action until some sort of accommodation between the intentions of the action researcher and the intransigence of the context can be achieved. This is true for those in positions of influence and those who work at the chalkface. Some critics question whether people outside positions of power can successfully influence change. However, achieving the aim of creating a community of researchers has its own tensions for people in authority and many action researchers have reported the painful and difficult decision to let go ownership of a particularly loved project when they have encouraged others to take over. I share the optimism of John Elliott (1993) who says that we must always believe that we can alter things for the better in the light of our values within the constraints that affect us.

# ACTION RESEARCH IS A RIGOROUS FORM OF ENQUIRY THAT LEADS TO THE GENERATION OF THEORY FROM PRACTICE

A strength of action research is that practitioners have a subjective understanding of the issues; a problem with this is that it is difficult to see things objectively. It is not easy to stand back from the action and describe events clearly. Personal values and interpretations interfere with getting an all-round picture which includes the perspectives of others. So-called 'subjective' research, which depends on the researcher's insider understanding of a situation, demands even more rigorous methods of enquiry than so-called 'objective' research, where the researcher stands back from the data.

The action research cycle is a useful conceptual tool for organizing data. It enables the researcher to document different stages of the research in terms of planning, acting and evaluating in a way which is different from a chronological time line. Some researchers have developed intricate diagrams to show the relationship of different parts of a research project that are not necessarily chronological. Others have devised diagrams illustrating the messiness and complexity of most action research, where many different events and issues impinge on a central enquiry (McNiff, 1988). In Figure 11.1 a number of research cycles are shown to shape and focus the planning, acting and reflection on complex practical management issues. Bone, as headteacher of a special school, aimed to implement a collegiate working style. He monitored his strategies for identifying shared values and a shared view of collegiality. This meant encouraging senior staff to get involved in living their values in their practice, and developing his own role as headteacher.

Action researchers must be persistent about monitoring and collecting a variety of data. They need to sample many viewpoints on the same event to get a comprehensive description. The data are needed for further reflection as part of the action research cycle and later as 'evidence', authenticating the research. They need to explain how they have grouped the data and what alternatives existed. To 'appreciate' the action, they need to interrogate the data, identifying patterns and themes. These are the 'green shoots' of theory, grounded in the events described. Successful action research leads to increased knowledge and not just successful action; it is able to generate theory from careful scrutiny of practice (see Winter, 1989, for an extended discussion of this).

The importance to action researchers of developing their reflective skills in a systematic way by subjecting their work to continuous critical review is self-evident. They must be able to question their own assumptions and to analyse an argument in a way which exposes and questions its assumptions. An advantage of practitioner research is that theory and practice are closely linked, so there is less chance of being sidetracked by irrelevant theory. Engagement with practice enables action researchers to develop theory from their practice,

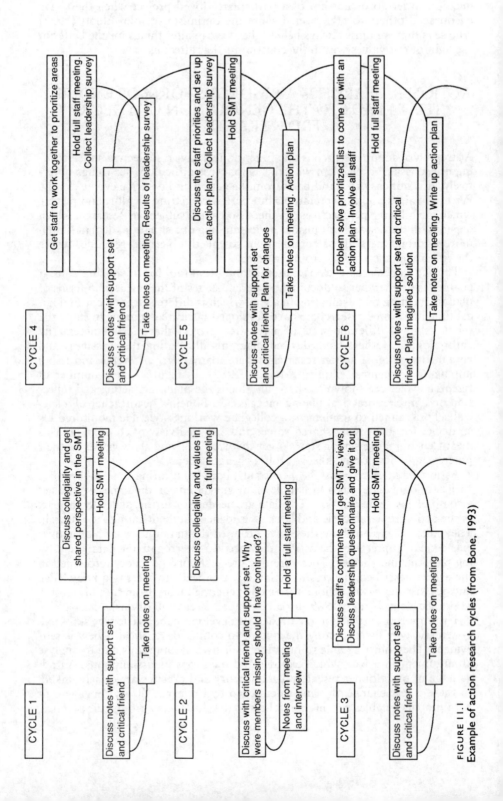

FIGURE 11.1
Example of action research cycles (from Bone, 1993)

giving them a platform from which to choose the most appropriate of established theories, although in choosing they must be conversant with other theories and ideas.

## ACTION RESEARCH NEEDS CONTINUOUS VALIDATION BY 'EDUCATED' WITNESSES FROM THE CONTEXTS IT SERVES

The validation process in action research is about sharing ideas, interpretations and conclusions with an 'educated' audience who are able and willing to judge the authenticity and relevance of the work to a professional context. Validation is an ongoing event rather than a one-off at the end of a project. A preliminary stage involves the researcher in deciding if her research represents a 'true' account of her own practice. Once she is confident in the explanations being generated she should involve others in their validation. This means establishing the relevance of the work in the professional community. At the start this involves justifying it within professional knowledge which may be available through others' research. As the research progresses it will involve testing it out with professional colleagues both within and outside the research context.

During each cycle of action, the researcher can involve co-researchers by getting them to experience vicariously the arguments and evidence in the light of their understanding of the professional practice being scrutinized. Ideally these peer validators should comment on all aspects of the research: the questions and plans; monitoring techniques; and interpretation. Most importantly, they should consider the researcher's values and practice and help pinpoint contradictions.

Going public, convincing others about the truth of our claims, is an important aspect of validating action research. Apart from co-researchers and colleagues in the place of work, some action researchers are part of support groups and networks that will provide a forum for critical debate. In some contexts, like those at Bath and Kingston Universities, validation meetings are quite formal events with the validation panel carefully selected in order to provide a range of different perspectives from which to view the research. In these contexts the validation group contains people who know the context of the work or are able to empathize with the context; people who come from outside the context and can provide an outsider view; and people who are familiar with the methodology of action research but not necessarily with the situation in which it is being practised.

Whatever the validation procedure, the researcher should be proactive in making critical debate possible. The researcher must seek critical feedback and must take account of feedback. Demonstrating the validity of action research means demonstrating high-quality awareness of the issues. This depends on being skilful at self-critical reflection. It means demonstrating systematic personal and interpersonal development. It means demonstrating the interplay of theory and practice. It means using contradiction constructively. It means triangulation, where more than one account of an event is sought, and replication, where actions are repeated in order to establish their value. Questions that might be answered include: Are the outcomes significant? For whom and why? Do you like them? Has there been practical change? Can it be justified as educational change? Have you developed professionally? Have you exposed the assumptions and contradictions of your results? Is the evidence to support your analysis and explanation sufficient and appropriate? Are your claims 'authentic' to your colleagues? Can you insert your findings into a critical professional debate?

The dangers in action research are where issues are not sharply delineated; where the focus is one sided and oversubjective; where the researcher is unaware of projection; and where there is insufficient outsider involvement to compensate for possible insider collusion, that is, where practitioners have a vested interest in getting a specific outcome.

Validation which enables action researchers to test their claims has improved their practice. As a result of presenting evidence to a sympathetic but critical audience the researcher should develop an enhanced understanding of the research and should be able to formulate further plans for action. Cox (1993) describes the meeting set up to validate her claim to have made her county middle-school more bullyproof.

> I wanted to provide a context, state my concerns and the reasons for them and give a clear synopsis of my research project, finishing with my claims and listing the supporting evidence. . . . At the validation meeting in addition to my course tutor, there were three members of my support set, and BM who was also there in his capacity as my critical friend. TS attended as an 'occasional' critical friend. I had invited three colleagues from school who had been closely involved in the research project. . . . I had displayed on the walls, for easy reference, a chart showing my action research cycles, some children's charters and reflective writing from THE BOOK. Other evidence was also available for examination. My presentation included the use of video and my three colleagues joined in and elaborated various points when appropriate.
>
> (Cox, 1993, p. 71–2)

# CONCLUSION

Action research is different from the professional practice in which good practitioners engage as a matter of course. Action is both informed and committed. Values are made explicit and practices are monitored to see that discrepancies are minimized. Other people are involved and empowered. Claims to know are validated as work progresses. As well as the five principles discussed, a sixth principle might be that action researchers should be obliged to bring their good professional practice into the public arena so that others can judge the quality of the professional work in which they have engaged. This arena might be a small one such as the specific workplace or it might be throughout an institution. Ideally it should be the whole professional community through publication.

# REFERENCES

Adelman, C. (1989) The practical ethic takes priority over methodology, in Carr (1989) op. cit., pp. 173–82.

Atkinson, P., Shone, D. and Rees, T. (1981) Labouring to learn? Industrial training for slow learners. Reprinted in R. Gomm and P. Woods (1993) *Educational Research in Action*, London: Paul Chapman.

Bone, D. (1993) How can I develop a collegiate management style in the school and encourage the senior management team to involve staff fully? Unpublished M.Ed. dissertation, Kingston University.

Busher, H. and Smith, M. (1993) *Managing educational institutions: reviewing development and learning,* Sheffield Hallam University for BEMAS.

Carr, W. (1987) What is an educational practice? Reprinted in Hammersley (1993) op. cit, pp. 160–76.

Carr, W. (1989) *Quality in teaching.* Brighton: Falmer Press.

Cox, G. (1993) Making the school more bullyproof. Unpublished M.Ed. dissertation, Kingston University.

Elliott, J. (1993) Educational studies and research in the context of competency-based teacher education. Paper presented at SCSE Annual Conference, November, 1993.

Griffiths, M. (1990) Action research: grassroots practice or management tool? in Lomax (1990) op. cit., pp. 37–51.

Griffiths, M. and Tann, S. (1991) Ripples in the reflection, in Lomax (1991) op. cit., pp. 82–101.

Halsey, A., Heath, A. and Ridge, J. (1980) *Origins and destinations.* Oxford: Clarendon Press.

Hammersley, M. (1993) *Educational research: current issues.* London: Paul Chapman.

Kemmis, S. (1988) Action research. Reprinted in Hammersley (1993) op. cit.

Lomax, P. (1990) *Managing staff development in schools.* Clevedon: Multi Lingual Matters.

Lomax, P. (1991) *Managing better schools and colleges.* Clevedon: Multi Lingual Matters.

Lomax, P. (1993) Managing change and the empowerment of schools, in Busher and Smith (1993) op. cit.

Lomax, P. (1994) Standards, criteria and the problematic of action research within an award bearing course, *Educational Action Research*, Vol. 2, no. 1.

Lomax, P. and Jones, C. (1993) *Developing primary schools through action research,* Bournemouth: Hyde Publications.

McGougan, S. (1993) How I used action research to develop the facilities and improved use of the playground during breaktime. Unpublished MA dissertation, Kingston University.

McKen, D. (1993) An action research enquiry into a collaborative exercise to encourage ownership and empowerment of the monitoring and evaluation process in a college of further education. Unpublished MA dissertation, Kingston University.

McNiff, J. (1988) *Action research: principles and practices.* Basingstoke/Macmillan.

Murgatroyd, S. and Morgan, C. (1993) *Total quality management and the school.* Milton Keynes: Open University Press.

Smith, H. (1993) An action research enquiry into the introduction of the national curriculum into a humanities department. Unpublished M.Ed. dissertation, Kingston University.

Stevens, J. (1993) Total quality management. Unpublished M.Ed. dissertation, Kingston University.

Winter, R. (1989) *Learning from experience.* London: Falmer.

Whitehead, J. (1993) *The growth of educational knowledge.* Bournemouth: Hyde Publications.

# PART THREE

# *Methods of Data Collection Analysis and Presentation*

# CHAPTER 12

# *Planning Small-Scale Research*

### DAPHNE JOHNSON

[. . .]

## THE NEED TO PLAN SOCIAL RESEARCH

Are you a planner by nature? Or do you prefer to take life as it comes? Whatever your temperament, when undertaking research of any type or scale, planning is a vital preliminary.

When embarking on *social* research, a category which, of course, includes educational research, investigators cannot assume that because a particular form of social life – perhaps school life – is going on all around them, they are in a position to 'research' it. However qualitative or flexible research is intended to be, some structure must be imposed on everyday social experience. Even that indefatigable chronicler of social intercourse and activity, James Boswell, took pains so to order his social life, travels and correspondence that he met and spent time with the great literary men who were so important to his view of the world and made sure to be present to observe the events which he wanted to record. As a result, he has left us, in his writings,[1] a sparkling and apparently unpremeditated account of eighteenth-century life, but one in which the careful reader can discern the hallmarks of skilled social research – the negotiation of access, the recording of data, their analysis, and the effective writing up and dissemination of what has been learned. On a smaller scale – perhaps a *much* smaller scale – the present-day social researcher must impose a structure on social experience, and give thought to planning the research which can feasibly be carried out.

## WHAT IS MEANT BY RESEARCH PLANNING

The fundamental principle of planning effective research is to match the research design to the resources available for its completion, and to the particular characteristics of the topic under consideration. Silvey (1975) considers that a research plan is at best a compromise between the aims of the research, the resources available and the feasibility of the area of study. His definition is realistic rather than pessimistic. Research is unlikely to be successful if the design is drawn from a textbook on research methods, but takes no account of the time available for its execution, the amount of help which can be recruited, and the special requirements of those whose activities are being studied – for example, the frequent requirement that the researcher protect the anonymity of those who are the subject of the research.

Later in this chapter consideration will be given to the selection of a research method from among the established range of quantitative or qualitative approaches. But this is only one aspect of research planning. It must be decided in the context of the whole projected investigation.

## THE STAGES OF CARRYING OUT AN INVESTIGATION

The inexperienced investigator, faced with the need to 'do some research' as part of a course of study or to give a wider perspective to personal experience, may welcome the security of a list by which to order the research activity. The following has been found useful in classifying the stages of activity which must be worked through in carrying out and completing an investigation.

(1) Establishing the focus of the study.
(2) Identifying the specific objectives of the study.
(3) Selecting the research method.
(4) Arranging research access.
(5) Developing the research instrument.
(6) Collecting the data.
(7) Pulling out of the investigative phase.
(8) Ordering of the data.
(9) Analysing the data.
(10) Writing up.
(11) Enabling dissemination.

Each stage will be discussed in turn, bearing in mind that the investigation in question is likely to be small scale. Most of the examples used will be drawn from educational research, and the assumption will be made that the investigation is being undertaken as a means to a particular end (of academic qualification or occupational advancement) rather than as part of a continuing and professional research career.

### (1)   Establishing the focus of the study

When students are questioned about a preferred subject for a mini-project or research-based dissertation, they may say 'I'd like to do something about Saturday schools', or 'I've always been interested in pastoral care'. They are halfway towards deciding on the general area for their study, but have many more questions to ask themselves before they have established its focus. Are they interested in examining Saturday schools as institutions for the perpetuation and promotion of particular cultures (in which case they might want to look at Polish schools and Hebrew schools, as well as the more recently established Saturday schools for Asian or West Indian children)? Or are they interested to establish the part played by parents in the setting up and resourcing of a Saturday school? In this case examples of recently established schools would give better access to memory and documentation than would a long-running school, the contributions of whose founding fathers and mothers have been overlaid by the sediment of rules and traditions. Does the student interested in pastoral care want to investigate it in terms of its implications for the career patterns of teachers? Or perhaps as an example of the cross-fertilization of ideas between the independent and maintained schools? Or in terms of the use of a pastoral care system to identify and help withdrawn pupils? All of these ideas, and many more, may be in the background of a student's 'interest' in a topic, but they cannot all form the subject of the same investigation.

It is true that, when set down in words, the focused subject of an investigation may sound as dry as dust. This is probably why so many dissertations, theses and projects have sub-titles, explaining the scope of the study, but preceded by a more eye-catching and evocative main title. For example:

SCHOOL CLOSURE – A Study of Changes in Governing Body Membership and Activity During a Programme of Secondary School Closures in One Local Authority.

The sub-title makes it plain what the investigator has set out to do, and what kind of information the reader can expect to be given. The overall title reassures them both that the investigation contributes to understanding of an important social phenomenon, and that this wider context is not forgotten in the account given of the investigation.

It is not until the investigator has so concentrated the subject of the study that it can be expressed in one sentence, that he or she can be said to have established the focus of the investigation and be ready to move to the next stage.

## (2)   Identifying the specific objectives of the study

The cynical investigator's approach to the setting of specific objectives is to 'wait until you have finished, see what you've managed to achieve, then say this was your objective'. Whilst it is to be hoped that this practice is rarely followed in any wholesale way, some minor *post hoc* modification of objectives probably contributes to the cut-and-dried tidiness of many a research account.

But the attempt to define specific objectives in advance should not be abandoned for fear they will not, in the event, be met. Identifying particular objectives helps the investigator along the road to choosing the research method and deciding on the forms of access needed, and may contribute to the selection and development of a suitable research instrument.

The background reading, or review of the literature, which is an essential contextual element of any piece of research, will ideally take place at this stage, so that it can influence the formation of research objectives. In practice, literature relevant to the subject of investigation may prove to be scanty, or may only be identified later in the research.

If the investigator has a particular personal interest in, and commitment to, the subject of study, one way to identify specific objectives is to ask 'What will I be disappointed not to have learned (or had experience of) when the study is over?' For example, in a study of home–school relations the researchers were particularly eager to learn how secondary schools were viewed from the point of view of the home, to complement the many accounts of home–school relations given from the point of view of the school.[2] One of the specific objectives of the study was, therefore, to recruit parental opinion, and to do this away from the milieu of the school. In fieldwork terms, this meant devoting nearly all the resources of the project to setting up and carrying out home interviews with parents. But meeting this particular objective of recruiting parental opinion also satisfied the researchers that they had not missed the opportunity to explore an aspect of home–school relations which they held to be neglected in other accounts (Johnson and Ransom, 1983).

[. . .]

## (3)  Selecting the research method

This is the next stage in planning the study. Ideally the research method should not be decided until the focus and objectives of the investigation are clear. In practice, professional researchers tend to prefer those methods of investigation in which they have a cumulative expertise, and will tailor the subject of study to make possible the use of their well-tried research techniques. Inexperienced or self-supporting researchers may also feel tempted to decide on a research method before giving detailed consideration to the subject of their investigation. The requirements of their course of study, or the sparsity of research resources may, in fact, rule out the use of certain methods such as, for example, some of the 'unobtrusive measures' discussed by Webb *et al.* (1966) which have to be recorded over a lengthy period. Nevertheless, the selection of the research method is a crucial element in the planning of an investigation. A range of possible methods and some guidelines for choosing between them are discussed in a later section of this paper.

## (4)  Arranging research access

If an entirely quantitative method is to be used, such as the issue of a postal questionnaire, the notion of arranging research access may seem superfluous. People cannot prevent the post being delivered to their home or place of work. Nevertheless, even in such a case the investigator must give thought to what can be done to improve the receptivity of the addressee to the questionnaire, and hence increase the likelihood that he or she will complete and return it.[3] In one way or another the envelope, covering letter and questionnaire itself must perform the tasks which the investigator might otherwise carry out in person, when arranging research access. These tasks can be summarized as:

(a) imparting the conviction that the investigation is a worthwhile piece of work and the investigator a competent person to carry it out;
(b) explaining why the investigation seeks the co-operation of the person or institutions being approached;
(c) indicating the use to be made of the eventual research material.

In the case of educational research the negotiation of research access is unlikely to be a once-and-for-all event. The investigator must be prepared to reiterate, to a succession of audiences, the purposes, style, scope and utility of the proposed research, and these explanations may have to be communicated in a number of different ways. For example, to make a study of secondary school responses to the behaviour of disaffected pupils (Bird *et al.*, 1981), getting research access entailed formal correspondence with selected chief education officers, meetings at local authority offices with particular headteachers, debate (and defence) of the proposed research in the staffrooms of their schools, and face-to-face assurances regarding the scope and confidentiality of the research to individual teachers and pupils who were asked to take part. This was a sizeable piece of research involving four researchers, and on a sensitive topic. However, the investigator whose chosen sphere is education is likely to find that almost any topic is deemed 'sensitive' by some of those asked to take part.

In setting up a single-handed study within the confines of one's own school or college, as many teacher-investigators are likely to do, there will still be a need to get the formal agreement of the headteacher and relevant heads of departments, and the active co-operation of any teachers, ancillary staff or pupils whose help is required. Depending on the subject of study, the headteacher may consider that the approval of parents must also be sought, and it is to be hoped that he or she will agree to obtain this by telephone or letter, on behalf of the investigator.

If documentary research is being undertaken, and the access required is to files and papers rather than individuals or situations, then it is with the keepers of the archives in question that access must be arranged.

Whatever the research method being used, the investigator will find that agreement to research access must be kept in good repair throughout the enquiry. Even if agreement has been given, the careless or offhand investigator may become *persona non grata* during the course of the research, and be unable to complete it. If files are left in disarray, papers borrowed and not returned, or respondents subjected to too lengthy or frequent interviews, at inconvenient times, the researcher's welcome will be worn out. All social researchers are to some extent mendicants, since they are seeking a free gift of time or information from those who are the subject of study. But researchers who bear this fact in mind, and who, without becoming the captive of their respondents, can contrive to make the research experience a helpful and profitable one, will almost certainly be gratified by the generosity with which people will give their time and knowledge.

## (5)   Developing the research instrument

The research instrument may be an interview schedule or a postal questionnaire. Or it may be a set of guidelines for an unstructured interview, or a pro forma for the classification of information selected from records. In some cases, the research instrument may be the trained capacity of an individual to make notes about the circumstances and content of a meeting. (A tape recorder, it should be stressed is *not* a research instrument. It is simply a means of enabling the reiteration of audible material in a place and at a time other than when it was recorded. The researcher's essential task of selection from and analysis of that material still remains to be done.)

The important point about research instruments is that they require development – they do not spring to hand in a perfect form, fully adapted to the particular investigative task. All formal texts on research methods mention the desirability of a 'pilot study', and this is one way in which a research instrument can be honed to its particular task. Trying out an interview schedule on a sample of respondents with similar characteristics to those of the intended survey population, for example, may quickly reveal gaps in the logical sequence of questions, or the incomprehensibility to the respondent of the wording used. 'I had no idea a Rising Five was a *child*', said one school governor. 'I thought it was something to do with fishing tackle.'

The luxury of a genuine pilot study, which tries out in miniature the viability of an envisaged investigation, is unlikely to be available to the student planning a small-scale short-term piece of research. But at least some attempt at 'trying it on the dog' should be made. Questionnaires and interview schedules in particular must be tried out on *someone* – friends, relations, neighbours. The investigator will get valuable feedback, for example, on whether 'closed' questions can readily be answered in the terms of the suggested range of replies.

Experience will be gained of how long it will take a respondent to fill in the questionnaire, or for an interview schedule to be worked through – important information for the overall planning of the investigation. Such *ad hoc* trials will confirm the need for any questionnaire or schedule to go through several draft stages, the number of which will depend on the time available.

In the case of a pro forma for recording information extracted from files, for example pupil records, the design of such a tool may have had to take place without prior knowledge of the range of information likely to be available. Teachers researching in their own institution will be more fortunate here, as they will have some notion of what is usually recorded. But if access is negotiated to the pupil records of *another* school, the range of information available may be different again, and the pro forma has to be rapidly adapted. Complete redesign may be needed in some cases, and it is to be hoped that the files can be studied on more than one occasion.

It can be seem that development of the research instrument may take place either before or during its use. Where the instrument is the researcher's own capacity to observe and record, this will certainly develop in the course of research experience. However, short-term small-scale investigations may provide only brief opportunities for 'learning on the job'. The investigator should do everything possible to prepare for the event to be observed. For example, in the case of a meeting the observer should try to sort out the names and roles of those present before the meeting starts or, if this is impossible, at least note some identifying physical characterstic of each person, and where they are sitting in relation to others. After the event, whether it be a case conference or a governing body meeting, a helpful informant may then be prepared to help the observer discover the identity and contribution of each person.

One factor influencing the eventual form of any research instrument must be the form of anlaysis which is to be applied to the data after they have been collected. For example, the tables it is intended to draw up using collated information from questionnaires or schedules, should be decided on and listed at the time the research instrument is designed. If these decisions are left until after the fieldwork has been done, the investigator may find that a question vital to the analysis has not been asked. And although qualitative forms of investigation may be seen as exploratory, with the intention that any analytic theory shall be grounded in the research material which comes to hand during the fieldwork, interviewers or observers should still, at this 'research instrument' stage, provide themselves with guidelines which ensure the coverage of what are likely to be the eventual analytic themes of the research account.

## (6)  Collecting the data

Developing the research instrument may, as we have seen, lap over into data collection, but for many research designs the fieldwork period is a distinct and discrete phase of the investigation. Its clear demarcation may, in fact, be essential to the successful completion of the whole enquiry. This is the period during which the researcher is likely to be investing most in the study, by way of time and personal involvement. Marking out a definite period during which the fieldwork is to be pursued helps concentration and commitment to the task in hand, for the fieldwork period is one when other customary social or work activities may well have to be set aside, reduced or postponed.

What the fieldwork actually consists of will depend upon the research design. It may be interviewing, documentary study or observation – all are forms of data collection which, in a small-scale study, are likely to entail the personal involvement of the investigator. Only in the case of a postal questionnaire will there be a 'breather' for the researcher while the research instrument is in the field. In this particular case the pre- and post-fieldwork periods are likely to be the busiest, when the questionnaire is being designed and developed before its issue, and when the completed questionnaires are being studied after they are returned.

One problem for the researcher whose fieldwork takes the form of interviewing or observation is that the period set aside for fieldwork may, fortuitously, prove not to be a good time for the study of the social phenomenon he or she has set out to investigate. In social research there is rarely an opportunity for the use of a controlled experimental model. Social life is untidy and episodic, and although investigators may, like Boswell, contrive to insert themselves into the milieux in which they are interested, during a given period there may be few opportunities to acquire data by the method planned. A Master's student investigating the education provided to adolescents in hospital for short-term treatment had as one objective the interviewing of such patients, as well as the study of the organizational infrastructure of hospital schooling (Smith, 1981). From the point of view of the investigator it was a disappointment that during the period allocated for fieldwork only a few patients within the eligible group were, in fact, admitted to the hospital under study. The student had to make the most of her small available sample – but also had to resist the temptation to extend the fieldwork period, in the hope that more patients would be admitted.

For not only must the researcher decide when to *start* the fieldwork, but a decision must also be made when to end it. This is the essence of the next stage to be discussed.

## (7) Pulling out of the investigative phase

Under this heading we can also discuss the whole question of 'getting away with the data', for the novice researcher may find it is just as difficult to pull out of a single interview as to say 'finis' to the fieldwork period as a whole.

To deal first with this problem of ending an interview, it is always the responsibility of the interviewer to do this, rather than waiting for the respondent to call a halt, however unstructured and relaxed the interview situation may be. It may have been difficult to negotiate access and to get in in the first place, but the interviewer who, once in, stays until [she or] he is thrown out, is working in the style of investigative journalism rather than social research.[4] [. . .] This sort of practice breaks one of the ethics of professional social research, which is that the field should not be left more difficult for subsequent investigators to explore by disenchanting respondents with the whole notion of research participation.

There are other questions of more personal ethics to be borne in mind, when private interviews are being conducted. Respondents become vulnerable during the course of extended sympathetic interviewing, and if the interview is unduly prolonged may begin to say things they will subsequently regret[5] or talk themselves into a despondent frame of mind, if the interview has focused on problems. The interviewer may feel increasingly unable to terminate the interview and leave the depressed respondent alone, and is in danger of losing professional control of the situation by stepping out of the role of social enquirer to become the confidant of the person being interviewed. The writer makes it a rule, for example when conducting home interviews with parents, not to leave respondents in a worse state than that in which she found them. This can mean keeping an eye on how time is passing and devoting part of the available period to winding-down conversation which diverts the respondent from problems discussed to more positive aspects of their life experience.

Difficulties of this kind may perhaps be unlikely to crop up in small-scale research in which fieldwork may well be confined to interaction with known colleagues. Nevertheless, the novice researcher should be alert to the possibilities that such difficulties may occur, and may perhaps be precipitated by overlong research contact with one individual. A problem which all will encounter, however, is the wider one of calling a halt to the investigative period as a whole.

Can the researcher be flexible about how long to wait for questionnaires to come back? Can use be made of those which come trailing in long after the rest? If a meeting which it was hoped to observe is postponed, should efforts be made to attend it when it is reconvened? If the target population proves thin on the ground during the period set aside for interview, can that period be extended? In the case of small-scale research, the answer to any of these questions must usually be 'No'. The fault from which many amateur investigations – and some professional ones – suffer is that of an open-ended period of data collection. Almost all social enquiries produce more data than can subsequently be made use of, however short the fieldwork period. And if this is endlessly extended, perhaps the researcher has become fascinated with the phenomenon under study, there is a danger that none of the material may be adequately taken through the outstanding stages of the investigation. Research which is not completed is no research at all; a point we shall return to later in this chapter.

## (8)   Ordering of the data

All research material, however collected, should be set in order and stored in a form in which it would be comprehensible to others, were they to be given access to it. Some kind of research archive or data bank must be established. However slender the data their sole repository must not be between the ears of the investigator, or a fundamental tenet of research – that the material must be testable and contestable by others – is not being met. Questionnaires and interview schedules must be collated and classified, field notes must be written up, and a reckoning should be kept of the timing and incidence of the field-work. Researchers must be prepared to be accountable for the investigations they have undertaken, even if they are never called to render that account.

A further reason for putting the data together in an orderly form is applicable both to large- and small-scale research. The disorganized investigator is in danger of making disproportionate use of the more striking or memorable research material and neglecting to balance this with other more humdrum data. When moving to the tasks of analysis the totality of the acquired data needs to be surveyed.

## (9)   Analysing the data

The main general point to be made about this stage is that it must exist and be allowed for in the overall research programme.[6] An investigator should not move directly from data collection to writing up, however small-scale the study. A weakness of many dissertations or theses is that, although considerable pains may have been taken to set up and carry out an effective piece of fieldwork, little use is made of the data collected in the eventual discussion of the thesis topic. Instead, discussion appears to be chiefly based on the investigator's background reading and/or preconceived ideas about the subject of study. In such cases it is likely that the student has not allowed sufficient time to muse on and learn from the research material. The broad analytic themes of the study will, as we have already indicated, have had to be identified before embarking on the fieldwork. But the data collected must be drawn on to illuminate those themes, and may well call into question the researcher's implicit assumptions about the topic.

## (10)   Writing up

This is perhaps the most difficult, but potentially the most satisfying, phase of the research. By putting words on paper about [the] research the investigator makes it available to other scholars and, in the classic phrase, pushes back the frontiers of knowledge, however minutely.

Technical advice on the format of research accounts is fairly readily available and cannot be included here. Important features are that the text shall be understandable and unambiguous, the referencing punctilious and accurate, and the overall conclusions or 'message' of the research be summarized in an assimilable and memorable form.

Writing up research can never be simply an exercise in handing on the data to the reader for his or her consideration. In a quantitative study tables may be compiled which, to the investigator, may seem self-explanatory, but some discussion of them must appear in the eventual text. In a qualitative study, quotations may be selected from the research material for inclusion in the research account, but these do not render superfluous a clear summative statement by the researcher of the beliefs or sentiments which the quotations serve to illustrate. The essence of an effective research account is that it conveys to the reader something of a researcher's empirical experience, together with [her or] his reflections on it.

## (11)   Enabling dissemination

Although the active and continuing dissemination of research findings may not be a feasible part of a small-scale investigation, the investigator has a duty to make dissemination possible. Writing an account of the research may be all the investigator can do, but some thought should be given to the number and durability of copies of that account, and the formal and informal circulation of them which can be arranged or permitted.

Various methods exist by which the dissemination of research material can be agreed with those who participated in the enquiry. The non-confidentiality of the materials may have been clearly accepted by participants from the outset, in which case no further negotiation is strictly necessary regarding the open circulation of the eventual research report. Nevertheless, it is courteous to supply a draft copy for comment to the principal 'gatekeeper' who allowed the research to go forward.

It has already been pointed out that almost all educational research is felt to be sensitive by some of those taking part. If individuals or institutions are to be named in the research account, explicit 'clearance' of the document by those concerned is desirable and advisable.[7] Where anonymity has been required as a condition of the investigation, this should be scrupulously preserved by the use of pseudonyms and the editing of descriptive material in such a way as to make identification of individuals or institutions at least difficult, if not impossible.[8] This professional practice should not be regarded by the student investigator as unnecessary for a research account which 'no one will see'. The whole point of a research account is that someone other than the writer shall see it, and it may well prove of interest to a select or extended circle of researchers and/or educationalists.

By taking the trouble to meet the requirements of the research participants with regard to clearance or confidentiality, the investigator has made possible the wider dissemination of the research findings and given some protection to informants in the event of the account being circulated or reproduced without the researcher's permission. (Such practices, whilst undesirable, are not unknown.)

Verbal dissemination of research findings (supplementing, but never replacing, a written research account) may prove useful, and is perhaps especially desirable in the case of small-scale means-to-an-end research which does not lead to published work. Whilst it cannot be regarded as an essential stage of the research enquiry, the teacher-investigator may find it worthwhile to prepare a short list of key issues arising from [the] research which can form the basis of formal or informal discussion with colleagues or, where appropriate, pupils. Any other feasible form of dissemination should also be considered since, in addition to meeting the academic requirements of an enquiry, dissemination to some extent redresses the balance of researcher–participant indebtedness. [. . .]

# COMPLETE RESEARCH

The many stages of a research inquiry which we have worked through may seem daunting to a novice investigator. For our purposes, the chief usefulness of such a list of stages is as a basis for research planning. The list underlines the necessity, already pointed out, of tailoring the enquiry to the resources available for its completion. If the research is *not* completed it would be preferable that it had not been begun. Aborted research wastes time and dissipates goodwill.

It is not only small-scale, 'amateur', investigations which stand in danger of not being completed. Many well-funded professionally staffed research projects have foundered because the investigative task has not been realistically appraised in the light of the time available for its completion, and the temperament and capacity of those intended to carry it out.[9] The means-to-an-end investigator, such as we are considering here, who undertakes research as part of a course of study or to give a wider perspective to personal experience, is likely to be well motivated to press through with the task, and if single handed will not need to adjust to the differing work pace and methods of personal organization of colleagues. But the need to plan out one's own use of the resource of time cannot be overstated. If there is a deadline by which, to be acceptable or usable, the research must be completed, that is all the time there is for *all the stages of the research* – including the writing up. Novice planners will be well advised to identify sub-deadlines for each stage – for establishing the focus of study, access negotiation, development of research instruments and so on – since the inevitable need to be flexible about one or more of those deadlines will keep them alert to the passage of time and the continuing drain on this major resource. Arranging access, for example, may well take longer than anticipated, and perhaps the only way to adjust to this is by reducing the time to be spent on developing the research instrument, or by reducing the scope of the proposed fieldwork. The sub-deadline to be preserved at all costs, however, is the one which marks the end of the investigative phase. In the concluding stages of a research enquiry, one more interview, or one more meeting attended, does not equal the value of an hour or two's reflective analysis and writing.

# SINGLE-HANDED RESEARCH

The need to make measured use of the resource of time has been stressed because failure to do this is so common, and has disastrous consequences for the effective completion of research, whether large or small scale. Novice investigators who know they will be pressed for time and will also be 'single handed' in their research inquiry, may feel the required research task is well-nigh impossible. Some words of encouragement can, however, be offered which will aid positive thinking about the actual resources at their disposal.

The man or woman power resources available for the research task should not be appraised solely on a quantified basis, as the term 'single-handed' research appears to do. Researchers should consider what particular strengths or attributes they have which will contribute to the research. Examples may be a network of personal or professional contacts which will help them gain entry to a particular field of enquiry; seniority or standing in an institution which will add persuasive power to requests for information; experience in meeting the public or in the analysis of documents which will be of use in the empirical stage of an investigation. 'Sponsors', if prestigious, may also lend strength to the single-handed researcher's arm.

Professional researchers frequently make sure that their sponsors, such as a research council or a charitable foundation, are mentioned in any account they give of a proposed research enquiry. Student researchers may not have sponsors of this kind, but could perhaps truthfully claim that they have been seconded by the local authority to undertake the work in hand, or mention that their enquiry has the approval of a senior colleague.[10]

In summary, single-handed investigators should carefully appraise what personal and political resources they have which are relevant for the research. For the means-to-and-end investigator it is sensible to design the research, perhaps even select its topic, so as to make maximum use of those resources.

## CONSIDERATIONS OF METHOD

In this section we briefly consider a range of research methods, and discuss some criteria for choosing between them. More detailed discussion of particular modes of research will be found elsewhere in this book.

We have seen that research design has to take account of the aims of the study, the resources available and the general feasibility of the study area. But before embarking on the compromise which, this chapter has stressed, is a characteristic of effective research design, it is as well to remind ourselves of the main forms of research method. [. . .]

Research methods can be broadly divided into *quantitative* methods, taking a *positivist* approach, and *qualitative* methods which are *relativist* in their perspective. Researchers in the positivist tradition (Durkheim, 1895) take the view that social facts exist and can be ascertained. They may hypothesize that these facts occur together in certain patterns and are subject to particular causes. Their research purpose will be to measure the occurrence of these phenomena in such a way as to test their hypotheses.

Relativist researchers, on the other hand, are less confident of the existence of social facts. Their own view of the world, they believe, has developed cumulatively, contributed to by their particular life experience. They postulate that the world may look different to other people, and in their research they set out to understand more about the view of the world which some other people (or 'actors') (Silverman, 1970) have. Their purpose is not to obtain a set of facts, but to gain insight into a perspective.

As we have said, quantitative methods are usually associated with positivist research, and qualitative methods with relativist research. However, this is not always so. For example, while participant observation is held to be a qualitative research method, some early occupational and industrial sociology which used participant observation was undoubtedly positivist in its form of analysis (Roy, 1963). Equally, and almost quintessentially, the survey method is defined as quantitative. But some small-scale survey work is so detailed, exploratory, and sensitive that it illuminates a perspective on the world rather than providing a set of facts. Nevertheless, for the most part it can be asserted that surveys, using structured interviewing or postal questionnaire, come up with quantifiable facts, while participant observation in all its forms (Denzin, 1978) and exploratory interviewing, provide a qualitative perspective.

[. . .]

Which of these two broad types of research – qualitative or quantitative – is the most suitable form of research to inform a dissertation, or piece of required course work? Both have their attractions and their disadvantages.

The intensive but flexible mode of qualitative research has obvious attractions for the slenderly resourced single-handed investigator. But qualitative methods are slow, and may be anxiety creating because of the lack of structure or even an end goal, in the research design. Moreover, since the research question is being developed and refined during, rather than prior to, the research, it is more difficult to plan the research programme as a whole and get some parts of it (for example, establishing the framework of analysis) out of the way early on. Nevertheless, as this whole paper has attempted to make clear, the requirement to plan and allocate resources of time and effort cannot be set aside, however flexible the research approach.

Quantitative methods also have their attractions. For the novice investigator they appear more clear cut, with more obvious boundaries around the fieldwork phase. Researchers undertaking a quantitative study may find that it temporarily occupies their waking hours, but it is less likely to invade their way of life than, for example, the more participative and reflexive style of qualitative work (Whyte, 1955). But, to meet the requirements of its underlying positivist philosophy, quantitative research must be scientifically 'respectable', a requirement which entails rigorous design, administrative control and clerical accuracy. Moreover, it must be moderately large scale, in order to justify collation of the comparable material and enable some subtlety of analysis. At the least, there should be *some* respondents in each of the cells of a simple table (which might, for example, seek to sub-divide a pupil population by sex and reading age).

A few points should be made about *documentary research*, as this does not fall neatly into either the quantitative or the qualitative group of methods. Much depends on the type of document and the use made of it. It may provide a statistical, quantified input to back up or supplement a quantified study. (Here the researcher should bear in mind that the statistics being drawn on may not have been collected for the same purpose as the researcher's own data and may not therefore be entirely comparable.) Alternatively, documentary material may be used to provide another perspective on and area of qualitative study. For example, Gill (1977) used police records to give another angle on the activities of some young people, activities in which he had been a semi-participant observer.

Files and records are frequently an untapped source of data which have never been used for anything other than administrative purposes, but which would repay analysis for a number of research purposes. Almost all social populations are in danger of being over-researched, so the small-scale investigator should never rush out to do yet another survey without considering whether a survey has in fact already been done, and the material be lying uncollated in the file of an institution to which he has access. For example, a Master's student worked extremely hard at carrying out and following up a questionnaire survey of 'drop-out' students from the evening institute with which he was connected. When he came to compare his small and hard-won sample findings with records from previous years, it became evident that the records already contained the raw data for a much fuller analysis of student drop-out, which had never been undertaken by the institute in question (Delahunt, 1979). Any novice investigator who has full access, through work or voluntary activities, to records, all the weaknesses and strengths of which are already familiar, should think carefully whether they are potentially a body of data for survey analysis.[11]

## THE REWARDS OF SMALL-SCALE RESEARCH

Many of the difficulties inherent in social research, especially for the slenderly resourced novice investigator, have been stressed in this paper. The imperative need to work to a research plan, and to tailor the scope and duration of the investigation to the resources available, has been repeatedly emphasized. What are the rewards of undertaking an activity so fraught with problems? Are those rewards worthwhile?

In the case of small-scale investigations, carried out for a dissertation or piece of course work, it is more likely that the rewards of the work accrue to the investigator rather than to the investigated. Nevertheless, most people find it of some interest to take part in a survey whose purpose they understand. In the case of face-to-face enquiries of an exploratory kind, it is not unusual for the person interviewed to comment that they have found it helpful to their own thinking to be required to focus on a particular aspect of their life experience and discuss it with someone less closely involved than themselves.

So far as novice investigators themselves are concerned, the experience of carrying out a piece of social research may benefit them by uncovering certain skills they did not know they had – these skills may be analytic, literary or administrative, or they may be skills in social relations. But the chief benefit – and the reason why so many courses of study require the student to carry out some sort of social enquiry – is that to do so fosters the enquiring attitude which is a prerequisite for successful academic work of any kind. The whole exercise of planning and carrying out a piece of social research forces the recognition, and usually the questioning, of the investigator's own assumptions about social life.

## NOTES

1. See, for example, Boswell, J. (1791) *The life of Samuel Johnson*, Dilley, London; also Harris, M. (ed.) (1982) *The heart of Boswell*, McGraw-Hill (a distillation of the first six volumes of the Yale edition of the private papers of James Boswell).

2. See, for example, McGeeney, P. (1967) *Parents are welcome*, Longman; Lynch, J., and Pimlott, J. (1976) *Parents and teachers*, Macmillan; Harris, R. (1980) Parent teacher contacts: a case study, in Craft, M. *et al.* (eds.) *Linking home and school*, 3rd edition, Harper & Row.
3. A classic source on this subject is Scott, C. (1961) Research on mail surveys, in *Journal of the Royal Statistical Society*, A.124, pp. 143–205.
4. Bernstein, in Bernstein, C., and Woodward, B. (1975) *All the President's men*, Warner Books, p. 65, gives a vivid account of how an interview with a key informant was prolonged by the request or acceptance of numerous cups of coffee.
5. There is always a need to protect research respondents from the consequences of verbal indiscretions not relevant to the research. See Johnson, D. (1975) Enlisting the participation of teachers in educational research, in *Research Intelligence*, Vol. II.
6. Useful technical advice on the analysis of quantitative data is contained in Silvey (1975) Chapters 1 and 2 (see References).
7. For a description of methods of 'clearance' see Johnson, D., Ransom, E., Packwood, T., Bowden, K., and Kogan, M. (1980) *Secondary schools and the welfare network*, Allen & Unwin, Methods Appendix.
8. 'Informed guesses' as to the identity of anonymized schools or local education authorities participating in research may always be made by educational *cognoscenti*, but the use of pseudonyms will prevent unequivocal identification.
9. Platt, J. (1976) *The realities of social research: an empirical study of British sociologists*, Sussex University Press, gives a fascinating and salutory account of university research projects which failed to be completed. Team research seemed especially susceptible to problems of non-completion.
10. However, in a classic paper, Deming points out that knowledge of the 'auspices' or sponsors of a piece of research may bias response. Deming, W. E. (1944) On errors in surveys, in *American Sociological Review*, Vol. 9, pp. 359–369.
11. Questions of confidentiality and anonymity must, of course, be fully considered if existing records are used in this way.

# REFERENCES

Bird, C., Chessum, R., Furlong, J., and Johnson, D. (eds) (1981) *Disaffected pupils.* Brunel University.
Delahunt, D. (1979) Continuing education for adults: investigating one local authority adult centre. Unpublished dissertation, MA in public and social administration. Department of Government, Brunel University.
Denzin, N. K. (1978) *The research act: a theoretical introduction to research methods.* McGraw-Hill, Chapter 7.
Durkheim, E. (1895) *The rules of sociological method,* English translation edited by Catlin, G. E. C. (1950). Free Press of Glencoe.
Gill, O. (1977) *Luke Street: housing policy, conflict and the creation of the delinquent area.* Macmillan.
Johnson, D. and Ransom, E. (1983) *Family and school.* Croom Helm.
Roy, D. (1963) Efficiency and the 'fix' – informal intergroup relations in a piecework machine shop, in J. A. Litterer (ed.) *Organisations: structure and behaviour.* Wiley.
Silverman, D. (1970) *The theory of organisations: a sociological framework.* Heinemann.
Silvey, J. (1975) *Deciphering data.* Longman.
Smith, J. (1981) An exploration of the schooling of pupils aged 13 to 16 who have to spend a short time in their local general hospital. Unpublished dissertation, MA in public and social administration. Department of Government, Brunel University.

Webb, E. J., Campbell, D. T., Schwartz, R. D., and Schrest, L. (1966) *Unobtrusive measures: non-reactive research in the social sciences.* Rand McNally.
Whyte, W. F. (1955) *Street corner society: the social structure of an Italian slum* (2nd edn). University of Chicago Press.

# CHAPTER 13

# Diagnosis, Data Collection and Feedback in Consultancy

### PHILIP HOPE

## PART I: DIAGNOSIS AND INFORMATION GATHERING

### 1. What is Diagnosis?

Diagnosis is the process of understanding and describing the issue or problem you and the participants from the organization want to address. As a result of the diagnosis you are aiming to be clear about the problem requiring a solution, to have identified the forces that are causing it to exist and to have the basis for choosing an effective way of bringing about change to resolve the problem.

TABLE 13.1

*The purpose of diagnosis. Diagnosis in consultancy aims at generating action, not achieving understanding*

| The researcher wants a full understanding of the situation, and therefore: | The consultant wants to create action, and therefore: |
|---|---|
| seeks to identify all relevant factors and frame a comprehensive understanding of the situations. | seeks to identify the factors which the client can influence, and establish a satisfactory understanding as a basis for action. |
| tries to base the investigation on objective data interpreted in the light of theoretical knowledge. Is sensitive to criticisms of bias and intuition. | tries to incorporate their bias and intuition into the investigation, preferring to call them judgement and expertise. |
| is not concerned to obtain approval of the research findings, and can do the study without having anyone from the organization working as a researcher. | is crucially concerned to get the client to approve of the findings and recommendations, and so tries to involve the client as a research colleague throughout the consultancy. |

SOURCE: *Based on a formulation by Peter Block (1981).*

Crucially, the purpose of diagnosis is to generate insight, understanding and a motivation for action about a problem. Diagnosis in a consultancy is not the same as research. In particular there is an overt recognition that the diagnosis of the problem involves someone – you and/or the participants – making a judgement about the problem and what to do about it. The difference is summed up in Table 13.1.

## 2.  Steps in the diagnostic process

The basic steps that you and the organization will take in carrying out a diagnosis will be:

- Step 1. **Identifying the presenting problem.** This is the problem as **the participants** see it.
- Step 2. **Choosing a limited number of areas to be examined.** Deciding what particular questions the participants want answered on the 'technical' problem.
- Step 3. **Deciding who will be involved.** This is both you and the participants deciding who will take part in the consultancy process and the roles you will play.
- Step 4. **Choosing how the information will be collected.** Interview – individually or in groups; group activities; questionnaires; diagnostic tools; document analysis; observation.
- Step 5. **Collecting the information.**
- Step 6. **Funnelling, summarizing and analysing the information.** This is the key part of the process including: focusing on the important pieces of information; drawing together the key points; analysing what it means and its implications.

## 3. Starting points

*The participants' starting point*

The participants may have done a lot of diagnosis and information gathering about the problem they want to tackle during the process of deciding what they want to use a consultant for, selecting a consultant and agreeing a contract. However, if they have chosen a consultant fairly quickly they may have spent only a limited amount of time exploring the problem they want to address and gathered a limited number of relevant views, opinions and factual information. The consultancy contract may even be solely about doing a diagnosis.

*The consultant's starting point*

Whatever the participants may have done by way of diagnosis, you, the consultant, will want to continue to explore deeper and deeper layers of the problems to be tackled. That's your job.

You will want to be sure that the participants' preconceived ideas about the issues are tested out and that you and they arrive at a shared analysis. There may well be sectional interests within the organization who are in dispute about the problem or have different perceptions of need. You will want to identify what these are.

You may have carried out some diagnosis during the contracting process, but the time limits and constraints inherent in agreeing a contract will mean you will want to spend more time diagnosing the problems at the start. Depending on the nature of the consultancy task and the relationship you have created, you and the participants will continue to be diagnosing what is happening, why, and what to do about it through the contract.

## 4. Who does the diagnosis?

Your primary concern is to get both a good diagnosis of the problem *and* to ensure *the participants* own it. You can use the most advanced consultancy tools for analysing a problem in an organization but unless they are willing to act on that analysis it is wasted work. There are three basic approaches to getting participants to make use of your diagnostic skills and methods: self-diagnosis, joint diagnosis and independent diagnosis.

### Self-diagnosis

You can act as a facilitator to participants undertaking their own diagnosis. You can assist them to carry out the interviews, discussions and fact finding and you can provide them with techniques to analyse the results. In this approach you will ensure greatest ownership of the outcome by the participants. But it runs the greatest risk of being a self-fulfilling process because the participants may not be fully challenged about their preconceived ideas, or not take full account of experiences and knowledge outside their organization.

### Joint diagnosis

A collaborative approach to diagnosis involves you and the participants collecting information, jointly analysing the problems and both contributing suggestions for change. This gives the organization the benefit of your knowledge and experience about the issues or problems but requires you to have techniques for helping participants to undertake this process themselves. This approach combines the two roles at opposite ends of the consultancy spectrum – process facilitator and policy advocate. As such it is hardest to make work. It requires careful negotiation at the outset and constant attention when under way to both the problem being addressed and to your relationship with the organization.

### Independent diagnosis

A wholly independent diagnosis hands over to you the task of gathering information, making an analysis and suggesting solutions. This places greatest emphasis on the importance of your technical expertise on the problem, but runs the greatest risk of the participants rejecting it as their ownership of your findings will be at its lowest.

## 5.  Diagnosing how the participants are dealing with the problem

During the diagnostic process you and the participants need to focus on issues to do with both the technical problem on which you are working and how the problem is being dealt with (working relationships, management style, where power is located and how it is used, attitudes to social equality and so on). Whilst gathering and analysing information about the technical problem you should reflect on the behaviour of the participants. What does this tell you about the changes needed in how the organization is run in order to implement the 'technical' solutions to the problem?

> *When the consultant was interviewing a middle manager about the management structure, he realized that the answers were all geared towards ensuring that the person moved away from being line managed by one of the regional directors. The issue here was not necessarily to do with structure but was to do with management style and a conflict of values. Specifically, it was to do with the values of the middle manager being interviewed and the way he responded to people. Whilst there was a benefit in carrying out a restructuring of the organization, unless the consultant and the participants identified and dealt with the relationship problems, these problems would remain and simply surface elsewhere in the new structure.*

## 6.  Reviewing how the diagnostic stage is going

At every stage in your relationship with an organization you should review how the relationship is going – both formally and informally. There are three reasons for this. Firstly, it is important that you and the participants feel the work is going the way you want it to. You might want to renegotiate the contract as it proceeds. If you feel, for example, that in the light of what you have found to date you want to interview other people in the organization who were not included in the original contract, then this should be done only through a review and an agreement. You should also assess the extent to which you are doing what they expected and doing so in a way that reflects the values you hold and you understood were agreed. Are you behaving in ways that have integrity, feel to them to be empowering and creating ownership? A second reason is that it will reveal information about how the organization as a whole or individuals within it deal with problems. You should pay a lot of attention to how you are treated by organizations. This is not only because you are concerned to ensure the consultancy is successful but because the way the participants handle you gives you information about how they might deal with other people and problems in their organization. This is important information that you can use to diagnose action in order to help resolve the 'technical' problem.

> *The consultant had been asked to help a social work staff team improve the quality of their practice in dealing with child abuse cases. The consultant found that when at the start of the contract he began analysing the existing practice his credibility as a consultant kept being questioned. After clarifying his knowledge and experience twice, the consultant asked the staff team to reflect on what their rejection of him revealed about their attitudes to accepting new ideas and new ways of working generally. This focus on the*

*relationship between the consultant and the team enabled them to examine the cause of their defensive behaviour towards other agencies and practice developments. This led to a positive discussion about relationships with other staff teams and other organizations which in turn created a more open approach to improving the quality of their practice.*

Thirdly, are there aspects of your behaviour that could be a model for them to use in the way individuals are relating to each other? Do you use techniques such as writing on flipcharts for recording views that they could use in their meetings? Do you have ways of intervening that assist group discussion such as asking for a round of individual opinions that the participants could experience and adopt? Are there ways you operate that are not effective role models and need to be avoided?

## 7. Techniques for gathering information

In order to make a diagnosis of the problem, its causes and how it is being dealt with, you and the participants need to gather together a variety of facts, opinions, statistics, assumptions, clues, signs and signals. It is unlikely that one method of collecting such information will be sufficient or appropriate. The six methods that consultants frequently use are:

(i)    interviews – individually or with groups;
(ii)   group activities;
(iii)  written questionnaires;
(iv)   written diagnostic tools;
(v)    document analysis;
(vi)   observation.

You can also use your experience of working with the participants as a significant source of information about the organization and how it handles problems.

The choice of which combination of information-gathering methods to use will depend on the key questions you will have already explored along with:

- What methods will give the best information we need to achieve the analysis?
- How many people need to be involved or consulted?
- Should everyone be involved or a sample?
- How much time do we have?
- How much will it cost?
- What methods fit the culture of the organization?
- What effect will doing the data collection have on the organization?

### (i) Interviews

*Individual interviews*    Table 13.2 summarizes three layers that you might seek to work through during a more exploratory diagnostic interview. You begin with asking about the 'presenting problem', move on to the person's perceptions about how other people are contributing to the problem, and finally arrive at what the person you are interviewing is doing that contributes

TABLE 13.2
*Layers of analysis*

| LAYER | CONSULTANT'S QUESTION | ISSUE BEING EXPLORED |
|---|---|---|
| TOP | What's the technical or business problem you are experiencing? | The presenting problem will most often be expressed in organizational or technical terms: 'We aren't achieving our aims, my group isn't going well, the system isn't working.' |
| SECOND | What are other individuals or groups in the organization doing to either cause or maintain this problem at its current level of severity? | The person's perceptions about how others are contributing to the problem is the next level. 'People are more interested in the processes than the product of this organization, two members of the group do all the talking, the people don't understand the system.' |
| THIRD | What is your role in the problem? What is there in your approach for ways of dealing with the situation that might be contributing to the problem or getting in the way of its resolution? | This is a statement of how a person sees his or her own way of contributing to the problem. The person may be contributing by certain conscious actions or by simply not giving the problem attention. It is vital as it brings responsibility closer to the person involved. Instead of expressing the situation in terms of forces outside the person which are creating problems, the focus is moved a little more internally. |

SOURCE: *Block (1981).*

to the problem. Each of these layers interact and you may want to explore, for example, the person's working relationship with others in the organization.

*Resistance to analysis*   You can analyse people's behaviour when you interview them to consider whether they are really working with you to explore the problem fully or whether they are consciously or unconsciously resisting the process:

- Are they only talking about the behaviour of others and resisting talking about themselves, and their behaviour?
- Are they tending to go off on side issues and diverting attention away from the real issue?
- Are they being silent or giving very short answers and avoiding the questions?
- Are they going into too much detail and so clouding the issue?
- Do they keep saying they are confused about why this interview is happening even thought you've explained it to them twice?

- Are they moralizing about other people and what they should be doing rather than thinking about the fact that they disagree with them and how this conflict with their views can be dealt with?

Reflect on how the person is responding to the interview. Try to help them by restating something you've said, disclosing a similar experience, asking open-ended questions and testing out how they might be feeling. If you believe their response is resistance, you could describe what you see them doing – as a means of helping them to reflect on their behaviour and return to the problem.

*Group interviews and discussion*   The group interview and discussion reveals information in two ways – the content that people give and the process or behaviour in the group. If the group is a team in the organization – or a group of managers who need to work together – then the behaviour in the group could well provide more important information about the problem than what they say. But if the group have been drawn together for a discussion simply to save time, the diagnosis may be of less importance. You can lead a group interview in the same way as a one-to-one interview. The group dynamics may mean that this is a harder task as you seek to ensure that everyone has a chance to give their viewpoint and different people resist the exploration in different ways at different times.

A diagnostic group discussion should not be confused with a group planning an implementation process. The purpose is different and the process will be different too. However, it is often the case that once a group has begun to share information and views and analyse their responses, they may be in a position and mood to identify options and agree ways forward. You may want to use techniques that encourage group discussion and analysis. Examples of techniques that can be used for a group information sharing and analysis of a problem include:

- **Brainstorming.** People are encouraged to give ideas or viewpoints that are written down on flipchart paper without being challenged. This list is then discussed, key areas highlighted, issues that fall into similar categories marked, and so on.
- **Structured brainstorming.** People discuss their views or thoughts in pairs and the points are written up one point per pair until all the issues are identified.
- **Rounds.** Each person is invited in turn to say what their view is about the issue, or the process that is happening in the group.
- **Talking walls.** A series of open or closed questions are written up on flipcharts for people to walk round and complete. The information is then discussed by the group as a whole, or a subgroup takes the answers from a section of the wall and prepares a summary of the findings to feed back.
- **Index cards.** There are many ways of using index cards in groups for exploring problems. One method is as follows. Each person writes down on each of the three cards three reasons why they think the problem exists. These are laid out on a table or floor so that everyone can see them. Everyone picks up two cards that they think are the two most important causes of the problem. If their first two choices are picked up by someone else, they can pick up just one or none at all. The cards chosen are laid out again

(the rest are discarded) and everyone turns over any card they disagree with or which they want clarified. All the cards left uppermost are statements of the cause of the problem that everyone agrees with – these should be written up on a sheet of flipchart paper. The group then works through each of the turned-over cards with the person who wrote it, saying why they think it is a cause of the problem, and the person who turned it over responding to this point. The card is then either added to the list of agreed statements, amended and added, or listed as a point of disagreement.

### (ii) Group activities and exercises

Group physical activities that reveal information about a problem are commonly used in consultancy for diagnosing issues relating to team development but could be more widely applied. One example is called 'sculpting' whereby the people in a group place themselves around a room in positions and stances that reflect a particular theme such as power that they want to explore. This kind of activity can have considerable impact and needs to be handled carefully by consultants with experience of working on questions of group work and team relationships. For example:

*The consultant asked the team to arrange the furniture and themselves to reflect their relationship with the volunteers and committees in their organization. The physical distance between the staff and the chairs, and the position of the organization's director, graphically illustrated why there were problems of lack of trust and confidence between staff and the rest of the organization – an issue that might not otherwise have been so readily identified, but having been so could no longer be avoided.*

*A variation on this sculpting theme is to use drawing. The consultant asked each member of the team to draw a picture of the team with each person being a petal and the size and position of the petal representing their influence in the team.*

*Each person then presented their picture explaining who each person was in the picture and why they had drawn them that way. The difference in perception based on these drawings provided a useful starting point to resolve issues of the way people operated in the team and how others reacted.*

The major benefit of sculpting and drawing is that they show simply and easily the complex problem which people find it difficult to express verbally. The physical nature of the activity also makes it more memorable and is a shared experience to which participants can readily refer back in later discussions.

## (iii) Written questionnaires

Simple written questionnaires asking for facts or opinions are a tool often used by consultants for gathering information. They are discussed in Chapter 17. One dilemma in the use of survey questionnaires is the undue weight that can be placed upon them. Once the information is analysed and presented in graphs it can gain a status that places it above the 'softer' data of observation and interviews, even though it may not be complete or in sufficient depth. To avoid this it is important to place the survey results alongside all the relevant information about a particular area of concern, to draw out only the key aspects of that information and to use judgement with integrity in analysing the data and drawing conclusions.

## (iv) Written diagnostic tools

Written diagnostic tools are also used by many consultants when seeking to understand the nature of problems in organizations. Although a pen-and-paper procedure, they differ from ordinary questionnaires where you need to analyse and interpret the information you collect. Written diagnostic tools contain a diagnosis within their structure. They ask participants questions and then interpret their answers.

Consultants differ markedly in their approach to such diagnostic tools. Some view them as telling 'the truth' and believe that variables such as different organizational settings, cultural differences among the participants or simply people's mood when completing them have been taken into account through extensive field testing of their content and use. Others are more sceptical and use such instruments only as an additional way of gathering insights into the overall picture being built up through interviews, observation and so on.

It is important that you do not use such diagnostic tools to place you in some special position of being the person with mysterious knowledge or mystical analytical powers. That does not empower the participants and anger is likely to reinforce their dependence on you, the consultant.

## (v) Document analysis

Depending upon the nature of the task, you may want to see the organization's published documents such as annual reports, newsletters and so on; and internal documents such as minutes of meetings, internal reports, and policy statements. You may have a specific aspect in mind when reading them such as the images portrayed, the content, or factual data. Or you may wish to gain a more general picture of what the organization is about and how it has developed over a period of time. It is also a way for you to develop an understanding of how an organization communicates internally and externally and makes decisions.

## (vi) Observation

Depending on the nature of the task, you will very often find it useful to observe what an organization does and how it is managed. Although 'expensive' in the time it takes, observation gives you first-hand information that can be reviewed and discussed later as a shared experience. Both you and the participants need to be clear about why you are there and what is being observed. Other people need to be told in advance that you will be attending and why. You may need to be introduced and your presence explained at the start of the session. You need to have agreement about whether you will make notes or in other ways record what you are observing at the time or afterwards; and how these observations will be used. Your presence will affect what happens. What you observe may not be 'representative' of what happens every day. This is not necessarily a bad thing. It may be that a meeting that is normally a disaster goes very well in your presence. This is the time to ask what was different. What did they do in front of you that they don't normally do? More importantly, what did they *not* do that normally happens? In this way you can use the effect of your presence to produce learning and, hopefully, change for the better – a good use of you as a consultant.

## 8.   Funnelling, summarizing and analysing the information

This is the tricky bit. There is a pile of interview notes, a stack of questionnaires that have been analysed, the write-ups from some group discussions, a box of internal documents that have been read, a file of relevant statistical data and the notes from observing a series of staff meetings. What happens now? The task is to funnel, summarize and analyse the information in order to focus on the key items that are important to the organization, can be changed by the organization, and which people in the organization want to change.

One approach is to take each of the key issues to be addressed and summarize the main points and facts about that issue that have been gathered via the different information collection methods. There is an element of 'living with the data' for a period until you can see the patterns within it. Having summarized them, analyse them to develop suggestions for action or ways forward on dealing with them – a process that is often better done by two or more people together (see Figure 13.1).

You might expect consultants to be very rigorous in applying detailed and systematic approaches to analysing the information they have collected. But most avoid this approach. The reason for this is to repeat that consultancy is not research. It is about making a judgement about what is important – not being comprehensive or overly detailed. This is summed up in the way one consultant described his approach:

> You may have devised a rational, logical process to sort out and categorize the data, but the selection of what is important is essentially a judgement on your part. This is what they are paying you for. Trust your intuition, don't treat it as bias. If you are an internal consultant, you are often familiar with all the organization, the people and how they operate. Use this information in condensing the data.
>
> When I am struggling to decide what is important in a pile of notes, I will sometimes read through all the notes once, then put them away. On a blank sheet of paper I will then list what I think is important in the data – usually about four or five items. I let that be my guide on what to report and how to organize the report. I have faith that what I can remember is what is really

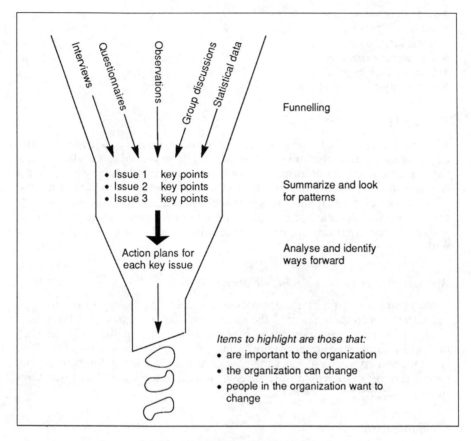

**FIGURE 13.1** Funnelling, summarizing and analysing the information

important. Since a person can only absorb a limited amount of data, what stands out to me is what I want to stand out to the client. Let the information that stays in the background become part of an appendix, but don't clutter the feedback meeting with a complete list of everything you found out.

That approach may seem simplistic but it reflects the essence of what consultancy is about – not research, and not justification, but focusing on the key items that are important, can be changed and which people want to change.

## 9.   Diagnostic dilemmas

You should be aware of some of the pitfalls that can occur in the diagnostic phase of a consultancy contract. The main dilemmas are:

- the time and cost;
- appropriate methods;
- contamination;

- over-diagnosis;
- under-diagnosis;
- crisis diagnosis;
- threatening diagnosis;
- favourite diagnosis;
- culturally biased diagnosis.

### Time and cost

Whilst interviews can be very effective they are expensive in both the amount of participants' time they take and your costs. You should not underestimate the amount of written information the organization will already have that is relevant to the problem and that should be made available to you. Similarly, observation of participants' meetings or work does not take up more of the organization's time but can give a lot of information to you about what goes on in the organization, how people behave and how problems are dealt with.

### Appropriate methods and contamination

Some methods of collecting information may feel wholly inappropriate to an organization's culture. You and the participants have a choice – to avoid such methods because they seem to be inappropriate or to deliberately use such methods to begin to counter the prevailing culture. Using new ways of working is a common approach for creating change at the stage of implementation but carries the risk of increased resistance when used in the initial diagnostic stage of a consultancy.

### Contamination

Asking basic questions about why people do what they do, stimulates thinking and inevitably creates change. If you view consultancy as research, this is a dilemma. But consultancy is not research; it is about giving advice and support in order to take action to resolve problems. The question is not how to avoid the information-collection methods having an influence but to ensure they have an influence that is congruent with resolving the problem being addressed.

### Over-diagnosis

There are two kinds of over-diagnosis. Firstly, too much time can be spent collecting information and analysing it and not enough time taking action to resolve the problems. It is important to get the balance right when planning the consultancy process and to avoid the diagnosis itself becoming a ritual of continual analysis.

Secondly if there are too many things to tackle and too many alternatives about how to approach them, you can lose sight of what are the most important ones and which need to be dealt with first. To avoid this, concentrate on funnelling the information so as to focus on the key areas, summarize them and be clear about what the implications might be for future action.

## Under-diagnosis

Arriving at a diagnosis and making recommendations for change on the basis of insufficient information can also be a difficulty. It is essential that you are provided with the information you need if you expect to do a reasonable analysis. The organization has a lot of control both in determining the information collection methods and in being open with you when you have started work. It can be easy for participants to play games with you by not giving you information they know is vital or, for example, challenging the statistical validity of the data you do collect because they don't like the results. It is important to remember that the purpose of diagnosis is action, not research. Unlike research, consultancy means drawing on both 'hard' and 'soft' data and mixing it with personal judgements to arrive at a diagnosis.

## Crisis diagnosis

You can fall into the trap of responding to the immediate crises you see; conducting your interviews or group discussions, you could be diverted away from the underlying problems by the short-term and very visible issues you meet. In analysing the information collected you need to feel able to 'get up into the helicopter' and look at the overall picture of what is happening. Action should be focused on the factors that are causing the symptoms rather than on responding to the immediate problems presented.

## The threatening diagnosis

The extent and depth of change required in some organizations to ensure their survival can be dramatic. But you want to avoid a situation in which the consultancy operation is a success but the organization dies. It is of little value if the changes, or the ways in which you present your proposals for change, are so overwhelming and dramatic that the organization suffers badly.

A different kind of threatening diagnosis is one that imposes an alien set of organizational 'cultures' on to an agency. You should not deliberately avoid 'threatening' change or change that requires a massive shift in an organization's culture. But unless you have been specifically asked to take a particular approach you should at least map out several options and their implications, one of which might require fundamental change.

## The favourite diagnosis

In your exploratory meetings and in agreeing a contract you may have already disclosed your particular bias or way of looking at the organizational world. A dilemma that you will need to consider is whether the diagnosis you have made only reflects that original bias (and hence may be missing an important aspect) or genuinely endeavours to analyse the problem from a variety of viewpoints and approaches.

It may be that a tendency to use your favourite diagnosis is an inevitability. If you always see problems as rooted in structure, you will inevitably find structural solutions to the problems that organizations have. If you view organizational problems as fundamentally to do with how people relate and communicate with each other, then it won't be surprising if you recommend solutions based on improving relationships and team-building. And if you are an expert on reorganizing services into devolved and competing profit centres, then you are not likely to make proposals for services based on sharing resources towards co-operatively agreed plans.

### Culturally biased diagnosis

You can fail to recognize that your diagnosis is culturally biased in that it fails to take account of the perspectives of the problem held by women or black or disabled people. The original planning and contracting process should have raised this issue, and the way you carry out the consultancy should involve collecting the views of individuals and groups inside and possibly outside the organization who reflect these perspectives. The feedback and action planning phase provides an important opportunity to check out and remedy any bias. Where you feel it is not possible or where it is even undesirable to eliminate such 'cultural' bias this needs to be clearly acknowledged with clearly stated reasons.

## PART 2: FEEDBACK, ACTION PLANNING AND IMPLEMENTATION

## 1. What is feedback?

### The purpose of feedback

Unless you have been contracted to act solely as a facilitator, you will want to give feedback to the organization or participants about the problem being addressed. The purpose of feedback is for you to give information in order that the participants make a commitment to take action. Your task is to present a clear picture of the current situation and your recommendations, and to encourage them to focus on doing something about the problem.

### Types of feedback

Your feedback may be a written report, a written summary or verbal feedback. It may happen once, on two or three occasions as part of a regular cycle of doing–reviewing–implementing (see Figure 13.2), or live as the situation demands. It may be a formal meeting or it could be an informal discussion. Your choice of feedback will depend largely on the nature of the consultancy task, the expectations of the participants as agreed in the original contract and your personal preferences.

### The audience and access to the feedback

You and the organization need to decide who has access to any feedback from you – be it verbal or in a report. The decision about who has access is largely in

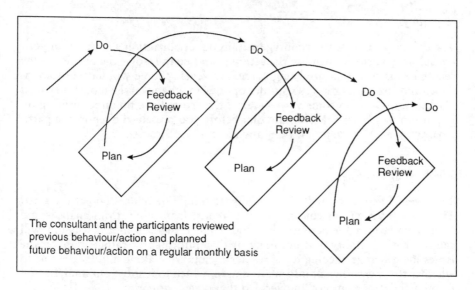

The consultant and the participants reviewed
previous behaviour/action and planned
future behaviour/action on a regular monthly basis

FIGURE 13.2 The do-review-plan cycle

the organization's hands and it may be something you agreed with them right
at the start of the contract. When making this decision the main groups of
people who have a stake in the outcomes of your work – the stakeholders – to
consider are:

- **Those who have the power to make decisions about the action recommended.** Unless these people directly receive your feedback, commitment
  to do something is less likely.
- **Those who are directly affected by the feedback and recommendations.** You
  may not *have* to involve others in your feedback but a decision not to do
  so gives big signals to them about the organization's approach to handling
  the problem. Trade union involvement may be important and you have
  the option of giving presentations to the various relevant groups and
  concluding in a final presentation that includes their reactions.
- **Those who have taken part in the consultancy.** Circulating a summary of the
  key points will demonstrate the organization's commitment to the process,
  its willingness to be open and its self-confidence about moving forward.

## 2. Content

*The problem and how you are dealing with it*

You will want to give feedback on all aspects of the problem – both the
technical aspects and how you are dealing with it. If you are giving a written
report, you might verbally feed back problems relating to how individuals are
behaving because of the damage that could be caused by putting this down on
paper and it being widely circulated. But this approach must not be used as a
means of avoiding dealing with the issue.

*Accuracy*

The debate you want to encourage within the organization as a result of your consultancy needs to focus on the action proposed to resolve the problem – the recommendations that are being made. However, people will have less confidence and less motivation to consider options for change if the report they read is factually wrong in some way – even if the errors have no direct bearing on the recommendations. Make sure that before you present the report the participants have a chance to put right any factual inaccuracies.

*The level of detail*

The level of detail you will give in a report should be understood at the start. The more information you include in a report (as distinct from analysis and recommendations for action), the more chance there is that discussion will centre on the validity and accuracy of that information rather than on the issues identified as needing to be resolved. You are making a judgement as to whether there is sufficient information upon which to justify your analysis and recommendations but not an overload that diverts attention.

## 3.   Expectations and surprises

*Expectations*

It is crucial that the type of feedback you will give is clear and agreed with the organization during your negotiation of the consultancy contract. If you give feedback in a form or way that the participants were not anticipating you could at best be disappointed with their reactions and at worst have a serious problem to deal with.

*Surprises*

You know you have failed in your task if you wait until the feedback meeting to worry about whether the participants will accept your diagnosis and recommendations. By that time in the process you should have a good idea of whether they share your analysis and where the differences in views between different participant lie. The meeting, and in particular a report, should be a confirmation of something you both know needs to be resolved and is realistic, practicable and clearly understood by all concerned. Failing that, you should know that they will disagree with your views and be ready for a meeting in which you will 'agree to differ'.

Whilst what you say may well be very challenging, you should not spring a big surprise on participants at a feedback meeting. The way that you conduct the interviews, group discussions and so on should indicate the direction of your thinking. As well as gathering views and exploring the issues, you will have been testing out reactions to different options and alternatives as to the problem, its causes and ways of resolving it.

## 4.  Feedback meetings

If the consultancy contract is structured to include a separate session for receiving feedback (as distinct from live feedback during a team-building session), then you should be clear about the style and structure you want for that meeting and be aware of how you and the participants might behave.

### Style

Different consultants have different approaches to giving feedback. You should make clear the extent to which you want the feedback meeting as a collaborative discussion in which participants can make suggestions and proposals of their own, prompted by what you have to say; or whether you expect it to be a them-and-us approach where you make a presentation and they decide what to do.

### Structure

Whilst the nature of the feedback you give will vary according to the consultancy task, the basic format and style of the feedback meeting can be planned in advance to make it as productive as possible. Your objective is for the participants to agree with and take ownership of the recommendations. The key is to ensure that the feedback you give focuses on a few main points and avoids going into too much detail.

A general format you might use for a feedback meeting, derived from the work of Peter Block (1981), might be as follows:

1. remind participants of your original task;
2. present your report, focussing on diagnosis and recommendations;
3. discussion of diagnosis and recommendations;
4. review of meeting;
5. decisions on action;
6. close.

In this format, the bulk of the time – 60% or even more – should be spent discussing your diagnosis and recommendations and deciding what to do. Your presentation should not take up more than 15–20% of the total time available.

Having a review of how the meeting is going half-way through is important because if it is not going in the way you or the participants want, there should be the opportunity to say so whilst there is time to do something about it.

The end of the feedback meeting is a chance to check that the participants have sufficient commitment to go ahead and to consider any future involvement you might have in the process.

### Behaviour

*The consultant's behaviour*  You may well be nervous at a feedback session because you are worried they will reject your findings and criticize you personally. If you are anxious, you may assume they are anxious. This nervousness might surface as undue defensiveness about your diagnosis and recommendations.

However, you should not be aggressive or submissive but be assertive. An assertive style means giving your views without putting the participants down or making yourself seem superior. You should not collude with them by avoiding difficult areas. You should present them with issues you know they will find hard to accept. And you should confirm where you believe things are going well.

*The participants' behaviour*   You should expect participants to be resistant to your findings. They have every right to disagree with your diagnosis and recommendations but that is not the same as behaving in ways that resist change or avoid taking action about the real problem. Something you can look out for is playing games in feedback meetings. Here are some of the favourites you might find participants doing:

- '*Beat the Consultant*'. Participants continually challenge, question or criticize you with the purpose of blocking progress. There will be times, of course, when your competence or style may need to be challenged, but this is only of value when the intent is to assist the process. It rarely is.
- '*Yes, but . . .*' They agree with what you have recommended but continually find reasons why it wouldn't work. Victory is achieved when you agree the problem is insoluble.
- '*We've Tried that Before*'. They dismiss suggestions or proposals for change by citing similar attempts from the past which failed – particularly useful if they have deliberately kept this experience from you during the diagnostic stage.
- '*Immediate and Complete Acceptance*'. They instantly agree with everything but their commitment is only skin deep. As soon as you leave the room they will find reasons why it was not such a good idea after all.
- '*When did you last Visit a Family Centre?*'. They find reasons why the suggestions are impractical and unworkable and ask whether you have even worked in a family centre (or youth club or whatever the problem is related to).
- '*Give Me more Detail*'. They keep asking for more and more detail about the information you have presented to avoid discussing the key issues and the recommendations.
- '*Not enough Detail*'. They condemn the findings as giving insufficient grounds on which to base a judgement but helpfully propose a delay whilst more data is collected. A tempting trap if you need the work.
- '*Is that Based on Likert's Linchpin Theory of Management?*'. They move the discussion from action to solve the problem into an intellectual debate about theory. They might even be able to put you down if you have never heard of Likert but know their current structure is falling apart.

*Your response*   Your feedback, their response and your response to them are key points in the whole process. It is the point at which the transfer of responsibility for action or work occurs from you, the consultant, to them. You should respond to questions about your diagnoses and recommendations in good faith. Twice. If the same question appears a third time you might suspect it is resistance. So as a rule of thumb give two straightforward replies to their questions about issues such as level of detail, practicality, validity of the data and so on. But thereafter begin to interpret their questions as a way of avoiding the issue or problem, or as hidden disagreement.

At this point you could name the resistance as it happens. Don't do this to expose people or score points but use it as a way of assisting them to realize what is happening and to put the focus back on to the problem. If they disagree with the analysis or the recommendations, then encourage them to say so clearly rather than play games to disguise their views. When giving feedback to groups, you should also try to respond to the concerns and anxieties of every individual. But you need to make a judgement about how much time and effort to invest in the one person or group who is continually resisting as compared to the many others who are taking ownership and want to move on.

## 5. Taking action

The action participants take as a result of a consultancy will depend on the task. They may take action on their own, having said goodbye to you after receiving your feedback and planning what to do. Or you may have negotiated a specific role for yourself in the action they are now ready to take. This can include ongoing consultancy support and progress reviews.

### Ongoing consultancy support

If they continue to use you in the implementation phase, your one key task is to offer support. They have decided what to do and you can support them in doing it. The way you can support them can vary from offering skills and knowledge about the issue, to offering skills and knowledge about the process of implementing change.

But there should be a shift (if it has not been happening from the start) from you offering them knowledge about the issue to using your skills to support them in developing their own knowledge and implementing change. If at support and review meetings they are relying on you to come up with the answers about what to do next, then the consultancy has failed. It has failed to help them develop the skills, knowledge and confidence to move forward on their own.

### Progress reviews

One common use of consultants during the action phase is to facilitate a review of progress. You will have a genuine interest in how they have got on and because of your previous involvement may be in a good position to help them in a review. You can arrange to meet with the participants after a number of weeks or months to review progress and to help them answer key questions such as:

- Did we do what we set out to do? If not, why not?
- Did we do things other than we agreed and planned? If so, why?
- Did our actions achieve the outcomes we intended?
- What other outcomes resulted from the changes we implemented?
- How well did we manage the process of change?
- What do others think about what happened – other staff, volunteers, users, committee members?

The valuable thing about inviting you, the orginal consultant, back to facilitate a review of progress is that your starting point is where you last saw them. They will have moved on. Things will have changed. What they are doing in six months' time will seem natural to them and as though it was never different. But you can remind them of where they were and what they planned to do then and assist them to track the path they have taken to where they are now. Figure 13.3 gives five examples of the ways that you can support organizations to take action.

---

### Group process facilitator

A consultant used his process skills to assist an organization arrive at a new five-year plan. He then met with an implementation group on a regular basis for the first 12 months to assist the participants develop their skills and confidence in implementing and amending the strategy, and to review progress.

### Skills trainer

A consultant used her conflict resolution skills to help staff decide what to do about improving the working climate in their organization. The consultant was then asked to provide the training identified as being needed among staff and committee members in communication and negotiation skills.

### Non-managerial supervisor

A consultant with specialist knowledge of management structures was used to draw up plans for a new structure with the organization. The consultant then met the director on a regular basis to continue to develop their knowledge and skills in implementing the new structure and to review how it was working in practice.

### Team development consultant

A consultant met a team for several sessions at regular intervals. At each session participants had the opportunity to share their views and insights, reflect on them, use activities to develop and extend their skills and learning and prepare for a further period of practical action that could be reviewed at the next session. In this approach a cycle of do–review–plan was used in which the participants and the consultant moved from diagnosis to implementation and back to diagnosis over several sessions.

### Progress reviewer

The consultant facilitated a one-day review meeting for an organization with whom she had worked before. The consultant began by reminding the participants of the agreements and action plans they made six months previously. She then drew a line on a large piece of paper representing the six months that had passed and asked people to annotate that line with statements of their feelings about events that had happened over that period. This subjective picture of events was then referred to in a systematic analysis of what had actually happened.

---

FIGURE 13.3 Ways that you can support organizations to take action

## Implementation dilemmas

Being involving in the implementation stage creates its own set of potential dilemmas of which you should be aware.

*Becoming a manager*  Involvement in implementation is the point at which you are most likely to find yourself being asked to make that all-important shift from consultant to manager. Don't do it. You will no longer be their consultant if you start to take responsibility for implementation.

*Letting go*  Consultancy is giving advice or assistance to improve a situation. One of your goals is to work yourself out of a job – to get them to a position where the situation is improved and they no longer need you. But you and the organization may resist ending the relationship you have developed. They get security from the support you provide and you enjoy the feeling of being needed and being paid. Consequently it is worth developing time-limited contracts. At the end of the period the contract can then be reviewed and a decision taken to end, amend or continue the contract for a further period.

*Deskilling the staff*  The presence of a consultant who brings specialist help or knowledge can imply that people in the organization do not have the resources or competence to solve the problem. The role you play is crucial to ensuring that they make use of your expertise without making them feel deskilled in the process. You should recognize the impact of your presence and use it to empower the people in the organization. You cannot pretend you don't exist or don't have an impact but you need to work in ways that reinforce and support participants in carrying through their plans and not take them over.

*Dealing with the unexpected*  You will get anxious if issues and problems emerge that you feel you are not equipped to handle or if you find yourself in very bitter situations. When you are confronted with a new or unexpected issue, you need to make judgements about whether to:

- go with that issue of concern and give whatever help you can;
- stop the work on that issue and stay within the boundaries established by the contract;
- re-negotiate the contract to take in the new issue;
- create a balance between working on the new issue and keeping to the contract;
- disclose to the group your own fear/being out of your depth, and trust the group to deal with it.

When choosing what to do you need to make a judgement about whether the unexpected issue is a diversion, or is so overwhelming it cannot be ignored, or whether the group will gain strength from your disclosure of anxiety. You can help the participants to help you by encouraging them to recognize the dilemma, to avoid using you as a scapegoat for the problem that has emerged, and to state how they are feeling and what they are experiencing.

## REFERENCE

Block, P. (1981) *Flawless consulting*. University Associates.

# CHAPTER 14

# *Using Success Criteria*

KATH ASPINWALL, TIM SIMKINS, JOHN F. WILKINSON
AND M. JOHN MCAULEY

*This material has been abridged*

[. . .] Terms such as success criteria, performance indicators and target setting have recently gained currency in the world of education. This kind of language is traditionally associated with the culture of commerce and industry, and is viewed with suspicion by many educationalists. Those who hold this view argue that this kind of langauge implies an emphasis on formal accountability, on a product-centred view of the task at hand, and a preoccupation with quantifiable findings, whereas educational organizations are dealing not with a product but with the complex process of educating and developing people which cannot be represented in such relatively simple ways.

There are many who view this apparent culture clash as irreconcilable. However, such a view often represents more a rejection of the language being used than a desire to be uncritical or unaccountable. Good professionals are invariably looking for evidence of success and indicators of their level of performance. In simple terms, they constantly pose the question 'How are we doing?' This question in turn implies a need for clarity about what we are trying to achieve and about how we shall know whether we have achieved it. This may lead to the design and use of fairly hard, quantitative 'performance indicators'; often, however, this will be inappropriate and softer approaches will be necessary. Whatever particular method is used, however, it needs to be based on a systematic approach. This chapter attempts to provide this. [. . .]

## DESIGNING AND USING SUCCESS CRITERIA AND INDICATORS

All evaluation is in some way comparative. Either explicitly or implicitly, information gathered through ongoing monitoring processes or from specific pieces of investigation will incorporate ideas about the standards or criteria against which performance should be judged and about the kinds of information which represent evidence of success or otherwise in achieving these standards. This is the world of performance indicators. These may be specified in a fairly 'soft' or subjective way, or they may be embodied in apparently 'harder' and more objective measures. Hopkins and Leask offer the following definition of a performance indicator:

> A performance indicator is a statement against which achievement in an area or activity can be assessed; they are also useful for setting goals and clarifying objectives. For some performance indicators, a brief statement is sufficient; for others the statement should be more specific and refer to supplementary processes which would give a measure of depth, quality and/ or commitment in a particular area. In our view there is a place for both quantitative and qualitative indicators.
>
> (Hopkins and Leask, 1989, pp. 6–7)

The development and use of success criteria and indicators is not necessarily a complex technical task, although there are many examples of performance measures in education which do require a good deal of specialist knowledge for their application and interpretation. [. . .]

However, if success criteria are to be of maximum benefit, they need to be developed and used in a systematic way which takes account of the pitfalls that can arise. A systematic approach can best be developed by working through a number of key questions in relation to a programme or activity.

## Question 1: What is it trying to achieve?

This is the central question, and will require considerable thought and discussion. It needs to be addressed within the context of the specific purposes for which the evaluation is being undertaken. So, for example, the criteria will be very different if the main concern is to monitor the implementation of a project over time than if it is to assess the impact of a change in teaching method on students' learning. [. . .] Two examples of approaches to the identification of performance areas are given in Figures 14.1 and 14.2. One is taken from the schools sector, and the other from further education.

---

1 *Academic progress*
   What proportion of pupils in the school have made above average levels of academic progress over the relevant time period?
2 *Pupil satisfaction*
   What proportion of pupils in the school are satisfied with the education they are receiving?
3 *Pupil–teacher relationships*
   What proportion of pupils in the school have good or 'vital' relationships with one or more teachers?

---

FIGURE 14.1 Sheffield University school success criteria. *Source:* Gray and Jesson (1990)

1 *The staff:student ratio* based on full-time equivalent (fte) student and academic staff numbers.
2 *Non-teacher cost* per enrolled student.
3 *Cost per fte student* enrolled on a course.
4 *Completion rates* for students enrolled on courses, and the cost per fte student completing a course.
5 *Rates of target qualifications* gained for students enrolled on a course, and the cost per qualified fte student.
6 *Rates of employment or progression* to further and higher education for students completing appropriate courses.

FIGURE 14.2 The Joint Efficiency Study's success criteria for further education. *Source*: DES (1987) The Joint Efficiency Study

It will be seen that the two approaches differ substantially in their emphasis. That proposed for schools explicitly identifies three performance areas and defines a focusing question for each one. In contrast, the Joint Efficiency Study moves straight to the specification of six performance areas: although these are based on two core performance areas, 'efficiency' and 'effectiveness'. The study defines efficiency as the relationship of inputs to outputs and effectiveness as the extent to which objectives are being achieved. Thus criteria 1 to 4 broadly relate to the area of efficiency and 5 to 6 to that of effectiveness.

There are other differences. The school criteria make no reference to resource utilization or cost whereas three of the further education (FE) criteria, with their concern for efficiency, do. In contrast, two of the school criteria are concerned with process whereas none of the FE criteria is. And, whereas the FE criteria are all relatively straightforward to define and easy to quantify, two of the school criteria are quite difficult to represent other than in a qualitative way.

These differences, though important, should not be allowed to detract from the main point, which is that any success criteria should be based on an analysis of what the key dimensions of achievement are. Only when this is done is it safe to proceed to a consideration of more specific indicators of success.

## Question 2: What would be appropriate indicators of success?

Having identified our area of concern, we need to identify one or more phenomena about which information can be gathered and which will help us to answer our chosen question: what would indicate success in this particular area? [. . .]

An example of how broad performance areas can be translated into more specific success indicators is the 'Quality of Learning and Teaching Profile' developed by the Scottish HMI in relation to further education (Scottish Education Department, 1990). This translates five areas – relevance, access, responsiveness, appropriateness and standards – into 17 'quality statements' (QS) (see Figure 14.3).

**Relevance**

QS1 There is a planned portfolio of programmes which is broadly consistent with the identified needs of clients.

QS2 The overall content of each individual programme is suited to its aims and purposes.

QS3 Programme content is accurate and up-to-date in its treatment of employment practice and new technology.

**Access**

QS4 Potential clients receive clear, accurate, and comprehensive information about programmes on offer and have the opportunity to clarify their goals in order that students enrol for a suitable programme.

QS5 The prior learning of students, whether certificated or experiential, is adequately taken into account.

QS6 Circumstantial restrictions on access, such as those arising from the timing and location of courses, are minimized.

**Responsiveness**

QS7 Innovative programmes or modifications to existing programmes for employers and community users are provided with a minimum of lead time.

QS8 There is liaison and collaboration with employers and community users in the delivery of programmes.

QS9 Students have access to sources of information, advice, and support which assist them to meet their learning needs, cope with difficulties and progress satisfactorily from a programme.

QS10 Programmes are negotiable and components are selected to meet individual needs.

QS11 Students are able to progress at their own pace.

QS12 Clients have the opportunity to evaluate provision.

**Appropriateness (of learning and teaching approaches)**

QS13 There is a climate of purposefulness and rapport, and a concern for individual student achievement.

QS14 The learning resources and environment are well planned and organized with regard to the accomplishment of learning outcomes.

QS15 Learning and teaching methods are appropriate to learning outcomes, emphasize student activity and responsibility, and are varied.

**Standards**

QS16 Assessment approaches cover all the learning outcomes and performance criteria and are applied to the work of all students.

QS17 The standards, as set out in descriptors, are correctly applied and systematically moderated.

Note: Terminology tends to vary among different kinds of educational provision. In reading these quality statements 'programme' should be deemed to include 'courses', and 'learning outcomes' to include 'outcomes' and 'learning objectives' and so on.

FIGURE 14.3 Quality of Learning and Teaching (QLT) Profile. *Source:* Scottish Education Department (1990)

It is important that a systematic framework is developed for thinking about performance, so that all major performance areas are defined and suitable indicators are developed for each. This might be done in a number of ways, depending on the programme or activity being considered. The QLT Profile is just one approach. Another classification which is often advocated is that of 'input', 'process' and 'outcome'. Each of these three dimensions focuses on a different aspect of provision. *Input* concerns the scale and appropriateness of the resources devoted to a programme. It includes such considerations as expenditure, costs and the appropriateness of teacher skills. *Process* is concerned primarily with the quality of interactions between, and experiences undergone by, those involved in the programme. It might include, for example, the degree of active learning undertaken by pupils or the range of teaching methods used on a course in further education. Finally, *outcome* concerns the results of the programme – learning achieved, entry to further education or work, and so on. In each of these areas it is possible to think of indicators of success which are both quantitative and qualitative. Each of these three areas can be developed in a variety of ways, depending on the objectives and priorities of the programme under consideration. Such an approach can be used at a variety of levels from the individual activity or programme to the whole institution. [. . .]

The definition of performance areas and the derivation of indicators for each can best be considered as an iterative process. The systematic identification of performance areas can provide a framework for deriving indicators appropriate to each (for example, using the QLT Profile or the input/process/output model); on the other hand, the generation of a large number of indicators can lead to the refinement of performance areas or the identification of new ones. [. . .]

## Question 3: How should data be gathered and processed?

There are usually many ways of gathering and processing data on a particular phenomenon. This may involve measuring things. Consider academic achievement, for example. One possible measure of this is examination performance, perhaps in GCSE, or test results. Is it sufficient to measure the number of passes, or passes at a particular level, or should different weightings be applied to different grades of pass? If the latter, what should the weightings be? As a measure of efficiency of staff utilization, too, the SSR can be measured in a variety of ways: for example, at different times in the year, or by weighting part-time students in particular ways. Where such choices exist, different measures are likely to show different patterns of performance.

To choose a suitable way of gathering and processing data we may need to refine our criteria of success. For example, is 'success' enabling a high proportion of less able students to obtain passes at GCSE, or is it maximizing the number of students who obtain passes at grades A and B? The former would best be assessed by a simple measure of total passes; the latter would need the results to be weighted heavily in favour of the higher grades. A department which performs well on one criterion may not do so on the other, and vice versa.

Statistics of examination results, of staff deployment or of anything else, are not the only kind of data which might be collected as indicators of success, however. In its work on the Quality of Learning and Teaching Profile, HMI suggest 10 evaluation instruments (EIs) which combine a variety of interviews, questionnaires and recording schedules (Scottish Education Department, 1990, p. 20). These are:

EI 1  User Survey (postal questionnaire)
EI 2A  Student Survey: guidance (questionnaire)
EI 2B  Student Survey: learning and teaching (questionnaire)
EI 2C  Student Survey (interview)
EI 3A  Staff Survey: guidance (questionnaire)
EI 3B  Staff Survey: learning, teaching and assessment (questionnaire)
EI 4  Programme Analysis (recording schedule for analysis of documentation and interview findings by a team of evaluators)
EI 5  Module Analysis (recording schedule for analysis of 'extended' modules and findings from discussion by evaluators)
EI 6  Analysis of Student Work (recording schedule for analysis of assessed student work by evaluators)
EI 7  Analysis of Teaching (recording schedule for analysis of findings arising from observation of learning and teaching in classrooms, workshop, etc. by evaluators)

These evaluation instruments are then related to the 17 quality statements as shown in Figure 14.4. Evidence from instruments such as these is just as valid as more traditional statistics – indeed it may be more so for particular purposes. Data from such sources will still need to be aggregated in a suitable way, however, to produce usable information. [. . .]

## Question 4: With what can the results validly be compared?

However well the success criteria have been designed and however well the data have been gathered and processed, information about performance in relation to a particular development at a given point in time is of little value on its own in answering the question 'How are we doing?' It has to be placed in comparative perspective. The statements 'We're doing OK' or 'We could do better' implies the existence of some standard against which performance is being judged.

It is common to use three main types of standard for making judgements about achievements:

- *Comparative:* How are we doing in comparison with similar developments elsewhere?
- *Progress:* How are we doing compared with how we have done previously?
- *Target:* How are we doing compared with a specific standard or target(s) which we have set ourselves, or which others have set for us?

Each of these approaches has its attractions. Comparison with similar programmes elsewhere ensures an outward-looking approach to evaluation and guards against parochialism. An emphasis on our own progress demonstrates the importance of development and potentially can be extremely motivating. The development and utilization of specific targets encourages the development of clear links between plans and performance assessment. Perhaps the best advice is to use a combination of all three approaches in an attempt to get the best of all worlds.

| Quality Statement (abbreviated) | Evaluation Instrument | | | | | | | | | |
|---|---|---|---|---|---|---|---|---|---|---|
| | 1 | 2A | 2B | 2C | 3A | 3B | 4 | 5 | 6 | 7 |
| **Relevance** | | | | | | | | | | |
| QS1 Relevant portfolio of programmes | ✓ | | ✓ | | | | ✓ | | | |
| QS2 Appropriate programme content | ✓ | | ✓ | ✓ | | ✓ | ✓ | ✓ | ✓ | ✓ |
| QS3 Accurate, up-to-date content | ✓ | | ✓ | | | ✓ | | ✓ | ✓ | ✓ |
| **Access** | | | | | | | | | | |
| QS4 Appropriate pre-entry guidance | ✓ | ✓ | | | ✓ | | | | | |
| QS5 Recognition of prior learning | | | | ✓ | ✓ | | ✓ | | | |
| QS6 Circumstantial restriction on access minimized | ✓ | | ✓ | ✓ | ✓ | | ✓ | | | |
| **Responsiveness** | | | | | | | | | | |
| QS7 Innovative programmes provided quickly | ✓ | | | | | | ✓ | | | |
| QS8 Collaboration with employers in programme delivery | ✓ | | ✓ | ✓ | | | ✓ | | | |
| QS9 Appropriate continuing guidance | | ✓ | | | ✓ | | | | | |
| QS10 Programme re-negotiation | | ✓ | | | ✓ | | ✓ | | | |
| QS11 Self-spaced learning | | ✓ | | | ✓ | | | ✓ | | |
| QS12 Evaluation by clients | | ✓ | | | ✓ | | ✓ | ✓ | | |
| **Appropriateness of learning and teaching methods** | | | | | | | | | | |
| QS13 Purposefulness and rapport; concern for individual achievement | | | ✓ | ✓ | | ✓ | | ✓ | | ✓ |
| QS14 Appropriate learning environment and resources | | | ✓ | ✓ | | ✓ | | ✓ | | ✓ |
| QS15 Appropriate learning and teaching methods | | | ✓ | ✓ | | ✓ | | ✓ | | ✓ |
| **Standards** | | | | | | | | | | |
| QS16 Comprehensive assessment approaches | | | | | | ✓ | | ✓ | ✓ | |
| QS17 Correct application of standards; moderation | | | | | | ✓ | ✓ | ✓ | ✓ | |

FIGURE 14.4 The quality statements addressed by each evaluation instrument.
*Source:* Scottish Education Department (1990)

## Question 5: What other information is necessary to put the results into context?

The availability of information which can be used for comparative purposes, while essential, may not be sufficient to enable appropriate conclusions to be drawn from evaluation data, however. The question still remains: 'Is the comparison valid?' or 'Is like being compared with like?' There may be many reasons why a comparison with similar developments elsewhere may not be valid. Differences in examination performance, for example, often reflect differences in student ability rather than teaching quality; or perhaps a relatively low SSR reflects the need to teach a higher than average proportion of students with special needs in small groups. Our own progress over time may have been affected by staff shortages or a changing student profile. And the targets we have set, or been set, may have been based on quite unrealistic expectations deriving from experience in very different circumstances.

It is essential that performance assessment takes account of such qualifications. It is important too, however, that they are used in a sensible way. Too often in education it is argued that our achievements cannot be assessed because our situation is unique. Interestingly, uniqueness is more often claimed to excuse apparently poor performance than to explain good! Where there are concerns about comparability, a number of strategies are possible:

- Use statistical techniques to attempt to take account of the sources of difference. For example, it may be possible to take account of differences in student ability in comparing examination results.
- Seek other comparators. For example, look for schools, colleges or departments whose characteristics most closely resemble your own. Or alternatively, move to a self-determined progress or target model rather than an externally imposed comparative one.
- Seek a wider variety of information which captures different aspects of achievement.

The discussion and development of these kinds of approaches not only increase the likelihood of drawing valid conclusions; they also enhance in a more general sense our understanding of the problem of assessing 'success'.

## Question 6: What conclusions can legitimately be drawn?

We can now begin to put the elements of the development and use of success indicators together. These elements are:

- identification of *performance areas*, with one or more focusing questions for each;
- identification of a number of *success criteria* for each area;
- determination of the *kinds of data* which need to be collected and analysed to present evidence in relation to the chosen criteria;
- determination of the basis on which the level of performance is to be judged (the basis for *comparison*);
- consideration of any *particular circumstances* which may need to be taken into account in interpreting performance.

|  | Example A<br>*(Primary school)* | Example B<br>*(Further education)* |
|---|---|---|
| Performance area | Pupil-centred learning | Efficiency of staff utilization |
| Success criterion | Pupil–pupil co-operation | Staff:student ratio |
| Data collection | 1 Observation schedule<br>2 Teacher interview | Annual Monitoring Survey data |
| Comparator(s) | Progress over time | 1 DES target<br>2 Other similar colleges |
| Contextual factors | Class sizes have increased | The college's work is biased towards staff-intensive subjects |

FIGURE 14.5 Developing and using success criteria

Figure 14.5 shows the process of analysis for two very different areas of concern.

[. . .]

Once the analysis gets to this point, conclusions should be emerging. However, at this stage it is worth reviewing the process which has been undertaken so far:

- Have the correct areas of performance been identified?
- Have criteria been identified which adequately represent these areas?
- Have data been gathered and processed in appropriate ways to assess achievement against these criteria?
- Have comparisons been made with the right things?
- Has account been taken of particular circumstances that may limit the validity of comparisons?

It may be helpful to draw up in relation to each of these questions a list of the strengths and weaknesses of the process through which success criteria have been defined and in relation to which evidence has been gathered. While doing this, it is desirable to consider how far the information which has been obtained meets a number of basic quality tests:

- Is it *relevant* to the focusing question or questions? It is too easy to collect information on the basis of convenience or cost rather than in relation to clearly defined questions. There is also a danger of collecting far more information than is necessary to form judgements about the performance area in question. It is essential, therefore, that the most rigorous standards of relevance be applied. With resources scarce, it is not acceptable to collect information because it appears 'interesting'.
- Is it an *adequate* response to these questions, in the sense that it reflects the full range or complexity of the issue or does it present a limited view? We have already pointed out the danger of omitting important performance areas from the analysis. This is particularly likely to occur if only one stakeholder is involved in the discussion. For example, teachers may give quite a low priority to assessing the efficiency of a programme in which

they are involved; conversely, administrators may not always be too concerned about educational quality provided the resource sums look right.

- Is it *valid*, in the sense that it adequately represents what it is supposed to represent? Perhaps the biggest, and most common, criticism of the performance indicators approach to collecting evidence for evaluative purposes is that quantifiable measures tend to drive out the less quantifiable dimensions of performance, and that the essence of educational quality cannot be captured by such measures either at all (the extreme position) or alone. One problem here is that quantified and standardized measures are much easier to treat comparatively, and external comparison is an important dimension of accountability in education.
- Is it *reliable*? Would similar conclusions be drawn if the information was obtained by somebody else or by some other method? This is a tricky area. Again, quantitative indicators are often more reliable than more qualitative ones, although as the previous paragraph suggests, their reliability may be bought at the expense of their validity. Where reliability is a problem, there is advantage in using more than one kind or source of data in relation to a particular criterion: [this is known as] 'triangulation'. [. . .].

## Question 7: What action follows?

[There are] four ways in which information might be managed. Briefly, these [are] using information *symbolically*, or as a *scorecard*, or in an *attention-directing* way, or for *problem-solving*. Information arising from monitoring and evaluation processes, including that relating to success criteria, can serve any of these four purposes. It is often tempting to concentrate on collecting and providing symbolic and scorecard information, especially where this is sufficient to ensure a quiet life! However, such an approach is not consistent with the kinds of values outlined earlier. It will do little to encourage and facilitate processes of development and even the accountability function will be quite restricted. Performance information, if it is to be of value, must be attention-directing and it must be supplemented by processes which ensure a problem-solving approach to the identified areas of concern. Such a philosophy, however, is not a cosy one. It challenges and it may threaten. It is essential, therefore, to consider carefully the behavioural implications of information management.

## INFORMATION AND BEHAVIOUR

A key characteristic of the mangement of information is that it affects behaviour. Often its effects are intended – when, for example, a teaching approach is changed in response to negative feedback by students. Frequently, though, the methods used to collect or disseminate information have behavioural consequences which not only are unexpected but are the exact opposite of what was hoped for. It is essential, therefore, that those responsible for developing and using success indicators concern themselves not merely with the *technical* adequacy of their information – in terms of its relevance, validity, reliability and so on – but also with the *behavioural* appropriateness of the methods they are using to manage the evaluation process. Questions of perception, expectation and motivation are just as important as those of research design.

Individuals view information management processes, including monitoring and evaluation, in terms of their impact on themselves and their work. They attempt to interpret the purposes of those who are managing the process and they also attempt to envisage the likely consequences of these processes for their position in the organization. They may accept the 'official' view about these things. Or they may develop their own alternative understandings on the basis of their previous experiences or their perceptions of how the process of monitoring and evaluation is proceeding. For those managing evaluation, therefore, it is important that the 'style' adopted is consistent with the philosophy espoused. Often this is not the case, and then a number of possible behavioural consequences follow. This can be illustrated by the kinds of responses which may arise in relation to success indicators whose design or use have been ill-judged (Lawler and Rhode, 1976, Ch. 6). Some responses are legitimate, although they are not in the best interests of the organization and were not intended by those designing the evaluation process. For example:

- Individuals may respond in a *rigidly bureaucratic* way, changing their behaviour uncritically in response to the type of performance implied by the indicator. The often-cited fear of 'teaching to the test' is a good example of this.
- They may adopt *strategic behaviour* designed to make them look good in terms of the indicator. This may involve spending up at the end of the financial year on anything which is available, when 'spending to budget' is an indicator of success and funds cannot be carried over. Or it may mean limiting examination entries to the most able students to ensure a good pass rate.

Other responses are normally considered to be illegitimate, but may still be engaged in by those who feel their interests are threatened:

- *Reporting invalid data* which puts the performance of an individual or group in a good light. An example of this might be the marking of absent students as present on class registers when attendance is used as an indicator of success.
- Attempting to *subvert* the whole information-gathering process by ridiculing it, overloading it and so on.

Such responses arise because information is often used in situations where conflicts of interest exist and people are consious of the potential impact of information on key decisions. These concerns can be addressed in part by ensuring that indicators cannot easily be manipulated in these ways – the design issue. But this is not always possible, especially where, as is often the case in education, the factor which is being assessed is complex. Furthermore, there is always the danger of a vicious cycle setting in, with 'unacceptable' responses giving rise to tighter restrictions, which led in turn to new methods of getting round the system being invented. Most of these examples relate to the use of success indicators for accountability purposes alone. Where the developmental dimension dominates, the dangers are fewer, but still they cannot be ignored. People may have differing views about what comprises desirable development. In these circumstances it is necessary to think about the behavioural as well as the technical dimension of information management.

# MANAGING SUCCESS INDICATORS

If success indicators are to be used effectively, a number of issues need to be considered carefully before the process of designing them begins.

## 1. Keep them simple and clear

Success indicators can be developed at a number of levels and in a variety of ways. At the level of the organization, it is possible to develop very long lists, such as the list of school performance indicators promulgated by the DES (DES, 1989) or the indicators developed by the Department of Employment for evaluating TVEI (Department of Employment, 1991). The general consensus, however, is that such lists are of limited use except as stimuli to creative thinking. The aim should be to develop a relatively small number of indicators which capture the key dimensions of success for the programme or activity which is being monitored or evaluated.

The argument for simplicity, however, should not be used as an excuse for unjustifiable reductionism. For example, unadjusted examination scores do not 'speak for themselves'; and examination success will rarely be acceptable as the only dimension of performance which needs to be measured. The point being made here is about obtaining a realistic focus, not an inappropriate oversimplification.

## 2. Set them after discussion

The best success indicators are those which have been developed by or in partnership with those who work in the are where performance is to be assessed, or who have an interest in the area. Such a process ensures that the indicators have credibility and authority, and this in turn reduces the likelihood that the undesirable consequences outlined above will occur. Success indicators developed in this way will:

- be built upon the educational objectives of the programme which is to be assessed, although they may also take account of externally determined requirements;
- take account of local circumstances, although they will also take account of good practice in comparable circumstances elsewhere to ensure that expectations are not set unrealistically low (or high!).

Put another way, success criteria should take full account of what a programme is trying to do and the circumstances in which it is being done, but they should also put performance in the broader context of the expectations of others and the experience of what is being achieved elsewhere. Those running a programme are key stakeholders, but they are rarely the only ones.

## 3. Ensure openness

It is important that all those stakeholders who have a legitimate involvement have a shared understanding about the kinds of information that is being gathered and the purposes for which it will be used. This is not always the case. There is a need to be clear about:

- what criteria are to be used;
- why they were chosen;
- what information is to be collected in relation to them;
- how the outcomes of the process will be used.

Information about these things should be communicated in ways appropriate to the particular audience. This is not always easy, especially if the indicators involve a good deal of technical calculation or analysis. It should always be possible, however, with sufficient thought.

## 4. Use the indicators for developmental purposes

The driving force for the development of success indicators is commonly that of accountability. Those who manage us, or from whom we obtain resources, commonly set the pace or call the tune when indicators are being designed. Even when we take the initiative, it is because we wish to pre-empt the issue before others set the agenda for us. It is highly desirable, however, that indicators are viewed from a developmental perspective whoever takes the initiative and whatever the prime motivation for their development. The intelligent use and interpretation of information about performance can be a powerful influence for change and development.

It is important, therefore that the use of success indicators is seen as an integral part of the monitoring and evaluation *process*, not simply as a parallel activity which is necessary to meet external requirements.

## 5. Keep them under review

Success indicators may be used for monitoring and/or as part of a review or in-depth investigation. In either case, but particularly for monitoring, it will probably be appropriate to use the same indicators for a period of time, perhaps for a number of years. This has advantages. Not least, a consistent time series of information enables progress to be charted in a helpful way. On the other hand, there is always the danger that the same information will continue to be routinely gathered, despite the fact that objectives have been modified or external factors have changed so as to render any comparison of performance meaningless. It is important, therefore, that the success indicators being used are reviewed regularly.

[. . .]

## CONCLUSION

[. . .] Some [readers of this chapter] will have been reinforced in their concerns about the dangers of adopting approaches to evaluation in education which are too hard-nosed and which embody dangers of serious misuse. As Mrs Angela Rumbold, Minister of State, said in introducing the DES's list of performance indicators for schools in 1989:

> Those of us advocating the use of performance indicators in education must always attach a 'Government Health Warning'. Considered in isolation they are open to misinterpretation and misuse and can damage the health of a school.

(DES, 1989)

We share these concerns. The view that all indicators should carry a 'health warning' is a valid one, and we have tried to indicate in this chapter the kinds of issues that such a warning might address. However, it is also our view that in a world where legitimate pressures for accountability in education are increasing, it is important that educators are as clear as possible about what they are trying to achieve and the ways in which they wish to demonstrate success. Such clarity is not just valuable in rendering an account, however; it can also provide the basis for gathering information which can really contribute to successful development.

# REFERENCES

DES (Department of Education and Science) (1987) *Managing colleges efficiently.* London: HMSO.

DES (Department of Education and Science) (1989) Performance Indicators: an aide-memoire from the DES, *Education*, 8 December, pp. 514–15.

Department of Employment (1991) *Guidance on TVEI performance indicators.* London: HMSO.

Gray, J. and Jesson, J. (1990) The negotiation and construction of performance indicators: some principles, proposals and problems, *Evaluation and Research in Education*, Vol. 4, no. 2, pp. 93–108.

Hopkins, D. and Leask, M. (1989) Performance indicators and school development, *School Organisation*, Vol. 9, no. 1, pp. 3–20.

Lawler, E. E. and Rhode, J. G. (1976) *Information and control in organisations.* Pacific Palisades, CA: Goodyear.

Scottish Education Department (1990) *Measuring up: performance indicators in further education.* London: HMSO.

# CHAPTER 15

# Literature Searching: Finding, Organizing and Recording Information

## SALLY BAKER AND JOAN CARTY

## INTRODUCTION

Beginning the task of finding published information and other resources for a project can appear daunting if you are not sure where to start. You may wonder how you can find out what has been written on your subject, and how to obtain and record the information so that it is easily accessible when you need it. Our aim is to help you to find the most direct route through the information maze so that you do not have to expend more time and effort than is necessary. We will be telling you about:

- the most useful *secondary* sources – bibliographies, indexes and abstracts – which you can use to track down references to the *primary* sources – the books, journal articles and so on which contain the actual information you need to use;
- the libraries in which you may be able to consult and obtain these primary and secondary sources;
- how to record for later use the details of the books and articles in your research area.

Thus, when you have read this article you will know how to adopt a systematic approach to literature searching, which types of library may be available to you and how to keep track of the information you have found.

You will need to use libraries for the kind of literature search described below. However, Brindley (1992) dispensed with this type of search altogether: 'I decided instead to start from my own fairly random collection of photocopies of articles and untidy piles of read and "waiting to be read" reports in my study at home.' Similarly, you may prefer to make use of the resources which are readily available to you, such as books and journals which you, your colleagues, your school, your teachers' centre or local adviser may have. You may already have been provided with some help in the form of reading lists from your tutor or supervisor, in which case you may still need to use a library to either consult or obtain what has been recommended.

## LIBRARIES

You may be fortunate enough to have several libraries available to you in your area. Everybody has the right to use the public library service where they live and work, and in addition most academic, and local institutes' or schools' of education libraries can usually be used for reference purposes.

Your literature search will progress through various stages, and spending a little time familiarizing yourself with the library layout will make it easier to find:

- the bibliographies which you need to use at the start of your search;
- the library catalogue where you check whether the specific books and journal titles which you have noted down from the bibliographies are held by the library;
- any relevant books and journals which you have found that the library holds;
- where you make inter-library loan requests for books and journals not held by the library.

Some of the books and journals you wish to consult may not be available for you to borrow. If this is the case, remember that you will normally be able to photocopy, though at a cost, journal articles and sections of books, within the limits of copyright law of course. In some library catalogues – such as OPACs (On-line Public Access Catalogues), for example – you can check the holdings of other libraries convenient for you to use. This can be helpful if your library has not got the items you are looking for, either because they have not been purchased or because they are out on loan.

### Academic libraries

Although these institutions primarily exist to serve the needs of their own staff and students, most provide a limited service to non-members. In some cases this will extend only to the consultation of library stock, in others, borrowing a few items may be permitted free of charge or, as is more likely, after payment of a fee. External borrowers are occasionally permitted to make inter-library loan requests, although the institutions which offer this facility often charge a high price per item. Some schools and institutes of education operate policies which are especially liberal towards teachers. However, as academic libraries' rules concerning external users vary tremendously, it is worth contacting any institution relevant to your needs, or convenient for you to use, to explain your circumstances and requirements.

Most academic libraries have a wider range of secondary sources, or bibliographies, than public libraries, and staff will be able to tell you whether you have to consult these in hard copy or on microfiche, or whether some or all are available on CD-ROM (Compact Disc – Read Only Memory). In some libraries, you will have to book or queue to use the CD-ROMs, and some may not allow you access to them, unless you have registered as an external user and paid a fee. Similarly, you may be able to request an on-line search, though charges for this are often more than the actual cost of the search itself, to cover the staff time involved.

## Public libraries

These range from mobile or small, part-time branch libraries to very large central libraries, where CD-ROM and on-line searching may be available. As the collections in all but the fairly large libraries will of necessity be general, you will probably have to visit a central library to be able to find the books and journals you need, as well as the bibliographies used to trace them. However, you will be able to place inter-library loan requests at any public library irrespective of size. A fee will be charged for this service. Inter-library loans often take some time to arrive, and, for this reason, it is a good idea to make your request well in advance if you can and to let the staff know if you need something urgently. Some libraries offer a fast route service, but the cost of this, per item, may be quite high. As the arrangement of the stock varies from library to library, and indeed some bibliographies frequently used by librarians may not be on open access, you may like to ask at the enquiry desk for some help and advice before you start.

## LITERATURE SEARCHING

The techniques of searching are the same whether you are carrying out large- or small-scale projects, but the more advanced the research, the more exhaustive the literature search will need to be. The sources which we suggest below are only a selection of the wide range of bibliographies, indexes and abstracts available for tracing the titles of books and journal articles, but they are likely to be the most easily accessible and useful for a small-scale project. We are concentrating on the retrieval of information about books and journal articles as these are usually the most productive primary sources. However, there are other bibliographies which can be used for tracking down specific types of materials, such as dissertations, government publications, newspaper articles, or audiovisual media and so on. If you feel that information from these additional types of material might be useful, then you can consult some of the bibliographies listed in *'Finding other information sources'* (p. 228). When time is limited, an approach to a few carefully chosen sources will probably produce more than enough references, especially as, once traced, all the material selected as potentially useful has to be read.

You will find that any one bibliography may be available in one or several formats, such as hard copy, microfiche, CD-ROM, or on-line. *PsycLIT*, for example, is the CD-ROM version of *Psychological Abstracts* which is in hard copy, whilse *PsycINFO* is the on-line name. In the sections dealing with finding books, journal articles and other sources of information, we have given you the hard copy or microfiche titles of bibliographical works, but many of them are also available as CD-ROMs or on-line databases. You can ask at the library enquiry desk for advice on what is available, and in what format, when you are ready to begin your search.

## Planning the search

When carrying out a literature search, the aim is to identify all those items which deal specifically with your topic and to exclude irrelevant material. This may seem perfectly obvious and simple to apply in theory, but, in practice, it is very easy to become sidetracked and waste a lot of time following up items of marginal interest. In order to maintain your focus and to ensure that you retrieve relevant references, you will find it helpful to break your topic down into its component parts or sets. Taking as an example the topic 'fair selection of staff', Figure 15.1 shows diagrammatically that the relevant references occur at the intersection of the three sets.

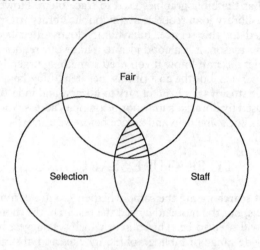

FIGURE 15.1 Fair selection of staff

In reality, searching solely under the three terms in the model will make the focus too narrow and thereby restrict the number of references retrieved. By analysing each concept group, or set, you can compile a much broader list of synonyms and related terms for use in your search. These will more accurately reflect the depth of your topic. As it can be difficult to think up terms, a thesaurus will help you to find additional words. Two specialized publications are *British Education Thesaurus* and *Thesaurus of ERIC Descriptors* (ERIC is the Educational Resources Information Center based in America) where you will find terms (broader, narrower and related) listed systematically in appropriate categories. If you also use your own subject knowledge, you should be able to build up an extensive list of keywords to search under. Example 1 shows terms which may be relevant within each of the component sets of the topic.

---

**Example 1**

TOPIC TITLE: *Fair Selection of Staff*

1. 'Fair' includes a number of issues concerned with equality such as gender, age, religious beliefs, race, disability, sexual orientation, and personal prejudices.
2. 'Selection' could include interviews, personnel selection, recruitment, appointment, job applications.
3. 'Staff' could include teachers, headteachers, deputy heads, support staff, ancillary staff.

---

You may not be interested in all these aspects of this topic. However, having ranged widely, you can then focus down on your particular sphere of interest with greater confidence that you have a reasonably comprehensive list of search terms. If you are using bibliographies in hard copy or microfiche, you will need to look up each of the subject terms which you have decided is significant to your project, and choose from among the references you find those which you think are relevant. You can then note down the details of these for later use (see RECORDING INFORMATION, p. 233). If you are carrying out a computer search, which is discussed again at the end of this section, you will be able to type in groups of related concepts and print out the results.

## Finding books

You can find out what books are held by your library by using the library catalogue. This can range from a traditional card catalogue, through microfiche to an OPAC. Whichever type you use, you will be able to adopt a subject approach to finding relevant books held by the library. However, the catalogue can only lead you to the books which that particular library has in stock, whereas bibliographies will list what has been published, or is in print, irrespective of any one library's actual holdings. We are, therefore, going to suggest some general bibliographical sources which should be available for consultation in most types of library, to enable you to find book titles on your subject. As you come across relevant references you can note them down so that you can check, via the library catalogue, whether the library holds them.

### Bibliographies

*British National Bibliography* (BNB) includes material published in the UK, mainly books and some government publications. Use the index to find references by author, title or subject.

*American Book Publishing Record* (ABPR) covers American book production, and is arranged by subject, author and title.

If the above are not available to you, *Whitaker's Books in Print* can be used in a very general way. Its indexing is mainly by author and title, but there is limited subject access by title keyword.

In the next section we talk about the use of indexes and abstracts for finding journal articles. Some indexes and abstracts, however, also cover books. It is worth bearing this in mind when you are doing your subject search.

## Finding journal articles

Because of their frequency of publication, journals tend to contain more up-to-date information than books, and a search for articles is essential if you are not to miss important material that is often not published in books. Looking through individual issues of relevant journal titles is a time-consuming way to find out what journal articles have been published on your research topic. Although you will be able to check which journals are held in stock by looking at the catalogue or a holdings list, or asking the staff, a more systematic way of retrieving a greater range of articles is to consult indexes and abstracts.

*Indexes and abstracts*

These publications enable you to trace articles within journals, although there is usually a delay of a few months between an article being published and its appearance in a secondary source. Indexes list the bibliographical details of articles by subject, and abstracts additionally summarize the article content. Abstracts are particularly useful because in many cases they will help you to decide whether you need to see the article or not. Coming to such decisions is not easy, but it is one way to avoid creating a massive list of references.

After the first three publications below, which are more general in scope, we list a selection of subject-specific abstracts which, according to your project topic, you may find useful. All are international in coverage, but, where necessary, we give the country of origin in brackets after the title to show the main emphasis.

- *British Education Index* provides an index, by author and subject, to mainly British periodicals.
- *British Humanities Index* lists by subject articles from newspapers and journals. Until the end of 1992, *BHI* was merely an index, but from 1993 abstracts have also been provided.
- *Current Index to Journals in Education (CIJE)*, despite being called an 'index', also provides abstracts to the journal articles it lists. As an American publication, its emphasis is on the USA but titles from other countries, including the UK, are covered.
- Subject-specific abstracts: *Educational Administration* (US); *Educational Technology Abstracts* (UK); *Exceptional Child Education Resources* (US); *Language Teaching* (UK); *Multicultural Education Abstracts* (UK); *Psychological Abstracts* (US); *Research into Higher Education Abstracts* (UK); *School Organisation and Management Abstracts* (UK); *Sociology of Education Abstracts* (UK); *Special Educational Needs Abstracts* (UK); *Technical Education & Training Abstracts* (UK).

## Finding other information sources

You may not wish to restrict your range of resources to books and journals only, and for this reason we are going to provide a brief guide to some of the bibliographies which will help you trace other forms of material. As the list is not exhaustive, you could ask at your library for additional titles if you wish to investigate something in more depth, or consult a written guide to bibliographical sources in education such as Smeaton (1993).

*Government publications*

Most libraries will have some government publications, but, as tracking down those of interest to you can sometimes prove quite difficult, it is worth seeking help at the enquiry desk if you do not find what you are looking for. The two bibliographies which, in combination, will cover the majority of official publications are *HMSO Annual Catalogue* and *Catalogue of British Official Publications Not Published by HMSO*.

## Newspapers

Newspapers can be a good source of both current and historical information. We have already mentioned *British Education Index* which includes coverage of *The Times Educational Supplement* and *The Times Higher Education Supplement*, and *British Humanities Index* which selectively covers articles from the 'quality' press such as the *Financial Times, The Guardian, The Independent*, the *Observer, The Sunday Times* and *The Times*. Comprehensive coverage to their own newspapers is provided in *The Times Index* and *The Guardian Index*.

## Audiovisual media

Many libraries have collections of videotapes. These may be for viewing on the premises only, or also available for loan. *British National Film and Video Catalogue* provides details of both fiction and non-fiction films and videos available in Britain for loan or purchase. It includes educational and training films, documentaries, feature films and television programmes. Entries tell you from which distributor the film or video can be obtained, and give a summary of content and intended audience.

## Research and dissertations

Perhaps you will not have enough time or even need to investigate what research has already been done on your topic. Dissertations can be difficult to obtain because you will either have to order them through the inter-library loan system, or read them in the library in which they have been deposited. However, finding a fully referenced dissertation specifically covering your field can save you a great deal of time and effort. For this reason, we are including a few bibliographies which list research being carried out or completed: *British Education Theses Index; Dissertation Abstracts* (US); *Index to Theses with Abstracts Accepted for Higher Degrees by the Universities of Great Britain and Ireland and the Council for National Academic Awards* (commonly known as ASLIB Index to Theses); *Register of Educational Research in the United Kingdom*.

# Computer searching: CD-ROM and on-line

Although computer literature searching via a remote database host (i.e. on-line) has existed for a long time, it has been the arrival of the CD-ROM which has made this type of searching more accessible. On-line searching usually incurs a cost, according to the databases used, the amount of on-line time, and the number of references retrieved, but services are now becoming available, such as BIDS (Bath Information and Data Services) and OCLC FirstSearch, where a global fee is paid in advance, by the institution, for unlimited access. Thus, like CD-ROMs, which are also paid for in advance, they are often free at the point of use, though sometimes a charge is imposed.

If you have access to CD-ROMs in your library, you will probably find that you are expected to do the search yourself. This is generally quite straightforward as CD-ROMs have become increasingly user-friendly through the use of menu-driven systems. At each stage of your search you will be prompted by the computer to carry out an appropriate action either by selecting from a list of options or by entering a piece of information such as a keyword. The list of terms you prepared when planning your search can be utilized here.

If you are able to access CD-ROMs, some of those which are likely to be most useful to you are listed below:

- *Bowker-Whitaker Global Books in Print Plus* combines the records of books drawn from every country where English-language publishing exists.
- *BHI PLUS* (for coverage of *British Humanities Index*, see above).
- *British Newspaper Index* covers a selection of the 'quality' press as well as *The Times Higher Education Supplement* and *The Times Educational Supplement*.
- *ERIC* includes both *CIJE* (see above), and *Resources in Education* which lists documents other than journal articles, such as conference proceedings and reports related to the field of education.
- *International ERIC* has extensive educational coverage as it includes *Australian Education Index, British Education Index, British Education Theses Index, Canadian Education Index*.
- *PsycLIT* provides access to international journal articles in psychology and related behavioural social sciences.

Similarly, if you have access to BIDS and OCLC FirstSearch, you will be able to search:

- *Social Sciences Citation Index* (BIDS);
- *Education Index* (OCLC);
- *ERIC* (OCLC).

Example 2 is a literature search drawn from a small selection of secondary sources with a few examples of what was found in particular years.

---

**Example 2**

With the ending of indefinite exclusion of pupils in September 1994, the impetus was provided to rethink school discipline policy and the underlying causes of the disaffection which leads to exclusion. A possible project topic might examine measures to prevent the need for exclusion, by suggesting new ways of anticipating or dealing with discipline problems.

**Preparing a list of search terms**

In *British Education Thesaurus*, 'exclusion' was used to define suspension for non-disciplinary reasons, whereas the *Thesaurus of ERIC Descriptors* omitted 'exclusion' altogether but included 'suspension'. In the end, a list of terms was compiled using the 'related' and 'broader' terms headings under each word in both thesauri, and a few more were added from *Roget's Thesaurus*. The search terms divided into two groups:

1. DISCIPLINE POLICY; SCHOOL EXCLUSION; SUSPENSION.
2. AGGRESSION; ALIENATION; BEHAVIOUR PROBLEMS;
   BULLYING; DISAFFECTION; DISCIPLINE PROBLEMS;
   DISRUPTIVE BEHAVIOUR; LEARNING DIFFICULTIES.

The list increased as more bibliographies were consulted and additional headings were found. Some rechecking was necessary of previously checked sources in order to ensure that all relevant headings were searched. It is a good idea to impose an initial limit on the number of years searched, say to the last five years. This can always be extended if insufficient references occur, or narrowed if the amount of material found is too great. Starting with the most recent issues and working backwards will quite often be self-limiting.

### Searching for books

The list of terms checked in Volume 2 (indexes) of *British National Bibliography* 1992. Below are examples of the entries under 'Schools':

| | |
|---|---|
| Schools. Discipline | 371.5 |
| Schools. Discipline | 371.50942 |
| Schools. Disruptive students | 371.93 |

The numerals refer to the class numbers under which the book details are arranged in Volume 1 (subject catalogue) of *British National Bibliography*. Two of these entries are shown below:

#### 371.5

**Lawson, Bridget**. Pupil discipline and exclusions in
schools / Bridget Lawson. - Harlow : Longman,
1991. - 63p ; 22cm. - (Longman - AGIT school
governor training series)
Includes bibliography
ISBN 0-582-08384-2 (pbk) : £7.95

#### 371.50942

**Discipline** in schools : psychological perspectives in the
Elton report / edited by Kevin Wheldall. - London :
Routledge, 1992. - xiii,103p ; 23cm
Includes index
ISBN 0-415-06245-4 : no price

### Searching for journal articles

Below are examples of articles referenced in *British Education Index* 1993 (hard copy), including the subject keyword under which they were found:

### Behaviour Problems

A circular response to the Elton Report: a social context for improving behaviour / Jenny Mosley *Education Section Review*, Vol. 15, no. 2: 91 p68-74.

### Bullying

Students themselves tackle the problem of bullying / Helen Cowie and Sonia Sharp *Pastoral Care in Education*, Vol. 10, no. 4: Dec 92 p31-37.

### Discipline Policy

The exclusion of pupils: is it the most appropriate way of dealing with indiscipline? / David Sassoon *Education and the Law*, Vol. 4, no. 2: 92 p55-59.

The CD-ROM version of *ERIC* (Dialog on Disc) was searched to give an international perspective on the problem and its solution. Using the easy menu search option, the following results, shown step-by-step, were obtained:

1. 505 Records with Word/Phrase Index of DISRUPTIVE
2. 281 Records remaining, Limiting to those with Word/Phrase Index of PUPILS or STUDENTS
3. 616 Records total, also Including those with Word/Phrase Index of BULLYING or DISAFFECTION or "DISCIPLINE PROBLEMS"
4. 136 Records remaining, Limiting to those with Word/Phrase Index of "DISCIPLINE POLICY" or SUSPENSION
5. 37 Records remaining, Limiting to those with Year of Publication of 1990 or 1991 or 1992 or 1993 or 1994.

An example of one of the 37 records is given below:

12 of 37 Complete Record
EJ425739  EC600386
An Examination of the System-Wide Use of Exclusion with Disruptive Students.
Bain, Alan; MacPherson, Anita
Australia and New Zealand Journal of Developmental Disabilities, v16 n2 p109-23 1990
ISSN: 0726-3864
Available from: UMI
Language: English
Document Type: JOURNAL ARTICLE (080); POSITION PAPER (120)
Journal Announcement: CIJSEP91
The paper presents the view that many Australian students excluded from school for disruptive behavior may require special services on the basis of a disabling condition. Descriptive data for 124 students (ages 10-17) and a case study are presented to support this position, along with discussion of legal and service delivery implications associated with exclusion. (Author / DB)
Descriptors: *Behavior Disorders; Case Studies; Delivery Systems; *Disabilities; Discipline; Elementary Secondary Education; Expulsion; Foreign Countries; Handicap Identification; Legal Responsibility; *Suspension
Identifiers: *Australia

### Searching other information sources

As the Elton Report was mentioned in examples from both *British National Bibliography* and *British Education Index*, it might prove a valuable source of additional information. The *HMSO Annual Catalogue* was therefore checked year by year for the full reference which was found in the 1989 edition:

**Committee of Enquiry into Discipline in Schools**
**Discipline in schools:** Report of the Committee of Enquiry chaired by Lord Elton. - The Lord Elton (chairman). - 292p.: 30 cm. - 0 11 270665 7 £10.00

Finally, *the Times* and *the Sunday Times* (CD-ROM edition) for 1993 were searched, as newspapers often provide a general perspective from outside the mainstream of educational literature. Using the keywords 'school' and 'exclusion' produced several references, one of which was entitled *Schools to be 'fined' £2000 for every pupil they expel* (24 April 1993). This provides some statistical information on exclusions as well as reviewing the factors which may shape future policy.

## RECORDING INFORMATION

As your literature search progresses it will become increasingly difficult to remember what you have searched and what you have found. It is advisable to try to establish a system, early on, of recording the details you will need later for making references or citations, and also for jogging your memory about the content and usefulness of what you have read. It is tempting, when under pressure to write your project, to leave this until the end because it does not seem a priority. But, if you do make the effort from the start, then recording accurately the bibliographical detail of materials you have found will ultimately save you a lot of time. For example, if you wish to order items on inter-library loan, you will already have all the necessary detail to hand. Similarly, as you write your project, it will be easier to prepare your references to the works you have cited in your text. Finally, it is important to keep a record of all the items you have looked at, whether useful or not, to avoid wasting time obtaining again an item with a fruitful-sounding title which, on inspection, you had previously rejected.

### Creating your records

You can keep your records in any format which suits you – in notebooks or on computer, for example – but a separate card for each item provides a flexible and portable option. There is a general consensus about the individual pieces of information which should be included in your record, as shown in the following examples.

---

**Example 3:** *book record*
HITCHCOCK, G. and HUGHES, D. (1989) *Research and the Teacher: a qualitative introduction to school-based research*, London, Routledge.
Source of reference: *British National Bibliography* 1989.
Annotation: Very useful for school-based action research; covers a variety of methods; whole chapter on interaction in schools and classrooms; NB remember to check through extensive bibliography for extra references.

---

**Example 4:** *journal article*
SASSOON, D. (1994) 'Out of school, out of mind?', *Education: the voice of education management,* Vol. 183, no. 9, p. 170.
Source of reference: *British Education Index,* 1994
Annotation: Suggests six reasons for the steep rise in pupil exclusions; brief discussion of a project to provide a constructive alternative educational programme which includes counselling and individual learning support.

---

You can vary the format and the content of the annotation according to your own preference, but it will be to your advantage to be consistent.

## Citations, references and bibliographies

Above, we mentioned using your records to prepare your references. You will come across the terms *citation, references* and *bibliography* in the course of your research, and perhaps it would be useful to give a general definition here. *Bibliography* has a number of meanings, and up to now we have used it to describe publications that contain details of books or other materials on a particular subject, or from a particular country. The secondary sources we have referred to in other sections are bibliographies of this kind. The term can also mean a list of sources used in the preparation of an essay, thesis, book, article, and so on.

A citation occurs in your text to identify the source of a paraphrase or direct quote from the work of another author. It alerts the reader to the fact that another author's work has been used and that full identification of the source can be found in another place, that is, in the list of references. Thus, references give details of books or articles you have cited in your text, while a bibliography is a list of works you have consulted for your project but have not necessarily cited.

There are several different referencing styles, of which we will give a brief outline of the two most commonly used. Both include the same pieces of information, but differ in the manner in which the citation is made in the text, and the order of the pieces of information within the reference. The first, which is the less complicated to use, is known as the Harvard system. The citation is given by inserting the author and the date of publication, in parentheses, in the text, e.g. (Hanson, 1992). To differentiate between works published by the same author in the same year, a letter is added to the date, e.g. (Hammersley, 1992c). Page numbers are given when you are making a specific, rather than a general, citation. The complete set of references is given in alphabetical order by author at the end of your text.

The second system indicates that a reference has been made by marking the place in the text with a numeral, either superscript or in parentheses, which refers the reader to a note containing the reference, and sometimes comments or other information. The notes occur in numerical order, and if a work is cited more than once, the reference can either be repeated or the number of the earlier reference cited again.

When a citation has been made within your text, the order in which the elements of the accompanying reference – author, title of book or article, date, journal title, volume and part numbers, pages and so on – are given, and how they are punctuated, differs between the two systems. Fuller descriptions, with examples, are set out in British Standards Institution (1989) and a brief guide in British Standards Institution (1990).

## Bibliography formatting software packages

There are several software packages available, such as *Pro Cite, Reference Manager, EndNote Plus, Papyrus* and *Bib/SEARCH*, which will assist you in setting out your references in accordance with either one of several predetermined formats or your own format (Hanson, 1992, p. 46). The '. . . software manages details such as choosing which elements of the citation to include, placing the elements in the correct order, placing the proper punctuation between the elements, placing punctuation within elements, and handling formats of authors' names' (Stigleman, 1992). The features available within some 40-plus bibliography formatting software packages are listed by Stigleman. This type of software may be available for use in some libraries.

## CONCLUSION

The importance of carrying out a literature search will perhaps only become apparent after it is completed and the resulting information has been incorporated into your project. Finding precisely what you want is not an easy task, but to discover a reference closely centred on the precise nature of your own inquiry can be the most valuable find in any independent investigation. However, if at the end of your literature search you have not made such a discovery, nevertheless the very process of investigating the literature will have given you a broad overview of the current situation and made you better informed about your field of research.

## REFERENCES

Brindley, L. (1992) Information and innovation, *British Journal of Academic Librarianship*, Vol. 7, no. 3, pp. 163–75.

British Standards Institution (rev. edn 1989) *Recommendations for references to published material: BS 1629*. Milton Keynes: BSI.

British Standards Institution (2nd edn 1990) *Recommendations for citing and referencing published material: BS 5605*. Milton Keynes: BSI.

Hanson, T. (1992) Libraries, universities and bibliographic software, *British Journal of Academic Librarianship*, Vol. 7, no. 1, pp. 45–54.

Smeaton, R. F. (1993) *Researching education: reference tools and networks*. Librarians of Institutes and Schools of Education.

Stigleman, S. (1992) Bibliography formatting software: a buying guide, *Database*, Vol. 15, no. 1, pp. 15–27.

# CHAPTER 16

# Analysing Documents and Records

## COLIN ROBSON

*This material has been abridged*

## USING DOCUMENTS

Although the use of physical trace measures has never achieved much more than curiosity value in the social sciences, there has been particular interest in the use of a particular kind of artefact: the *document*. By this is meant, primarily, the written document, whether this be a book, newspaper or magazine, notice, letter or whatever, although the term is sometimes extended to include non-written documents such as films and television programmes, pictures, drawings and photographs.

This *documentary analysis* is commonly referred to as CONTENT ANALYSIS. It [. . .] is *indirect rather than direct*. Instead of directly observing, or interviewing, or asking someone to fill in a questionnaire for the purposes of our enquiry, we are dealing with something produced for some other purpose.

This is an example of an *unobtrusive measure* [. . .], that is, the nature of the document is not affected by the fact that you are using it for the enquiry. Another way of saying the same thing is to refer to it as *non-reactive*. There are exceptions. You may be asking respondents to fill in diaries or some other account for your project, and these may well be amenable to content analysis. In this case it is not an unobtrusive technique. The fact that a person is filling in a diary for the project may in some way alter their behaviour; in other words, there is a possible reactive effect.

Content analysis has been defined in various ways. Krippendorff's (1980) definition, that 'content analysis is a research technique for making replicable and valid inferences from data to their context' (p. 21), while perhaps over-inclusive in not making clear that we are dealing with certain kinds of data (those coming from documents of various kinds), does have the virtue of stressing the relationship between content and context. This context includes the *purpose* of the document as well as institutional, social and cultural aspects. It also emphasizes that reliability and validity are central concerns in content analysis.

It is possible to do other things with documents over and above analysing their contents. Such approaches, for example focusing on the authenticity of the document, or the intentions of the writer, are derived from the methods of historians. They are essentially concerned with the problems of selection and evaluation of evidence (see Barzun and Graff, 1977; Marwick, 1970). [. . .]

The checklist of criteria suggested by Gottschalk *et al.* (1945), in relation to the use of personal documents in history, anthropology and sociology, covers important concerns relevant to the accuracy of all documents:

(1) Was the ultimate source of the detail (the primary witness) *able* to tell the truth?
(2) Was the primary witness *willing* to tell the truth?
(3) Is the primary witness *accurately reported* with regard to the detail under examination?
(4) Is there any *external corroboration* of the detail under examination? (p. 35)

Content analysis is in several senses akin to structured observation. This similarity is particularly evident when structured observation is carried out on a recording of the situation observed. A video-recording of such a session appears to be a very similar kind of artefact to, say, a video-recording of a television programme. The main difference is that in the former case the intention is to obtain a closely equivalent picture to that which the 'live' observer would have seen in the situation. Selectivity of focus and direction will be made with the needs of the observer in mind. The edited picture making up the TV programme appears under the direction of the programme maker who has her own agenda, which is unlikely to include the needs of the content analyst.

This illustrates a general problem in content analysis. The material to be analysed is not only unstructured, or at least not structured with the needs of the observer in mind; it will in general be a document with a purpose. And that purpose is important in understanding and interpreting the results of the analysis. A distinction is sometimes made in documentary analysis between *witting* and *unwitting* evidence. Witting evidence is that which the author intended to impart. Unwitting evidence is everything else that can be gleaned from the document.

## Uses of content analysis

Content analysis came to prominence in the social sciences at the start of the twentieth century, in a series of quantitative analyses of newspapers, primarily in the United States. In a debate prefiguring current concerns in this country about the tabloid press, campaigns against 'cheap yellow journalism' were bolstered by statistical studies showing how 'worthwhile' news items were being increasingly dropped in favour of gossip, sports and scandals (Krippendorff, 1980, pp. 13–15 provides details). This type of content analysis was subsequently extended to radio, and then to television, and continues unabated in, for example, studies of advertising, and of pornography and violence in the media.

Similar studies have attempted to assess bias in school textbooks, and the depiction of favourable or unfavourable attitudes to blacks, females and homosexuals both in texts and other publications. While the main interest has probably continued to be in the field of mass communications, content analysis has more recently been used in a wide variety of psychological and sociological areas. In particular, the approach discussed here can be readily adapted for use in the analysis of qualitative interview and questionnaire data (e.g. in the coding of open-ended questions in surveys) and of direct observation (typically through coding of tapes and transcripts).

Documents themselves cover a very wide range, including for example:

- minutes of meetings;
- letters, memoranda, etc.;
- diaries;
- speeches;
- newspapers and magazine articles.

Particular contexts generate specific types of document. Studies involving schools or other educational establishments might include:

- written curricula;
- course outlines and other course documents;
- timetables;
- notices;
- letters and other communications to parents.

Remember also that 'document' is taken to include such non-written forms as:

- films;
- television programmes;
- comic strips and cartoons;
- photographs.

These require somewhat different approaches to analysis from those discussed below, although the basic principles remain the same (see Fetterman, 1989; and Walker and Adelman, 1975, specifically on using photographs).

The main focus here is on the use of content analysis as a secondary or supplementary method in a multi-method study. This does not preclude carrying out a study based solely on content analysis, but there are substantial difficulties and deficiencies (see Box 1 below on 'Advantages and disadvantages of content analysis'). On the other hand, it is often possible to 'acquire' copies of documents of a variety of types in conjunction with interviews and observations which may be used for triangulation purposes, or to provide something of a longitudinal dimension to a study when a sequence of documents is available extending back in time.

## How to carry out a content analysis

[. . .] Content analysis is 'codified common sense': a refinement of ways that might be used by lay persons to describe and explain aspects of the world about them.

### 1. Start with a research question

Once again, the effective starting point for the process is the research question. Perhaps 'Is there a greater emphasis on sex and violence in the mass media now than there was 10 years ago?' A different research question might derive from the comment, commonly heard in listeners' responses to radio programmes, that there is political bias in radio programmes. For example, the BBC Radio 4 *Today* programme seems particularly adept at generating near apoplexy in right-wing listeners. Note here that, while the communication here is initially 'on the air', in practice any study of the programme's content will be likely to be based on a transcript of what is heard. It may be, however, that an audio-tape will also be helpful, enabling you to judge from intonation whether a particular comment is to be taken in a sarcastic or ironic sense.

There may be occasions when you have documents but no properly formulated notion of what you are looking for. In many methodology texts, this so-called 'fishing trip' is severely frowned on, e.g. for example: 'content analysis cannot be used to probe around a mass of documents in the hope that a bright idea will be suggested by probing. Content analysis gets the answers to the question to which it is applied' (Carney, 1973, p. 284). However, in the general spirit of 'exploratory data analysis' which is advocated in this text (Tukey, 1977; Marsh, 1988), this prohibition on 'fishing' appears unnecessarily limiting. Obviously, the choice of data is justified by what you want to know: but to suggest that there is a difference in value between the research of one enquirer who starts out with the question, and that of another who gets the idea for the question from peeking at the data, verges on the metaphysical. Either we have good evidence about the question from the data, or we haven't.

## 2. Decide on a sampling strategy

It is usually necessary to reduce your task to manageable dimensions by *sampling* from the population of interest. [. . .] Thus, in the case of the *Today* programme, it might be considered appropriate to take a random sample of, say, 20 programmes from those transmitted over a three-month period. Or, possibly, some form of stratification might be considered – perhaps ensuring that all presenters of the programme are equally represented in the sample. A different approach would be to have as one's sample all the programmes transmitted over an extended period, but to focus, from the point of view of the analysis, on a small part of the content, say, on references to a particular incident or type of incident.

There may be situations where the relevant documents are so rare or difficult to get hold of that sampling in this sense is inappropriate.

## 3. Define the recording unit

In addition to deciding on categories, it is necessary to select a *recording unit*. The unit most commonly used is probably the *individual word*. In the simplest version, all occurrences of the word would be treated as equal, and counts of them made and compared. A somewhat more sophisticated approach would differentiate between the different sense of words that have multiple meanings (e.g. 'right' as 'correct'; or as 'non-left') and code phrases constituting a semantic unit (e.g. 'ice cream' or 'Houses of Parliament'). It is also common to use *themes, characters* (i.e. the actors or individuals mentioned in the document [. . .]), *paragraphs* or *whole items* as the recording unit.

Other possibilities suggest themselves for particular tasks. For example, when analysing newspaper or magazine content these might be:

- number of stories on a topic;
- column inches;
- size of headline;
- number of stories on a page;
- position of stories within the page or paper as a whole;
- number and/or type of pictures;

and so on. For some purposes, it may be necessary to examine the *context* in which a recording unit is set in order to categorize it. Although you may have fixed on the word as recording unit, if you are interested in coding whether a treatment is positive or negative, favourable or unfavourable, it is likely that you will have to take into account the sentence in which the word appears.

There is some argument in content analysis circles about the degree of inference which coders should 'be called upon to make when categorizing items. This is sometimes expressed in terms of *manifest* and *latent* content, corresponding essentially to low- and high-inference items respectively. Manifest items are those which are physically present (e.g. a particular word); latent content is a matter of inference or interpretation on the part of the coder. At its simplest this may just require a judgement of warmth, favourableness etc., but some might require use of a complex personality typology. As with other techniques of data collection, it is obviously likely to be more straightforward to achieve reliable results with low-inference systems. However, the research question should determine type of system you are using, and it may well be that a high-inference system is appropriate. This then puts greater stress on ensuring that you can demonstrate reliability through the use of independent coders, or by some other means such as triangulating with data obtained through other sources.

## 4. Construct categories for analysis

It is difficult to give helpful general comments here, as there is such a wide range of possible types of research question for which content analysis might be used. Holsti (1969) lists several types of categories. Thus, in looking at what is said in the document, categories might be concerned with:

- *subject matter*   what is it about?
- *direction*   how is it treated, e.g. favourably or not?
- *values*   what values are revealed?
- *goals*   what goals or intentions are revealed?
- *methods*   what methods are used to achieve these intentions?
- *traits*   what are the characteristics used in describing people?
- *actors*   who is represented as carrying out the actions referred to?
- *authority*   in whose name are statements made?
- *location*   where does the action take place?
- *conflict?*   what are the sources and levels of conflict?
- *endings*   in what way are conflicts resolved (e.g. happily)?

[. . .] It is highly desirable that these categories are *exhaustive* and *mutually exclusive*. The former ensures that everything relevant to the study can be categorized (even if you have to resort to a 'dump' category for things that you don't know how to deal with). The latter means that anything to be analysed can only be categorized in one way; if it is categorized in one particular way it can't also be categorized as something else.

The categories also have to be *operationalized*: that is, an explicit specification has to be made of what indicators one is looking for when making each and any of the categorizations. *Sorting Out The Categories is the Most Crucial Aspect of The Content Analysis.* As Berelson (1952) points out, 'since the categories contain the substance of the investigation, a content analysis can be no better than its system of categories'. [. . .]

### 5. Test the coding on samples of text and assess reliability

This is the best test of the clarity and lack of ambiguity of your category definitions. It is highly likely that this process will lead to the revision of your scheme. With human (as against computer) coding, at least two persons should be involved at this stage. When the scheme appears workable, tests of reliability should be made [. . .]. If the reliability is low, further practice is necessary and it may also be necessary to revise the coding rules. The process should be repeated until the reliability is acceptable. If computer coding has been used, it is necessary to check for errors in computer procedures.

### 6. Carry out the analysis

In formal terms, the analysis is equivalent to the set of activities you carry out when using and analysing a structured observation schedule. The statistical analysis of the data obtained can follow exploratory data analysis procedures or more conventional hypothesis testing approaches. The most common approach is to relate variables from the content analysis to other 'outside' variables (e.g. gender of the persons producing the documents; or type of school from which they come). More complex procedures involve the use of factor analysis, as either an exploratory or a confirmatory tool, to identify themes in texts; and the subsequent use of techniques such as analysis of variance to outside variables.

Box 1 lists advantages and disadvantages of content analysis.

## Computers and content analysis

Content analysis can be extremely laborious and time-consuming. It is a field where computerization has led to substantial benefits. Analyses which would have been beyond the resources of small-scale research can now be completed routinely given access to a reasonably powerful microcomputer and specialized software. The text can be easily manipulated and displayed in various ways (e.g. showing all sentences, or other units, containing a particular word or phrase). The availability of optical character recognition (OCR) devices can transform a document directly into a computer file without the necessity for typing.

A major methodological advantage of computer-aided content analysis is that the rules for coding the text have to be made completely explicit, or the

BOX 1

---

*Advantages and disadvantages of content analysis*

*Advantages*

(a) It is an 'unobtrusive' measure (Webb *et al.*, 1966). You can 'observe' without being observed.
(b) The data are in permanent form and hence can be subject to re-analysis, allowing reliability checks and replication studies.
(c) It may provide a 'low cost' form of longitudinal analysis when a 'run' or series of documents of a particular type is available.

*Disadvantages*

(a) The documents available may be limited or partial.
(b) The documents have been written for some purpose other than for the research, and it is difficult or impossible to allow for the biases or distortions that this introduces (note need for triangulation with other accounts, data sources to address this problem).
(c) As with other non-experimental approaches, it is very difficult to assess causal relationships. Are the documents causes of the social phenomena you are interested in, or reflections of them [. . .]?

---

computer will not be able to carry out the task. Once these rules have been established and written into the software (itself no mean task) then it is possible to work through a range of documents and achieve results which are formally compatible with each other. At the same time, once the development stage has been completed, and any 'bugs' removed from the system, the computer provides perfect coder reliability in applying the rules built in to the program.

This does not mean that all problems have been solved. Little matters of validity, interpretation and explanation remain. You also still face the inescapable fact that content analysis is concerned with *data reduction*. You throw away much of the information in a document to see the wood for the trees. Weber (1985) provides a good review of ways in which the computer can help in carrying out content analysis and these related ground clearing tasks.
[. . .]

## USING DATA ARCHIVES

An archive is simply a record, or set of records. Some records are in the form of documents containing text, as covered in the preceding section. Others may contain quantitative statistical information. Such archives share an important feature with the documents just discussed in that they have been produced for some other purpose than for your use as a researcher. They will have been collected and paid for by someone else (though there is also the possibility of revisiting a study you carried out previously, with a view to carrying out a different or extended analysis). The 10-yearly National Census is an archetypal example, but there are many recurrent and one-off surveys (e.g. the Current Population Survey, General Household Survey, British Social Attitude Survey, American General Social Survey, British Workplace Industrial Relations Survey, British Crime Survey, and others; Hakim, 1987, Ch. 7, provides details).

[. . .]

It is, of course, perfectly possible to focus one's research solely on the *secondary analysis* of such data. This is defined by Hakim (1982) as 'any further analysis of an existing data set which presents interpretations, conclusions or knowledge additional to, or different from those presented in the first report' (p. 1). This can be an attractive strategy as it permits you to capitalize on the efforts of others in collecting the data. It has the advantage of allowing you to concentrate on analysis and interpretation. Baker (1988, pp. 254–60) discusses the issues involved and presents examples.

Archival research is not limited to the re-analysis of survey data. Bryman (1989, Ch. 7) gives varied examples from the field of organization studies. A frequently quoted study is by Grusky (1963) who analysed the performance of sports teams in relation to turnover of personnel such as team coaches and managers. Later studies have followed related themes – in part, one suspects, because sports performance is an area where there is a surfeit of published statistical information.

## Using administrative records and management information systems

Many small-scale real life studies involve in some way relating to an organization, such as an office, school or hospital. A feature they all have in common is the collection of records and other information relating to their function. Such records can form a valuable supplementary resource, and it is often possible to obtain access to them. (The usual ethical principles apply in relation to confidentiality, and there may be particular problems associated with information collected for one purpose being used for a different one.)

The records are, however, unlikely to provide direct answers to the questions we are interested in when carrying out research. Indeed, they may form a tempting distraction, with pages of descriptive statistics on individual measures, and cross-tabulations between measures, amassed to little or no purpose. Simply to know that there are 73% of males on an innovatory programme, or that 23% of the males and 48% of the females are from low-income families, carries little meaning in its own right. The issue is, *what light can this information throw on our research questions?* We may be interested in answering questions on recently introduced crèche facilities, or different access arrangements, and this kind of routine data may in such circumstances be of direct value. Nevertheless, a thorough exploratory study of existing data may suggest questions, or act as a starting point for unforeseen lines of enquiry. It is well worth while spending a fair amount of time looking at and playing with data from record systems. Patterns may suggest themselves and trends emerge which had not previously occurred to you.

Typically it will be necessary to rearrange the data in various ways, so that, for example, you can compare data over different time periods. Your research questions assist in selecting from what can easily be a data mountain. If, as is increasingly the case, these routine systems have been computerized, your task *may* be simplified. It is, for example, usually relatively easy to provide suitably anonymized extracts from computer records. Previously it would have been necessary to go through filing cabinets and record cards to obtain the information you need. This has the possibility of introducing transcription errors, and may also require that the researchers have access to confidential or private records. Access to computer records should be subject to strict controls and any necessary clearances must be obtained. Remember, however, that there is no guarantee at all that the computer system designed to cope with routine data collection has the flexibility to deliver the comparisons or selections that you need.

Hakim (1987, Ch. 4) discusses the design of studies based exclusively on administrative records. She makes the point that they have to be designed 'back to front'. That is, instead of designing the study and then, collecting the data, the researcher starts by finding out what data are available in the set of records and then identifies a possible research model. The situation is rather

## BOX 2

*Issues in using administrative records for research purposes*

(1) *The quality of the data must be assessed.* Generally, information central to the activities of an organization will be of better quality than more peripheral items. Check on what actually happens (e.g. are large batches of forms filled in cursorily long after the event?). Find the views of the persons entering the data. If they think that 'the yellow form always goes into the dustbin' (actual quotation from a social worker) then they are unlikely to fill them in conscientiously.

(2) *Careful study of existing record systems may allow you to avoid unnecessary duplication in data collection.* Informants in studies are often busy people and it is highly desirable to minimize the extra load you put on them for the purposes of research. Even though an existing question may not be asking for exactly what you had in mind, it may provide you with a close enough approximation of the information you need. It is sometimes feasible to add temporary 'research' questions to standard administration forms.

(3) *Sampling from administrative records may well be needed.* A variety of approaches may be possible (e.g. time samples, sampling of individuals, sampling of items).

*Note:* As administrative records often give information on a rigidly defined set of topics over considerable periods of time, they lend themselves to some form of time series analysis.

BOX 3

---

*Example of the use of administrative records in an evaluation*
(*Source*: Robson *et al.*, 1988.)

The evaluation focused on the effects and effectiveness of a widely used training package on the use of behavioural techniques in the education of persons with severe learning difficulties (the EDY package; see Foxen and McBrien, 1981).

A main aspect of the evaluation involved a substantial postal survey of persons who had completed the course, and their instructors. The second main aspect involved a series of case studies of the use of the package in a range of different settings.

The instructors of persons who had successfully completed the course had been, since its inception, invited to send in a request form to the sponsoring institution. Providing their performance reached certain criteria they were then sent an official certificate. The request form incorporated useful information which was analysed as part of the evaluation. This included biographical and career information which established the representativeness of this sample in relation to the survey sample.

There were also indices of the trainees' performance at an early stage and on completion of the course. It was appreciated that the 'demand characteristics' of this situation on the instructors might lead to an under-reporting of the latter. Nevertheless, useful corroborative information was gained. For example, early high scores, in connection with some skills covered in the course, supported evidence from the case studies and assisted in framing recommendations for the revision of the course.

---

different in a multi-method case study. If administrative records are available, they are examined to see what additional corroboration or other light they can throw on the case. If they don't help with your research questions, then either don't use the administrative records, or consider whether it makes sense to modify what you are after in the light of what they can tell you.

Box 2 lists some issues to be taken into account when using administrative records from management information systems; Box 3 gives an example of their use.

[. . .]

# REFERENCES

Baker, T. L. (1988) *Doing social research*. New York: McGraw-Hill.
Barzun, J. and Graff, H. F. (1977) *The modern researcher*. New York: Harcourt Brace Jovanovich.
Berelson, B. (1952) *Content analysis in communications research*. New York: Free Press.

Bryman, A. (1989) *Research methods and organisation studies.* London: Unwin Hyman.

Carney, T. F. (1973) *Content analysis.* Winnipeg: University of Manitoba Press.

Fetterman, D. M. (1989) *Ethnography step by step.* Newbury Park and London: Sage.

Foxen, T. and McBrien, J. (1981) *The EDY course for mental handicap practitioners.* Manchester: Manchester University Press.

Gottschalk, L., Kluckhohn, C. and Angell, R. (1945) *The use of personal documents in history, anthropology and sociology.* New York: Social Science Research Council.

Grusky, O. (1963) Managerial succession and organisational effectiveness. *American Journal of Sociology,* Vol. 69, pp. 21–31.

Hakim, C. (1982) *Secondary analysis in social research: a guide to data sources and methods with examples.* London: Allen & Unwin.

Hakim, C. (1987) *Research design: strategies and choices in the design of social research.* London: Allen & Unwin.

Holsti, O. R. (1969) *Content analysis for the social sciences and humanities.* Reading, Mass.: Addison-Wesley.

Krippendorff, K. (1980) *Content analysis: an introduction to its methodology.* Newbury Park and London: Sage.

Marsh, C. (1988) *Exploring data: an introduction to data analysis for social scientists.* Cambridge: Polity.

Marwick, A. (1970) *An Introduction to history.* Oxford: Oxford University Press.

Robson, C. Sebba, J., Mittler, P. and Davies, G. (1988) *Inservice training and special educational needs: running short school-focused courses.* Manchester: Manchester University Press.

Tukey, J. W. (1977) *Exploratory data analysis.* Reading, Mass.: Addison-Wesley.

Walker, R. and Adelman, C. (1975) *A guide to classroom observation.* London: Methuen.

Webb, E. J., Campbell, D. T., Schwartz, R. L. and Sechrest, L. (1966) *Unobtrusive measures: nonreactive research in the social sciences.* Chicago: Rand McNally.

Weber, R. P. (1985) *Basic content analysis.* Newbury Park and London: Sage.

# CHAPTER 17

# Designing and Using Questionnaires

## M. B. YOUNGMAN

## 1. THE IMPORTANCE OF PLANNING

Popular conceptions of survey research often see the use of questionnaires as a mechanistic exercise requiring minimal thought, especially if compared with qualitative approaches, for example. But the effective use of questionnaires demands a clear understanding of the overall research context. This is seen most starkly in the extent to which the ultimate analytical interpretations exhibit confusion or lucidity, scepticism or conviction. Certainly to compile and distribute a large number of questionnaires may seem, and indeed sometimes be, a straightforward clerical exercise requiring very little research skill. Unfortunately, this simplicity is too often exaggerated, to the extent of assuming that analytical considerations are irrelevant until the pile of returns grows. Such an approach will almost inevitably result in the introduction of difficult, and even insurmountable, problems for the analysis. The solution lies in accepting that the initial and concluding stages of a survey are not independent; the questionnaire structure must include all the facilities deemed to be necessary for successful analysis. So the treatment of various types of non-response (questions refused, pages missed, or even whole questionnaires not returned) should be considered from both the coding and analysis standpoints. Similarly the role of open-ended questions should be decided in advance; failure to do so may result in the loss of essential factual information. Probably the simplest safeguard is to plan the questionnaire coding, before distribution, to take into account as many of the analyses as can be anticipated. Inevitably some will depend upon the outcome of preliminary tests, but the majority of analytical requirements can be accommodated with a reasonable amount of prior thought. Overriding all these considerations, though, is the invaluable protection of always having in mind the aims of the research study. Questions or hypotheses – they repeatedly focus the form and purpose of all stages of questionnaire use.

Before proceeding to the essential steps in questionnaire usage it should be mentioned that researchers must satisfy themselves that this method is likely to be more effective than other approaches such as interviews, observation or some combination of them. [. . .] The remainder of this article assumes that the decision has been made in favour of questionnaires although many of the issues covered [. . .] could quite likely apply to structured interview schedules as well.

## 2. QUESTION SPECIFICATION

The variety of question structure, and the numerous problems associated with them, makes it vital to give careful consideration to all aspects of question specification. Failure to appreciate the degree to which the research outcome may hinge upon the strengths or weaknesses of individual questions could easily invalidate an entire study.

### 2.1 Source of questions

Dreaming up interesting questions might seem an enjoyable and acceptable approach to determining questionnaire content, but for worthwhile results a much more rigorous procedure is necessary. As with any other attempt to isolate pertinent research data, the prime source must be the working hypotheses and the literature survey that contributed these hypotheses. This implies two possibilities; either the literature study will have revealed specific questions, or more generally it will have suggested important areas needing more detailed investigation. Either way, there should be some theoretical justification for including a particular question, beyond superficial appeal.

### 2.2 Fact or opinion

Fact and opinion can usefully be taken to represent two extremes of question content and as a result they often require different formats. Frequently factual information can be elicited using a simple YES/NO question.

EXAMPLE 1

Do you have a child at Higginthorpe Primary School?

| YES | |
|-----|--|
| NO  | |

Assuming that the respondent does not confuse the three terms Infant, Primary and Junior, and assuming also that 'child' has been suitably defined to allow for stepchildren, foster children and so on, it should not be difficult to produce a reliable answer. But what about:

EXAMPLE 2

Does your child regularly do homework?

| YES | |
|-----|--|
| NO  | |

The interpretation of 'regularly' is extremely arbitrary, and there is no indication regarding who supplies the homework. To turn this into a factual question both of these ambiguities must be removed. Even more doubtful is a question like this:

EXAMPLE 3

Does your child expect to stay at school after 16?

| YES | |
|-----|--|
| NO  | |

The potential factuality of this question is very carefully disguised! At the other extreme, opinion or attitude questions are easily spotted:

EXAMPLE 4

Do you consider your child's school to be co-operative?

| YES | |
|-----|--|
| NO  | |

From this example it should be clear that opinion is usually a matter of degree, making it unlikely that a simple YES/NO response will be satisfactory. One final warning about factual questions is that although in *theory* a question may be factual, in *practice* it may not be so. A good example concerns school size:

EXAMPLE 5

How many children are in your school?

Given that school numbers fluctuate, at what time is the count to be made? More important, though, is the hint of precision in the question. Few teachers would know the answer to within 10 and the apparent need for an exact answer may be confusing. Since it is likely that broad size bands would be sufficient, the question should be phrased accordingly, or offered as a different type of question, usually categorized.

## 2.3 Structured or open

To some extent the deliberation over whether open or structured questions are required will have already occurred. In opting for a questionnaire rather than an interview approach, the assumption must be that the *bulk* of the information to be collected is accessible via structured questions. Consequently an open question like:

EXAMPLE 6

What are the essential skills
education should provide?

should tend to be used as an adjunct to the main theme of the questionnaire. For example, it could allow the respondent to elaborate upon an earlier more specific question, such as:

EXAMPLE 7

| Is modern education suited to the needs of Britain today | for all children? | |
|---|---|---|
| | for most children? | |
| | for many children? | |
| | for few children? | |
| | for no children? | |

Another valuable use for the more open type of question is to put the respondent at ease. Excessive structure can progressively generate a feeling of repression or even resentment, simply because respondents feel they are not doing justice to their opinions. Open questions inserted at the end of major sections, or at the end of the questionnaire, can act as safety valves, and possibly offer additional information. However, they are best not used to introduce a section since there is a risk of influencing later responses.

The area where open questions are especially valuable is in pilot studies. Many researchers use a more extended approach at the pilot stage, on the understanding that subsequent refinement will allow a more convenient structure to be used in the main study.

## 2.4 Question structure

Questionnaires can encompass a multitude of response formats although many of these are best treated as specific but separate methods. So a series of scaled attitude questions may be included in a questionnaire, but the analysis would need to bear in mind the principles implicit in scaling methods. [. . .] Nevertheless, at the stage of questionnaire design it would be unnecessarily restrictive to assume that questionnaires only contain YES/NO questions, or indeed, only questions.

**Statement or question.** In question form Example 7 above seems rather awkward. Particularly where opinions are involved, it may be better to ask for an indication of level of agreement with a statement.

EXAMPLE 8

| Modern education suits the needs of Britain today | for all children | |
|---|---|---|
| | for most children | |
| | for many children | |
| | for few children | |
| | for no children | |

Not only is the item structure less complicated, often it is shorter, making design and response that much easier.

**Descriptions.** The apparent simplicity of an item of the form:

EXAMPLE 9
Describe your school _____

_____

belies the considerable difficulty of analysing the responses it generates. Even though analytical difficulty is not a sufficient reason for avoiding a technique, the value of purely descriptive items should be considered carefully beforehand.

**Lists.** After descriptions the next level of structure is listing.

EXAMPLE 10
List what you feel are the GOOD and BAD things about your school.

| GOOD | BAD |
|------|-----|
| _____ | _____ |
| _____ | _____ |
| _____ | _____ |
| _____ | _____ |

However, similar problems remain, particularly those of classification, completeness (what can you deduce about something not mentioned?) and the varying lengths of the lists suggested. A simple solution to the last problem is to ask for a fixed number of comments.

**Checklists.** Many of the difficulties associated with listing can partly be overcome by supplying the statements to be checked off (that is, answered YES). This really becomes feasible if relatively few items (up to 30) are presented. If a large number of items is needed, [. . .] the subsequent classification may be a substantial undertaking [. . .] requiring knowledge of specialized analytical methods.

**Categories.** If certain important categories of response can be identified sufficiently early in a research design then it should be possible to improve the rather loose structure of the checklist by formulating more direct questions incorporating these broader response categories.

EXAMPLE 11

Which of these things do you
DISLIKE about your new school?

| | | |
|---|---|---|
| 1 | BUILDINGS | |
| 2 | TOO MANY CHILDREN | |
| 3 | TOO MANY TEACHERS | |
| 4 | THE NEW SUBJECTS | |
| 5 | HOMEWORK | |
| 6 | SPORT | |

Since a relatively small number of categories (up to 20) is usually sufficient for most questions, some simplification is achieved compared with the earlier structures. Further benefits are achieved if the number of choices is fixed (for example, 'indicate the WORST THREE things' . . .). In many cases it will be legitimate to ask for a single choice, although this will normally only apply to factual questions.

EXAMPLE 12

| What type of school do you attend? | 1 | COMPREHENSIVE | |
|---|---|---|---|
| | 2 | GRAMMAR | |
| | 3 | SECONDARY | |
| | 4 | INDEPENDENT | |
| | 5 | OTHER* | |

\* If other, please specify

**YES/NO questions.** These are really no more than an alternative way of describing some of the methods already described. So in Example 11, when an unspecified number of choices is allowed, another way of obtaining the same information would be to treat the six categories as six separate YES/NO questions. This would certainly make most statistical analyses easier. The important benefit from the YES/NO formulation is that both possible responses, YES and NO, are explicit. This is particularly valuable in scale construction because some of the problems of response bias (for example, people's stronger tendency to agree than to disagree) can be overcome by a judicious grading of positive and negative constructs.

EXAMPLE 13

| | | | | |
|---|---|---|---|---|
| (a) Are the teachers helpful? | YES | | NO | |
| (b) Is it easy to consult teachers? | YES | | NO | |

A parent with reservations about school contacts would be more likely to disclose this via the second question than the first.

**Partial agreement.** When the starkness of a YES/NO response becomes too restrictive, some gradation of response is necessary. The commonest rating system uses levels of agreement, usually with five response categories. It is the Likert scale.

EXAMPLE 14

Teachers are usually helpful

| Strongly agree | Agree | Neutral | Disagree | Strongly disagree |
|---|---|---|---|---|
| | | | | |

Notice that the wording of the question needs to allow for the possibility of varying levels of agreement. If the statement had been presented in the form: 'Teachers are *always* helpful', then responses would be forced towards the disagreement end purely through logicality. A further consideration in choosing response categories concerns the *intermediate response*. If it is included, it must be clearly differentiated from responses such as failure to understand the question, disagreement with the possibility rather than the tenor of the statement, or pure indecision. With a carefully piloted questionnaire it should be possible, and analytically preferable to do without an intermediate response *so long as* it is made clear to the respondent how non-response is to be indicated.

**Semantic differential.** Here the level of agreement is elaborated even further in that even more gradations are offered, and the constructs themselves are finer and usually more personal. The respondent indicates his or her level of support for a construct defined in terms of opposites.

EXAMPLE 15

### SCHOOL IS

| difficult | 1 | 2 | 3 | 4 | 5 | 6 | 7 | easy |
| important | 1 | 2 | 3 | 4 | 5 | 6 | 7 | unimportant |
| long | 1 | 2 | 3 | 4 | 5 | 6 | 7 | short |
| useless | 1 | 2 | 3 | 4 | 5 | 6 | 7 | useful |
| interesting | 1 | 2 | 3 | 4 | 5 | 6 | 7 | boring |

The more personal nature of such items makes the semantic differential a useful device for examining individual reactions over a broad range of personal involvements. As with the previous method, the instructions supplied to the respondent are an important part of the instrument. Anywhere from five to twelve categories have been used, but again a middle point may cause problems of interpretation.

**Ratings.** A slightly more conventional form of the semantic differential arises when a single, relatively commonplace, construct is used to evaluate a range of situations:

EXAMPLE 16

Rate the IMPORTANCE of the following, using 1 to indicate of little or no importance, 4 as very important.

| IMPORTANCE FOR PROMOTION | LOW | | | HIGH |
| --- | --- | --- | --- | --- |
| Education | 1 | 2 | 3 | 4 |
| Intelligence | 1 | 2 | 3 | 4 |
| Specialized training | 1 | 2 | 3 | 4 |
| Qualifications | 1 | 2 | 3 | 4 |
| Personality | 1 | 2 | 3 | 4 |
| Luck | 1 | 2 | 3 | 4 |

Instructions are again important, especially regarding the numerical link. As the rating method is largely arbitrary, a general rule in coding is to associate high numbers with positive constructs (that is, 4 = very important) since this produces a more natural interpretation at the analysis stage, particularly when correlations are involved.

Rating dimensions are chosen and defined to meet the research objectives. So typical reference constructs may be importance, seriousness or prevalence. It is usually better to try to offer specific terms for each rating point, rather than rely on subjective interpretations of positions between named extremes. The more behavioural these terms are, the less subjective they become. For example, using Importance assessed on a four-point scale, the four rating points might be Essential/Very/Fairly/Not. Prevalence or incidence scales are best related to explicit frequencies (twice per week, termly, etc.) wherever possible. Care should be taken to avoid reducing the effective range of the scale which can result from offering virtually impossible extremes. The commonest examples are using Always or Never in situations where those frequencies are highly unlikely to occur within the survey sample.

**Rankings.** These should *not* be confused with ratings. For rankings the responses are placed in *order*. However, the treatment of ranking does raise response and analysis problems and preferences should usually be for ratings. [. . .]

Before becoming committed to ranked questions it is advisable to decide how responses are to coded or scored, and subsequently analysed. If a workable method cannot be devised, an alternative question format should be sought.

This summary of question structures is by no means exhaustive. The general benefit of such an outline is that many of the points relating to the methods covered apply equally well to other question forms.

## 2.5 Difficulty

When questions are formulated in such a manner that response becomes difficult, the reliability of the whole questionnaire can become suspect. For a start an intelligence dimension may be introduced unintentionally, and this could distort the responses of low-ability children. Difficulty also has the effect of alienating the respondent, often to the extent of producing flippant or even aggressive responses. Almost inevitably an ambiguous question will be unreliable through a tendency to generate random responses. One effective way of detecting potentially difficult questions is to pilot them by administering the questionnaire personally, *timing* each response. Any questions which take substantially longer to answer than others quite likely are too complicated. They should be reworded, or broken down into separate parts.

**Response overlap.** This is a common error particularly with factual questions, but it is also easily remedied.

EXAMPLE 17

| | 1 | 2 | 3 | 4 |
|---|---|---|---|---|
| What is your age? | UNDER 20 | 20–25 | 25–29 | OVER 30 |
| | | | | |

What answer does a 25-year-old give? Category 2 should really be 20–24. There is, however, the opposite, namely of leaving a gap. Categories 3 and 4 omit age 30. Probably Category 4 should be 30 or over. [. . .]

**Excessive precision.** The danger of implying excessive precision has already been mentioned. Usually any numerical answer is best categorized within the question, rather than at the analysis stage. Simply ensure that minimum precision is achieved.

**Impossible questions.** Even though certain questions may seem to request straightforward information, often it can be impossible to supply an answer, either because the wording is too precise or because the information is inaccessible. An example of an excessively precise question has already been offered in relation to school size, but any numerical answer is prone to this difficulty. Age, distance, salary or IQ are all cases where banding is a more appropriate structure. Inaccessibility occurs when the respondent does not have access to the information sought. Usually this involves attitudes, especially other people's, rather than factual data [. . .] But it can arise when the time or effort required by the respondent to locate the information effectively renders the data inaccessible.

**Complexity.** Excessively complex questions can usually be reduced to two or more simpler questions, thereby improving response ease and reliability.

EXAMPLE 18

What course in education are you currently studying?

PGCE   B.Ed F/T   B.Ed P/T   Dip.Ed F/T   Dip.Ed P/T   M.Ed F/T   M.Ed P/T
☐         ☐            ☐             ☐               ☐               ☐           ☐

A better form would be:
(a)  What is your mode of Study?                    Full-time ☐    Part-time ☐
(b)  What is your course?            PGCE            ☐
                                     B.Ed            ☐
                                     Dip.Ed          ☐
                                     M.Ed            ☐
                                     Other           ☐
                                     If other, please specify

**Double negatives.** Most adults experience difficulty in handling double negatives and so there is little chance of children coping reliably with them. Question (d) of Example 19 is a relatively common double negative but it does require some care in answering. Occasionally people tackle a double negative by switching *both* negatives (i.e. *with* a PTA you *can* . . .) and then assuming that the same answer applies. Clearly that tactic would not necessarily be logically valid.

EXAMPLE 19

(a) Having a parent–teacher association makes it
    more difficult to get all types of parents to help
    in school activities                                  SA   A   N   D   SD
(b) The whole of your life is affected by your
    education                                             SA   A   N   D   SD
(c) Teachers deserve great praise for the way they
    manage such large classes                            SA   A   N   D   SD
(d) Without a parent–teacher association you
    cannot talk things over as equals                    SA   A   N   D   SD
(e) Schools should use religious education to help
    children learn what is right and wrong               SA   A   N   D   SD

**Double questions.** Questions sometimes contain two separate propositions and then there is the problem of knowing to which the answer refers.

EXAMPLE 20

Education after 15 is too specialized and should
only be compulsory for clever children                   SA   A   N   D   SD

This is rather obvious in its extremity but more subtle double-barrelled questions are common. Question (c) of Example 19 is not explicit in what is meant by 'the way they manage large classes' – management can be good or bad. Question (e) is another one where there is a distinct danger of only part of the question being answered.

**Excessive elaboration.** The principle of parsimony is a very effective rule of thumb for question design. The longer a question is, the greater the chance of introducing some of the problems already discussed. Question (a) of Example 19 offers an instance of an unnecessarily elaborate question, gradually compounding difficulty. 'Having a . . . more difficult . . . all types of parents . . . to help in' are all grammatical and semantic formulations that are not immediately obvious by themselves, never mind in association. There is often a good case for sacrificing a degree of literary finesse if the meaning of the question can be made more accessible. For instance, with schoolchildren, colloquial expressions such as 'get on', 'OK', 'sweets' and 'bike' are likely to communicate more effectively than their more grammatical equivalents.

**Consistency.** Whilst it is reasonable, and indeed useful, to vary the structure of different sections of a questionnaire, there is a danger of confusing the respondent if variety is carried to extremes.

EXAMPLE 21

| (a) I find a lot of school work difficult to understand | Yes often | Sometimes | Hardly ever |
|---|---|---|---|
| | | | |
| (b) I should like to be one of the cleverest pupils in the class | Yes | Not sure | No |
| | | | |
| (c) I work and try very hard in school | Always | Mostly | Sometime |
| | | | |
| (d) I am very good at sums | Always | Sometimes | Hardly ever |
| | | | |
| (e) I don't always get on well with some of the children in my class | Yes, true | Not sure | False |
| | | | |

Within the space of five questions the child is expected to cope with five different response systems. Each requires extra thought and quite likely introduces an element of uncertainty in the child, for little real benefit. Better to forgo some of the specificity and instead to devise a more universal set of answer categories, such as YES/SOMETIMES/NO.

In addition to difficulty resulting from the form of individual questions, there is a further likelihood of confusing the respondent within the overall design of the questionnaire. Before dealing with that topic there is the trap of impertinence.

## 2.6 Impertinence

Literally, impertinence refers to question content that is not pertinent to the main research theme. At the extreme questions of this kind also become impertinent in the everyday sense because respondents may take personal offence, and react accordingly. Questionnaire designers need to be aware of both possibilities, not only because response rate and reliability may be affected, but also because respondents do have rights which should be respected [. . .]

## 2.7 Suggestion

The risk of suggesting suitable responses is not so strong in questionnaires as it is with interviews. Nevertheless it is wise to be aware of the possibility of subconsciously implanting your own wishes in the question structure. This is most likely to arise as a result of not offering a sufficiently broad range of options in response categories [. . .] (Gaskell *et al.*, 1993).

## 3. QUESTIONNAIRE DESIGN

Placing this section after Question Specification does not imply that design need not be considered until late in the research; the reality is that the design cannot be finalized until some idea of the content is known. Having examined the range of possible question structures, it then becomes easier to produce the overall questionnaire form.

### 3.1 Theme

The general theme of the questionnaire should be made explicit, either in the covering letter, or in the questionnaire heading, or both. This ensures that the respondents know what they are committing themselves to, and also that they understand the context of their replies.

### 3.2 Appearance

The surest way of deterring a potential respondent is to send out a hastily constructed and untidy questionnaire. Appearance is usually the first feature of the questionnaire to which the recipient reacts. A neat and professional look will encourage further consideration of your request, increasing your response rate. In addition careful thought to layout should facilitate both completion and analysis. There are a number of simple rules to help improve questionnaire appearance.

(1) Liberal *spacing* makes reading easier.
(2) *Photoreduction* can produce more space without reducing content.
(3) *Consistent positioning* of response boxes, usually to the right, speeds completion. It also avoids inadvertent omission of responses.

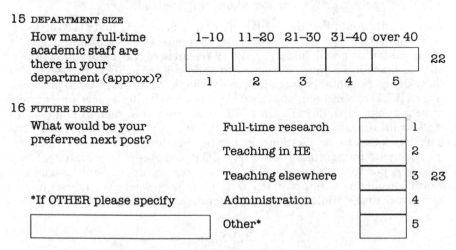

FIGURE 17.1 Sample layout using a simple text-based word processor

| Please provide the information requested below, by ticking relevant boxes, or writing your response | | | MEd Enquiry and Research CODING EXERCISE | |
|---|---|---|---|---|

| | | | | | COMPUTER |
|---|---|---|---|---|---|
| 1 | **gender** | | Male | ☐ 1 | ☐ |
| | | | Female | ☐ 2 | |
| 2 | **area** | Which of the areas listed is (or has been) your main area of employment? | Formal education | ☐ 1 | |
| | | | Vocational education | ☐ 2 | |
| | | | Support services | ☐ 3 | |
| | | | Other please specify | ☐ 4 | ☐ |
| | | | _____ | | |
| 3 | **ages involved** | What ages do you teach or support? | up to 11 | ☐ 1/2 | ☐ |
| | | | 11–16 | ☐ 1/2 | ☐ |
| | | | over 16 | ☐ 1/2 | ☐ |
| 4 | **MEd options** | Which other MEd options are you studying? | Educ Psychology | ☐ 1/2 | ☐ |
| | | | Management in Ed | ☐ 1/2 | ☐ |
| | | | SEN | ☐ 1/2 | ☐ |
| | | | Language in Ed | ☐ 1/2 | ☐ |
| | | | Curriculum | ☐ 1/2 | ☐ |
| | | | Other(s) | ☐ 1/2 | ☐ |

FIGURE 17.2 Sample layout using a word processor with standard font and graphics capability

(4) Choose the *type face* to maximize legibility. If photoreduction is to be used capitals, being bigger, are more legible.

(5) *Differentiate* between instructions and questions. Either lower case and capitals can be used, or responses can be boxed.

(6) Allow space for any *computer coding* if it is intended.

There is little doubt that the availability of text-processing and DTP (desk-top publishing) facilities via PCs (personal computers) has introduced greatly enhanced layout possibilities. For survey researchers one important consideration is likely to be your own access to appropriate facilities. The two insets show design possibilities ranging from the simplest text-based word processor (Figure 17.1) to a medium power word processor offering a range of fonts and some graphics capability (Figure 17.2). Some programs, such as Pinpoint for the Archimedes, already have a questionnaire format which is linked to a database. Responses to the questionnaire can be directly entered into the computer questionnaire format for analysis. With DTP packages near professional level quality is possible with practice. If, for any reason, doubts still remain, it is worth considering having a master version of the questionnaire typeset professionally, with the printing being carried out separately.

## 3.3 Size

There may be a strong temptation to include any vaguely interesting question, but this should be resisted at all cost. Excessive size can only reduce response rates. If a long questionnaire *is* necessary then even more thought must be given to appearance. Photoreduction helps, if only by making the task of completion look smaller. Pages are best left unnumbered; to flick to the end and see 'page 27' can be highly disconcerting.

## 3.4 Mixture

Mixing questionnaire content is another way of encouraging responses. A continuous sequence of YES/NO questions can be very tedious. By switching betweeen two or three different question structures and topics, interest is more easily maintained. However, the danger here is of excessive variation. If the respondent never has time to adjust to a particular response format frustration may be induced, along with the accompanying unreliability. The semantic differential is especially valuable since it is intrinsically appealing, and at the same time it allows a lot of information to be supplied quickly.

## 3.5 Order

Probably the most crucial stage in questionnaire response is the beginning. Once the respondents have started to complete the questions they will normally finish the task, unless it is inordinately long or difficult. Consequently the opening questions need to be selected with care. Usually the best approach is to ask for biographical information first. This tends to be the easiest because the respondents should know all the answers without much thought. Furthermore, interest should immediately be aroused since most people enjoy talking about themselves.

Another benefit is that an easy start provides practice in answering questions. On the other hand there are situations where biographical data can have the opposite effect. For example, some teachers are sensitive about their qualifications. A rather more important consideration, however, is whether the insertion of biographic content will disturb the continuity of points made in the covering letter. If the theme has been clearly established in this letter, it may be advisable to continue that line of questioning in the opening sections of the questionnaire itself. Once the introduction has been achieved the subsequent order will depend on many considerations, some of them such as mixture having already been mentioned. One possibility to be aware of is the varying importance of different questions. Essential information should appear early, just in case the questionnaire is not completed. For the same reason relatively unimportant questions can be placed towards the end. If any questions are likely to provoke the respondent (questions about marital status or ethnicity for example) these may best be left out altogether.

## 3.6 Instructions

Anyone who has played the game where you describe an object such as a bicycle, using only words, will know how difficult it is to provide clear and unambiguous verbal instructions. The questionnaire designer cannot avoid this problem. Usually questionnaires are self-report instruments which means that the only guidance available to the respondent is contained in the letter, the instructions and the clarity of the document. Within most questionnaires there are *general instructions* and *specific instructions* for particular question structures. It is usually best to separate these, supplying the general instructions as a preamble to the questionnaire, but leaving the specific instructions until the questions to which they apply. The response method should be indicated (circle, tick, cross, etc.). Wherever possible, and certainly if a slightly unfamiliar response system is employed, an example helps greatly in confirming that the verbal instructions have been understood. This applies particularly to children. One trivial but effective instruction is to ask the respondent to complete the questionnaire using a *colour* other than black (assuming that the form is printed in black). Bright colours such as red or green make the subsequent coding and analysis substantially quicker.

The importance of questionnaire instructions is often underestimated. Certainly the piloting should test the clarity of the instructions as well as the questions and method.

## 3.7 Automation

Much as the arrival of piles of completed questionnaires might seem to signal the end of the road, in reality there remains considerable work to be done. This can be alleviated if proper care is given to question structure and response provision. In particular, respondents can often be asked to supply an answer code, substantially reducing coding time. [. . .]

## 3.8 Thank you

Respondents to questionnaires rarely benefit personally from their efforts and the least the researcher can do is to thank them. Even though the covering letter will express appreciation for the help given, it is also a nice gesture to finish off the question with a further thank you:

THANK YOU FOR COMPLETING THIS QUESTIONNAIRE

If at all possible information should also be made available to interested participants. A final comment to the effect that a summary of the findings is available on request is evidence of genuine gratitude.

## 4. PILOTING

Piloting is an integral part of any research and a questionnaire survey is no exception. Indeed, the strong dependence upon the instrument rather than the researcher makes pilot assessments even more critical. These need to evaluate the instructions, the questions and the response systems. Also, if a novel distribution method is to be adopted (see next section) that too must be tested. And on top of all that it is likely that more than one pilot will be needed because any changes suggested by the first pilot will themselves require testing, albeit less extensively.

Although the piloting of a questionnaire might seem rather laborious, it would be wrong to assume that the effort is unproductive. The information collected at the pilot stage can itself be of value. For example, if everyone says

YES to a question, then that question can usually be dropped from the main study because the answer is known, and because it has no discriminatory value. A second benefit is that the pilot data can be used to test the coding and analytical procedures to be performed later. Indeed, wherever possible all the anticipated coding and analytical procedures should be tested using the pilot data. Any alterations resulting from this test can then be incorporated in the final form of the questionnaire. To try out the analytical procedures it will be necessary to select appropriate statistical methods [. . .]

*Pilot procedures* normally involve a small-scale application of the main method, but with questionnaires some modification of this pattern may be desirable. In particular it is usually advisable to administer some questionnaires personally so that the respondent can be observed, and questioned if necessary. By timing each question it becomes possible to identify any questions that appear inordinately difficult, and also a reliable estimate of the anticipated completion time can be obtained for inclusion in the covering letter. The standard concepts of *reliability* and *validity* have limited relevance in questionnaire design. Validity is typically assessed in terms of face validity, more often than not a euphemism for doing nothing. If any more objective measure is available (for example, groups of respondents expected to show different responses) then it should be considered. Reliability is slightly more accessible. Often some of the information is available elsewhere (on school records, for example) and checking may be practicable within the small pilot sample. Alternatively the respondents can be questioned personally to see how far these more lengthy responses match their earlier questionnaire answers. In general, piloting is far too often ignored, and the resultant disaster becomes all too predictable.

# 5. DISTRIBUTION AND RETURN

[. . .] The researcher using questionnaires for data collection remains heavily dependent upon response rates. Since the best guarantee of efficient sampling is a high response rate, distribution and return arrangements become vital parts of the research design.

## 5.1 Method

Cost, effort, delay and willingness are just a selection of the factors affecting choice of distribution method and therefore no single ideal procedure can be offered. Usually relative advantages and disadvantages will have to be offset and a compromise solution reached. However, it is possible to isolate three main considerations.

**Personal or postal.** Although postal distribution is perhaps the most popular method, there may be situations where it becomes preferable or even essential to deliver the questionnaire personally. Two obvious examples are where the sample is small, making a high response rate vital, or as a follow-up after postal circulation has failed to produce an adequate repsonse. Whilst postal circulation is usually cheaper, personal contact is often quicker. Telephone contact is also becoming an accepted procedure, although the costs involved probably prevent sole researchers using it to any great extent.

**Direct or indirect.** Where the sample members fall into convenient groups such as schools, classes or colleges, it may be possible to contact them indirectly using an agent within the group. This can be particularly helpful at the return stage, since the agent can usually be enlisted to remind or encourage some of the more reluctant participants. However, the indirect contact may not be possible if anonymity is an important consideration. The general problem of anonymity is discussed later in Section 5.5.

**Nominated or chance.** In most instances the subjects will have been identified individually beforehand. Occasionally, however, all that is required is a suitable number of responses and then it may be possible to avoid the effort and expense of nominating specific subjects. Instead, chance respondents are obtained, either one-by-one, or by distributing batches of questionnaires to suitable collection centres. The main disadvantage of the chance method is that being self-selected, chance respondents may not be representative in respect of the characteristics the sample was intended to cover. Consequently the need to make some attempt to assess representativeness becomes even more important in the quest for validity. In specifying the precise method to adopt these three considerations are taken independently, so that, for example, the final choice might be for a *postal indirect nominated distribution*. Furthermore, the return can be different from the distribution. Thus the above distribution example might favour an alternative return method, say *postal direct*. The distribution and return procedures are separate, and should be considered on their own merits.

## 5.2 Contents

As well as the *questionnaire* itself it is normal to send a *covering letter* and possibly a *stamped addressed envelope*. Freepost and business reply services are especially valuable since only returns are charged. If the questionnaire is especially complicated it may also be necessary to supply a separate set of *instructions*. The questionnaire should be checked for *completeness* to ensure that all pages are present and that none is blank or illegible. The covering letter should be reasonably explicit regarding the aim of the inquiry. It should admit that the request does make certain demands of the respondent's time, offering an estimate if possible. The letter should not be effusive or ingratiating. Instructions for *return* should be included but those for completion should be on the questionnaire. The *return date* must be obvious; the easiest solution is to print it in block capitals on a separate line:

'. . . It would be appreciated if you could return the completed questionnaire by:

TUESDAY 17th JANUARY
if at all possible . . .'

Notice that both day and date are given since the day of the week acts as a stronger reminder. It is rarely worth allowing more than two weeks from receipt of the questionnaire because longer times only encourage procrastination. The covering letter should also include an assurance of *confidentiality* specifying the range beyond which the information will not pass (usually the research team only). Also if *official permission* or support has been sought, for example from the Local Education Authority, it is advisable to mention this. Certainly where parents are involved, they are unlikely to co-operate fully in a survey which does not have the blessing of the school head or the Authority. They may not be interested in helping even if they are aware of official support, but that is a different matter.

## 5.3 Returns

Returned questionnaires, completed or otherwise, usually show an initial surge, followed by a gradually decreasing flow, the later ones often taking four or five times as long to arrive as the early ones. To make best use of this period processing should begin as soon as the first ones are received. Arrival date should be noted and the questionnaire numbered, unless it is already. The contents should be checked for completeness since it may be possible to return a questionnaire if any sections have been inadvertently missed. [. . .]

## 5.4 Follow-up

It will rarely be possible to accept the initial response as sufficient without some effort to increase it. The follow-up request should not be left too long otherwise what little interest the non-respondent had will have disappeared altogether. The tone of the follow-up letter should acknowledge the difficulty that person might have in complying with your request, but it needs to emphasize the importance of every single questionnaire. A replacement questionnaire should be included 'in case of misplacement or loss'. Occasionally, as a last resort, it may be practicable to supply a shorter follow-up questionnaire, covering only the essential areas.

Should the response rate still be unsatisfactory, even after the follow-up, it may be worth considering a personal visit or telephone call, rather than a further letter. Follow-up requires some method of respondent identification and therefore if an agent is used for distribution, or if anonymity is essential, special arrangements may be required. In extreme cases follow-up may not be possible at all.

## 5.5 Anonymity

Some identification system must be devised initially if only to enable any necessary follow-up to be made. There may also be a need to link data collected on different occasions. Usually, however, all that is required during processing is an index number. Consequently it is preferable to limit recorded identification to this number, apart from maintaining a private master list relating these numbers to individuals.

Questionnaires should be kept secure, and destroyed at the earliest opportunity, although the practicability of this will depend on the efficiency and completeness with which the responses can be coded. [. . .]

## 6. CONCLUDING COMMENT

The later stages of a questionnaire survey are often characterized by a reduction in the amount of control the researcher maintains. It is advisable to take all reasonable steps to minimize the effects this change might have on the quality of the outcome. In general, a continuous and systematic handling procedure is recommended. For example, a clear record of the returns should be kept, and processing should be carried out as soon as possible after receipt of the questionnaires. Even storage should be treated with the same degree of care; I recall one research study that lost a quarter of its responses because a carelessly stored box of questionnaires was thrown away by the cleaners!

## REFERENCES

Gaskell, G., Wright, D. and O'Muircheartaigh, C. (1993) Reliability of surveys, *The Psychologist*, Vol. 6, no. 11, pp. 500–3.

Kerlinger, F. J. (1973) *Foundations of behavioural research* (2nd edn). New York: Holt, Rinehart & Winston.

Oppenheim, A. N. (1966) *Questionnaire design and attitude measurement*. London: Heinemann.

Tuckman, B. W. (1972) *Conducting educational research*. New York: Harcourt Brace. Jovanovich.

# CHAPTER 18

# *Conducting and Analysing Interviews*

### E. C. WRAGG

## INTRODUCTION

Interviewing is the oldest and yet sometimes the most ill-used research technique in the world. Person A wishes to find out information, Person B has a point of view, is in possession of relevant facts or has undergone certain experiences. What could be more straightforward than Person A simply seeking out Person B, asking [her or] him a direct face-to-face question and noting down the answer?

Yet consider the following pitfalls which describe but six out of countless opportunities for inaccuracy or distortion in interviewing.

**Pitfall 1:** Interviewer bias
An interviewer's question can lead the respondent in a certain consciously or subconsiously desired direction. For example: 'Is there too much sex and violence on television and what are you going to do about it?'
**Pitfall 2:** Sample bias
An investigator interviews mothers in a shopping centre and conclude that 'few parents understand [LMS]'.
**Pitfall 3:** Hired interviewers
Some studies of people hired to conduct interviews show that they may fake answers when subjects are unco-operative.
**Pitfall 4:** Race bias
It is frequently the case that black pupils respond differently to a black interviewer than to a white one.
**Pitfall 5:** Straitjacket interview
Some tightly structured interview schedules permit little latitude. For example: 'Are you in favour of corporal punishment?' YES/NO
**Pitfall 6:** Respondent bias
Respondents frequently give the interviewer an answer which is more public relations for their own group than an accurate response. For example when Mildred Collins (1969) interviewed heads and asked what they did for probationers they tended to say they were always helping, ever a cheery word. The probationers during interview reported lack of interest and few contacts.

## WHY INTERVIEW?

Researchers need to begin not so much by saying, 'I am doing research into home/school relations so I shall interview 50 parents', but rather by carefully outlining questions to which answers are sought, and then deciding which data-gathering techniques are most appropriate. In some cases questionnaires or tests will be better than interviews; in other cases interviews may be *complementary* to other modes of enquiry.

Suppose, for example, you are studying teachers' praise and children's learning, arguing that the better readers in the class receive more praise than the poorer readers. You might interview teachers, ask them who are the best readers and who are the poorest readers, and then require them to tell you how often they praise various children. A much more effective strategy, however, would be to use reading scores derived from an objective test, classroom behaviour description obtained from live observation or lesson transcripts, and use interviews to supplement this information.

Equally, if you have a lot of simple questions requiring short answers or ratings on five or seven point scales, a mailed questionnaire might reach a much wider audience and produce much more information. Alternatively if your questions are such as to require a great deal of careful thought or research rather than an off-the-cuff reply you should elicit a written response.

On the other hand, if your target population consists of small children, illiterates or poorly educated people, you may obtain better results from talking to them rather than expecting them to write.

## WHERE TO INTERVIEW?

Environment is most important in our daily lives. Even professional people, used to meeting officials, attending meetings, using telephones, feel on their guard when interviewed in an office with the questioner behind a desk. Such things usually only happen in a crisis or in the Income Tax Office.

Much more relaxed is the interview in a home or in comfortable chairs. Not that this is always perfect, as many people [. . .] may be so overconfident as to give false information. What you need to ask yourself is what location, given the nature of your interview, makes most sense.

Confidentiality is also an important element. Few people will be frank if they are in earshot of an 'audience'. If you interview parents in a school, for example, it should be, wherever possible, away from other parents, teachers and their own children, unless their presence is desirable. When interviewing children, especially adolescents, it is also important to do this away from their peers, in whose company they often feel they must play a certain role. Investigators studying adolescents often find that in a group interview they strike a strong 'anti-school' note, whereas in individual interviews they are more likely to admit to being interested in their work and resenting their colleagues' attempts to disrupt lessons. Small children, however, may not communicate at all unless in the company of their parents or friends.

# WHOM TO INTERVIEW?

Sampling is a problem throughout educational research. A single or a few respondents may be atypical, and a cast of thousands may be equally unrepresentative if badly selected. [. . .]

Basically the choice is between a *random sample* and an *opportunity sample*. An opportunity sample consists of those whom it is convenient to interview, either because they are willing to talk or because they come your way. The group of mothers out shopping referred to in Pitfall 2 above comprised an opportunity sample. The investigator was wrong, therefore, to make inferences about 'parents' when his sample may have been predominantly of one social class or background, and when fathers had not been interviewed at all.

A random sample gives everyone an equal chance of being interviewed. If you were studying 10-year-old children in a school and wished to interview a quarter of them you might, for example, interview every fourth child from an alphabetical list starting with one of the first four children in the alphabet chosen arbitrarily. However, your final sample might, by chance, contain many more boys than girls. You might prefer, therefore, a *stratified random sample*. To obtain a stratified random sample you specify in advance, as part of your research design, which subgroups of the whole sample might be important. This is usually decided on the basis of previous research findings or professional judgement.

Suppose you are interviewing secondary school children and can manage 60 interviews in a school, you might specify age and sex as being important subcategories of the whole school population. A stratified random sample might produce the following six subgroups, allowing you to interview equal numbers of boys and girls and of 11-, 13- and 15-year-olds. The 10 children in each 'cell' would then be selected randomly from all those in that category. (The principle is that you select numbers of children in each cell in proportion to the total. Here, the author has assumed equal numbers of boys and girls in the school population, and also equal total numbers in each year.)

|  | Boys | Girls | Total |
|---|---|---|---|
| 1st year | 10 | 10 | 20 |
| 3rd year | 10 | 10 | 20 |
| 5th year | 10 | 10 | 20 |
| Total | 30 | 30 | 60 |

Stratified random sample of secondary pupils

This design would be very simple with six 'cells' each containing 10 children. Beware of too many stratifications. If you wish to add colour of eyes, social class, IQ, or personality you could find yourself with a 200- or 300-cell design and either have empty cells (e.g. no pupils in the female, 1st year, blue-eyed, middle-class, low IQ, introvert' category) or several thousand people to interview.

One further point to bear in mind is that you need to be open and honest about your sample. When a random sample is selected it is customary to have a 'reserve list' in case anyone drops out of the sample or refuses to be interviewed. Interviewing in some areas invades well-defended privacy, and on topics to do with taboo subjects the refusal rate might be high. Consequently if many people drop out or refuse to be interviewed, and are replaced by others, one has an opportunity sample of people willing to be interviewed, rather than a genuinely random sample.

It should be said that there is nothing wrong with an opportunity sample provided that (a) the investigator states clearly that this is what he [or she] has chosen, and (b) he [or she] does not make over-bold claims or inferences from his interview data. Many interesting pieces of research based on interviews have used opportunity samples.

## WHEN TO INTERVIEW?

This may seem a pointless question to ask, and yet it can be a quite critical issue, particularly if the interview is part of a battery of data-gathering devices.

Suppose one is interested in knowing something about how student teachers change during their training. Any preliminary interviews designed to elicit information about their attitudes, experience or behaviour would need to take place immediately before or at the very beginning of their course. If these were left until after the course had commenced important changes might already be under way. People's attitudes and behaviour often do transform over a period of time, a phenomenon which some researchers into personality call 'function fluctuation'.

A second consideration is the frailty of human memory. When respondents are being asked to describe or evaluate events, they should be interviewed as close to those events as feasible. A good example of this occurs in research into classroom interaction. If one tape records a lesson and plays it back to a teacher for discussion, this interview should take place within a very short time of the lesson. Some investigators have returned to the school some days later and been surprised at how little teachers could recall of the lessons in question. Teaching is a busy job and many thousands of incidents occur every day.

A third trap concerns extraneous circumstances, sometimes beyond the investigator's control. Children interviewed about 'authority' might have a quite different view of it if a teacher has just arbitrarily punished the whole class than if they have just returned from a relaxed residential field course. It is not always possible to do anything about such circumstances, but grossly unsuitable timing should be avoided, and people should not be interviewed when markedly upset or euphoric unless this emotional condition is the subject of or central to the enquiry. [. . .]

Other aspects of timing are self-evident. Late evening is a time when both investigator and respondent may be fatigued. Parents who are shift workers are not always accessible at times when other workers can be found at home. Pupils in rural areas may not be available after school because of the prompt departure of school buses. These and other small but significant points of timing should be clarified before any programme of interviewing is undertaken. One experienced interviewer engaged in an evaluation of a national curriculum package made the mistake of interviewing a group of teachers after they had been to a meeting. He found that many used identical phrases in their replies, as these were fresh in their minds from the meeting they had just attended.

## USING INTERVIEWS IN PILOT STUDIES

One common use of interviews is at the early stage of an enquiry which may or may not go on to use interviews in its main phase. Three typical examples are given below.

### Example A

An investigator intends to study teachers' attitudes to new curricula. He hopes to use an attitude questionnaire, but in the first instance he interviews a sample of teachers known to be either hostile or particularly receptive to new ideas. He notes down actual phrases used in conversation, and eventually uses these as part of a pool of possible items for an attitude inventory. He also interviews the small group of teachers who respond to the pilot version of the attitude scale to see how they regard it.

### Example B

A primary and a secondary school head are interested in making the transition from one school to the other as smooth and trouble-free as possible. Their principal intention is to establish and monitor an experimental programme for one year, but preparatory to this they interview a number of pupils, parents and teachers from each school to help them discover more about children's anxieties, any lack of communication between the two schools, teachers' ideas, parents' problems and so on. The experimental programme is then substantially influenced by what was discovered in the interviews.

### Example C

A classroom researcher wishes to observe and study probationer teachers at work. One of his concerns is to know what to observe. He interviews several experienced teachers, getting them to describe their job. From these interviews he assembles a checklist of items such as 'marking books', 'preparing materials', 'asking pupils questions', 'dealing with misbehaviour', 'ordering equipment', etc. which he then uses to categorize the type of jobs various probationers find themselves doing in a day.

## TYPES OF INTERVIEW

Three kinds of face-to-face interview are commonly distinguished: the *structured, semi-structured* and *unstructured* interview.

| | Can you give me a few details of the people in this family? How many children are there? (pre-school) (at school) Can we start with the youngest? | | | | | | |
|---|---|---|---|---|---|---|---|
| | Christian name | Relationship to informant | Sex M | F | Age on 1.12.77 | Name of school | Office use |
| A | | | | | | | |
| B | | | | | | | |
| C | | | | | | | |
| D | | | | | | | |
| E | | | | | | | |
| F | | | | | | | |
| G | | | | | | | |
| H | | | | | | | |

FIGURE 18.1 Demographic grid

## Structured interviews

These are based on a carefully worded interview schedule and frequently require short answers or the ticking of a category by the investigator. They are often like a written questionnaire in form, and indeed it is common for a sub-sample of people who have been given a questionnaire to be interviewed, partly to amplify and partly to check their written answers. The structured interview is useful when a lot of questions are to be asked which are not particularly contentious or deeply thought provoking. If the area under investigation does require more profound deliberation the respondent may become irritated at being press-ganged into one word or category answers. In such a case the semi-structured interview would be far better. Typical items in a structured interview schedule require yes/no answers, some quantification of time such as 'always, often, sometimes, rarely, never' or a demographic grid such as the one in Figure 18.1.

Since this sort of information can so easily be collected by questionnaire method there is no reason to interview unless face-to-face questioning really is a superior method.

## Semi-structured interviews

Again a carefully worded interview schedule is assembled, but in this case much more latitude is permitted. Often there is an initial question followed by probes. The schedule may contain spaces for the interviewer to record notes, or a tape recorder may be used. A semi-structured interview schedule tends to be the one most favoured by educational researchers as it allows respondents to express themselves at some length, but offers enough shape to prevent aimless

Since last September, have you or your husband helped at home with arithmetic or other subjects? (circle code as appropriate).

|                   | W | H |
|-------------------|---|---|
| Yes, often        | ① | ④ |
| Yes, occasionally | 2 | 5 |
| No, or hardly ever| 3 | 6 |
| No mother/father  | 7 | 8 |

If *YES (1) (2) (4) (5)

(a) what sort of things do you do?

HUSBAND _____

WIFE _____

(b) how does _____ feel about it?

If *NO (3) (6) why not? _____

* Footnote: The numbers in brackets after YES (1) (2) (4) (5) and NO (3) (6) refer back to the codes at the beginning of the item, i.e. if the respondent answers the first question 'yes, often' or 'occasionally' for husband or wife, the interviewer goes on to ask 'what sort of things do you do?'

FIGURE 18.2 Item from a semi-structured schedule

rambling. A typical item from a semi-structured schedule used during an enquiry into home/school liaison is shown in Figure 18.2.

## Unstructured interviews

Depth interviews require considerable skill and in areas such as psychotherapy practitioners receive extensive training in the necessary techniques. Consequently it is not something which can be undertaken lightly or by anyone not well informed about procedures or hazards. Yet, sensitively and skilfully handled, the unstructured interview, sometimes lasting for two or three hours, can produce information which might not otherwise emerge. One national manufacturer of prams once engaged a group of psychologists to give depth interviews to young mothers. Whereas the conventional market research interview might be concerned with price, shape, colour or convenience, the unstructured depth interviews produced information of a different kind. Some young mothers eventually talked about their fears of babies suffocating, their conflicts with grandmothers who preferred coach-built prams and other examples of deep-rooted attitudes or anxieties such as would only emerge during skilful questioning. In general the novice interviewer is best advised not to embark on this kind of interview until [she] can confidently handle a more structured situation, and not before [she] is fairly clear about [her] own value system.

# GROUP AND TEAM INTERVIEWING

So far we have considered the common one-to-one interview, but, despite the warnings given earlier, it is sometimes useful for more than two people to be involved, provided this does not overawe the subjects.

## Group interviews

These involve several respondents. Despite the problem of undue prominence being given to the statements of the very articulate or vociferous, an interview with a small group of perhaps three or four people can be quite useful. For example, if an investigator wishes to get a picture of classroom life this can often be assembled quite accurately with a small group. Pupils will correct each other on points of detail until a consensus is established. Nevertheless caution must be exercised. The consensus might still be fiction.

## Team interviews

These normally involve two interviewers working in partnership. In some contexts, say a study of sex roles in adolescents, it might be useful to have a man and a woman present. Certainly, it would be extremely unwise in a study of adolescent sex, for example, for a male investigator alone to conduct an interview with a girl adolescent. Similarly in a multiracial context a white and a black interviewer might work in tandem. The advantage of the team interview is threefold. Firstly it may facilitate responses from some subjects; secondly it allows one person to ask questions and the other to make notes, or to observe certain aspects of the respondent's behaviour; thirdly, since interviewing can be such a subjective process, it allows two people to make separate records of the event and then compare their two versions.

# MORE THAN ONE INTERVIEWER

Sometimes, usually in funded research, a group of interviewers might embark on an interviewing programme. This occasionally happens in small-scale research where the investigator has friends or colleagues – fellow teachers, a spouse, a group of student teachers – who are willing to help out and increase the sample being studied. It is most important that training should be given to such collaborators. Ideally they should be given an explanation of the purposes of the research, told how to use the schedule and supervised whilst conducting a pilot interview. All should use whatever form of words is agreed for each question and not improvise. A videotape of an interview can be shown, and each person can use the schedule as if he [or she] were the interviewer. Careful scrutiny of the responses should show if different interviewers are misusing the schedule or not recording accurately. Differences between interviewers cannot be entirely obliterated, but they can be minimized. If there are preliminary and follow-up interviews lists can be exchanged so that interviewers do not see the same respondent on both occasions, unless this is desirable on other grounds.

# DEVISING AN INTERVIEW SCHEDULE

It is a highly skilled job to devise an interview schedule which elicits relevant information, contains no redundant items and eliminates questioner bias. Even a watertight schedule cannot totally excise the kind of bias inherent in tone of voice, gesture and facial expression.

The investigator needs first of all to make a list of areas in which he [or she] requires information. These should then be translated into actual questions and probes, bearing in mind the age and background of the respondent. Professional jargon should be left out unless the person being interviewed is fully familiar with it.

---

In October last, parents were invited to a meeting where the teachers explained their teaching methods – one meeting for the second year pupils and one for the fourth years. Were you invited to either of them?

|  |  |
| --- | --- |
| Yes | 1 |
| No | 2 |
| Don't know | 3 |

| If YES (1) Did you or your husband go? | W | H |
| --- | --- | --- |
| Yes, attended second year meeting | 4 | 9 |
| Yes, attended fourth year meeting | 5 | 10 |
| No, did not attend either | 6 | 11 |
| Don't know | 7 | 12 |
| No father/mother | 8 | 13 |

If YES (4) (5) (9) (10)

   (a) What can you remember of it?

   (b) How did you feel about the meeting?

   (c) Did you learn anything from it at all?

If NO (6) (11) Why did you not go?
[. . .]

---

FIGURE 18.3

Let us take the example of an investigator studying home/school liaison in junior schools in a working-class area. Some schools have held meetings for second and fourth year parents to demonstrate and explain teaching methods, and the interviewer wants to know about these. He could ask, 'What did you think of the meetings?', but this might merely elicit non-committal answers such as 'not bad' or 'quite interesting'. He might enquire, 'How do you evaluate the school's attempts to communicate the principles of Science 5–13 to parents?' and receive a blank stare or a polite smile from most respondents. 'Presumably you went . . .' suggests the person must reply in the affirmative. What he should rather do is build up an item until it meets his requirements, bearing in mind the following:

(1) Some parents might not have gone to the meetings because their children never delivered the invitation.
(2) In some cases only one parent might have attended, in others none or both. Why do people not go? Is it shift work, baby-sitting problems, lack of interest?
(3) Some parents might say they were present because it looks negligent not to have attended, so they should be asked to describe what happened. Often people who say 'Yes' in the first instance, retract when asked about the event.
(4) If some information is to be coded for later data processing a code might be built in for easy circling and transfer to punched cards. For example:
    Yes        ①
    No         2
    Don't know   3

Consequently the final item, question, probes, data codes and all, would look like Figure 18.3.

## PILOT INTERVIEWS

When you have assembled a schedule always do two things:

(a) *Pass it on to experienced people for comment.* What is straightforward to you as the investigator may be baffling to another person not fully in the picture. Sometimes you are too close to something and others can be more objective.
(b) Do one or more pilot interviews. Try out your completed schedule with one or two typical respondents. Do not make the mistake of trying it out on a sophisticated colleague or friend and then using it with children or less sophisticated people. If necessary ask one other person to use the schedule and offer comments. Be prepared to modify it, considerably if necessary, in the light of informed comment. *Pilot the modified version again.* There are many instances of investigators committed to a round of interviews who only discover the ambiguity or other inadequacy of their instrument after the first few subjects have responded. By then it is often far too late to modify it.

# ORGANIZING TIME AND TRAVEL

Pilot interviews can also give you some rough ideas about the amount of time you will need. Many investigators, even experienced ones, are hopelessly unrealistic about the amount of time needed to complete an interviewing programme.

Suppose, for example, someone conducting research into children's leisure activities cheerfully decides to interview 100 sets of parents to collect background information. Since it is fairly difficult to conduct an interview properly in less than an hour, and can take as long as two or three hours, perhaps one and a half hours should be allowed on average. One then needs to add travelling time and 'abortive visit' time, when no one is at home and one has to try the next person on the list.

Consequently it is difficult, particularly for the part-time investigator usually working evenings and weekends, to do more than one interview a day. A full-time researcher might manage up to three. Clearly, therefore, assuming a part-time investigator can give up to three evenings a week, the proposed 100 interviews would take most of a year. In some enquiries it might be undesirable to aggregate data collected in September with that assembled the following March. The plan for 100 interviews would thus be unrealistic in this context. A far better plan would be to select a smaller number of parents for intensive interview and collect the rest of the data in other ways. [. . .]

It is well worth the time spent in planning the interview visits carefully. [. . .] Find out when teachers are free if they are to be interviewed, or make sure you know which lesson and classroom the children are in if they are involved. Check that your visits do not coincide with Sports Day, medicals, prize giving or half term. Then if Lassa Fever strikes suddenly, at least you did your best.

# ANALYSING INTERVIEWS

Analysis time is also frequently underestimated even by experienced investigators. [. . .]

If one tape records a one-hour interview, play-back time alone will be one hour. Transcribing will take much longer. A skilled audio typist would need about two hours, allowing for stopping and starting the machine, etc. A shorthand typist would need three hours, and a well-meaning two-finger typist more like five hours. Indeed, it might even need as much as seven or ten hours. The investigator then has a transcript containing perhaps 5000 words and running to 15 or 20 pages. These then have to be read and inferences drawn from them. Thus our optimist who earlier embarked on 100 interviews may have as much as 700 hours of transcribing time and lengthy analysis time. By the time he reports, his research may be out of date.

It is not essential to transcribe interviews, and many interviewers rely on handwritten notes assembled during the interview. These need to be subjected to content analysis, a matter too complex to discuss in any depth here [see Chapter 16]. Suffice it to say that it is important for subjective content analysis to be double checked. The first reader might deduce from reading interview transcripts that certain points are being stressed by subjects. A second reader should independently make his list of salient points. Areas of disagreement can then be discussed and analysed further.

It is also useful to think of content analysis as being a two- or three-stage operation. Usually the investigator knows why he is asking certain questions, but when all interviews have been completed other matters of importance often emerge. A first rapid reading of all transcripts by two independent readers can be used to decide how the main analysis should be conducted. There may even be a 'sandwich' model whereby this major analysis is followed by a final rapid reread to see if anything has been missed or become distorted.

# VALIDITY AND RELIABILITY

These concepts apply to interviews as much as to any other data-gathering device. [. . .]

## Validity

Does the interview measure or describe what it purports to measure or describe? How does the evidence collected compare with other sources of evidence such as written self-reports, questionnaires, test scores, or observation data? Are the constructs employed meaningful ones? (e.g. would experienced practitioners regard them as important? Are they based on the findings of previous investigators?) Is the evidence collected in any way predictive of future behaviour or events?

## Reliability

Test-retest and split-half types of reliability are not always feasible or relevant. Nevertheless one should ask: would two interviewers using the schedule or procedure get similar results? Would an interviewer obtain a similar picture using the procedures on different occasions? [. . .]

# CONDUCTING THE INTERVIEW

A great deal of common sense needs to be employed when interviewing people. The style should be a balance between friendliness and objectivity. The tight-lipped interviewer with a sphinx-like expression can alienate just as readily as the affable, matey interviewer, who too readily agrees with what his respondents say, can distort.

The beginning of an interview is very important. First of all you should carry some kind of credentials [. . .] A letter from the head of the school or from a research supervisor on headed paper explaining that you are a bona fide investigator will usually be sufficient.

Secondly, make sure all the spadework has been done. If a head is writing to parents or telling class teachers, then do not commence your interviews until you know the ground is cleared.

Thirdly, explain to the subject the purpose of your interview. For example: 'I'm interviewing several parents in the area to try to find out what they think about their children's schooling', or 'I'm talking to a lot of children in your class about what they do in their spare time'. Avoid a tendentious opening like: 'Most young people are browned off with school nowadays, so I'd like to know how you feel' or 'There's been a lot of publicity about falling standards lately, so I'd like to know what you think about it'. Incidentally do not be put off too easily if doing home interviews. Many parents, for example, will tell you that they are too busy, and when you explain 'It won't take long' are so glad of the chance to talk they will scarcely let you out of the house. It is not a bad idea to start off with easier personal questions which arouse interest and do not put off people apprehensive of authority figures.

Fourthly, always remember to ask at the end of the interview if there is anything the subject would like to ask you. You have probably asked a lot of questions and it is the least you can do.

Finally, and most important, assure the subject that the interview is confidential. Do not under any circumstances break this promise. Although educational research does not have a professional code which, if broken, leads to dismissal from a profession, it does have a set of ethics which should be followed. For some investigators this code of ethics requires that the interview 'picture' should be given to the respondent for comment. In other words if you conclude that a person is for or against something he should have the chance, subsequently, of amplifying what he has said, or correcting it if it is erroneous. You need to use your judgement about when this is an appropriate procedure. Incidentally many interviewers, particularly when interviewing in a home or a school, write up a little 'scenario' describing in fairly free form the location and the interview. This can be useful supplementary material and refreshes the memory at a later date.

## DIFFICULT TOPICS

Some topics, particularly to do with sex, religion, politics or private lives, may be too difficult to handle unless you are an experienced interviewer. Others are difficult but not impossible.

Sometimes one needs to use projective techniques or other devices to elicit an accurate picture. These are too involved to describe briefly, so below are four examples where the investigator uses a particular device to get round a difficult problem.

### Example 1. 'Guess who' technique

A researcher investigates under-age smoking. He knows that few children will admit to it, so he says, 'Guess who this describes. The person often smokes secretly. Without telling me the names look through this class list and tell me how many people it might be.' If a whole class come up with a number like 12, 13 or 14 the investigator would have a rough idea of how many were involved without anyone having given away [their] friends.

## Example 2. Critical event

When people talk about some issues their language is often vague. For example, teachers often talk about classes being 'busy' or someone 'having a firm grip'. A clearer picture of what this means can emerge if the person is asked to describe a few 'critical events', that is things which happen in a lesson which indicated that the class was 'busy' or that a certain teacher had 'a firm grip'.

## Example 3. Rank ordering

Small children often have no idea if you ask them whether they are the best, the 15th or the worst reader in a class. Roy Nash in his *Classrooms observed* (1973) gave the children a class list and asked them to say of each member whether that child was a better or a poorer reader. What transpired was a rank order very similar to that assembled by the teacher.

## Example 4. Projection

People are often reluctant to talk about their own fears or desires, and projection offers a device which may produce valuable information. With young children the interviewer may say, 'This is a picture of a little boy who looks worried about something. Can you tell me what he might be worried about?' Many children rapidly begin to talk about themselves, some even switching to the first person. This needs skilful handling both in administration and interpretation and the advice of a good clinical psychologist should be sought.

## STEREOTYPES TO AVOID

Interviewing is a complex if enjoyable way of collecting information [. . .] If you decide to do interviews avoid the following stereotypes. They may read like crude exaggerated caricature, but rest assured they are alive and well. Try to avoid swelling their numbers.

**The ESN Squirrel.** Collects tapes of interviews as if they are nuts, only does not know what to do with them other than play them back on his hi-fi.

**The Ego-Tripper.** Knows in [her] heart that [her] hunch is right, but needs a few pieces of interview fodder to justify it. Carefully selected quotes will do just that, and one has no idea how much lies on the cutting room floor.

**The Optimist.** Plans 200 interviews with a randomly selected group of secondary school heads by Christmas. Is shortly to discover 200 synonyms for 'get lost'.

**The Amateur Therapist.** Although ostensibly enquiring into parents' attitudes to lacrosse, gets so carried away during interview he tries to resolve every social/emotional problem he encounters. Should stick to lacrosse.

**The Guillotine.** Is so intent on getting through [her] schedule [she] pays no attention to the answers and chops [her] respondents short in mid-sentence.
[. . .]

# A CHECKLIST

Finally, if you still intend to interview, go through the checklist below. It highlights many of the points brought out in this chapter. If there are too many NOs you ought not to be interviewing. If the answer to question 1 is NO don't bother with the rest.

## BEFORE

| | | |
|---|---|---|
| 1. Is interviewing really the best procedure for the research? | YES | NO |
| 2. Is the purpose of the interview clear? | YES | NO |
| 3. Have I made the best decision about whether to use a structured, semi-structured, unstructured or mixed interview format? | YES | NO |
| 4. Have the relevant authorities been consulted and permission obtained? | YES | NO |
| 5. Has the sample, random or opportunity, been properly assembled? | YES | NO |
| 6. Is the time schedule realistic? | YES | NO |
| 7. Is the travelling efficiently planned and manageable? | YES | NO |
| 8. Has the schedule been skilfully assembled? | YES | NO |
| 9. Is the language level suitable? | YES | NO |
| 10. Has a data processing coding been built-in? | YES | NO |
| 11. Are the procedures for administration of the interview clear? | YES | NO |
| 12. If other interviewers are involved, have they been properly trained and their reliability checked? | YES | NO |
| 13. Has the schedule had a pilot run? | YES | NO |
| 14. Have other people used and commented on the proposed schedule? | YES | NO |
| 15. Am I aware of my own possible bias on the issues? | YES | NO |
| 16. Have appropriate analysis and data processing procedures been worked out? | YES | NO |
| 17. Is there a clear relationship between the interview and other data-gathering devices such as questionnaires, tests, or observations? | YES | NO |
| 18. Have I decided whether to record by hand or by tape recorder? | YES | NO |

## DURING

| | | |
|---|---|---|
| 19. Is the timing of the interview right? | YES | NO |
| 20. Is the location favourable? | YES | NO |
| 21. Is the rapport sufficiently good for the respondent to be truthful and at ease? | YES | NO |
| 22. Does the subject know the purpose of the interview? | YES | NO |
| 23. Is there privacy? | YES | NO |
| 24. Have I asked all the questions? | YES | NO |

## AFTER

| | | |
|---|---|---|
| 25. Are the schedules properly completed? | YES | NO |
| 26. Is data processing going to take place as soon as possible? | YES | NO |
| 27. Is content analysis properly conceived with safeguards against too subjective an interpretation or report? | YES | NO |
| 28. Should the interview report be fed back to the respondent for comments? | YES | NO |
| 29. Have I respected my promise of confidentiality? | YES | NO |
| 30. Are the interviews properly written up in the research report? | YES | NO |

# REFERENCES

Collins, M. (1969) *Students into teachers: experiences of probationers in schools.* London: Routledge and Kegan Paul.
Nash, R. (1973) *Classrooms observed.* London: Routledge and Kegan Paul.

# CHAPTER 19

# Telephone Interviewing

BRIAN FIDLER

## INTRODUCTION

The telephone has only recently begun to be widely used for survey research in the USA. In the UK its use is increasing but it is hardly used at the moment in educational research (Powney and Watts, 1987). This paper argues that the objections to using the telephone for surveys is misplaced and that it represents an untapped resource for surveys in schools.

## BACKGROUND

For many years [. . .] the telephone was seen as an inadequate survey device for a number of reasons:

(a) inadequate sampling frame
(b) technically poor quality communication;
(c) response rate;
(d) lack of visual information during the interview.

[. . .]

Technically the quality of communication has improved a great deal as has the ease of dialling, redialling, random digit dialling and using direct computer entry of the results.

For general surveys the extent of telephone coverage has undoubtedly been an influential factor in increasing the use of the telephone to the extent that it is now the dominant and most popular survey technique (Frey, 1989). This growth in interest has stimulated a number of investigations into response rates and how to improve them and how to make best use of the limited channels of communication. These will be pursued in more detail later.

## THEORY

Summarizing a number of writers Frey (1989) states three norms of telephone behaviour. When a call is made, each respondent feels:

- an obligation to answer;
- an obligation to negotiate termination; and
- a pressure to carry on an active conversation.

Much of the success of telephone interviews depends on these three norms. Only the appearance of telephone answering machines and call diversion [have begun] to redress the imbalance between caller and respondent.

Dillman (1978) develops a theoretical basis for maximizing the success of telephone surveys using 'social exchange'. The basis is that people undertake activities because of the rewards they hope to get. These rewards can be of various kinds including social [. . .] and may be dependent on the discretion of the giver. The behaviour is likely to be governed by a cost-benbefit analysis. 'Thus there are three things that must be done to maximize survey response: minimize the cost of responding, maximize the rewards for doing so, and establish trust that those rewards will be delivered' (Dillman, 1978, p. 12).

## ADVANTAGES OF TELEPHONE INTERVIEWS

In many ways the telephone interview lies on a spectrum of data collection methods between postal surveys and face-to-face interviews. It lies between the two in terms of (a) cost, and (b) response rate. An important advantage of telephone interviewing is speed. The time taken to conduct the survey and obtain working results is the least of all survey methods and if directly using a computer can be very swift indeed.

On the issue of data quality, there has been a reappraisal of the value of telephone compared to conventional interviews. Cannell (1985) confesses: 'While we think our enthusiasm for the telephone was in the first place mainly financial, we are now coming to the conclusion that this may be an inherently better way of collecting data' (p. 70). His comments are based upon comparisons of large-scale studies in the USA on telephone versus interviews on medical matters which showed great similarity in the findings. On the other hand, comparisons of interviewer effects on face-to-face interviews show a fair measure of variability which is reduced in telephone surveys. He argues that it is a matter of improving both face-to-face interviews and telephone interviews, not of getting the latter to be as good as the former.

Indeed, Lavrakas (1987) argues that one of the biggest advantages of telephone interviewing is the ability to control quality throughout the process: 'When properly orgnaized, interviewing done by telephoning most closely approaches the level of unbiased standardization that is the goal of all good surveys' (p. 12).

## DISADVANTAGES

### Limited channel capacity

Communication is limited to verbal and paralingual utterances. Cannell (1985) recommends that interviewers should not converse more in the spaces in the conversation but should indicate feedback by 'harmless' things to say – 'Yes, I heard you', 'I see', 'Uh, uh', 'I understand' and so forth. Complex questions can be aided by posting copies of visual aids before telephoning although evidence on the acceptable degree of question complexity without visual aids is reassuring (Sykes and Hoinville, 1985).

Clearly verbal communication is at a premium. Initial motivation and interest has to be conveyed in the first few seconds of the interaction. Many factors influence this and Cannell cites evidence of differences of up to 30% in response rates to certain voices (60–90%). Experience seems to help also.

## Response rates

A large study in the USA in the late 1970s by Groves and Kahn (1979) found that response rates were typically 5% lower on telephone interviews than face-to-face interviews but higher than postal questionnaires. A large-scale investigation (600 interviews) in this country (Sykes and Hoinville, 1985) set out to test the effects of length of interview and preparation by letter on response rates. On a general study of social attitudes they found that:

(i)    only 65% of households could be contacted by phone;
(i)    7% higher refusals from those telephoned;
(iii)  a 20-minute interview had a better response rate than one of 40 minutes;
(iv)   prior information by letter increased the response rate by 4%;
(v)    about 5% terminated the interview early;
(vi)   the results from telephone and face-to-face interviews were very close;
(vii)  sensitive issues appeared to lead to less inhibited responses on the telephone.

# OTHER USES OF THE TELEPHONE

Sykes (in Frey, 1989) lists the following:

(1) as a reminder to postal respondents;
(2) to set up face-to-face interviews;
(3) to screen for a sample which has a rare characteristic for face-to-face interviews;
(4) to provide advance notice of mail questionnaires (can also be used to transmit answers);
(5) to resurvey after a mail questionnaire.

Mixed-mode surveys can also be undertaken using telephone interviews for those with telephones and face-to-face interviews for those without.

# POTENTIAL USES OF THE TELEPONE IN RESEARCH IN EDUCATION MANAGEMENT

The telephone can be used: (1) as the sole means of collecting survey data, and (2) in conjunction with other data collection methods.

## Stand-alone

Using the telephone as the sole means of data collection appears to have advantages over conventional postal surveys when

(a) *speed of response is crucial:* collecting opinions about potential policy changes in order to influence the changes could only be done sufficiently quickly by using the telephone; rapid evaluations of innovations can be similarly speeded (Dicker and Gilbert, 1988);

(b) *a high degree of control is required:* in a telephone interview the ordering of questions is fixed by the interviewer unlike a postal survey where the respondent can peruse the qustionnaire before replying which may contaminate responses: the respondent is required to give spontaneous replies without time to prepare;

(c) *selective probing questions can be used:* if particular replies are given these can be followed up, as can ambiguous answers;

(d) *response rate is critical:* any postal survey's validity is undermined without an adequate response rate. Telephone surveys generally give a higher response rate and there is instant feedback about the response rate rather than a delay before the responses begin to come in. Thus in cases where an adequate postal response rate is in doubt, the telephone interview has advantages;

(e) *postal survey saturation:* in cases where respondents receive so many postal questionnaires that they cease to respond, the telephone may provide a way in. It has a novelty value but it may also be possible by using personal contact with an interviewer with appropriate credentials, to elicit participation. A pilot for this was carried out using a headteacher to ask heads in Cambridgeshire about training for [Local Financial Management].

All these possibilities are open to the individual or small-scale researchers when the numbers involved are about 50 or less and the time to carry out the interviews is not prohibitive.

## In conjunction with other methods

These may involve use of the telephone;

(a)  before data collection;
(b)  as part of the data collection process;
(c)  as follow-up to data collection.

### Before data collection

*Identifying the sample*   Where members of the population have to be traced, the telephone can help identify the population and/or sample. In order to identify teachers leaving schools at a particular time, phone calls to schools to ascertain if there are any teachers leaving that school and to request their names may be the only way of identifying individual members of the population.

*Identifying respondents*   If the members of a sample are organizations, the telephone may be used to target a postal questionnaire at the most appropriate member of the organization. LEAs, in particular, being large organizations with individually different structures present problems in targeting questionnaires. They can be sent to the chief education officer but risk lying in an in-tray pending a decision on which of three people should receive the questionnaire first. The telephone can be used to collect the names and designations of appropriate people.

*Preparing respondents for a postal questionnaire*   The telephone can be used to make contact with and seek to interest and motivate potential respondents of postal questionnaire. This is most likely to increase the response rate.

*Setting up face-to-face interviews*   Potential face-to-face interviewees who can be contacted by telephone [may be more co-operative if there has been] a personal contact to set up an interview.

## As part of the data collection process

Telephone interviews may be used to supplement either postal questionnaires or face-to-face interviews. They can add to postal questionnaires by giving a greater depth of knowledge from a sub-section of respondents on the same issues, whilst they can supplement face-to-face interviews by increasing the numbers covered and the geographic spread of participants.

## As follow-up to data collection

Telephone interviews may be used to clarify or supplement postal questionnaires or face-to-face interviews. Ambiguities or potential mistakes can be checked and intriguing responses can be probed.

# RECENT SMALL-SCALE INVESTIGATIONS

## Advance notice of postal questionnaire

On a study of the problems facing heads of small primary schools, a prior contact by telephone to interest heads in the study and alert them to the arrival of a relatively long postal questionnaire achieved an 83% response rate (Brock, 1991).

## Identification of teachers leaving

A study of primary teachers leaving at the end of the Christmas term in 1990 when no central records were available required the identification of schools which had leaving staff. A postal questionnaire identified the majority of the 300 schools with leaving staff but non-respondents had to be followed up by telephone to ascertain whether they had teachers leaving and to obtain their co-operation in distributing a postal questionnaire. Some discrepancies were discovered in county records which were available later (McElwaine, 1992).

## Reasons for probationary teachers leaving

A study of the reasons for probationary teachers leaving an LEA required swift action at the end of the summer term 1990 before contact with the teachers was lost. Forty-seven teachers were identified as leaving. Telephone interviews lasting about 15 minutes were conducted with 40 of the population. These were set up and conducted entirely by phone.

- The technique was piloted.
- The purpose, length of interview and guarantee of confidentiality were given.
- A structured interview schedule was used with minimum deviations.
- Prompts and ambiguities were given only if requested.
- At the end of the interview respondents were given the opportunity of elaborating and adding to their views.

One unanticipated issue was the degree of privacy in which the interview was conducted. Others may have been within earshot and with hindsight it would have been wise to try to ensure that the interview was taken in a private location (Newnham, 1991).

## CONCLUSIONS

Telephone interviewing appears to have a great deal of potential for research in education management. If contact with respondents is via their workplace then the potential sampling frame problems are virtually eliminated since educational institutions will be accessible via the telephone network. However, it should be recognized that this is, in effect, cluster sampling.

The advantages of quicker results and a higher response rate compared to postal questionnaires, and lower costs, lower interviewer bias and improved geographical coverage compared to face-to-face interviews, make telephone interviews worthy of consideration. There is emerging knowledge about how to make telephone interviews successful.

However, genuine educational researchers using the telephone will need to find ways of distinguishing themselves in the future from what is likely to be a developing vehicle for market research by educational institutions. Too much use of the telephone for research purposes will lead to saturation some time in the future. At the moment though this is the beginning of a very fruitful research technique.

## REFERENCES

Brock, P. (1991) Small school headship and the dual function. Unpublished MSc dissertation, University of Reading.

Cannell, C. F. (1985) Interviewing in telephone surveys, in T. W. Beed and R. J. Stimson (eds) *Survey interviewing: theory and techniques.* Sydney, NSW: Geo Allen & Unwin.

Dicker, R. and Gilbert, J. (1988) The role of the telephone in educational research, in *British Educational Research Journal,* Vol. 14, no. 1, pp. 65–72.

Dillman, D. A. (1978) *Mail and telephone surveys: the total design method.* New York: Wiley.

Frey, J. H. (1989) *Survey research by telephone* (2nd edn). Newbury Park, Cal: Sage.

Groves, R. M. and Kahn, R. L. (1979) *Surveys by telephone: a national comparison with personal interviews*. New York: Academic Press.

Lavrakas, P. J. (1987) *Telephone survey methods: sampling, selection, and supervision.* Newbury Park, Cal: Sage.

McElwaine, P. (1992) The retention of teachers in primary schools. Unpublished MSc dissertation, University of Reading.

Newnham, D. (1991) The new teacher in school – but for how long? Unpublished MSc dissertation, University of Reading.

Powney, J. and Watts, M. (1987) *Interviewing in educational research*. London: Routledge & Kegan Paul.

Sykes, W. and Hoinville, G. (1985) *Telephone interviewing on a survey of social attitudes: a comparison with face-to-face procedures*. London: Social and Community Planning Research.

# CHAPTER 20

# *Exploring Institutional Images Through Focus Group Interviews*

TRUDY H. BERS

Market research in higher education can benefit greatly by using qualitative methods to generate new insights and provide a deeper understanding of perceptions and behaviours. This chapter shows how focus group interviews are appropriately used in market research. It describes their implementation, and it discusses their benefits and drawbacks. Briefly, focus group interviewing is a qualitative research technique in which a small number of respondents – generally eight to ten – and a moderator participate in an unstructured group discussion about selected subjects. A typical discussion session lasts for one to two hours. Focus group interviews elicit in-depth, albeit subjective, information to help researchers understand the deeply held perceptions of students or other groups of policy importance to a college or university. The method is best used to identify attitudinal dimensions and not to quantify the extent to which these are held in any population or subgroup.

A growing body of literature describes the processes and uses of focus group interviews in a variety of settings. Few articles, however, are grounded in research theory. An exception is Calder (1977), who provides a typology from a philosophy-of-science perspective. Calder suggests that focus group interviews can be characterized by three general types of approaches. The first approach is exploratory, to generate hypotheses and constructs for subsequent testing using quantitative research techniques or to help confirm the results of earlier quantitative research. The second approach is clinical; here focus group interviews are undertaken to understand the 'real' underlying causes of behaviour detected through the 'clinical judgement' of specially trained moderators. The third approach is phenomenological, to help researchers or other observers intuitively know and understand how individuals in the group experience their world, to see the world through the respondents' eyes without evaluating the accuracy or correctness of that view. Calder argues that each approach necessitates different decisions with regard to such aspects of focus group interviewing as selecting the moderator, selecting the respondents, conducting the discussion sessions, and using the results.

Hess (1968) presents the relative advantages of focus group interviews as compared to individual, in-depth interviews. Among the advantages to the respondent are synergism, that is when a group's combined effort will produce more than the sum of individual responses; snow-balling, the process by which one person's comment triggers a chain of responses from others; stimulation; security; and spontaneity. Advantages also accrue to the sponsor of the research. These include serendipity, when an idea pops out spontaneously; specialization, in the case of using a well-trained moderator who would be too expensive to use for individual interviews; scientific scrutiny, available through direct observation of a group or a tape of its session; structure, obtained through the control exerted by a moderator; and speed.

Langer (1986) provides guidelines for conducting qualitative research and reminds researchers not to be surprised when respondents are inconsistent, different from model or idealized subjects in the population being studied, uncaring about a college or university, angry about some aspect of an institution, or uninformed. Goldman and McDonald (1987) [examine] the principles and practices of focus group interviews, and Higgenbotham and Cox (1979) provide a variety of research examples. Many other articles and books about focus group interviews are available, the majority of which are recent – testimony to the relatively new status of focus group interviewing as a viable and appropriate market research technique.

## INITIAL PLANNING OF FOCUS GROUP STUDIES

As with any good research method, focus group interviews entail more planning and thought than is immediately apparent to those who think of it as simply a couple of hours of informal group discussion. In this section and the next, I examine the elements of a successful focus group study. Examples are drawn from focus group marketing research using adult students conducted at Oakton College in spring 1986 (Bers and Smith-Bandy, 1986).

### General approach and specific purpose

Before conducting a focus group study, it is important to clarify the general research approach. Calder's typology may be useful here. The specific purpose of a focus group study must also be clearly identified. Among the possible purposes related to market research in higher education are the following: to investigate the perceptions of an institution by constituent groups such as potential students, parents of potential students, and high school counsellors and teachers; to examine the evaluations by potential recipients of college brochures, other promotional materials, and alternative marketing campaigns; and to generate new ideas for improving or adding services (such as registration, and child-care).

To clarify the approach and purpose of a focus group study, researchers need to discuss these issues with relevant college personnel. It is important that a consensus be achieved before proceeding further if the research is to be successful. The approach and purpose of a study will determine most of the other aspects of the design and conduct of the research.

The Oakton College study was undertaken to generate hypotheses for a future quantitative study of college choice and evaluations and to get in touch with or learn more about the phenomenology of non-traditional students. Its purpose was to examine the college choice decision-making processes of adult students and their impression and attitudes about Oakton College's programmes and services. While many factors affected the decision to use focus group interviews in this study, the most important was that no one at Oakton College had consciously talked to non-traditional students to ask about their experiences in selecting the college or evaluating its programmes and services.

## Respondents

Once the general approach and specific purpose of a focus group study have been determined, appropriate respondents must be recruited. Researchers should be aware that if care in recruiting respondents is not taken, the accuracy and usefulness of information will be compromised. Depending on the specific study and the nature of the institution, various criteria will probably need to be followed to ensure that respondents are members of the populations of interest. For example, a selective college wishing to conduct research on potential students will want to ensure that respondents meet minimum academic standards for admission. Also, having participated in other focus group interviews ought not by itself to disqualify a potential respondent.

A question related to recruiting respondents is whether livelier or more perceptive discussions arise in groups that are heterogeneous or homogeneous in the characteristics qualifying respondents for inclusion. In general, the more researchers wish to understand a group's shared perspective (the phenomenological approach), the more important it is that the group be homogeneous. When the approach is exploratory, heterogeneity is more acceptable.

The Oakton College study used recently enrolled women and men who were age 25 or over during their first terms at Oakton College and who had earned at least 15 credits. This was done so that the discussion sessions would consist of students who were familiar with and had shown some commitment to the college. Separate sessions for women and men were conducted, but there was no attempt to differentiate by such factors as major, age, or credits earned.

For some types of focus group studies, researchers might well look to college employees as potential respondents as well as to those outside the institution. For example, an institution that wishes to generate ideas about improving the way in which it presents itself to campus visitors might conduct focus group interviews with employees such as security guards, maintenance personnel, and receptionists and secretaries. They will be familiar with problems and can offer insights into possible solutions from very different perspectives than their supervisors. Improved commitment to the institution and higher morale are additional positive effects generated by employee participation.

## Moderator

Once the approach, the purpose, and the respondents have been decided on, a moderators' guide needs to be prepared. Such a guide lists important topics to be covered in a discussion session and may even contain suggested questions to ensure that important terminology is included and relevant points are probed. It is important to remember, however, that the guide is that, and not a structured questionnaire or interview schedule. One of the primary benefits of focus group interviewing is that it allows researchers to explore and obtain elaborations on subjects pertinent to a study but not anticipated in advance.

A skilled moderator familiar with the study should be able to cover virtually all of the issues in the guide yet take advantage of new subjects that arise spontaneously. When a study includes more than one group, all topics will not be discussed in every group, since the natural flow of conversation might make introducing some topics too artificial or even divert a group from a more fruitful line of discussion. If it is imperative to cover certain topics or questions with a group, the moderator should be made aware of this in advance. A moderator normally does some combination of the following in a discussion session (Mariampolski, 1984):

- rapport building, in which the moderator establishes rapport with the respondents and orients them to the general task at hand;
- exploration in which very general questions are posed such as, 'What comes to mind when I mention XYZ College?' or 'What do you think of when you imagine your ideal college?'
- probing, in which the moderator narrows the discussion for elaboration on specific topics and introduces new issues to expand the discussion;
- closing, in which respondents are given a final opportunity to add to the discussion by answering such general questions as, 'Is there anything else you want to say about XYZ College?'

Other things that might be added include task accomplishment, in which respondents are to be asked to perform a task such as ranking suggested promotional themes, and evaluation, in which respondents are asked to evaluate such test items as brochures and advertising designs.

While most respondents are co-operative and expressive, moderators must be prepared to cope with those who are unusually verbose, hostile, passive, or obnoxious. Bers and Smith-Bandy (1986) have categorized such respondents and offered suggestions for dealing with them:

- axe-grinder, who dwells on a very negative experience. The moderator should say that a particular concern has been heard and need not be repeated, and avoid eye contact to discourage repeated discussion.
- Self-styled expert, who claims absolute knowledge. The moderator must weigh the benefit of correcting misinformation with the risk of discouraging participation from others who fear they will be corrected if their comments are 'wrong'.
- Single-issue respondent, who fixates on a topic. The moderator should treat this person as an axe-grinder, but may need to make direct statements that the single issue in question is not on the group's agenda.
- Adviser, who tells the college how to improve, but whose ideas are in fact trite and have probably been implemented already or are impossible. The moderator must tolerate this, lest others be discouraged from offering their ideas.
- Special case, who deviates from the norm, often through aberrant behaviour or perceptions. If possible, known cases should be screened out unless there is a real interest in talking to them. Outside moderators may not recognize the special case.

- Non-participant, who attends but doesn't talk. The moderator should use smiles, nods of approval, and even gentle but direct invitations to participate.

## Number of groups

A frequent concern is how many different groups of respondents to include in a single study. One rule of thumb is to hold at least two groups to reduce the chances of an atypical group providing all the input. A second rule of thumb is to continue to hold sessions until virtually the same discussion is repeated. If a study is being done to brainstorm ideas, however, one group might suffice, regardless of how atypical the respondents appear.

## CONDUCTING FOCUS GROUP STUDIES

After initial planning, several decisions related to the actual implementation of a focus group study must be made. There are few right or wrong decisions; rather, such factors as those just described as well as the resources and time available will influence the way in which a study is conducted.

## Location

Typically discussion sessions are held in small rooms equipped with a conference table and comfortable chairs or couches. Hot and cold drinks and, depending on the time of day, snacks or a light meal are provided. Sessions are generally taped, and, when watching the reactions of respondents to physical or visual materials is important, video-taping is recommended. Commercial focus group facilities, [. . .] also provide a viewing room for observers (which is of course necessary only if observers are part of a study). The viewing room is behind one-way glass and enables a person to watch a session in progress. Respondents should be told they are being taped or observed; there is generally no resistance or effect on their behaviour, since taping equipment is unobtrusive and observers cannot be seen.

## Observers

It has become common practice for representatives of a college or university to observe discussion sessions. This is not necessarily important, however, particularly when a study's general approach is to explore new ideas rather than to provide decision makers with a 'feel' for the kinds of people in whom they are interested. When observers are present and they are unfamiliar with focus group interviews, there is a tendency for them to jump to conclusions or target a particular phase or idea as a generalizable finding. One way to discourage this is for the study director to hold an immediate debriefing with observers at the conclusion of each session to permit them to share their first reactions and be gently reminded of the ways in which the results might be properly and improperly used. [. . .]

## Moderator

Moderators are either selected from college personnel or hired from outside. If a study is following an exploratory or clinical approach, the moderator should have some scientific training (Calder, 1977). Regardless of the approach, it is imperative that the moderator understand the research so that he or she can appropriately select statements to probe and further explore topics, guide the discussion away from irrelevant issues, and take advantage of spontaneous or unexpected comments that are germane to the project. At a minimum, the moderator needs to be a good communicator who puts respondents at ease and encourages them to share their ideas candidly. The moderator should also be empathetic and capable of participating without biasing the results or leading respondents, and he or she must be able to provide the college or university with insightful observations (Welch, 1985).

Skillful moderators rely on numerous tactics to draw out reticent respondents and to prevent those with strong personalities from dominating a discussion session. For example, useful statements to elicit comments include, 'I'm interested in your thoughts on that, Joe,' 'That's an interesting observation, Joe; will you elaborate a bit?' and 'Can you tell us more about that?' Encouraging cues also include nods of the head, 'um hums,' and repeating statements as preludes to the next question. Tactics to discourage overbearing respondents include statements such as, 'Will you hold that thought for a minute, Joe? I want to hear the rest of what Jane is saying,' or 'Let's listen to Jane, now.' Avoiding eye contact, the implicit signal that permission to speak is being granted, and refusing to call on someone also aid in maintaining control.

## Use of service provider

Commercial firms provide an array of services for planning, implementing, and analysing focus group studies. Among such services (each, of course, for a fee) are providing a facility, recruiting respondents, making reminder phone calls or mailings, hiring a moderator, arranging refreshments for the respondents and observers, providing audio and visual tapes, preparing a written summary and analysis of the results, and writing thank you letters. The extent to which commercial firms are used will be influenced by the nature of a study and the availability of resources, including the ability of a college's researchers to conduct the discussion sessions.

## Respondents

Identifying and recruiting respondents is one of the most important elements in a successful focus group study. Often the suitability of respondents is not clear until a discussion session is under way. To improve the suitability of respondents for a study, various screening or qualifying criteria are generally employed. For example, a college interested in exploring its image among prospective students may draw respondents from its inquiry pool, assuming that these persons have at least heard of the institution. If there is concern about the size and quality of the inquiry pool, then respondents might be drawn from lists of high school juniors or seniors whose test scores indicate they would qualify for admission. In short, random selection of respondents is often unwise, since persons selected in this way usually have little to contribute. While some qualifying of respondents is recommended, applying stringent criteria will increase a study's costs if many contacts are needed before a sufficient number of qualified respondents can be recruited.

Because respondents are being asked to devote several hours of their time and must perhaps travel to a special site, incentives are usually provided. [. . .] The issue of monetary incentives is especially sensitive for public institutions whose administrations and boards are reluctant to allocate public funds for this purpose. Nevertheless, incentives may be essential for recruiting respondents and should be considered as analogous to printing and postage costs in a mail survey; they are simply part of the cost of doing research.

## ANALYSIS AND PRESENTATION OF RESULTS

As with any research, the results of a focus group study must be analysed. One common format is to identify broad themes that emerged in the discussion sessions and then to elaborate somewhat on each. For example, in the Oakton College study, several themes were identified from the four sessions conducted with returning women students, and these were described in detail. Returning women, for instance, did not engage in careful consideration of alternative colleges. Rather they decided to return to school *and* to Oakton College as one decision, and they based this overwhelmingly on the Oakton College's convenience. Only after they were enrolled did these students begin to assess the quality of the faculty or their choice of programme.

The results of a focus group study are usually presented in two types of reports. One type provides a general overview of findings, including brief sections on the nature of the research, recruitment and characteristics of respondents, and major themes that emerged. The second type is more extensive and includes numerous verbatim comments. Because results are qualitative in nature, neither type of report includes statistics; instead, terms like *some* and *most* are used.

## BENEFITS AND DRAWBACKS OF FOCUS GROUP INTERVIEWS

Focus group interviews are an effective research method, but they are not without problems. The following are among their primary benefits. First, focus group interviews enable college officials to observe people who may be very different from themselves as well as different from idealized or stereotyped models (Dickenson, 1986). For example, admissions directors may think of potential students as being goal-directed and knowledgeable about the college search process. Mail or telephone surveys that elicit responses to multiple-choice questions often perpetuate this image. Focus group interviews, however, may well reveal that potential students are disorganized, use irrational or very subjective reasons for selecting particular institutions, and know very little about college majors.

A second benefit of focus group interviews is their potential use as morale boosters when college personnel are involved as respondents (Fram, 1985). Since college staff members often possess critical information that is not systematically collected and may even feel ignored, inviting them to participate in focus group interviews serves both to obtain their ideas and to improve morale. A third benefit of focus group interviews is that they enable college personnel who are involved as observers to hear the language and vernacular used by respondents (Mariampolski, 1984). The importance of this cannot be overstressed, since successful promotional literature should address consumers using language and symbols they can and will interpret.

A fourth benefit of focus group interviews is that they permit the assessment of non-verbal responses. For example, body language, facial expressions, voice tone, and the physical handling of catalogues and brochures provide significant indicators about the way in which issues and materials are being perceived or used.

The drawbacks of focus group interviews include, first, the cost. Estimates of expenses per discussion session [vary widely] depending on the use and cost of outside service providers and incentives, difficulty of recruiting qualified respondents, and moderator costs. Travel and the staff time of observers may add significantly to this amount. A college or university that uses its own facilities and staff can substantially reduce costs.

A second drawback is the potential overenthusiasm over findings and a tendency to treat results as scientific and generalizable. The results of focus group studies should rarely be used alone; rather, they should be used in concert with findings from other types of research before expensive or irreversible decisions are made.

Third, recruiting appropriate respondents is more difficult than is immediately apparent. Consequently, it may be important to use an outside firm experienced at recruitment unless it is appropriate for a study to use accessible and easily identified participants such as currently enrolled students. Finally, some people are simply better able to express their ideas than others, and their comments may be given more credence or attention because they are more articulate.

## SUGGESTIONS FOR PLANNING FOCUS GROUP STUDIES

Most of the crucial steps in planning and conducting a focus group study have been identified in this chapter. Clearly, successful studies require thoughtful planning, careful implementation, cautious analyses, and the judicious use of findings. Additional points to consider are these:

- Clarify the general approach and specific purpose of a study before it is conducted, and be sure that all relevant parties in the institution agree on or at least understand them.
- Obtain consensus about the one thing those commissioning the study would most like to learn.
- Limit the number of topics to be discussed so that each one can be given sufficient attention. Focus group interviews are best at eliciting in-depth

information about one or two issues rather than superficial information about many (Hollander and Oromaner, 1986).

- Recruit and screen respondents carefully.
- Understand the limitations of focus group interviews – they are not a replacement for quantitative research.
- Give the moderator ample time to analyse the results; do not expect a thoughtful analysis in the immediate stimulation and excitement of a discussion session (Roller, 1985).
- Limit the number of observers, have a researcher present who can explain focus group processes to them and maintain a non-party atmosphere, and debrief observers at the conclusion of a discussion session (Smith, 1986).

## CONCLUSION

Focus group interviews can enable colleges and universities to understand their clientele, generate ideas for new and improved marketing programmes, and evaluate the effectiveness of such programmes. The insights gained from focus group interviews can prevent costly errors. Though their planning and implementation may appear casual and inexpensive, high-quality focus group studies require adherence to rigorous standards, skilled personnel, and adequate financial resources. Focus group interviewing is neither cheap nor easy, but when well done it is a powerful tool for market research and an important complement to quantitative studies.

## REFERENCES

Bers, T. H. and Smith-Bandy, K. (1986) College choice and the non-traditional student. Paper presented at the Association for Institutional Research Annual Forum, Orlando, Florida, June 22–25.

Calder, B. J. (1977) Focus groups and the nature of qualitative marketing research, *Journal of Marketing Research*, Vol. 14, pp. 353–64.

Dickenson, S. B. (1986) A little 'sensitizing' is helpful for marketers, *Marketing News*, Vol. 20, p. 50.

Fram, E. H. (1985) How focus groups unlock market intelligence: tapping in-house researchers, *Business Marketing*, Vol. 70, pp. 80–2.

Goldman, A. E. and McDonald, S. S. (1987) *The group depth interview: its principles and practices*. Englewood Cliffs, N.J.: Prentice-Hall.

Hess, J. M. (1968) Group interviewing, in R. L. King (ed.) *New science of planning*. Chicago: American Marketing Association.

Higgenbotham, J. B. and Cox, K. K. (1979) *Focus-group interviews: a reader*. Chicago: American Marketing Association.

Hollander, S. L. and Oromaner, D. S. (1986) Seminars fill gap in focus-group training, *Marketing News*, Vol. 20, p. 46.

Langer, J. (1986) Quoted in 'Focus groups aid search for new markets,' *Marketing News*, Vol. 20, p. 54.

Mariampolski, H. (1984) The resurgence of qualitative research, *Public Relations Journal*, Vol. 40, pp. 21–3.

Roller, M. R. (1985) Mental image of groups is out of focus, *Marketing News,* Vol. 19, pp. 21, 26.

Smith, A. (1986) Researchers must control focus group – and those behind the mirror as well, *Marketing News,* Vol. 20, pp. 33–5, 36.

Welch, J. L. (1985) Researching marketing problems and opportunities with focus groups, *Industrial Marketing Management,* Vol. 14, pp. 245–53.

# CHAPTER 21

# On Diaries and Diary Keeping

ROBERT G. BURGESS

The last two decades have witnessed the development of ethnography and case study research as approaches that are regularly used in studies of schools, classrooms, teachers and pupils (Burgess, 1984; Burgess and Ruddock, 1993). These approaches rest upon the first-hand collection of data using observation, participant observation and interviews of various kinds, with an emphasis upon an unstructured interview style alongside conversations (Burgess, 1984; Hammersley and Atkinson, 1983). To these methods, documentary evidence has been added. This can include ready-made documents that are available in many schools and classrooms, together with commissioned documents that researchers invite teachers and pupils to write on specific topic areas. Another important element that also constitutes documentary evidence is logs, diaries and journals.

Much writing about diaries has focused on the researcher's diary and the principles associated with it (Burgess, 1981, 1984). Here the focus is upon the kinds of data that are collected from research participants and then analysed. In particular, Burgess raises the following questions: What data do you record? How do you record them? What categories can be used in recording data? Should the diary be supplemented with interview transcripts, tape recordings and photographs? (Burgess, 1981, p. 76). The informant's diary, which is kept by people with whom the researcher works, might take the form of notes and jottings that address such questions as when, where, what and who, in order that the informant might record observations which will be of use to researchers. Some writers have also devoted attention to the keeping of personal professional journals by teachers (Holly, 1984, 1989) and also the use of the journal in collaborative work (Tripp, 1987). It is the purpose of this article to examine the use of diaries by teacher-researchers as well as those who work with researchers in order to engage in reflective practice and as part of 'action research' within schools and classrooms. Accordingly it is the diaries used by teachers and pupils that are the central feature of this article.

## LOGS, DIARIES AND JOURNALS

In many accounts distinctions are drawn between logs, diaries and journals (Holly, 1984, 1989). The log is seen as a record of information that relates to particular situations and circumstances. It is therefore an *aide-mémoire* rather than a continuous free-flowing piece of writing. Logs are distinguished from diaries, which are often less structured and include information that relate to the experiences of the writer. Mary Lou Holly concludes that:

> Because diary writing is interpretive, descriptive on multiple dimensions, unstructured, sometimes factual and often all of these, it is difficult to analyse. It is not easy to separate thoughts from feelings from facts and, as the writer, to extricate yourself from your writing.
>
> (Holly, 1984, p. 5)

She focuses upon the personal aspects of diary keeping and, in turn, goes on to distinguish journals in the sense that she argues that they are structured, descriptive and contain objective notes, as well as the free-flowing discursive aspects of the diary. While this may be useful analytically I would wish to combine the elements of all three documents and therefore refer to them all as 'diaries'. The 'diary' includes all three kinds of writing that have been identified by Holly. First, it includes a log of all the activities and decisions in which the writer has been engaged. This has the advantages of overcoming time problems in diary keeping that have often been commented upon by teacher-researchers (Elliott, 1982; Griffiths, 1985). Secondly, the 'diary' can involve a free-flowing account where the writer reflects on some aspects of the log at the end of a busy day by writing up some aspects in more detail. Finally, it may include a record of a particular situation or event in which the writer has been actively involved and wishes to describe.

## REFLECTIVE PRACTICE

There are a relatively small number of accounts about the ways in which teachers and teacher-researchers have kept diaries in order to examine their own practice. Among those which highlight teachers' work are diaries kept by teachers in primary school mathematics classes where the curriculum content was described (Burgess, 1985), and Gordon Griffiths' account of his work in a comprehensive school (Griffiths, 1985). In both cases, strategies needed to be devised to find ways in which the diary could be structured to avoid taking too much time for data recording while working in the classroom – an issue that Pollard (1987) has also raised. Some of these issues were also involved in a piece of research I conducted with teachers engaged in teaching adult education classes in a community college. Here I invited teachers to reflect on their own practice through a diary. The invitation for them to take part in diary keeping was framed in the following way:

> As part of my research I am interested in the adult education classes that you teach, and/or classes where adults are present. It would help if you could record details of these classes in the diary. In particular I would be interested in the content of the lessons and the events and activities that occur. You may wish to focus on a particular situation, for example, relationships between teachers and taught or relationships between adult pupils and school pupils or conversations that you hold with adults at the beginning and end

of classes. It would be useful if you could say who is involved, what is involved, when the lesson occurs and where it occurs. The period to be covered is 29th April to 24th May 1985. Please feel free to write any comments that you feel might be relevant. It may be that you would like to write a short piece reflecting on your work so far and where this particular block of four weeks fits in the programme. In addition you might care to reflect on your diary entries at the end of the period concerned. If you have any questions please do not hesitate to get in touch with me. Thank you for your help.

(Burgess, 1988, p. 195)

While this diary did not have a particular format, an implicit framework was provided within the instructions as teachers were invited to include:

- work with adult students;
- the content of classes;
- events, activities and relationships;
- conversations;
- a specific timespan;
- reflections on their work.

While no specification was provided about the style of writing, the suggestions were designed to offer some guidelines about the way a diary entry could be structured. As a result, one teacher wrote about teaching English to an adult student she called Susan. The way she recorded this in her diary is illustrated by the following entry:

Susan was receptive to 18th and 19th century literature in some ways more than the girls. Possibly she is wider read? Until I succeeded in 'turning them on' (how corny . . .) to Jane Austen the novel was universally disliked except by Susan. Now they do like it and can see some of the literary qualities. They can at least analyse why Fanny Price drives them crazy. Susan seems to have quite an empathy with Fanny's situation (I hope you've *read* the book, Bob) and at the beginning of our studies made many references to her own childhood, orphaning, isolation, etc. There were some interesting conversations between girls who were 16/17 – new to the 6th form – and this worldly wise woman. My teaching dilemma was to gauge its relevance to the lesson. You see I love a chat with the girls – it works wonders for your teaching if they relate/talk to you and I've got problems too; but it doesn't help if they don't know their stuff . . . As I am an experienced A-level teacher, I know I need 2–2 ½ terms to teach a text like *Mansfield Park* accurately and relatively clearly.

(Burgess, 1988, p. 201)

Such entries provide an opportunity to examine critically strategies that are involved in teachers' work.

## DEVELOPING DIARY USE

While the term 'diary' has been chosen to cover pieces of writing that are conducted by teachers and pupils much will depend upon the research context.

First, there is the question as to whether teachers or pupils are conducting the project and whether it is they who set the research agenda. Secondly, consideration needs to be given to whether teachers collaborate with researchers (Tripp, 1987) or pupils collaborate with researchers (Pollard, 1987). Thirdly, it is important to draw a distinction between situations where teachers and pupils keep diaries for their peers and where they do so for researchers. It is the latter that is among the most common of the contexts within which diaries are kept for research purposes. Accordingly we examine three different projects to highlight the different ways in which diary use and diary keeping occurs. The examples that follow suggest ways in which diaries can be used and some of the issues that diary keeping raises for teachers.

---

Dear [Name of pupil]

### A FOOD AND DRINK DIARY

I hope you will help me. I am a researcher who would like to learn more about what children eat and drink. If you write in this diary, it will help me to know more.

So, next MONDAY, TUESDAY, WEDNESDAY, THURSDAY, FRIDAY, SATURDAY, and SUNDAY, please write in your diary. It may help you to write if you think about answering these questions:

WHAT DID YOU EAT AND DRINK TODAY?
WHEN DID YOU EAT AND DRINK TODAY?
WHERE DID YOU EAT AND DRINK TODAY? (at SCHOOL, HOME, SOMEWHERE ELSE?)
DID YOU EAT ALONE or WITH YOUR FAMILY or WITH YOUR FRIENDS?
DID YOU GO ON A VISIT and EAT THERE?
DID YOU ENJOY A CELEBRATION? (like a BIRTHDAY, ANNIVERSARY)
DID YOU LIKE WHAT YOU ATE AND DRANK?
PLEASE WRITE ABOUT HOW YOU FELT.

Thank you very much for your help. Please return the diary to school after seven days.

Yours sincerely

MARLENE MORRISON
Research Fellow

---

FIGURE 21.1 Letter to pupils

## Pupils' food diaries

Among the projects that I am currrently conducting is a study on teaching and learning about food and nutrition in schools. The project consists of a series of case studies in primary and secondary schools and involves Marlene Morrison, the researcher who works on the project, conducting interviews and discussions with teachers, pupils, dinner ladies, parents and others. It also involves her making a series of observations in classrooms, corridors, dining halls and play-grounds. Within the data that have been collected, it is apparent that a number of contradictions exist about patterns of food and eating, both within school and between home and school (Burgess and Morrison, 1993; Morrison and Burgess, 1993). In this respect we considered that it was important to ask pupils to keep diaries about food use. However, in designing the diaries we had to take account of the context within which the work was conducted. Indeed, the first case study was conducted in a primary school and therefore a specific type of diary needed to be devised. First, it was important to talk with pupils to explain what it is that had to be done. Secondly, the time period over which a diary would be kept was limited to one week including one weekend. We also decided to limit the size of the diary and to make it look as near as possible to a specialist booklet. Inside the diary there were a series of instructions which were included in a covering letter addressed to each pupil as shown in Figure 21.1.

### Diary 1

*Breakfast.* cornflakes, orange juice. I ate it at home by myself.

*Lunch.* sandwiches with ham cheese lettuce crisp two chocolates and a drink. I ate at the Birmingham science museum with my friends.

*Tea.* Cup of tea with toast cakes and biscuits. Ate by myself.

*Supper.* chips vegetables beefburgers fish fingers gravy. Ate with my family.

### Diary 2

### 21/6/93

Today at dinner time I ate sandwiches, a chocolate, crisps and a drank some coke. In the morning I drank some tea. When I came back from school I ate rice pudding, chappati, and curry. Then later some fruit. I ate in the morning in the afternoon and at night. I ate at Birmingham museum and at home. At dinner time I ate with my friends, and in the morning and night I ate with my family. I went on a visit and ate there. No I did not enjoy a celebration. Yes I did like what I ate and drank today. I felt very hungry today.

**Diary 3**

---

*Monday 21th June 1993*

1) Today I ate 2 Turkey Batches, crisps, a bottle of pop.
2) I ate and drank at dinner time.
3) I ate and drank somewhere else.
4) I ate with my friends.
5) Yes.
6) Yes.
7) I liked what I ate and drank.
8) I enjoyed eating and drinking.

---

These diaries used the what? when? where? who? formula for collecting information. Yet the way this was interpreted varied between pupils as shown by the preceding examples taken from the first diary entries of three pupils.

These three diaries illustrate different styles of keeping an account of food and eating. In each instance the instructions have been interpreted in different ways. Accordingly, these diaries raise a number of issues. First, the use of diaries by the diarist. We have already seen how instructions to diary keepers may be closed or open ended – a feature that will influence the format chosen by the diarist as it helps to structure the material that is written. This also relates to a second important issue, namely the extent to which comparisons can be made between different diaries – a significant issue when wishing to trace similar issues such as patterns of decision-making, negotiations with teachers and use of time across several diaries when analysing their content. Finally, diary keeping is not without ethical problems. An ethical question that needs to be considered is the extent to which diary keeping constitutes intrusion, in the food diary example, into the lives of these children and their families.

## The supply teacher project

This study, on which I have worked with Sheila Galloway and Marlene Morrison, attempts to understand the experiences of teachers, substitute teachers, and pupils when regular teachers are unable to take a timetabled class and children are taught and/or supervised by another person. Within this project Morrison and Galloway (1993), who conducted the fieldwork, soon found they were dealing with a situation where supply teachers moved in and out of schools on a frequent and often irregular basis with the result that fleeting relationships were established with the teachers and their pupils. Supply teacher diaries allowed Morrison and Galloway to confront four major research challenges. They indicate that diaries allowed them to explore relationships between teacher substitutes, regular teachers and pupils, to make connections between public and private aspects of supply teachers' lives and to resolve the difficulties of observing situations that were relatively short and in unpredictable time periods. Accordingly, diaries allowed them to observe some

SUPPLY TEACHING DIARIES        DATE 18.6.92

| HRS 7.00 | MAIN ACTIVITIES | OTHER |
|---|---|---|
| 8.00 | Day 4 of exercises —— shower<br>Breakfast inside today. Up later not feeling totally together.<br>Watered garden.<br>Nursed rabbit for ½ hr. trying to get her to drink or eat. | No where yet to go so can set off to base at 8.15 and still be there before time. |
| 8.23<br>8.45<br>9.00 | Feeling a bit down (PMT and rabbit referred to in previous day's schedule)<br>Set off to base.<br>Arrive base. Chat to fellow supply – see how things are going. | |
| 9.05<br>9.25<br>10.00 | Just getting breath when message comes to go – but no age range given I & J school.<br>Set off.<br>Arrive school. Look for entrance & park.<br>School deserted – no sec. in office even. | Had to follow A–Z quite carefully. Hadn't been to this school for 2 yrs and then only for part of a day. |
| 11.00 | Eventually find hall – children in Assembly.<br>Teacher near door beckoned me in. When ready to go out same teacher pointed out the class – Yr 2 class.<br>Tells me they are worst in school – messed about.<br>10.00 go to class. Chat about self. Set them picture and writing to tell me about self. A lot of | Listened to end of Assembly. Introduced by the Dep. as Mrs A. at end of Ass.<br>10.40 Play. Went to staffroom for a coffee and put lunch away. |
| 11.30 | disruption. One or two quite difficult.<br>Collect children from playground. Took ages to get order – so much fuss. Back to class – for milk.<br>Lunch had been taken out.<br>Carried on writing – if finished did their maths.<br>Following Peak which I know. Heard some readers but difficult as children needed disciplining a lot.<br>Singing. | Got told at play that my class goes swimming after dinner. Singing – I was left with the 2 yr classes & a peripetetic pianist. Wow what a hard session. |
| 12.00<br>13.00 | Dismiss children. Quite a lot went home – unusual.<br>Mark work up to date & change any books. Get changed for swimming. Fill in a form for my mum. Ring Vet to book rabbit in. Ring bank – slight cash flow problem. Eat lunch in staffroom. Staff not particularly chatty but glad of the rest! | Ringing up took ages. Office locked – no idea where key was till found someone to tell me. |
| 13.10<br>14.00 | Children in. Did register. Didn't tally. Incorrect from morning!<br>Took ages to sort out some children's names difficult to pronounce. Reg. not very clear. Needed to be accurate for swimming. 13.20 Eventually set off. Took a while to get there as kept starting & stopping. Worn out when I arrived! | A mum came with me – a nice lady – very nice but not very effective. Very noisey in changing areas. I was dotting from one to the other. |
| | Eventually we got them down to the pool. Instructor. He took the more able group – leaving me alone with 20 children in small pool. We worked hard but they didn't tire. Changing took ages. Walked back better after a great lecture from me.<br>Got back 14.40. Too late for play. | I have never felt so worn after swimming. Only I had to get out of water for a short while. Miracles never cease. |
| 15.00<br>15.30 | I kept them out for 10 mins. play whilst I had a drink. An EMS teacher took a group for reading. I let rest finish off any work then get an activity whilst I heard readers.<br>Behaviour improving.<br>Dismiss children. Write note for teacher. | Didn't think they'd settle to a story and they hadn't read all week.<br>Dep. wished I was going back as I'd controlled class!! |
| 15.45 | Leave school after a chat with Dep. | |

| HRS 16.00 | MAIN ACTIVITIES | OTHER |
|---|---|---|
| 16.50<br><br><br>17.00 | Arrive home. 10 mins. walk for Ben. Rang Bill to tell him about rabbit. Collect rabbits. Go to vet's. Ben came for company. Female rabbit had to be put down.<br>I brought her home. | Not feeling wonderful! |
| 17.30<br>18.00 | Called at friend's for our weigh-in. I had not lost any weight from last Thursday!! Told friend about rabbit! | I stayed for longer than planned. |
| 18.30<br>18.45<br>19.00 | We had a chat over a red wine & tonic – much needed!<br>Call at friend's with a book I'd picked up for her.<br>Got home. Played with rabbit.<br>Had a bath. Soak! Soak! | |
| 20.00 | Ate nothing as no time!<br>Rang my sister to tell her about rabbit.<br>Mum rang.<br>Rang Bill to tell him. Got dressed. | My nieces had given me the rabbits for Christmas. |
| 21.00 | Went round to friend's house from my base school to a Pippa Dee. Very expensive for what it was. Resisted all the lovely cakes – just had a bit to taste as they were homemade (from a friend's piece).<br>Listened to the demonstrator telling us what a | Only bought some orange foam bath!!<br>Tried on some clothes with rest of base school – just for fun. |
| 22.00 | stressful day-time job she had.<br>She wasn't a teacher!!<br>Offered a coffee by hostess's daughter and gratefully accepted.<br>Just a few left – all base school staff. Had a chat and | I needed that! |
| 22.30<br>22.50 | laugh. Put the world to rights.<br>Set off home.<br>Arrive home. | |

**Anything before 07.00 hrs? Anything after 22.00 hrs?**

6.45 Got up later! Quickly walked dog-short walk.
Fed fish & checked rabbits.
Female very ill.

Cover rabbit.
Walk dog.
Have a bite to eat – literally.
Pack for Wales.
Flop to bed.

What was the most demanding task or situation with which you had to deal today? Any additional comments on today's activities? Please continue on the back of this sheet if you wish.

Singing  – not really fair to be landed after only 1 hr in a school with 2 difficult classes.
          Coped, but throat sore.
Swimming– Very dangerous situation – particularly at the baths., 1:20 ridiculuous.

FIGURE 21.2 Supply teaching diary

of the invisible aspects of supply teachers' lives. The diary was developed on a what? when? where? how? basis (Zimmerman and Wieder, 1977). However a time grid was also used to direct the teacher's attention to the day's events and allowed writers to develop detail on the most demanding features of daily activity as well as those that were considered more trivial.

The diaries were accompanied with instructions which provided a basis for identifying themes across activities and in turn follow-up interviews were also used. As in many other studies, the diaries gave access to events that the researchers were unable to observe, as shown by the diary kept by one teacher (Figure 21.2).

The format for the diary provides a grid within which teachers can distinguish their main activities from other events and in turn picks up the public–private dichotomy, taking into account issues that arise within and beyond their life in school and their life as a supply teacher. Here, several issues can be highlighted. First, there is a framework within which supply teachers can write but in turn they are given freedom to develop their ideas. In this sense, it is the diary writers who can place limits on the extent to which they give access to their world and their work. Secondly, the ethical questions about intrusion can be raised as the intention of the supply teacher diary is to gain access to material that would otherwise be hidden from the researcher's view. We might therefore ask: to what extent is such a device intrusive on the lives and work of teachers? This issue needs to be considered when inviting teachers and pupils to engage in diary keeping.

## The Interactive Video Project

The Interactive Video Project is an attempt to evaluate the use of interactive video for the purpose of school management training. This evaluation has been commissioned by the National Council for Educational Technology and requires our research team to look at the use of interactive video eqipment and interactive video disks in 21 sites. A number of different approaches are used

---

### DIARY OF INTERACTIVE VIDEO USE

CEDAR is collecting information about the use of interactive video equipment. This evaluation using a diary is being carried out at each of the sites in the project from the 1st February to the 28th February 1994.

Please complete an entry in this diary each time you use the workstation even if the interactive video facility is not used. Please include as much information as you feel you can.

If you have any questions or queries please contact Nicola Ramsay on 0203 523523 ext 2185 and leave a message for the project team.

*Evaluation of Interactive Video for*
SCHOOL MANAGEMENT TRAINING
by the
CENTRE FOR EDUCATIONAL DEVELOPMENT,
APPRAISAL AND RESEARCH (CEDAR)
University of Warwick
Coventry
CV4 7AL

---

FIGURE 21.3 Cover page of diary of interactive video use

to collect data: visits to the sites; telephone interviews; a conventional survey; and a series of case studies. One problem the research team has encountered is that the machines which have been given to the 21 sites are not necessarily on those sites, having been loaned to schools. It has therefore been difficult to discover something about the actual use of the machines. In these circumstances, the team decided to attach a diary to each machine to explore its use. Here, the diary is linked to the machines rather than the individuals who use them, so that all those who use a particular machine for whatever purpose (whether to play an interactive video disk or to use it for word-processing facilities are invited to record the information). The way in which the diary exercise was established was to write to the project co-ordinators at the 21 sites and to invite them to place the diaries next to the machines so that data could be collected for a whole month. In these circumstances it was important to include details of what was required but also to make it simple for individuals to comment. The cover page is shown in Figure 21.3.

The format for recording information was on a series of pages set out as a grid. The idea was to make the material easy to assemble, but to give the researcher information about the people who use the equipment, the date they used it, and the location (given that we were unsure whether the equipment was used by members of the site who obtained use of the equipment from NCET or whether it has been loaned elsewhere). Secondly, we asked for the duration of use by obtaining start/finish times. Thirdly, we required details of the interactive video disks that were used. Fourthly, we asked whether people were working in groups or working alone. Finally, an opportunity was given for a more discursive comment.

In these instances there was a lack of detail and depth associated with the diary as relatively few comments were provided. But the advantage that the diary gave was the detail about the location, frequency of use, and type of use for the equipment, thus showing the way in which the interactive video disks were or were not being used in relation to the equipment.

## ISSUES IN DIARY USE

As we have seen from the three research examples, diary use takes different forms. Much will depend upon the research question being posed and in turn the research context as to the way in which the diary is established and diary keeping is developed. In establishing the collection of any material using diaries it is important to give guidance on the topic areas that need to be covered. Secondly, the diary is one method of obtaining data and therefore needs to be linked carefully to other research activities. For example, the problem of time is very apparent when individuals are keeping diaries (Griffiths, 1985). Accordingly diaries may be linked to diary interviews in order that topics and themes developed by the diarist may be discussed in greater detail in the course of a diary interview (Burgess, 1981). In establishing diary interviews, it is important to take the words of the diarist and to build upon them so that the questions used in the diary interview relate directly to the diary entry. In a diary a teacher kept for me, he had indicated that student numbers were in decline – a topic I wished to explore so I started my diary interview with a comment from his diary:

RB:  You talk about the class and you say that one of the things is that it was important to keep the class going. Can you say why you felt that? Because from what I gather numbers have dwindled over the year, or numbers were small. We're talking about the Tuesday evening class.

(Burgess, 1988, p. 201)

In this way, further elaboration could be obtained on the situation (Burgess, 1988).

It is also apparent that the context for writing needs to be developed among those who keep diaries. If this is not done then the material obtained may be of limited use. Diarists therefore need to be encouraged to begin and end diary entries with reflective pieces that provide information on their work, their role, the social context within which teaching and school management occurs. Such contextual data may help when making comparisons between diaries and analysing the data as the context may help to advance our understanding of the social situation being examined. Finally, there is a series of ethical questions surrounding the use of diaries and diary keeping, especially as far as intrusion is concerned. In many instances, diaries are advocated as a means of gaining access to situations in which it would not normally be possible to obtain data. However, it could be argued that the researcher intrudes further into the lives and work of teachers and pupils in a far greater way than when observations and interviews are made in schools and classrooms. Here, the trade-off has to be considered between the information required and the degree of intrusion into the lives of individuals.

## FUTURE DIRECTIONS?

Researchers and teacher-researchers have been using diaries for a number of years in social and educational research. These diaries have taken different forms and have emphasized different kinds of activities. But what developments might take place? First, diary groups can be established when work is being conducted in the same school. Secondly, these groups can be given an agenda with which to work so they can discuss ways in which writing can be developed; can examine the content of writing and record keeping in relation to diaries; and can develop topic areas with a researcher or with each other. Members of a school senior management team might therefore meet as a group to discuss their day-to-day practice and use of time on the basis of record keeping through diaries. Such critical reflection may in turn lead to developments and changes in working practice. Accordingly, there appears to be considerable potential for developing the use of diaries within social and educational research so as to highlight features of educational activity that are beyond the scope of other methods, such as observation and interviews that are commonly used in schools and classrooms.

## REFERENCES

Burgess, H. (1985) Case study and curriculum research: some issues for teacher-researchers in R. G. Burgess (ed.) *Issues in educational research: qualitative methods.* Lewes: Falmer Press, pp. 177–96.

Burgess, R. G. (1981) Keeping a research diary, *Cambridge Journal of Education*, Vol. 11, no. 1, pp. 75–81.

Burgess, R. G. (1984) *In the field: an introduction to field research*. London: Allen & Unwin.

Burgess, R. G. (1988) Examining classroom practice using diaries and diary interviews, in A. Pollard and P. Woods (eds) *Sociology and teaching: a new challenge for the sociology of education*. London: Croom Helm, pp. 192–208.

Burgess, R. G. and Morrison, M. (1993) Ethnographies of eating in an urban primary school. Paper prepared for the European Interdisciplinary Meeting, Current Research into Eating Practices. Contribution of Social Sciences 14–16 October, Potsdam, Germany.

Burgess, R. G. and Rudduck, J. (1993) (eds) *A perspective on educational case study: papers by Lawrence Stenhouse*. University of Warwick, CEDAR.

Elliott, J. (1982) Action research into action research, *Classroom Action Research Network,* Bulletin no. 5, Cambridge Institute of Education, pp. 68–80.

Griffiths, G. (1985) Doubts, dilemmas and diary-keeping, in R. G. Burgess (ed.) *Issues in Educational research: qualitative methods*. Lewes: Falmer Press, pp. 197–215.

Hammersley, M. and Atkinson, P. (1983) *Ethnography: principles into practice*. London: Tavistock.

Holly, M. L. (1984) *Keeping a personal professional journal*. Deakin: Deakin University Press.

Holly, M. L. (1989) *Writing to grow*. Portsmouth, New Hampshire: Heinemann.

Morrison, M. and Burgess, R. G. (1993) Chapatis and chips: encountering food use in primary school settings. Paper prepared for an International Conference on Children's Food and Drink: Today's Market and Tomorrow's Opportunities at Chipping Campden Food and Drink Association, Chipping Campden, Gloucester, on 10 November 1993.

Morrison, M. and Galloway, S. (1993) Researching moving targets: using diaries to explore supply teachers' lives. Paper prepared for the British Sociological Association Conference, University of Essex, 5–8 April 1993.

Pollard, A. (1987) Studying children's perspective – a collaborative approach, in G. Walford (ed.) *Doing sociology of education*. Lewes: Falmer Press, pp. 95–118.

Tripp, D. (1987) Teachers, journals and collaborative research, in J. Smyth (ed.) *Educating Teachers*. Lewes: Falmer Press, pp. 179–91.

Zimmerman, D. H. and Wieder, D. L. (1977) The diary: diary-interview methods, *Urban Life,* Vol. 5, no. 4, pp. 479–98.

# CHAPTER 22

# *Observing and Recording Meetings*

## G. L. WILLIAMS

As members of organizations we all participate in a variety of meetings from informal discussions with colleagues to formal committee meetings with a chairperson and secretary. Rarely do we take the opportunity to observe what is going on in a meeting and work out why participants in the meeting are behaving in the way they are. Most of us complain about committee meetings and staff meetings but if you want to improve both individual and group performance in meetings then observing and analysing what is happening is the first stage in bringing about improvement.

Those carrying out research into behaviour or roles may also be interested in what happens in meetings. If you are observing a meeting as part of a project you need some way of recording your observations. But what should you observe? What sort of things should you look for? What affects the effectiveness of the meeting?

## CONTENT AND PROCESS

A fundamental distinction can be made in looking at a meeting between content issues and process issues. Content refers to what the group of people comprising the meeting is doing in terms of its purposes and objectives; process refers to the way in which the group goes about achieving its formal task – how it is carrying out its tasks.

## Content issues

When observing a meeting, it is important first to identify the type of meeting and then to decide what objectives are held by the members for the meeting, though objectives may vary from person to person and sometimes may be kept well hidden. As a result, observations tend to be incomplete. The main types of meetings are:

(1) **Command meeting.** A meeting called by a manager to instruct, co-ordinate or control his subordinates. The objectives specified for the meeting are those of the manager. Others may have conflicting objectives.
(2) **Selling meeting.** A meeting where one person or a group is trying to persuade or convince the other group members about some issue. The

objectives are concerned with persuasion. A subset of this type is where a person tries to 'sell' himself, that is by boasting or showing off in more or less subtle ways.

(3)  **Advisory meeting.** A meeting called for the exchange of information or the seeking of opinions. The purpose may be stated in terms of either giving or receiving information or both. [. . .]

(4)  **Negotiating meeting.** A meeting aimed at reaching a compromise/ agreement, or making a decision by bargaining, between two or more opposing sides with [. . .] different objectives but some overlapping mutual interests arising from their interdependence.

(5)  **Problem-solving meeting.** A meeting concerned with tackling a particular problem or problems. Usually the problem belongs to the whole group and all concerned are able to contribute towards the process. The meeting may have a limited focus on some aspect of problem solving, that is planning or decision making. Also the decision may be made outside the meeting following its recommendations or deliberations.

(6)  **Support meeting.** A meeting where the individual group members come together to give each other support in terms of such things as their emotional needs, learning and development, or individual problem solving. Usually each individual would have his own personal objectives although there would be more overlapping of objectives if this were a team-building session.

Some meetings may be of more than one type. In observing a meeting, details of the type of meeting and objectives or purposes can be recorded.

It is also interesting to record the types of meeting that a staff group holds over a period of time, and the balance between the different types of meeting. Do some types of meeting not occur (or only infrequently)? If not, why not? Could the balance between the different types of meeting be improved?

## Further analysis of content

Having analysed what type (or types) a meeting is, and what the objectives are, further analysis of the content of the meeting can be carried out by looking at how and/or how well the purposes of the meeting were achieved and what the various contributions were from members that influenced the achievement of objectives and purposes. Further analysis can be carried out by general checklists or by specific checklists for each type of meeting.

## General checklists

The starting point for analysis can be either the issues covered or the persons. For each issue in turn:

- Who speaks on that particular issue?
- For how long?
- What is the nature of their contribution?
- How effective is their contribution – particularly in helping to achieve the objectives of the meeting?
- What helped progress on the issue?
- What hindered progress on the issue?

For each person in turn:

- What did they contribute to the discussion?
- What was the nature of their contribution?
- How did they help in achieving the purposes or objectives of the meeting?
- How did they hinder the achievement of purposes or objectives?

Checklists can be drawn up for each type of meeting, but every meeting is different so the checklists given should be freely adapted to suit the particular meeting you are observing.

# PROCESS OBSERVATIONS

[. . .] There are many different types of processes that we can focus on. Some examples are:

- communication;
- decision making;
- problem solving;
- direction;
- functional roles (task and maintenance);
- self-oriented behaviour;
- norms.

## Communication

The communication process is one of the most important processes in any meeting. Basically communication is the transfer of information between people. However, the process itself is complex and in an apparently simple message a mixture of facts, feelings, opinions, insults, etc. can be communicated. In a face-to-face meeting verbal communication is always accompanied by non-verbal communication and the two types of communication may contradict each other. Some aspects of communication are easy to observe, others are more difficult and may have to be mainly inferred rather than observed directly.

Some of the simple-to-observe aspects of communication are:

- the relative contributions of individuals;
- who talks after whom;
- who interrupts whom;
- who individuals talk to.

### Relative contributions

Here what is observed is the relative frequency and duration of verbal communication. All that is needed for these observations is a list of group members and a mark placed against each name each time that person speaks. A different checkmark can be made if the same person is still speaking after a set period of time (i.e. half a minute) so that the length of communication is also measured (see Figure 22.1).

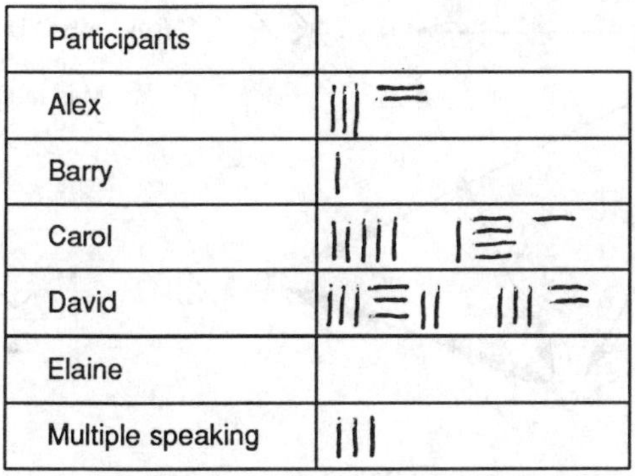

| Participants | |
|---|---|
| Alex | ‖‖ = |
| Barry | ‖ |
| Carol | ‖‖‖‖   ‖≡ ¯ |
| David | ‖‖≡‖   ‖‖ = |
| Elaine | |
| Multiple speaking | ‖‖‖ |

ǀ  indicates contribution

—  indicates communication continuing beyond a set time

FIGURE 22.1 **Relative contributions**

This type of analysis can be useful in highlighting the extent to which certain members may be dominating the meeting and indicating which members are not contributing very much.

## Who talks after whom

The analysis above can be easily extended to analyse who talks after whom and to plot the sequence of communication by using squared paper. After each communication a square to the right of the last square completed is used (see Figure 22.2).

There are often patterns of speaking so that one person tends to be followed by another particular individual. The next level of analysis is to identify what is happening between the two people. [. . .]

## Who interrupts whom

This is a particularly important category of behaviour which can also be plotted on the grid in Figure 22.2. Alternatively, a separate note can be made

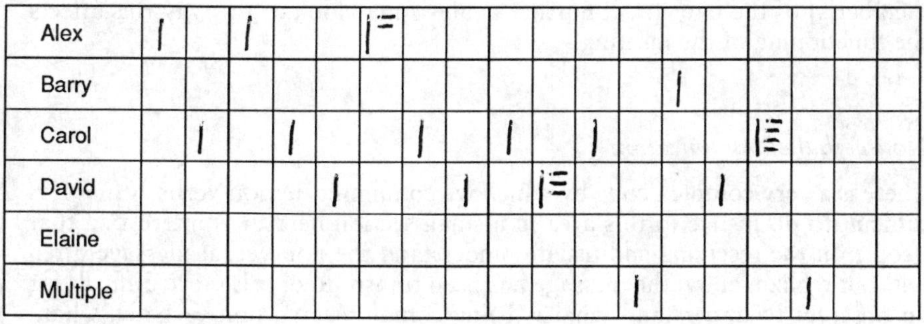

| Alex | ǀ | | ǀ | | ǀ= | | | | | | | | | | |
|---|---|---|---|---|---|---|---|---|---|---|---|---|---|---|---|
| Barry | | | | | | | | | | ǀ | | | | | |
| Carol | | ǀ | | ǀ | | ǀ | | ǀ | | ǀ | | | ǀ≡ | | |
| David | | | | ǀ | | | ǀ | | ǀ≡ | | | ǀ | | | |
| Elaine | | | | | | | | | | | | | | | |
| Multiple | | | | | | | | | ǀ | | | ǀ | | | |

FIGURE 22.2 **Sequence of communication**

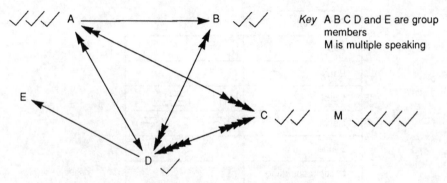

FIGURE 22.3 Who talks to whom

of instances of interruptions. This simple analysis usually needs to be supplemented with inferences about the causes of interruptions, usually using evidence from other observations such as non-verbal behaviour.

Interruptions often give us clues as to how people perceive their own power or status in a meeting relative to the others at a meeting. People who perceive themselves as of higher power or status or more important often feel free to interrupt those whom they perceive as of lower status. At a meeting of apparent equals, interruptions may indicate that one person feels that they are more important than certain, or all, others and this may lead to dysfunctional consequences.

### Who individuals talk to

A useful way of plotting who talks to whom is to use the system shown in Figure 22.3.

The letters represent group members. Each communication from one person to another is represented by an arrow or an additional arrowhead. Communications to the whole group are represented by a tick next to the person's initial. This gives an easy-to-read record of who has communicated to whom as well as the number of contributions from each person. Instances of multiple speaking can be recorded alongside the diagram.

This type of analysis can identify a type of pairing between individuals. If one person almost always addresses communications to another specific individual, the next level of analysis is to examine what is going on between the member[s] of the pair. [. . .] Further analysis may look at the way this affects the functioning of the meeting.

[. . .]

### Non-verbal communication

There is a very complex code by which we communicate non-verbally and it is difficult to do justice to this area in a small section here. It is interesting that people on the receiving end usually understand the non-verbal message often without realizing how the message has been transmitted. It is more difficult for an observer to understand what is being communicated non-verbally. Channels of non-verbal communication include:

- facial expression;
- gestures;
- changes in direction of gaze;
- eye contact patterns;
- tone of voice;
- posture;
- relative orientation between individuals;
- distance between people;
- touching;
  etc.

[. . .]

## Decision-making processes

It is not only on large issues that decisions are made. Decisions are made in meetings all the time, often without participants being aware of the process. It is important to be aware of what decisions are being made (often implicitly) and the way these decisions are made.

What are the different ways in which decisions are made in a meeting? There are a number of possibilities varying from very little involvement of group members through to total involvement of all.

(1) Lack of decision – even making no decision can be a type of decision.
(2) Decision by one individual – i.e. the expert or autocrat.
(3) Decision by minority group – i..e power group (inner cabinet) or sub-committee.
(4) Voting – taking a majority vote as to what to do.
(5) Consensus – giving everyone a chance to have their full say and to feel that they have made their position clear so that each individual can at least go along with the group decision to some extent even though they may not be in total agreement.
(6) Total agreement.

Further analysis might look at the quality and acceptability of the decisions that are taken by the meeting. The way that decisions are made tend to affect the quality and the acceptability of the decision. For example, in voting there is often a polarization in terms of acceptability. Those who voted for the decison may find it very acceptable but the minority who 'lost' the vote may feel that the group has made the wrong decision, and that they were right all along and thus they are not really committed to the decision made by the meeting and may even try to subvert it.

## Problem solving

Does the meeting tackle a problem in the best way? Some problems are best solved using a logical approach, other problems may be better tackled using creative techniques such as brainstorming. Many complex problems require both logical and creative approaches but used at the appropriate stage in the problem-solving process.

Does the group jump to quick solutions without finding out first what the real problem is?

Does the problem-solving process follow a reasonable sequence such as the following:

- identifying the real problem: where are we now? where do we want to be? how can we get there? what is problem and what is symptom?
- agreeing on the problem: checking everyone understands the problem;
- defining the problem: factors contributing to the problem, factors affected by the problem;
- generating alternative possible solutions: encouragement of differences, no evaluation or criticism at this stage;
- evaluating possible solutions: forecasting outcomes using good judgement, looking critically at the alternatives;
- taking the decision: being decisive;
- action planning: appropriate involvement of those who will implement, considering how to deal with adverse reactions and consequences;
- action;
- monitoring and evaluation of outcomes.

In recording problem-solving behaviour you can check the stages as they occur, indicating the sequence of stages and giving an effectiveness rating for each stage (see Figure 22.4).

Using the centre column identify the sequence in which the stages of problem solving occurred. Put a 1 by the first stage to occur, 2 by the second and so on.

| Stages of problem solving | Order of stages | Rating | | | |
|---|---|---|---|---|---|
| | | 1 | 2 | 3 | 4 |
| Identifying real problem | 3 | √ | | | |
| Agreeing on problem | 2 | | | √ | |
| Defining the problem | 1 | | | √ | |
| Generating alternatives | | | | | |
| Evaluating solutions | 4 | | √ | | |
| Taking the decision | 6 | | | √ | |
| Action planning | 5 | | | | √ |
| Action | 7 | | √ | | |
| Monitoring and evaluation | 8 | √ | | | |

*Key* 4 Carried out well
    3 Fair
    2 Attempt made but done badly
    1 Not done at all

FIGURE 22.4 Rating of problem solving

Often a meeting will not pass through all stages so some will be left blank. Using the 4 point rating scale, rate how well each stage that you have marked was carried out.

## DIRECTION AND RATE OF PROGRESS

Two of the main complaints about meetings are they often lack direction and take up far too much time. The two are often related in that if you are travelling in the wrong direction for part of the time it takes longer to reach your destination. In observing a meeting these two factors can be plotted together using a series of small arrows for set periods of time (i.e. three minutes) starting from S (for start) and hopefully (but not necessarily) ending up at G (for goal). The direction of the arrows indicates the direction of the discussion relative to the goal and the value given to each arrow indicates the speed of progress towards the goal on a 5 point scale (minus values are possible). Figure 22.5 gives an example of a meeting plotted in this way.

## FUNCTIONAL ROLES

Behaviour in a meeting can help the group in two different ways. It may help the group to achieve its task (task roles) or it may help the relationships between members or affect the climate of the meeting (maintenance roles). Both types of roles are important if the meeting is to be effective both in the short term and the long term. The roles can be played by anyone in the group and it is best if most roles are performed by most group members.

Types of behaviour concerned with the group achieving its task:

(1) Proposing: Proposing tasks or goals; defining a group problem; suggesting a procedure or ideas for solving a problem.
(2) Building: Making suggestions that build on or add to others' proposals.
(3) Presenting information or opinion: Offering facts; providing relevant information about group concerns.

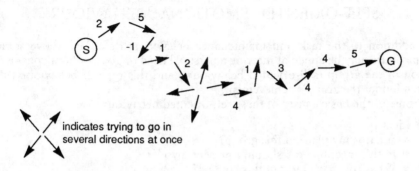

indicates trying to go in
several directions at once

FIGURE 22.5 Direction and rate of progress

(4) Seeking information or opinions: Requesting facts; seeking relevant information about group concern; asking for expressions of feeling; requesting a statement or estimate; soliciting expressions of value; seeking suggestions and ideas.

(5) Testing and clarifying: Testing for understanding and agreement; interpreting ideas or suggestions; clearing up of confusions; defining terms; indicating alternatives and issues before the group; testing of the quality of the group's procedures or achievements.

(6) Keeping group on course: Highlighting diversions and bringing the group back on track.

(7) Summarizing: Pulling together related ideas; restating suggestions after the group has discussed them; offering a decision or conclusion for the group to accept or reject.

Behaviours concerned with maintaining the group:

(1) Supporting/encouraging: Being warm, friendly and responsive to others; indicating by facial expression or remarks the acceptance of others' contributions.

(2) Gatekeeping: Helping to keep communication flowing freely; helping others to participate (bringing in); stopping others from monopolizing or disrupting (shutting out).

(3) Harmonizing: Attempting to reconcile disagreements, getting people to explore differences.

(4) Tension releasing: Reducing the build-up of tension where it is becoming dysfunctional, by joke or other mechanism.

(5) Showing attention: Indicating interest verbally or by body language, in what the group is doing, listening attentively.

[. . .]

Task and maintenance behaviours can be recorded using the form in Figure 22.6. It takes quite a lot of practice to be able to use the form for all group members and it is probably best to start by practising observation of just one or two group members until you have familiarized yourself with the categories.

Where categories are underutilized the next stage of analysis is to look at the reasons for and consequences of this. Would the meeting be more effective if these behaviours were more prevalent?

## SELF-ORIENTED EMOTIONAL BEHAVIOUR

In addition to the task and maintenance behaviours described above some behaviours may be aimed at meeting a personal need or goal without consideration of the group (self-oriented behaviours) and this type of behaviour will often hinder the group's achievement.

Some of the basic causes of these self-oriented behaviours are:

(1) Identity
  • What is my place in this group?
  • In this meeting how should I present myself?
  • What role have I got in this context?
  • What role should I play?

(2) Goals
- Which of my needs and goals can be met in this meeting?
- How can the meeting best help me to achieve my objectives?
- Which of the group's goals do I want to support?

(3) Power and control
- How much power, control and influence have I got in this group?

| | Group members | | | | | |
|---|---|---|---|---|---|---|
| **Task roles** | | | | | | |
| Proposing | | | | | | |
| Building | | | | | | |
| Presenting: information or opinion | | | | | | |
| Seeking: information or opinion | | | | | | |
| Testing Understanding | | | | | | |
| Agreement | | | | | | |
| Quality | | | | | | |
| Keeping group on course | | | | | | |
| Summarizing | | | | | | |
| **Maintenance roles** | | | | | | |
| Supporting/Encouraging | | | | | | |
| Gatekeeping: Bringing in | | | | | | |
| Shutting out +ve | | | | | | |
| Shutting out −ve | | | | | | |
| Harmonizing | | | | | | |
| Tension releasing | | | | | | |
| Showing attention (give comments) | | | | | | |

Fill in the group members' names at the top of each column. Each time a group member takes a particular role, put a tick alongside the category in the column for that individual.

FIGURE 22.6 Functional roles observation form

- How much do I want?
- How do I increase my power and influence?
(4) Acceptance and intimacy
  - How well am I accepted and/or liked by others at the meeting?
  - Do I accept and like them?
  - How emotionally close do I want to be to them?

These causes can lead to a further series of roles termed individual roles and these are aimed at satisfying individual needs. They are often irrelevant or dysfunctional to the task and maintenance functions. [. . .]

As the group develops and members' needs become more integrated with group goals, the proportion of self-oriented behaviour should decrease and there should be more task and maintenance behaviour.

Where you observe self-oriented emotional behaviour in a meeting, the categories above may help to give a possible interpretation of what is happening and why the individual is behaving in that particular way.

# NORMS

Some examples of the types of behaviour which might be classified as norms are:

- way of speaking (swearing, rudeness, politeness);
- following of procedure;
- dress;
- amount of participation;
- punctuality;
- innovativeness (or lack of it);
- aggression;
- rational approach;
- formality;
  etc.

Norms are shared expectations and attitudes. They are agreements about what should be thought, felt or done and the way in which actions should be carried out. The agreements may be explicit (verbalized) or implicit, and the implicit agreements may be either conscious or unconscious. In addition,

| Type of norm | Explicit | Implicit | |
|---|---|---|---|
| | | Conscious | Unconscious |
| Static | | | |
| Dynamic | | | |

FIGURE 22.7 Classification of norms

| General comments about the success or otherwise of the meeting | tick appropriate column for each item | strongly agree | mildly agree | mildly disagree | strongly disagree |
|---|---|---|---|---|---|
| 1. The purpose of the meeting was clear to all | | | | | |
| 2. There was agreement amongst members about their objectives | | | | | |
| 3. There was commitment by all to the objectives of the meeting | | | | | |
| 4. There was pertinent participation by all | | | | | |
| 5. Mutual interest was shown in all members' points of view | | | | | |
| 6. Individuals or subgroups did not dominate the proceedings | | | | | |
| 7. Disagreements were expressed and explained in order to try to resolve them | | | | | |
| 8. Any criticism was frank and constructive and perceived as such | | | | | |
| 9. The atmosphere was supportive and helpful | | | | | |
| 10. Group members were interested in the meeting | | | | | |
| 11. Decisions were taken when necessary | | | | | |
| 12. Everyone contributed fully to the making of decisions | | | | | |
| 13. The decisions taken were fully understood and supported | | | | | |
| 14. Problems were tackled in an appropriate manner including a full diagnosis | | | | | |
| 15. The resources of the group were fully used | | | | | |
| 16. Members were able to be creative where this was appropriate | | | | | |
| 17. The meeting was able to function in a flexible manner when necessary | | | | | |
| 18. The meeting did not stray off course | | | | | |
| 19. Time was used optimally and not wasted | | | | | |
| 20. The performance of the leader was appropriate to the task and the group | | | | | |
| 21. Both task and maintenance functions were fulfilled as necessary | | | | | |
| 22. Feelings were expressed freely and accepted | | | | | |

| | | | | |
|---|---|---|---|---|
| 23. No dysfunctional norms evolved or were present | | | | |
| 24. The group was cohesive | | | | |
| 25. Cohesiveness was channelled towards performance | | | | |

*Additional comments*



FIGURE 22.8 Meetings rating form

norms may be static or dynamic. Static norms are those that are accepted by everyone in the group and dynamic norms are the ones for which it is necessary for the group to bring pressure to bear on some individuals to make them conform to group norms. So in observing a meeting we can classify any norms that we see into the matrix in Figure 22.7.

The norms can be additionally classified by putting the letters U, H or N (unhelpful, helpful or neutral) after them depending on whether they help the group in its task or not.

The formation of norms often occurs around critical incidents. For example, someone may challenge the chairperson of the meeting concerning how the meeting is being run. What happens next may help to form group norms concerning the use of authority in the group and the 'legitimacy' of challenging that authority. As an observer, it can be useful to note critical incidents and their consequences.

## THE COMPLETE MEETING

So far we have looked analytically at a variety of specific issues which can be observed when studying meetings. It is useful to focus on these in order to study and improve what is happening in a meeting. However, it is difficult to carry out more than one or two of the types of observation for any one meeting unless this is done by several observers. A more global observation and rating of the meeting can be carried out using the meetings rating form in Figure 22.8. Being familiar with the issues above helps in completing the form. Using this form can be helpful in identifying which area to concentrate your observations on for future meetings of the same group.

One reason for studying meetings is for research purposes and to understand the behaviour that occurs in these settings. Other reasons for studying meetings are to bring about improvements in your own performance in future meetings and/or to help the group being observed to improve. Here we have just dealt with the observation and recording of meetings. [. . .] Where we want to improve the effectiveness of meetings it is important that the results of observations are shared in an appropriate manner with the members of the meeting.

# CHAPTER 23

# Observation Outside Meetings

## L. COHEN AND L. MANION

[. . .]

There are two principal types of observation – participant observation and non-participant observation. In the former, observers engage in the very activities they set out to observe. Often, their 'cover' is so complete that as far as the other participants are concerned, they are simply one of the group. [. . .]

Cover is not necessarily a prerequisite observation. In an intensive study of a small group of working-class boys during their last two years at school and their first months in employment, Willis (1977) attended all the different subject classes at school – 'not as a teacher, but as a member of the class – and worked alongside each boy in industry for a short period.

Non-participant observers, on the other hand, stand aloof from the group activities they are investigating and eschew group membership – no great difficulty for King, an adult observer in infant classrooms. Listen to him recounting how he firmly established his non-participant status with young children:

> I rapidly learnt that children in infants' classrooms define any adult as another teacher or teacher surrogate. To avoid being engaged in conversation, being asked to spell words or admire pictures, I evolved the following technique.
>
> To begin with, I kept standing so that physical height created social distance . . . Next, I did not show immediate interest in what the children were doing, or talk to them. When I was talked to I smiled politely and if necessary I referred the child asking a question to the teacher. Most importantly, I avoided eye contact: if you do not look you will not be seen.
>
> (King, 1979)

The best illustration of the non-participant observer role is perhaps the case of the researcher sitting at the back of a classroom coding up every three seconds the verbal exchanges between teacher and pupils by means of a structured set of observational categories.

It is frequently the case that the type of observation undertaken by the researcher is associated with the type of setting in which the research takes place. [. . .]

A number of factors intrude to make one or other of the observational strategies the dominant mode of enquiry in a particular type of setting. Bailey explains as follows:

In a natural setting it is difficult for the researcher who wishes to be covert not to act as a participant. If the researcher does not participate, there is little to explain his [sic] presence, as he is very obvious to the actual participants. . . . Most studies in a natural setting are unstructured participant observation studies. . . . Much the opposite is true in an artificial environment. Since there is no natural setting, in a sense none of the persons being studied are really participants of long standing, and thus may accept a non-participant observer more readily. . . . Laboratory settings also enable a non-participant observer to use sophisticated equipment such as videotape and tape recordings. . . . Thus most studies in an artificial laboratory setting will be structured and will be non-participant studies.

(Bailey, 1978)

## WHY PARTICIPANT OBSERVATION?

The current vogue enjoyed by the case study conducted on participant observation lines is not difficult to account for. This form of research is eminently suitable to many of the problems that the educational investigator faces.

The natural scientist, Schutz points out, explores a field that means nothing to the molecules, atoms and electrons therein (Schutz, 1962). By contrast, the subject matter of the world in which the educational researcher is interested is composed of people and is essentially meaningful. That world is subjectively structured, possessing particular meanings for its inhabitants. The task of the educational investigator is very often to explain the means by which an orderly social world is established and maintained in terms of its shared meanings. How do participant observation techniques assist the researcher in this task? Bailey (1978) identifies some inherent advantages in the participant observation approach:

(1) Observation studies are superior to experiments and surveys when data are being collected on non-verbal behaviour.
(2) In observation studies, investigators are able to discern ongoing behaviour as it occurs and are able to make appropriate notes about its salient features.
(3) Because case study observations take place over an extended period of time, researchers can develop more intimate and informal relationships with those they are observing, generally in more natural environments than those in which experiments and surveys are conducted.
(4) Case study observations are less reactive than other types of data-gathering methods. For example, in laboratory-based experiments and in surveys that depend upon verbal responses to structured questions, bias can be introduced in the very data that researchers are attempting to study.

On the other hand, participant observation studies are not without their critics (Stake, 1978). The accounts that typically emerge from participant observations are often described as subjective, biased, impressionistic, idiosyncratic and lacking in the precise quantifiable measures that are the hallmark of survey research and experimentation. Whilst it is probably true that nothing can give better insight into the life of a gang of juvenile delinquents than going to live with them for an extended period of time, critics of participant observation studies will point to the dangers of 'going native' as a result of playing a role within such a group. How do we know that observers do not lose their perspective and become blind to the peculiarities that they are supposed to be investigating?

These criticisms raise questions about two types of validity in observation-based research. In effect, comments about the subjective and idiosyncratic nature of the participant observation study are to do with its external validity. How do we know that the results of this one piece of research are applicable to other situations? Fears that observers' judgement will be affected by their close involvement in the group relate to the internal validity of the method. How do we know that the results of this one piece of research represent the real thing, the genuine product? [. . .] We can best illustrate the concern of participant observers for the validity of their data by giving a brief outline of a typical strategy in participant observation research. Denzin uses the term 'analytical induction' to describe the broad strategy of participant observation that is set out in Box 1.

## RECORDING OBSERVATIONS

[. . .]

### BOX 1

*Steps in participant observation (Source:* Denzin, 1970)

1. A rough definition of the phenomenon is formulated.
2. A hypothetical explanation of that phenomenon is formulated.
3. One case is studied in the light of the hypothesis, with the object of determining whether or not the hypothesis fits the facts in that case.
4. If the hypothesis does not fit the facts, either the hypothesis is reformulated or the phenomenon to be explained is redefined so that the case is excluded.
5. Practical certainty may be attained after a small number of cases has been examined, but the discovery of negative cases disproves the explanation and requires a reformulation.
6. This procedure of examining cases, redefining the phenomenon, and reformulating the hypothesis is continued until a universal relationship is established, each negative case calling for a redefinition or a reformulation.

BOX 2

*Field notes in observation studies (Source:* Lofland, 1971)

1. Record the notes as quickly as possible after observation, since the quantity of information forgotten is very slight over a short period of time but accelerates quickly as more time passes.
2. Discipline yourself to write notes quickly and reconcile yourself to the fact that although it may seem ironic, recording of field notes can be expected to take as long as is spent in actual observation.
3. Dictating rather than writing is acceptable if one can afford it, but writing has the advantage of stimulating thought.
4. Typing field notes is vastly preferable to handwriting because it is faster and easier to read, especially when making multiple copies.
5. It is advisable to make at least two copies of field notes.
6. The notes ought to be full enough adequately to summon up for one again, months later, a reasonably vivid picture of any described event. This probably means that one ought to be writing up, at the very minimum, at least a couple of single space typed pages for every hour of observation.

The recording of observations is a frequent source of concern to inexperienced case study researchers. How much ought to be recorded? In what form should the recordings be made? What does one do with the mass of recorded data? Lofland gives a number of useful suggestions about collecting field notes which are summarized in Box 2.

The sort of note-taking recommended by Lofland and actually undertaken by King (1979) and Wolcott (1973) in their ethnographic accounts grows out of the nature of the unstructured observation study. Note-taking, confessed Wolcott, helped him fight the acute boredom that he sometimes felt when observing the interminable meetings that are the daily lot of the school principal. Occasionally, however, a series of events would occur so quickly that Wolcott had time only to make cursory notes which he supplemented later with fuller accounts. One useful tip from this experienced ethnographer is worth noting: never resume your observations until the notes from the preceding observation are complete. There is nothing to be gained merely by your presence as an observer. Until your observations and impressions from one visit are a matter of record, there is little point in returning to the classroom or school and reducing the impact of one set of events by superimposing another and more recent set. Indeed, when to record one's data is but one of a number of practical problems identified by Walker, which are listed in Box 3.

BOX 3

---

*The case study and problems of selection*
(*Source:* Adapted from Walker, 1980)

Among the issues confronting the researcher at the outset of a case study are the problems of selection. The following questions indicate some of the obstacles in this respect:

1. How do you get from the initial idea to the working design (from the idea to a specification, to usable data)?
2. What do you lose in the process?
3. What unwanted concerns do you take on board as a result?
4. How do you find a site which provides the best location for the design?
5. How do you locate, identify and approach key informants?
6. How they see you creates a context within which you see them. How can you handle such social complexities?
7. How do you record evidence? When? How much?
8. How do you file and categorize it?
9. How much time do you give to thinking and reflecting about what you are doing?
10. At what points do you show your subject what you are doing?
11. At what points do you give them control over who sees what?
12. Who sees the reports first?

---

[. . .]

# REFERENCES

Bailey, K. D. (1978) *Methods of social research.* London: Collier/Macmillan.

Denzin, N. K. (1970) *The research act in sociology: a theoretical introduction to sociological methods.* London: Butterworth.

Lofland, J. (1971) *Analysing social settings.* Belmont, CA: Wadsworth.

King, R. (1979) *All Things Bright and Beautiful.* Chichester: Wiley.

Schutz, A. (1962) *Collected papers.* The Hague: Nijhoff.

Stake, R. E. (1978) The case study method in social inquiry, *Educational Researcher,* February.

Walker, R. (1980) Making sense and losing meaning: problems of selection in doing case study, in H. Simons (ed.) *Towards a science of the singular.* Norwich: Centre for Applied Research in Education, University of East Anglia.

Willis, P. E. (1977) *Learning to labour.* London: Saxon House.

Wolcott, H. F. (1973) *The man in the principal's office.* New York: Holt, Rinehart & Winston.

# CHAPTER 24

# Analysing
# and Presenting Quantitative Data

JASON HARDMAN

Statistical techniques are 'tools' used for the analysis and presentation of information or data. Like the tools of a mechanic, each statistical tool is fashioned for a specific job and thus, to be employed effectively, the potential user must understand its function. Just as one would not use a spanner other than to tighten a nut, statistical techniques cannot be used indiscriminantly when analysing and presenting data.[1] This chapter concentrates on **descriptive** statistical techniques which are used simply to summarize, and hence clarify, data. In doing so it is hoped to provide a guide as to when and why certain descriptive methods can and should be applied. More sophisticated statistical techniques which provide a means of estimating the likelihood that results from a particular sample (e.g. the percentage of female staff employed by a particular LEA) will reflect those of the parent population (e.g. the percentage of female staff employed by all LEAs combined), are beyond the scope of this chapter and, in any case, are not likely to be relevant when conducting relatively small-scale investigations.

The techniques to be examined do not require specialized mathematical knowledge beyond basic arithmetic; consequently all calculations can be performend by hand. However, a feature of this chapter which reflects the growing prominence of computers in the workplace is the recommendation that statistical software packages be utilized wherever possible. Such packages are becoming more 'user-friendly' (menu-driven, on-screen help facilities), and they bring both speed and accuracy to potentially laborious calculations. They also tend to incorporate facilities for creating very polished charts and tables which, depending on the package, can be exported and included in text documents.

---

1 A cautionary note worth sounding at this point concerns the 'social' nature of data. The process of research 'creates' data which are affected by the decisions, interests, and values of all those involved from researcher through to subject. Rather than standing alone, therefore, statistical data must be interpreted and presented **within the context of the study.** Such methodological considerations are given a full discussion by Reid (1987), who outlines several points to keep in mind when confronting statistical data. These amount to the recommendation that data be fully explained in terms of when, why and how they were produced and by whom. Moreover, presented material (e.g. text, tables, charts etc.) should be unambiguous in both form and content.

# VARIABLES – THE RAW MATERIALS OF RESEARCH

In collecting data you, the researcher, are essentially making *measurements* of certain *characteristics* of a particular population of cases; where a case may be a person, an event, an institution, etc. You may therefore wish to examine the gender of students at a particular university, the type of weather in London on each day during July, or the budget share of maintained schools in England and Wales. Such measures are referred to as **variables** to denote that individual cases may differ (i.e. take different values) with respect to the characteristic in question. Thus, each student at the above university will be attributed the value male or female; each day in July classified as sunny, cloudy, rainy, etc.; and each school in England and Wales measured in terms of its annual allocation of public funds.

Variables can be categorized according to a number of criteria. The most useful distinction concerns their **level of measurement** or **scale**. This criterion is important because it dictates the applicability of statistical procedures. In other words, certain procedures are only appropriate for certain types of data as defined by the scale of the relevant variable. Stevens (1946) delineated three levels of measurement, distinguishing between nominal, ordinal, and interval/ratio data. An example of each type of data should help to clarify the differences between the scales.

## Nominal data

An example of a variety measured on the nominal scale is gender. The values of this type of variable are labelled and *categorized* (e.g. 'male' and 'female'). The distinction between the categories is thus *qualitative* and no attempt is made to measure their size.

## Ordinal data

The values of an ordinal type variable are *ranked* in terms of size or magnitude. A typical ordinal scale is utilized when measuring an attitude towards something (e.g. the quality of food in the staff canteen), and usually comprises 5 or 7 points ranging from, for example, 'very poor' to 'very good'. Such scales are limited in that they *do not reveal the size of the difference between the different rankings*. Therefore, if Joe believed the food in the canteen to be 'very good', while Kath only rated it as 'good', it would be possible to state that Joe rated the quality of the food *more* highly than Kath but not by *how much* more. The relationship between ordinal values is thus one of order and not of quantity.

## Interval/ratio data

A distinction between interval and ratio data can and has been made. However, as it will be demonstrated below, in practice this distinction tends not to be important.

A variable classified as interval has *ordered values, the differences between which are equal*. A good example is temperature. If on 11 July the temperature is 24°C, while on 25 November it is recorded as 8°C, it is possible to say that the temperature on 11 July was 16° higher than on 25 November. Interval variables thus have a *standard unit of measurement* which enables the difference between values to be quantified.

However, it is incorrect to say that it was *three times* as hot on 11 July as on 25 November. This is due to the mathematical fact that such a *ratio* will only be valid when a scale has a true zero point, a property that the temperature scale lacks (i.e. 0°C does not mean that there is no temperature). Accordingly, a ratio scale of measurement differs from that of interval only because it has a *meaningful zero point*. This distinction between the two data types is, however, often overlooked because, as Reid (1987) pointed out, most social science variables have, at least theoretically, a zero point.

The order in which the scales are presented above is often viewed to reflect an increasing degree of sophistication. Thus interval/ratio scales allow quantitative assessments and are seen as the highest order of measurement in contrast to the simple, qualitative nature of nominal data.

In addition to level of measurement, variables are also frequently classified according to whether they are discrete or continuous. This classification has implications for the way data can be presented in a chart (see below). If the values of a variable are limited to a finite number of distinct observable categories, it is said to be **discrete**. That is to say the values of a discrete variable are units which cannot be logically subdivided, such as people (i.e. people can only be counted as whole units – the average family does not actually contain 2.4 children!). Inevitably, all nominal variables are discrete.

On the other hand, a **continuous** variable could theoretically take an infinite number of values such that between any two values it would always be possible to find a third (e.g. time). Consequently, when measuring (i.e. allocating a value to) a continuous variable the researcher must decide upon a suitable unit. For example, time to complete a task may be reported in minutes or seconds or milliseconds, etc. If minutes were chosen, a recorded time of 25 minutes would in fact cover all times which fell between 24.5 and 25.5 minutes. A consequence of this 'rounding up' when measuring continuous variables is that the data give the impression of being discrete. Therefore, to distinguish between a discrete and continuous variable the conceptual basis for the measurements must be borne in mind.

## PREPARING THE DATA FOR ANALYSIS

At this stage in the research process you should have data pertaining to all the relevant variables you wish to examine for each case to be included in the study.[2]

2 In fact it is unlikely, especially when dealing with a large sample, that you will have valid data on every variable for every case. It is often the case that some data will be missing. This could be for a variety of reasons – errors or omissions on the part of the respondent when filling out a questionnaire, failure of the researcher to ask a particular question in an interview, etc. In such cases the missing data is treated as a separate category or value.

## TABLE 24.1
*Career status data of employees at Cleverdick University*

| ID | GENDER | JOB CATEGORY | YEARS AS EMPLOYEE | GENERAL HAPPINESS |
|----|--------|--------------|-------------------|-------------------|
| 1  | male   | lecturer           | 7  | very happy     |
| 2  | male   | porter             | 4  | quite happy    |
| 3  | female | lecturer           | 4  | not very happy |
| 4  | female | lecturer           | 6  | quite happy    |
| 5  | female | research fellow    | 1  | very happy     |
| 6  | male   | librarian          | 5  | not very happy |
| 7  | female | head librarian     | 13 | quite happy    |
| 8  | male   | security guard     | 3  | very happy     |
| 9  | male   | research assistant | 2  | quite happy    |
| 10 | female | research student   | 1  | not very happy |
| 11 | male   | lecturer           | 5  | quite happy    |
| 12 | male   | cook               | 4  | quite happy    |
| 13 | female | receptionist       | 8  | very happy     |
| 14 | female | research assistant | 3  | quite happy    |
| 15 | female | secretary          | 4  | quite happy    |
| 16 | male   | lecturer           | 7  | quite happy    |
| 17 | male   | porter             | 6  | very happy     |
| 18 | female | secretary          | 14 | quite happy    |
| 19 | male   | librarian          | 5  | very happy     |
| 20 | female | lecturer           | 9  | quite happy    |

Throughout the rest of this chapter a hypothetical set of data will be referred to in order to illustrate the statistical techniques available for ordering and summarizing this data. These sample data are presented in Table 24.1. Each case is an employee of 'Cleverdick University' and the data cover a range of variables relating to the career status of each employee.

This sample is typical of the type of data which may be gleaned from a series of questionnaires or interviews. Of the twenty cases or respondents,[3] each has been assigned a value for the variables 'gender', 'job category', 'years as employee', and 'general happiness'. It should be noted that personal names are not included and that individual respondents are instead identified by a number – 'id'. The personal nature of the data under investigation warrants such confidentiality.[4]

A preliminary glance at the data in Table 24.1 reveals a wide variation in the values of the variable 'job category', many of which appear only once or twice (e.g. 'porter', 'research assistant', etc.). This poses a problem as it prevents the

3 This is a very small sample and is used merely for illustrative purposes.

4 It is often advisable to provide assurances that data will be kept confidential to the research team when recruiting respondents.

job category data from being adequately summarized. For this reason I have decided to simplify the values of the variable from specific job descriptions such as 'security guard' to more general categories – in this case 'non-academic staff', the other revised categories being 'lecturer', 'research staff', administration staff, and 'library staff'. Thus by decreasing the number of categories or values the distribution of employees' job categories is made more explicit. However, the advantage of limiting data in this way must always be balanced against the cost of sacrificing individual case detail.

One point worth mentioning here concerns the coding of data. This is the process, often employed by researchers, of systematically converting the values of each variable to numerical form prior to analysis. Bryman and Cramer (1990) state that data should be coded because 'it is easier to analyse data consisting of numbers rather than a mixture of numbers and other characters such as alphabetic letters'. Indeed it would certainly save time when preparing a summary of the data – as in Table 24.1 – if, for example, each job category was represented by a single number rather than a long string of letters. However, although this may be the case when handling a large amount of data, it is hardly necessary for a small-scale project.[5]

## DESCRIPTIVE STATISTICAL TECHNIQUES

Prior to analysis the data as they are presented in Table 24.1 are practically useless – the information they contain is unfocused and difficult to extract. It is the task of the researcher to try to make this information more explicit by revealing the way in which the sample is distributed with respect to the variables under investigation. In other words the data must be summarized, their patterns exposed, and some individual case detail sacrified to enable comprehension.

Several techniques have been devised for summarizing the properties of a sample, some of which are obvious while others are more sophisticated. All such techniques are categorized as descriptive statistics.

### The frequency distribution

The easiest way to summarize a set of data is simply to count the occurences of each value or category for the particular variable under investigation. For example, we may wish to know how many respondents from the Cleverdick University sample are men and how many are women. By merely totalling the number of cases that fall into each category (i.e. 'male' and 'female') a frequency distribution can be created thereby revealing the composition of the sample with respect to 'gender'. This can then be presented as in Table 24.2.

5 The statistical procedures outlined in this chapter do not require the data to be coded. The only data subject to arithmetic manipulation are those measured on the interval/ratio scale, which are numeric by nature. Moreover, non-numerical data are often suitable for use with modern statistical software packages.

TABLE 24.2
*Frequency distribution of gender* nominal

| VALUE | FREQUENCY |
|-------|-----------|
| male | 10 |
| female | 10 |
| Total | 20 |

Notice that the total frequency count corresponds to the number of respondents in the sample. With such a small sample the process of counting each case is relatively straightforward. However, when dealing with a much larger sample the use of computer software makes light work of an arduous task. Moreover, as long as the data file is free of error, the accuracy of any calculations made by the computer is assured.

The frequency distribution provides a basic means for ordering data, enabling the spread of the sample across the categories to be seen at a glance. It is possible to expand on the basic distribution by converting the frequencies to percentages, thereby revealing the relative size of each category.

Taking the variable 'job category' the inclusion of percentages in Table 24.3 enables us to see, for example, that lecturers constitute almost one-third of the sample, while only 1 in 10 of the cases examined are administration staff. For a small sample these calculations can be performed by hand; however, when using statistical software there is invariably an option for including relative percentages (as well as other measures) in a frequency distribution table.

For a variable such as 'job category' which can take several values, it is often useful to display the frequency distribution in the form of a chart. Charts tend to be more easily assimilated than tables of figures and help to emphasize the relative dimensions of each category.

TABLE 24.3
*Frequency distribution of job category* ordinal

| VALUE | FREQUENCY | RELATIVE PERCENTAGE |
|-------|-----------|---------------------|
| lecturer | 6 | 30% |
| research staff | 4 | 20% |
| admin. staff | 2 | 10% |
| library staff | 3 | 15% |
| non-acad. staff | 5 | 25% |
| Total | 20 | 100% |

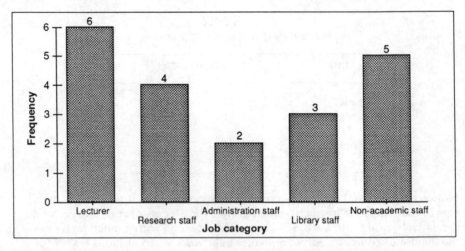

FIGURE 24.1 Bar chart of job category data

The **bar chart** in Figure 24.1 is an alternative to the frequency distribution in Table 24.3. It is usually inappropriate to include both in a report as they contain exactly the same information – in fact the chart is less informative in that it does not display the percentages. Each column or bar represents a different value or category of the variable. The height of the bars coincides with the number of cases in each category. For clarity each bar is labelled with the frequency it is representing.

To emphasize the discrete nature of the categories of the variable 'job category', the bars are spaced apart. This is in contrast to the way in which a continuous variable is charted with adjacent bars merging (see Figure 24.3).

An alternative to bar charts when presenting frequency data is the **pie chart** (see Figure 24.2). Here the total 'pie' represents the entire sample (100%) and each 'slice' a particular category or value. The area of each slice is proportional to the frequency of the category it represents and so the distribution of the sample amongst the various categories can be discerned.

The potential for distorting results if charts are constructed incorrectly is probably as good a reason as any for employing a computer. As long as the data it is working with is correct then a computer will produce accurate charts. In addition computer constructed charts can often be produced at the touch of a button and with very professional results. Charts will be automatically labelled and once created can be formatted to suit the researcher's requirements. Thus, for example, if the researcher wished to emphasize the proportion of lecturers in the sample as opposed to all other categories of staff, the relevant slice in the pie chart could be exploded as in Figure 24.2.

Perhaps the only drawback when using computer software to construct charts concerns the potential for over-elaboration. Most charting facilities allow effects such as shadowing and 3D, which can occasionally create pleasing results. However, if taken to extremes such decoration can clutter the chart or even obscure the result thus defeating the object of creating the chart in the first place. As Reid (1987) wisely pointed out, charts 'can be as simple or as

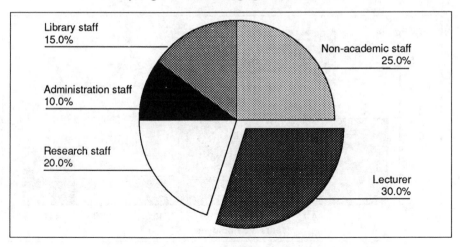

FIGURE 24.2 Pie chart of job category data

elaborate as the resources and the imagination of the researcher permits, but they must, ultimately, *increase* the accessibility of the information to other readers without sacrificing or compromising the accuracy of the original data.'

Frequency distributions in the form of tables or charts can be used to summarize data of any scale, not just the nominal variables used in the above examples. However, when a set of data covers a wide range of values, as is often the case for interval/ratio variables, they must first be grouped or aggregated into ordered categories in order to be adequately summarized. This can be demonstrated by using the variable 'years as employee'.

TABLE 24.4<br/>*Frequency distribution of years as employee*

| VALUE | FREQUENCY | RELATIVE PERCENTAGE |
|---|---|---|
| 1–2 years | 3 | 15% |
| 3–4 years | 6 | 30% |
| 5–6 years | 5 | 25% |
| 7–8 years | 3 | 15% |
| 9–10 years | 1 | 5% |
| 11–12 years | 0 | 0% |
| 13+ years | 2 | 10% |
| Total | 20 | 100% |

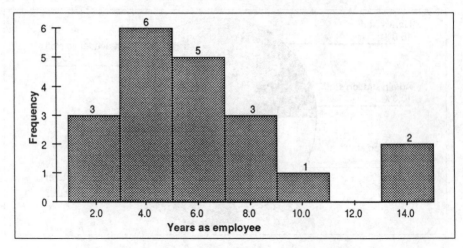

FIGURE 24.3 Histogram of years as employee data

Thus, rather than measuring individuals in terms of the specific number of years that they have been employed by Cleverdick University, each case is assigned to a *discrete* category which spans a number of years of employment.[6]

One effect of grouping the data in this way is to make it ordinal rather than interval. Thus, although they are now in a form that will help elucidate the spread of the variable more clearly, the sophistication of the data has been compromised. Reid (1987) urged caution when considering the tactic of aggregating categories: 'The general rule is to measure and categorize at the highest level possible so that your original "raw" data can later be aggregated if – but only if – it seems valuable to do so.'

To emphasize that 'years as employee' is a continuous variable, when it is charted, the bars are made to run into one another at the boundaries of each category. Such a chart is known as a histogram, and is presented in Figure 24.3.

The final variable in our sample – the ordinal variable 'general happiness' would also be presented as a histogram as it is measuring a continuum, albeit a theoretical one. However, unlike 'years as employee', the data relating to the 'general happiness' variable do not need to be grouped. In fact most ordinal variables have sufficiently few categories or values to allow an adequate frequency distribution to be constructed.

In summary, a frequency distribution

- is a versatile analytical tool which can be used with data of all scales;
- reveals the spread of the data across the values or categories of a variable;
- can be presented as either a table or a chart.

It is thus a useful preliminary technique that enables potentially interesting trends to be highlighted.

6 This aggregation of the data is necessary because the sample is very small and the distribution or spread of the variable 'years as employee' is wide. Thus there are a lot of categories all of which contain only one or two cases. If left in this form a chart or table of the data would reveal very much.

# Measuring the 'shape' of data

The main objective of descriptive statistics is to provide a *concise* description of a set of data without comprising its accuracy and informational value. This can be achieved to some extent, as we have seen, by ordering the data into a frequency distribution. However, in order to provide a basis for more sophisticated statistical methods it is necessary to be able to describe a set of data by a single figure.

The key feature of any set of data is revealed in the charts presented above. It is the shape of these charts or, more specifically, the way in which the data are spread or dispersed across the range of possible values, which defines the underlying data distribution. There are available several statistical techniques that allow this variability, or some aspect of it, to be measured. Accordingly, in order to describe a data distribution it is sufficient to be able to calculate one or more of these measures.

Measures of variability fall into one of two categories: (i) measures of central tendency; or (ii) measures of dispersion. When using these techniques the researcher must be especially mindful of the level of measurement of the data he or she is working with. Thus, there are three measures of central tendency, for example, only one of which is suitable for all levels of measurement.

## Measures of central tendency

Measures of central tendency all have a similar goal which is to establish the *average* value in a distribution. These techniques thus attempt to describe a set of data in terms of the typical or most representative value.

The most familiar measure is probably the **arithmetic mean** whereby the sum of all the values in a distribution is divided by the number of cases. Thus for the variable 'years as employee':

Arithmetic Mean = 110/20 = 5.5 years

This 'average' is comprehensive (it takes into account all the values in a distribution) and easily understood, however it has one or two drawbacks. It is only suitable for use with interval/ratio level data, and it is vulnerable to distortion when a distribution contains extreme values or outliers (this is especially so for small samples). Thus if, for example, employee number 10 in our sample had been employed for 40 years instead of 1 year, the arithmetic mean would work out to 7.45 years – quite a dramatic change. For this reason outliers may sometimes be excluded from analyses, although in doing so the researcher may in fact distort the results for the sake of a more 'representative' distribution.

The **median** is another measure of central tendency and is the value which divides a distribution equally in half (it is also known as the 50th percentile). Thus if the values of a distribution of, say, 145 cases were arranged in ascending order, the value of case number 73 would be the median. Where there are an even number of cases, as in our sample of 20, and thus no single middle case, the middle pair of scores are added together and divided by 2 (i.e. 'averaged') to provide a hypothetical midpoint.

The median is less intuitively understood than the mean and is based on only one case from the whole distribution. Furthermore it is only suitable for use with ordinal and interval/ratio based data. However, by emphasizing the middle of a distribution it is not susceptible, as the means is, to outlying values.

The final measure of central tendency is the most flexible (i.e. suitable for any data type) and is called the mode. It is simply the value in a distribution that occurs most frequently, and may therefore be derived from a frequency distribution table. The mode of the variable 'job category', for instance, is 'lecturer'. Despite its universal suitability and simplicity the mode is unpopular as it fails to take into account all the values in a distribution. Moreover, it is possible to have more than one mode in a distribution thus leading to problems in interpretation.

Although all three measures – mean, median, and mode – attempt to describe the typical value in a set of data, they do so in different ways and often produce different outcomes. Where the level of measurement permits, therefore, it is advisable to calculate all three to provide a more coherent picture of the distribution average.

## Measures of dispersion

Measures of dispersion are complementary to those of central tendency. They quantify the amount of variation in a set of data and thus, along with the average value, complete the description of a distribution.

The most intuitive way to describe the spread of a set of data is to simply state the highest and lowest values in the distribution – a measure of dispersion known as the range.[7] However, although easy to understand, the range is susceptible to outlying values which can contribute to a disorted result.

An alternative is the inter-quartile range. This concentrates on the middle 50% of values in a distribution and thus eliminates any extreme values. The procedure for determining this range is simple. First the distribution is ordered from lowest to highest and then divided into four equal parts. The first and last portions, which respectively contain the lowest and highest 25% of the values, are then discarded leaving a trunctuated range between the 25th and 75th percentiles. This is the interquartile range. Unfortunately, by ignoring 50% of the data this measure of dispersion loses a lot of information and may thus provide an inadequate description. The choice of which range to use is therefore dependent on the spread of the particular distribution, in particular the presence or absence of outliers.

Although the range and interquartile range can be calculated for data measured on an interval/ratio scale this is infrequently done. By far the most common measure of dispersion for this level of measurement is the standard deviation. This attempts to measure the spread or dispersion in a set of data by calculating the average amount of deviation from the mean.[8] It thus determines whether values are generally near or far from the mean.

7 In order to discern the highest and lowest values of a distribution, the data must be placed in order. Only ordinal and interval/ratio level data are therefore suitable for use with this technique.

8 The calculation of the standard deviation is quite long-winded and, given that the emphasis of this chapter is on the use of computers, it will not be given here. Nevertheless, the more adventurous reader will find the relevant procedure in any introductory text on statistics.

By providing information about the magnitude of the dispersion in a set of scores, the standard deviation places the mean value in context. It gives an indication of the degree to which values vary or fluctuate around this average figure. Moreover, the standard deviation enables a direct comparison of the amount of dispersal for comparable samples (i.e. different cases from the same population measured on the same variables), such that two samples may be found to have similar means but large differences in the amount of variation between values.

The standard deviation is subject to the pros and cons of employing all the values in a distribution. It thus loses no information but at the same time is at the mercy of outlying values. Also it is only suitable, as is the mean, for data measured on an interval/ratio scale. Nevertheless its importance dictates that whenever possible it should be calculated.

As may have been noticed the measures of dispersion outlined are all unsuitable for use with nominal level data. Basically this is because the qualitative nature of this data means that it is not amenable to mathematical manipulation. Accordingly the most appropriate way of examining the dispersion for data of this sort is probably via charts and histograms.

Each of the measures of central tendency and dispersion discussed above can be calculated, usually by a single command, using statistical software.

## Bivariate analysis

Up to now we have concentrated on techniques which describe the characteristics of a sample in terms of one variable. These techniques are known as univariate statistics. However, in addition to this we are frequently concerned with identifying *relationships* between variables. For example, we may wish to examine how 'general happiness' varies according to respondents' 'gender'. Here we are looking at the connection between *two* variables and so the relevant analytical techniques are called bivariate statistics. We will briefly examine the preliminary steps for identifying bivariate associations.

Taking the above example, the relationship between the variables 'general happiness' and 'gender' can be expressed using a technique called **cross-tabulation**. This procedure is useful with data such as these which are measured at the nominal and ordinal levels. The results are shown in Table 24.5.

TABLE 24.5
*Cross-tabulation of gender and general happiness*

|  | NOT VERY HAPPY | QUITE HAPPY | VERY HAPPY | TOTAL |
|---|---|---|---|---|
| Male | 1 | 5 | 4 | 10 |
| Female | 2 | 6 | 2 | 10 |
| Total | 3 | 11 | 6 | 20 |

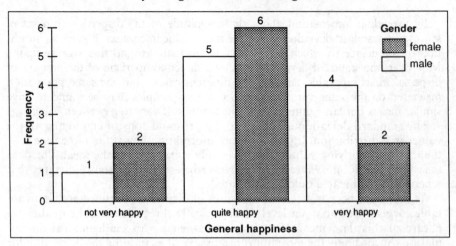

FIGURE 24.4 Bar chart of general happiness by gender

Table 24.5 details the pairs of values taken by each case for the two variables and is alternatively referred to as a contingency table. Each case is represented once, and only once, as evidenced by the grand total in the bottom right-hand corner which is equal to the number of cases in the sample. These data can also be presented as a chart as in Figure 24.4.

This is known as a compound bar chart. The frequency of each category of 'general happiness' is delineated according to 'gender' which results in the separate clusters of bars. In all other ways it is identical to the bar charts discussed earlier.

There are other ways to present this data, although they will not be detailed here. Suffice to say that presentations such as those above provide a preliminary profile of the relationship between two variables of nominal or interval scale.

As far as interval/ratio level data is concerned, when two variables of this scale are compared the number and diversity of values rules out a cross-tabulation. Instead the variables are plotted against each other to produce a scattergram. Thus if, for example, our sample contained the variable 'income', this could be plotted against the other interval level variable 'years as employee'. The result would then look something like Figure 24.5 below with each point on the scattergram representing each respondent's position in relation to the two variables under examination.

The interpretation of this graph in terms of the relationship between 'income' and 'years as employee' relates to the amount of dispersion or scatter of the points in the graph – the less scattered the points the stronger the relationship and vice versa. In this case the points are quite widely dispersed and for this particular sample there appears to be no relationship between the two variables. This is probably due to the fact that the plot includes people who fall into different 'job categories', a variable which no doubt intervenes between 'income' and 'years as employee' thus affecting their relationship.

This concludes our brief look at bivariate analysis – a vast topic which deserves a more thorough investigation if such techniques are to be employed.

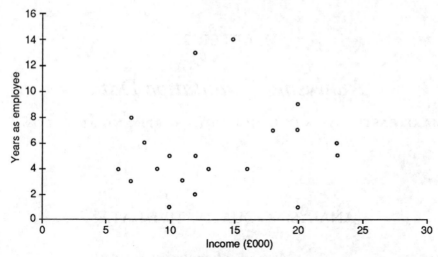

FIGURE 24.5 Scattergram of income versus years as employee

## CONCLUSION

In attempting to cover a wide range of techniques to suit various types of data this chapter has been limited to more general description. However, by introducing the more fundamental concepts of statistical analysis I hope to provide interested readers with a clear and straightforward guide as to how to go about the business of ordering and summarizing data.

As regards the use of computers, if you have the software available I would recommend that you use it. Relatively basic statistical software is available for all the major types of computer – PCs, Macintosh and Acorn. Once mastered, the benefits of this means of analysis are numerous. All the charts and tables in this chapter, for example, were prepared using a computer and in a fraction of the time needed had they been produced by hand.

## REFERENCES

Bryman, A. and Cramer, D. (1990) *Quantitative data analysis for social scientists.* Routledge.

Reid, S. (1987) *Working with statistics. An introduction to quantitative methods for social scientists.* Polity Press.

Steven, S. S. (1946) On the theory of scales of measurement, *Science,* Vol. 103, pp. 677–80.

# CHAPTER 25

# *Analysing Qualitative Data*

MARK EASTERBY-SMITH, RICHARD THORPE AND ANDY LOWE

## ANALYSING QUALITATIVE DATA

### Methods of analysis

To some extent the issues related to the analysis of qualitative data are a micro-cosm of those between positivist and social constructionist approaches. As one colleague once remarked, 'The debate is between rigour and rigor mortis'.

If the researcher is undertaking her research from a social constructionist perspective, then she will attempt as far as is possible not to draw a distinction between the collection of data and its analysis and interpretation. Indeed, the very word 'data', as something existing independently from the researcher, will be anathema. The nature of the problem being investigated and the philo-sophical stance taken will dictate the relationship of the research process. Exploratory research will place considerable emphasis on specifying research objectives. Research concerned with testing hypotheses will place emphasis on the data collection stage.

Secondly, within this apparently linear structure are a series of learning cycles. These have been described by Kolb (1986) as a four-stage process: concrete experience, reflective observation, abstract conceptualization and ac-tive experimentation. For example, the researcher might try out different ideas at one or a number of stages in the research process. She might then allow a period of time to elapse during which she can begin to think more clearly about the implications of her actions. The abstract conceptualization phase is where the researcher might use wider frames of reference to illuminate what she has experienced in order to allow her intellect and creativity to externalize the ideas in new and interesting ways. Finally, during the active experimentation stage the researcher might test out these new insights or ideas and so continue round the learning cycle until a clear understanding is reached.

Many researchers after collecting qualitative data spend a great deal of time turning it into numbers or otherwise attempting to quantify it. They recognize that numbers have a seductive air and sometimes, thinking politically of the acceptabil-ity of their findings, they gear their data to quantitative statements. Others argue that doing this spoils the richness of the data, often so painstakingly collected, and fails to give the holistic view so important in qualitative research.

TABLE 25.1

*Differences between 'content analysis' and 'grounded theory'*

| CONTENT ANALYSIS | GROUNDED THEORY |
| --- | --- |
| Bitty | Holistic |
| Go by frequency | Go by feel |
| Objectivity | Closer to the data, open much longer |
| Deductive | Inductive |
| Testing hypotheses | Testing out themes, developing patterns |

Even here at the analysis stage it can be seen how the philosophical links still remain, and for many managers or funders the political need for numbers wins through against the researcher's best intentions. These debates lead to two basic ways of analysing qualitative data. In one, often known as content analysis, the researcher 'goes by numbers' and 'frequency'; in the second, which we label 'grounded theory', the researcher goes by feel and intuition, aiming to produce common or contradictory themes and patterns from the data which can be used as a basis for interpretation. This second approach is much less bitty: researchers need to stay close to the data and any observations made have to be placed carefully in context. Classically, the data used in this type of research is kept out on the table and available for scrutiny. The main implications of these two approaches to data analysis are shown in Table 25.1.

### Content analysis

[This involves] certain key phrases or words being counted, and the frequencies analysed. The selection of these would depend on the hypothesis the researcher wished to prove or disprove. [. . .]

Richard [Thorpe] worked in a research team that used a similar kind of systematic approach. Firstly, material was read and themes and statements were collected. Early problems were encountered as field notes had been used rather than verbatim tape recordings. It was therefore necessary to assume that if something had been mentioned then it had happened, if it wasn't then it hadn't. This was far from satisfactory. Secondly, three sets of interviews that were good and fat were examined by a researcher, and coding was established from key interviews. This meant that key issues the researcher wished to explore in further interviews were marked down one axis and the interviewees' numbers across the other.

Thirdly, this frame, once established, was discussed with a number of researchers and modified in the light of apparent inconsistencies. Fourthly, following the pilot study, a workshop was organized at which a number of researchers met to agree the definition of terms and the interpretation that might be placed on the three sets of interviews used. A check then showed that errors had been reduced to an acceptable level between coders.

Reasons for the introduction of an incentive scheme

| Content analysis | 1 | 2 | 3 | 4 | 5 | 6 | 7 | 8 | Total |
|---|---|---|---|---|---|---|---|---|---|
| To increase profits | | | | | | | | | |
| To increase productivity | / | / | / | / | / | / | / | /// | 10 |
| To increase production/output | | | / | / | | | | | 2 |
| To increase efficiency | / | / | | / | | / | / | ++++ // | 12 |
| To increase labour flexibility | | | | | | | | / | 1 |
| To increase earnings | // | / | | / | | / | / | // | 8 |
| To increase employee identification with company | | | | | | | | | |
| To reduce production costs | | | | | | | | | |
| To reduce absenteeism | | | | | | / | | | 1 |
| To reduce wastage/rejects | | | | | | | | | |
| To reduce overtime | | | | | | | | | |
| To reduce labour turnover | / | | | | | | | | 1 |
| Not interested | | | | | | | | | |
| To improve timekeeping | | | | | | | | | |
| To provide an incentive | / | | | | | | | // | 3 |
| To pay a bonus | / | / | | / | | | / | | 4 |
| To alter differentials | | | | | | | | | |
| To alter relativities | | | | | | | | | |
| To prevent industrial unrest | | | | | | | | | |
| To circumvent incomes policy | | | | | | | | | |
| Not to circumvent incomes policy | | | | | | | | | |
| To change production organization | | | | | | | | | |
| To replace a previous scheme | / | | | | | | | | 1 |
| To keep people employed | | | | | | | | | |
| To allow employee profit sharing | | | | | | | | | |
| To stop threatened/actual strike | | | | | | | | | |
| To reduce the labour force | | | | | | | | | |
| To get more staff | | | | | | | | | |

43

FIGURE 25.1 Example of content analysis coding sheet

So far at least the information had all been derived from the data, although many of the themes for which we had searched had been assessed as 'relevant' prior to analysis. Following this, all the interviews were examined for the presence of the themes which were coded on sheets for computer analysis. New themes that occurred in later interviews were handled in a flexible way and added into the framework. An example of such a framework is included in Figure 25.1. At a later date, using this method, it was possible to compare answers derived from interviews with those derived from questionnaires, moreover it was possible to separate these into definite responses and probable repsonses.

In some ways the method is halfway between a positivist approach and a more grounded approach. This method is commonly used when frequencies are required from qualitative or unstructured data to be added to a larger computer model; similarly when open questions occur in an otherwise structured interview or questionnaire, responses will be coded and added into the larger analytic framework. However, one should still remember that if this type of content analysis is undertaken, although the researcher will be able to understand what the concepts are, he [or she] will be unlikely to understand why the ideas occur and why individuals interpret things or issues in their different ways.

## Grounded theory

This provides a more open approach to data analysis which is particularly good for dealing with transcripts. It recognizes that the large amounts of non-standard data produced by qualitative studies make data analysis problematic. In quantitative data analysis an external structure is imposed on the data, which makes analysis far more straightforward. With qualitative data, however, the structure used has first to be derived from the data. This means systematically analysing it so as to tease out themes, patterns and categories. As Jones (1987) comments, grounded theory works because 'rather than forcing data within logico-deductively derived assumptions and categories, research should be used to generate grounded theory, which "fits" and "works" because it is derived from the concepts and categories used by social actors themselves to interpret and organise their worlds' (p. 25).

The approach of Glaser and Strauss (1967) [to grounded theory] has been taken further by researchers such as Turner (1981, 1983) and we find his method useful in processing and sifting through volumes of non-standard data. In order to make the procedure more understandable we explain it in the following way, based on personal experiences and those of our colleagues. The method assumes that one is working with transcripts of in-depth interviews – one of the more intractable analysis problems. We consider that there are seven main stages to such analysis:

*(1) Familiarization* Re-read the data transcripts again. Doing this will enable some first thoughts to emerge: be aware and notice interesting things. When reading, draw on unrecorded information as well as recorded. This is where the fieldnotes and personal diary come into the analytic process. Note should be taken of, for example, the relationships established between the researcher and the people interviewed, the general attitude of the respondent, and the

level of confidence felt about the data that was offered. Nuances and intonation may also be important at this stage, so going back to the recorded interviews and listening to them again may be important.

The researcher may begin to doodle or jot down some first ideas. The stage, however, is essentially exploratory, where questions begin to be framed.

*(2) Reflection* At this stage desperation may begin to set in. There is usually so much rich data that trying to make sense of it seems an impossible task. Often researchers find that they have missed some crucial issues which should have been explored, but which for some reason were not. A process of evaluation and critique becomes more evident as the data is evaluated in the light of previous research, academic texts and common sense explanations. The kind of questions that researchers might ask themselves are:

- Does it support existing knowledge?
- Does it challenge it?
- Does it answer previously unanswered questions?
- What is different?
- Is it different?

In order to undertake this stage successfully it is often necessary to be aware of previous research, models and ideas. Cataloguing is important here so that previous research can be considered and evaluated. Ideas begin to be formulated and reformulated in the light of previous work. It is helpful if researchers begin to talk to other researchers or supervisors about provisional thoughts, hypotheses or ideas. This is a good way of 'testing the water' with an idea or emerging pattern.

The stage is distinctive for the volume and range of hypotheses, explanations or solutions which are still very much at the instinctive 'gut feelings' stage. These still need thinking about and might be substantiated, but haven't yet been rigorously tested.

*(3) Conceptualization* At this stage there is usually a set of concepts or variables which seem to be important for understanding what is going on. For example, in an examination of performance these might include: management style, technology, absence rates, demographic qualities of the labour force, locus of power and so on. These concepts which respondents mentioned are now articulated as explanatory variables.

However, at this stage the researcher will not be sure just how reliable or valid these concepts are: do they really relate in a consistent way to how the individual views an issue, or has there been misinterpretation of what has been said? What is needed, therefore, is for the researcher to go back to the data and search for them, methodologically highlighting them when they appear. There are a number of different ways this can be done but we find that different coloured pens are a useful device, or one can write code words in the enlarged right-hand margin of the transcript.

At this stage the researcher may well come across more concepts which were previously missed, and these can be added to the list.

*(4) Cataloguing concepts* Once it is established that the concepts identified do seem to occur in people's explanations, then they can be transferred on to

| *Labour turnover* | | | |
| *Interview* | *Page* | *Line* | |
| 4 | 3 | 7 | Others' motives |
| 11 | 2 | 18 | Effect on production |
| 4 | 9 | 23 | Management policies |

FIGURE 25.2 Index card for cataloguing concepts in interviews

cards as a quick reference guide. When this is done there is an issue of labelling. Do you use the language of the people concerned when labelling or do you use your own terms? Our view is that it is probably helpful at this stage to use your own terms, providing a trace is kept of how they were derived.

One way in which it can be achieved is by using a card index in which the concepts on, say, labour turnover are written down. The entry on the card needs to give the reference to its source in the transcripts, and it may be further elaborated with a word or phrase which indicates the content. Figure 25.2 shows an example of such a card.

However, it should be noted that, although it is systematically seductive, not everyone agrees that this is always a good approach. Writing on cards, or using a computer database tends to mechanize what ought to be an intuitive process, thus damaging the power of explanation and in a sense acquiescing to the need to 'play the game'. Even Turner (1981) concedes that the intuitive approach can produce 'brilliant material' and suggest that the card approach might be more suited to beginners to ensure that nothing is missed out.

*(5) Recoding* Now that all the references to particular concepts are known, it will be possible to go back quickly and easily to those places in the data to see what was actually said. It may, for example, be noticed that some concepts were used within different contexts or were used to explain different phenomena. Similarly, it may be found that what the respondent meant by a particular concept was different to what was understood by it. Or that different people in the same organization were defining differently what appear at face value to be similar concepts. It may even be the case that there are just too many concepts/variables to be manageable. This is an indication that the coding framework might be too refined, but an equal danger is that it is too crude, or too simplistic. For any of these reasons recoding will be necessary. When any recoding is undertaken, interpretation and analysis also take place.

For example, it may be the case that a number of people used the concept of flexibility as an explanation for why their organization survived the recession in the early 1980s. But on probing what people meant by flexibility, it might be found that some people were talking about labour mobility, some were talking about flexible working hours, while others were talking about flexibility in strategic directions.

So, at this stage, concepts are beginning to be redefined and recoded. As we indicated earlier it may well prove necessary to collapse some of the codes used into more general ones. This is called laddering. Laddering can take place both up and down – that is by enlarging or collapsing codes.

*(6) Linking*  By now the analytical framework and explanations should be becoming clearer, with patterns emerging and concepts spotted that could fit together. There should be a clearer hypothesis based on the evidence which has been gathered and organized. One can now begin to link all the variables which have been identified as important into a more holistic theory. This involves linking empirical data with more general models and it takes the form of tacking backwards and forwards between the literature and the evidence collected in practice.

This stage often produces a first draft which can be used to try out on others, thus exposing the argument and data to scrutiny. It is important therefore that this draft is presented to others, either to colleagues in the field, or to the respondents themselves.

*(7) Re-evaluation*  In the light of the comments of others, the researcher may feel that more work is needed in some areas. For example, the analysis may have omitted to take account of some factors or have overemphasized others. Following a consideration of issues such as these the first draft is rewritten, taking into account the criticisms made and contradictions highlighted. This stage may go on for a considerable period of time, and as with the other stages it may have to be undertaken more than once.

This approach can be applied to almost any kind of qualitative data. As with other methods of data collection a critical peer group of researchers can be useful in the early stages of research to suggest new categories as well as assist with interpretation of the data. The researcher may well feel that for much of the time the analysis of qualitative data is chaotic and extremely messy. A colleague of Richard's had his dining room out of commission for some four weeks whilst cards littered the table and floor and covered the walls. The themes he developed as a result were well worth the inconvenience. Bott (1971) has noted that 'one is caught in a dilemma between succumbing to confusion or choosing some simple, plausible but false explanation. We decided to succumb to confusion in the hope that it would be temporary.'

As with many systematic approaches, the method outlined is not without its critics. It can be argued that the systematic nature of the process to provide rigour for academic 'peer' assessment does harm to itself and in a sense becomes a reductionist approach. The argument is that research and analysis in qualitative data is about 'feel' and an implicit component of all research is the honesty of the person conducting the research.

## ANALYSING STRUCTURED INTERVIEWS OR QUESTIONNAIRES

The procedure outlined above is useful for a large volume of unstructured, in-depth data. The approach is time consuming and costly, and requires verbatim transcripts to be available.

But in applied research, especially where a large number of interviews may have been conducted by different people, a less time-consuming and more standardized approach is necessary. This must allow the researcher to draw key features out of the data, whilst at the same time allowing the richness of some of the material to remain for illustration purposes.

Miles and Huberman (1984) put forward a method of analysing qualitative data that is both simple and rigorous. For the method to be used effectively, the data needs to have been collected by means of a semi-structured questionnaire where respondents have been allowed to write their views on a number of open questions, or by means of a semi-focused interview as described by Merton and Kendal (1957). These methods are used when the researcher feels she knows fairly well what she is after but sees that a greater insight might be gained from permitting the respondent to choose his own path. The broad parameters though are very clearly set by the researcher.

In this type of analysis conceptual frameworks are encouraged and are used as boundary devices that need not work as strait jackets (Miles and Huberman, 1984, p. 29). Further, these frameworks can be revised to make them more precise as the research progresses.

Analysis of the data resulting from this method of inquiry is generally accomplished by drawing up the questions on a specially prepared matrix or analysis sheet. All the specific questions are drawn up along the top of the page, and the respondents are identified down one margin. The researcher then works through each interview or questionnaire in turn, cataloguing the various responses made to the main themes for which information is sought. What emerges from such analysis are visual patterns or themes that can either be qualified by reference to the individual transcripts, or quantified if numbers permit the use of statistical treatments. Those wishing to explore the various ways in which this might be done in relation to the particular focus of their study are recommended to read Miles and Huberman (1984).

[. . .]

# CONCLUSION

In this chapter we have attempted to provide an overview of some of the main ways of capturing qualitative data and making sense of it. A commitment to qualitative research is likely to derive from the researcher's view about which features of the world are significant and relevant to his enterprise. The key question is whether the quality of experience is more important than the frequency of opinions and events.

This choice is likely to be influenced by many other factors, including the nature of the research focus, and the politics of research funding and of individual careers. On the other hand the choice of methodological stance will constrain the uses to which research may be put. It is likely that qualitative research will relate to the needs and interests of those being researched. But this is by no means inevitable: it depends on the purpose and ethical positions of those conducting and sponsoring research.

Along the road of qualitative research there are also many dilemmas. There is the problem of public access to private experiences, and the difficulty of deciding how and when to impose any interpretive frameworks on this. There is the question of how accurate one's information is, and how 'accurate' it needs to be, or can be. And there is the continual tension underneath the research process between creating meanings and counting frequencies.

# REFERENCES

Bott, E. (1971) *The Family and Social Networks.* New York: The Free Press.

Glaser, D. J. and Strauss, A. L. (1967) *The discovery of grounded theory: strategies for qualitative research.* New York: Aldine.

Jones, S. (1987) Choosing action research: a rationale, in I. L. Mangham (ed.) *Organisational analysis and development.* Chichester: Wiley.

Kolb, D. A. (1986) *Experiental learning.* Englewood Cliffs, NJ: Prentice Hall.

Merton, R. K. and Kendal, P. C. (1957) *The student physician.* Cambridge MA: Harvard University Press.

Miles, M. B. and Huberman, A. M. (1984) *Qualitative data analysis: a source book of new methods.* London: Sage.

Turner, B. A. (1981) Some practical aspects of qualitative data analysis: one way of organizing the cognitive processes associated with the generation of grounded theory, *Quality and quantity*, Elsevier Scientific Publishing, Amsterdam: 15: 225–47.

Turner, B. A. (1983) The use of grounded theory for the qualitative analysis of organisational behaviour, *Journal of Management Studies,* Vol. 20, no. 3, pp. 333–48.

# CHAPTER 26

# Using a Computer for Personal Efficiency

ROSALIND LEVAČIĆ

The most significant technological development in my working life has been, without a doubt, the personal computer. The first lengthy piece of writing I did, a textbook on economics, was a product of the mechanical age. I borrowed from my husband-to-be an inherited sturdy pre-war Olympia typewriter which, despite its weight, claimed to be portable. I wrote and corrected by hand and then typed up the publisher's version. My typing, acquired in a short Pitman's course was, and still is, highly unreliable. By the time I had tippexed out all my mistakes the typewriter was clogged with white congealed globules and needed a complete overhaul. All the graphs had to be drawn carefully by hand using graph paper, ruler, protractor, compass and a set of plastic curves. All calculations were done on a simple handheld calculator. When I moved to The Open University, although I now had the services of a secretary, I found that as someone with illegible handwriting and a habit of crossing out words and rearranging clauses, it took a long time to prepare a manuscript which I could reasonably expect a secretary to cope with.

So the advent of the personal computer has been a major liberation and a great source of increased personal efficiency. Since I started to word process the pace of technological improvement has been wonderfully rapid. In 1984 I began with a BBC B computer, and a Japanese printer with a manual so incomprehensible that it took many weeks before we had fathomed out how to get page numbers printed out and never discovered how to get £ signs. The files were saved on tape and it took nine tapes to accommodate my first article.

Now, the accepted standard is a sophisticated word processor that has more features than I could ever need, a fast computer processor, a large hard disk and a high-quality printer which produces a standard and variety of print that far surpasses the typewriter. In addition I can do calculations on a spreadsheet and turn the numbers into graphs or into tables in the word processor. On my own at home I can now produce a quality of work that previously required a secretary, graphic designer and a print setter.

In this chapter I am going to outline the main tasks which one can undertake on a personal computer in order to produce professional reports and papers, starting with the recording and storing of information, through to its analysis and ending with the published product. Except where indicated all the forms of usage and related programs are suited to small-scale research.

# WORD PROCESSING

Being able to word process is becoming as necessary a skill in modern life as driving a car. It is much easier to be a poor typist if you are word-processing than if you are using a typewriter because you can so easily correct any mistakes. You can also use the spelling checker in the word processor to correct typing and other spelling errors. There are now even utilities which correct grammar. As I write this I am using my poor touch-typing skills and correcting mistakes as I see them come up on the screen. I found that it was surprisingly easy to make the transition from composing with pen and paper to writing directly to computer. I could not compose with a typewriter because it is so difficult to correct mistakes. However, when using a word processor one does tend to make typographical mistakes one would not make when writing by hand and which are not usually picked up by a spelling checker. For example when redrafting work, I sometimes fail to delete all the necessary words. It is therefore necessary to read through a piece which requires first-class presentation very carefully. I find it is most effective for spotting errors to read a hard copy and not from the screen and, if possible, to leave proof reading until a few days after completing the piece so that one comes to it afresh.

You can learn to type either by going to an evening course or by practising with a teach-yourself typing computer program. All word processor packages come with a set of tutorials which you can work your way through, as well as a manual and on-line help (in the word processor itself) for looking things up. There are also plenty of part-time courses on word processing and some employers, like The Open University, provide courses. However, it is not difficult to teach yourself to word process at least as far as the basics: I had been word processing for several years before I went on a course.

A word processor has a number of uses in research apart from writing out the final report and presenting it to a high standard. First of all it can be used to record information. The advantage of doing this rather than keeping records in handwritten or photocopy form is that you can rearrange the text very easily by moving it around the document or from one file to another. Notes you make of books and documents, such as summaries and selected extracts, can be stored on computer. You can even save yourself the trouble of typing if you can get hold of an optical scanner which will read the document directly into the computer. I transcribe taped interviews to computer. I do this myself since I have found using a secretary is no saving in time at all. Someone unfamiliar with the subject and who did not conduct the interview finds it much more difficult to transcribe the dialogue accurately. Consequently I found myself having to spend time going through the transcript correcting it and even having to play back the tape to fill in missing words. Ethnographic researchers claim it takes six to seven hours secretarial transcription time to one hour of interview whereas I find it takes me no more than a two to one ratio, given that I am not interested in transcribing every word with complete accuracy but with getting a reliable record of a person's views on a set of issues. Transcribing also ensures that I go through the interview material again and recall it. As it is a relatively mindless task, transcribing can be done when one is feeling tired or facing lots of domestic interruptions.

Having been stored in a word processor interviews can be prepared for analysis using the computer. This can be done in a number of ways starting from the simplest and extending to the use of special text manager computer programs. The simplest method is to categorize each interview under a series of subtopics. This is quite straightforward if you have used a structured or semi-structured interview schedule. For instance, in the interview of teachers I undertook for the case study on 'Improving student achievement by using value-added examination performance indicators' in Crawford *et al.* (1994), I collapsed the issues covered in the interview schedule to five topics: construct validity (of the performance indicator or PI), computation of the PI, student achievement, departmental PIs and departmental responses, and responses to teacher PIs. All relevant passages from each interview were copied and grouped under the appropriate heading in the 'analysis' document and labelled with a code for each interviewee. In this way I found it relatively easy to develop a structure for the report and to summarize the main findings under each topic and to select appropriate quotations.

Another method of 'managing' text is to use the 'FIND' command in the word processor in order to search through interview data or documentary material. You can just search through for key words and collect together all passages which refer to a given word or phrase, remembering to record their source (e.g. interviewee, site and date of interview). A more sophisticated approach is to code each paragraph of the original text with two or three key words, prefaced by a symbol such as @ so that @marketing is distinct from marketing. Provided you have labelled each paragraph with its source, you can then copy all paragraphs which refer to the same topic in one place, each labelled with its own source.

These forms of text management are quite adequate for small-scale research and a considerable advance on card indexes or cutting up several duplicate copies of written text in order to reorganize it. For larger-scale research, or for those already familiar with these programs, there are specialist 'text management' programs which enable you to code all your text using a complex set of hierarchically arranged topic codes. You can then assemble and print out different permutations of text under the same topic headings, with the source attached. A popular PC text manager is Ethnograph, while for Macintosh users there is Hyperqual which will directly manage text saved in Word. An alternative for expert users of a sophisticated word processor, such as Word for Windows, is to program it to act as a text manager. My 14-year-old son wrote a simple text manager in Word so all it takes is a willingness to learn the more arcane parts of the program.

Used in these ways a computer is a great aid to the analysis of qualitative data, but it cannot do the thinking for you. However, the ease with which you can rearrange and summarize text is a considerable aid to the process of analysis. For instance in a medium-scale study of the impact of formula funding, we coded interview data from 11 schools using Hyperqual and printed out the interviews rearranged under topic codes. In order to discover any patterns in spending decisions, I summarized the budget decisions under a set of common headings for all 11 schools set out in the matrix format in Table 26.1 – for just two of the schools. In this way one can absorb and make more sense of a lot of information because it is categorized and summarized. For further advice on using a personal computer for qualitative data anlysis you could consult Dey (1993).

*Improving Educational Management*

## TABLE 26.1

*Example of using a summary matrix when undertaking qualitative analysis using a word processor*

*continued*

| SCHOOL | RETIREMENTS | ESTABLISHMENT | NEW APPOINTMENTS | INCENTIVE ALLOWANCES AND CONDITIONS | HEAD'S/ DEPUTIES' PAY | SPECIAL NEEDS | INSET |
|---|---|---|---|---|---|---|---|
| Harrimore (lost £30– 40,000). Managed to stay on even keel | Deputy. Saved £22,000. Two temporary contracts | Deputy not replaced; savings used to fund LEA items: community tutor and school counsellor; family room; home–school links, primary/ sec. classroom. One teacher reappointed. Down from 53 to 51 teachers | 90/91 Permanent supply teacher appointed. Did not take out supply insurance. 91/92 Supply insurance (£3,000) | No change | | 1990/91 sustained at old level | |

| SCHOOL | RETIREMENTS | ESTABLISH-MENT | NEW APPOINT-MENTS | INCENTIVE ALLOWANCES AND CONDITIONS | HEAD's/DEPUTIES' PAY | SPECIAL NEEDS | INSET |
|---|---|---|---|---|---|---|---|
| Fenmore | | Priority to avoid redundancies. Technically overstaffed by 2 while science needs 1 more. Use of link hours. 91/92: pay for 1 FTE science and 0.6 languages from TVEI and lettings (£15,000). Unit teaching cost 1991/92 is £1,352. | | 1990/91: Unable to implement new agreed structure. Free meals and cover after 1 day kept – for staff morale. 1991/92: Some new IAs (£5,000). Withdraw plans to cut INSET | | Spent more than special needs allowance 0.5 short-term contract. 91/92 0.5 FTE appointed. £8,000 | Flexibility has helped |

## REFERENCES AND BIBLIOGRAPHIES

Computers have also replaced card indexes for keeping references and compiling bibliographies. I used to keep card indexes and would have several boxes for different subject areas in which I added references as I came across them. However, I could only assign each reference to one topic and not to the author unless I made out further cards for the same reference. Also if I ever wanted to reference the book or article in my writing I would have to write it all out again.

Using a reference program for a computer has a number of advantages: it saves space, it enables you to allocate several topics to one reference and you can search for and extract references either by topic or author and put them in a document, or make lists of references for further research or bibliographies. Hypercard on the Macintosh can be used for this purpose, or you can use a database program such as D Base III for the PC. You can also use the card index in Windows on a PC. However, these are not ideally set up for referencing as is a program written just for academic referencing. An example of a specific referencing program for the Archimedes is Archiver costing £10.00 (*Archimedes World*, September, 1993, p. 16). I use a program called Referencer programmed in Excel by my son. There are also a good number of dedicated bibliography software packages available, cited by Baker and Carty in Chapter 15.

## SPREADSHEETS AND GRAPHICAL PRESENTATIONS

A spreadsheet is a computer program for doing calculations and presenting the results either in tables or diagrams. At the basic level of doing simple arithmetic operations, a spreadsheet is easy to learn. I am therefore surprised at the extent to which professional people still do calculations by hand calculator and present the results in handwritten form. The great advantage of a spreadsheet is that, unlike a calculator, the figures once punched in can be saved for future use, such as checking the calculation. The raw figures or the descriptive statistics derived from them can be presented in a table complete with labels and headings, as Jason Hardman shows in Chapter 24. Spreadsheets can also, depending on their power, undertake statistical analysis and perform standard statistical tests. Many spreadsheets and word processors are now integrated so that you can take a table from the spreadsheet and copy it into the word processor. The major spreadsheets enable you easily to present your numerical data in graphical form, such as bar charts, pie charts and scatter diagrams, all labelled as you require. These can then be copied into a word processor document and so become fully integrated with your report.

## FROM QUESTIONNAIRE TO GRAPHICAL PRESENTATION TO THE FINAL REPORT

An example of how useful the integration of spreadsheet and word processor is for the do-it-yourself researcher is the work I undertook for the Resourcing Sheffield Schools project. Though this was a medium-scale project the examples I use from it concerning the manipulation and presentation of data could equally well be used for smaller-scale research.

The main purpose of the Resourcing Sheffield Schools project was to develop a needs-based funding formula for schools. One element of this development was to gather, analyse and disseminate to the authority's working party on the project information about the current level and pattern of resource use in Sheffield's schools. Consequently a questionnaire was devised and sent out to all primary and secondary schools. The secondary questionnaire was eight pages long and contained 15 questions, a sample from which is shown in the box below. I set up the questionnaire in Word, using its facilities for tables and boxes. However, there are specialist programs for setting up a questionnaire, and entering it in a database and analysing the results. One example is Pin Point for the Archimedes.

---

**Extracts from questionnaire**

QUESTION 2   HOW MANY PERIODS A WEEK DO YOU HAVE IN THE SCHOOL TIMETABLE?

QUESTION 3   FOR EACH YEAR GROUP STATE THE TOTAL NUMBER OF PUPILS AND TOTAL NUMBER OF TEACHER PERIODS PER WEEK FOR WHICH PUPILS ARE TAUGHT.

Include any team teaching (other than for special needs which is enumerated in question 14) by adding in the extra teacher periods. (Exclude any periods for withdrawing pupils with special needs since these are accounted for in question 14.)

| YEAR GROUP | NUMBER OF FTE PUPILS | NUMBER OF TEACHER PERIODS A WEEK |
|---|---|---|
| YEAR 7 | | |
| YEAR 8 | | |
| YEAR 9 | | |
| YEAR 10 | | |
| YEAR 11 | | |
| LOWER 6TH | | |
| UPPER 6TH | | |

QUESTION 9   HOW MANY PERIODS A WEEK NON-CONTACT TIME DOES THE SENIOR MANAGEMENT TEAM HAVE IN TOTAL? (Include head and deputies.)

QUESTION 10   HOW MANY NON-CONTACT PERIODS PER WEEK DO THE REST OF THE TEACHING STAFF (EXCLUDING THE SENIOR MANAGEMENT TEAM) HAVE IN TOTAL? (Exclude staff who are not funded out of the budget share.)

The main purpose of question 3 in the questionnaire was to find out the average class size across all subjects in which pupils in each year group were taught, since the allocation of teachers to pupils is the largest item of expenditure in school budgets. This issue is highly pertinent to formula construction since the average class size a pupil is taught in is the prime determinant of the amount of money needed per pupil. We were also interested in finding out how average class size varied with year group, with size of school and with the additional amount of extra funding then received in the formula for educational disadvantage, as this ranged widely across schools from an average of £17 per pupil to £362. In order to analyse the data obtained from question 3 (and related questions on the number of teacher periods a week) the data were entered into a spreadsheet. This was set out so that the schools were 'cases' appearing in the rows, while the figures reported in each question, such as number of pupils in Year 7 and number of teacher periods per week in Year 7 appeared as 'fields' in the columns. Average class size was worked out by multiplying the number of pupils times the number of weekly periods in the timetable (e.g. 35 if the school had seven periods a day) and dividing this multiple by the total number of teacher periods taught in the week. Clearly, the more teacher periods a week are taught the smaller must be the average class size, for a given number of pupils and weekly periods in the timetable. Such calculations are performed very quickly on a spreadsheet, in this case Microsoft Excel for Windows. This has a very good graphics facility so that one can quite easily display the numerical data in diagrammatic form. For example, Figure 26.1 displays the average class size across all secondary schools in each of the year groups. This shows three distinct bands of class size and provided evidence which the steering group used to recommend that the new funding formula weights for teaching costs should be the same for Years 7 to 9, higher but the same for Years 10 and 11 and still higher but common for Years 12 and 13. Previously the LEA had funded Years 7 to 9 differentially and had a steeper increase for Years 10 and 11.

As the LEA's existing formula contained a small-schools allowance as well as additional funding for educational disadvantage, it was important to investigate the relationship between average class size, size of school and amount of

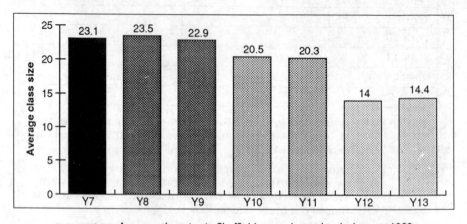

FIGURE 26.1 Average class size in Sheffield secondary schools: January 1992

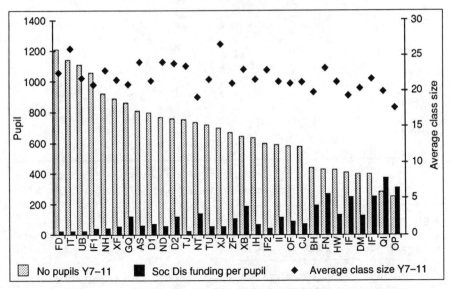

FIGURE 26.2 Class size compared to school size and social disadvantage funding per pupil

educational disadvantage funding per pupil. One way of doing this without using any statistical techniques is to graph the relationships, as is done in Figure 26.2. As this shows three variables in a two-dimensional graph, two of them are measured on the left-hand axis. These are the number of Year 7 to 11 pupils and the amount of educational disadvantage funding per pupil received by each school. Average class size, which is on a different numerical scale, is measured on the right-hand axis. Each school is represented by two bars, one for size and the other for disadvantage funding, and by a diamond, showing average class size at the school for Years 7 to 11. Schools are ordered from left to right by size and this shows the tendency for the smallest schools, which happen to be those in the inner city areas, to receive the most funding per pupil for social disadvantage. It can be seen that while some of the smallest schools with the highest proportions of socially disadvantaged pupils do have the smallest classes this is by no means universal. These data supported the recommendation to discontinue the small-schools allowance, since there was no evidence that smaller schools needed to run smaller classes in the lower years, whereas their need to run smaller classes to offer a range of options in Years 10 to 11 could be funded out of the educational disadvantage supplement.

The different choices between having smaller classes and a higher contact ratio for teachers or larger classes and a lower contact ratio which the survey revealed is shown in Figure 26.3. Four categories of school, differentiated according to the amount of educational disadvantage funding per pupil, are indicated by different symbols in the diagram. As one would expect, schools with higher amounts of educational disadvantage funding per pupil appear to the extreme left-hand side whereas schools with low amounts of educational disadvantage funding appear to the right. However, both high and low

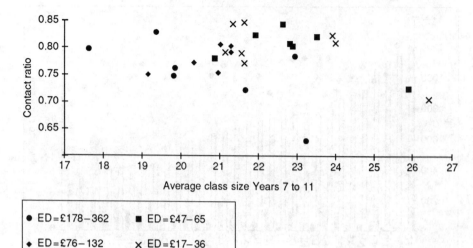

FIGURE 26.3 Average class size and contact ratio (for teachers who are not members of the senior management team) by schools grouped according to educational disadvantage funding per pupil

disadvantage funded schools are strung out from top left to bottom right, indicating that schools with both high and low disadvantage funding traded-off class size against teacher contact time. Not all schools with a high proportion of educationally disadvantaged pupils opted for small classes. One, in particular, chose to have much lower contact time. Similarly, schools with low disadvantage funding differed in their choices between class size and contact time.

When preparing the final report (Jesson and Levačić, 1992) it was possible to copy all the charts from Excel into Word, place them in appropriate parts of the text, as I am doing in this chapter, and to send off the disk to the authority to merge with the other contributions for their report for desktop publishing.

If you wish to illustrate your report with diagrams or other illustrations, not derived from numerical data, then you can use a drawing program, such as those supplied with Windows, Macintoshes and Archimedes. These also integrate with word processors. In addition images can be scanned into these programmes. One can even store and reproduce sounds in one's document given the required software and hardware.

## CONCLUSION

Personal computers are becoming steadily more powerful as well as cheaper. They are becoming more widespread in all educational institutions so enabling staff to have increased access to them. Many secondary schools are opting for PCs in order to use business standard software with students. However, Archimedes also has integrated word processing, spreadsheet and drawing packages.

To become a computer user does take some investment in time and also money, if your employer does not provide you with a PC, but it is an investment which is very worth while and which can be made gradually. Unlike driving, you can start computing with minimum competence without an instructor beside you and improve with practice. Being able to use a personal computer raises personal efficiency in tasks you do anyway, and opens up new methods of working that are not otherwise available without accessing the skills of other people. It enables you to present your work to a high standard, now increasingly expected of professional people. It also enables you to meet deadlines, without having to plan several weeks ahead because of the need to involve other people. Using a PC promotes personal efficiency, creativity and independence.

# REFERENCES

*Archimedes World* (Acorn) (1993) 'Archiver', September, p. 16.

Crawford, M., Kydd, L. and Parker, S. (eds) (1994) *Educational Management in Action*. London: Paul Chapman.

Dey, I. (1993) Introducing computers, in *Qualitative data analysis*. London: Routledge.

Jesson, D. and Levačić, R. (1992) Survey of current resourcing practice, *Resourcing Sheffield schools*, Sheffield City Council.

# CHAPTER 27

# *Writing the Report*

JUDITH BELL

## GETTING STARTED

When all the hard work of gathering and analysing evidence is complete, you will need to write the final report. Bogdan and Biklen, writing about the problems of getting started, offer the following advice:

> Novice writers are big procrastinators. They find countless reasons not to get started. Even when they finally get themselves seated at their desks, they always seem to find diversions: make the coffee, sharpen the pencil, go to the bathroom, thumb through more literature, sometimes even get up and return to the field. Remember that you are never 'ready' to write; writing is something you must make a conscious decision to do and then discipline yourself to follow through.
>
> (Bogdan and Biklen, 1982, p. 172)

All this is easier said than done, and it is not only novice writers who are procrastinators, but remember that a study is not finished until it is written up and, in your original planning, time has to be allowed for writing. That does not mean that you put off thoughts of writing until all the data have been collected. If you have followed some of the earlier advice, you will already have produced an evaluation of what you have read about the topic, so you will not have to waste time going back to books and articles read some time ago. You will have your bibliographical cards in good order, with notes and useful quotations to guide your writing, and you will not have started your project unless your objectives were clear, though you may have amended your objectives as your investigation developed.

Report writing is not, or should not be, a frantic activity carried out at the end of the project. It is a process of varied stages all of which need to be recorded at the time they are completed. Your first drafts will almost certainly need to be revised and in some cases completely rewritten, but the foundations for the report should have been established at the planning stage.

Writing a report or a dissertation requires discipline and even the most experienced of researchers need to impose some sort of self-control to ensure that the task is completed on time. We all have different ways of working and what suits one person may not suit another. By a method of trial and error, you will need to work out what is best for you, but the following guidelines, which derive largely from Barzun and Graff (1977), may provide a starting point for working out your own writing plan:

(1) *Set deadlines:* You will already have set deadlines and completion dates for different sections and for the whole report in your original schedule, but plans and ideas do sometimes change during the course of an investigation. With the help of your supervisor, set a deadline for the completion of the writing and keep that date constantly in mind.

(2) *Write regularly:* Many researchers find that they need to keep regular hours and to work in the same place. They find that building up an association between work and a particular place eases the difficulty of starting to write. The aim is never to miss a writing session.

(3) *Create a rhythm of work:* Barzun and Graff (1977, p. 325) suggest that the periods of writing should be 'close enough to create a rhythm of work'. It is tempting to stop to check a reference or because you have written a certain number of words that would seem to justify breaking off at that point, but resist the temptation. Keep the momentum going.

(4) *Write up a section as soon as it is ready:* Some sections of the research will be ready for writing up before others. Whatever sequence is attempted, it is a good idea to aim at writing a minimum number of words in each writing session.

(5) *Stop at a point from which it is easy to resume writing:* If you stop at a point when the next passage is difficult, it may discourage you from resuming work promptly for the next session. It is better to stop at a point when the next session's writing can get off to a running start. [. . .]

(6) *Publicize your plans:* You may need some help from family and friends to complete your report on time. We can all find good reasons for not getting down to writing, so tell everyone about your writing routine. With any luck, they will not tempt you with invitations to the pub or incite you to watch television. They may in fact put pressure on you to get to your desk. [. . .]

## STRUCTURING THE REPORT

Opinions vary as to the order in which sections should appear, but most researchers would agree with Nisbet and Entwistle (1970, p. 168) that a report or dissertation should include the following major sections:

(1) outline of the research;
(2) review of previous work;
(3) precise statement of the scope and aims of the investigation;
(4) description of the procedure, sample and tests of measurements used (if any);
(5) statement of results;
(6) discussion;
(7) summary and conclusions;
(8) references.

Many institutions also ask for an abstract, and so the final task should be to produce a brief, succinct statement which indicates what the research set out to do, the methods used and the results obtained.

# (1) Outline of the research

The main aim of this short section is to give a clear picture of the aims, methods and results of the research. It is intended to provide a frame of reference which will allow the nature of the research to be taken in quickly. Arguments and discussions are out of place here and only the essential points of the research should be indicated.

You may find it best to write this section last, to ensure that it accurately reflects what is in the main body of the report.

# (2) Review of previous research

Not all reports will include a review of previous research, though most will. You may have used your background reading mainly to support arguments throughout the report, but the value of a review to the reader is that it explains the context and background of the study. Remember Haywood and Wragg's warning that critical reviews can too often turn out to be uncritical reviews – 'the furniture sale catalogue, in which everything merits a one-paragraph entry no matter how skilfully it has been conducted' (Haywood and Wragg, 1982, p. 2). Selection has to be made, and only books and articles which relate directly to the topic should be included.

The literature review can be written first and, if you have managed to discipline yourself sufficiently well to write up sections and subsections as you have completed them, much of the work of this section will be ready for revision before you begin to collect data. You may find that you need to adapt your original version, but you should not need to start from the beginning by reading through notes to decide what should be included and what left out.

# (3) Precise statement of the scope and aims of the investigation

This should be a brief explanation of the purpose of the research. Explain the research problem in a few sentences and mention the proposed contribution to practical or theoretical issues. Draw attention to any limitations of the study at this stage. An individual researcher with only 100 hours or so to complete a project cannot hope to become involved in complex sampling techniques nor to interview hundreds of people. You cannot do everything in a small study, and your supervisor will know that, but in this section you should make it clear that you know what the limitations of your study are.

As in section 1, you will have considered and possibly outlined this section earlier in the project, but it is probably best to write the first version of section 3 last, together with section 1.

# (4) Description of the procedure, sample and tests of measurement used (if any)

This section explains how the problem was investigated and why particular methods and techniques were employed. Accounts of the procedure, size of sample, method of selection, choice of variables and controls, and tests of measurement and statistical analyses, if any, should be provided.

Nisbet and Entwistle (1970, p. 169) point out that it is unnecessary to describe in detail any standard tests or procedures that are well known and about which further information can easily be obtained, but if subjective assessments or individually devised measurement techniques have been used, then some explanation is necessary.

All important terms and variables should be defined precisely (Turney and Robb, 1971, p. 175) and any deficiencies in the methods mentioned. It is important to bear in mind that in certain kinds of investigation, the research needs to be repeatable, and a fellow researcher should be able to obtain enough information from this section to make this possible.

## (5) Statement of results

This is the heart of the report and will consist of tables or figures and text, depending on the nature of the project. [. . .]. The way results are presented is important. Tables, charts, graphs and other figures should illustrate and illuminate the text. If they do not, then there is no point in taking up space. The text, which should be written after the results are prepared, should highlight significant aspects of the findings (Travers, 1964, p. 526) so that all relevant facts are presented in a way which draws the reader's attention to what is most important. It is quite an art to achieve this balance, and you may find you need several drafts before you are satisfied with the result.

## (6) Analysis and discussion

It is often best to start this section with a restatement of the problem before discussing how the results affect existing knowledge of the subject. If your research aimed to test certain hypotheses, then this section should demonstrate whether they were or were not supported by the evidence. Any deficiencies in the research design should be mentioned, with suggestions about different approaches which might have been more appropriate. Implications for improvement of educational practice, if any, should also be drawn out.

Most researchers find it best to write sections 4, 5 and 6 in sequence to ensure continuity and logical progression. It is quite feasible to write some sections as discrete units at different times, but these three sections need to be considered as a whole. If you have to take a break from writing, make sure you reread everything that had gone before to ensure a smooth continuation and to avoid repetition.

## (7) Summary and conclusions

The main conclusions of the report that have been discussed in section 5 should be summarized here briefly and simply. Only conclusions that can be justifiably drawn from the findings should be made. That sounds (and is) obvious, but there is often a great temptation to drop in an opinion for which no evidence is provided in the report. Take care or you may spoil a good report by including a throwaway remark.

Before you write this section, read through the whole report and make a note of key points. Readers who want a quick idea of what your research is about will look at the abstract, possibly the introduction and almost certainly at the summary and conclusions. This final section should be sufficiently succinct and clearly expressed to enable readers to understand quite clearly what research has been done and the conclusions that have been drawn from the evidence.

## (8) List of references

All reports will require a bibliography, a list of references, or both. The term 'bibliography' has several meanings. It can be used to mean a publication listing the details of material about a subject, place or person. It can be a list of works by a specific author or it can be a list of sources consulted during the preparation of an essay, project or dissertation. If you are asked to produce a bibliography for your report, that will obviously mean that you are to provide a list of sources.

Lists of references are different. They will give specific details only about books and articles which have been cited or referred to in the report. Apart from page references to journals, page numbers are not included in bibliographies, but they may be included, where appropriate, in references. If you adopt the Harvard method, then references will appear in alphabetical order, which simplifies the process and avoids overlap. If you adopt the British or another numerical system, then references will appear in the order in which they appeared in the text.

The amount of time it takes you to produce either or both in your final report will depend on how meticulous you were when you made out your reference cards. This is the time when hard work and systematic recording really pay off.

## THE MECHANICS OF PRESENTING A REPORT

### Length

Guidelines about length will be provided by your supervisor, and many institutions produce leaflets which give information about the nuts and bolts of presenting a report. If you have not been told what length is expected, ask. If a maximum number of words is stipulated, stick to that number. You may be penalized for exceeding the limit.

### Title page

Include a title page, incorporating the title of your study and your name. The title should accurately reflect the nature of your study and should be brief and to the point. A main title and subtitle may be provided if the subtitle clarifies the purpose of the study.

### Acknowledgements and thanks

You may wish to acknowledge the help given to you in the preparation of your report. If so, acknowledgements and thanks come after the title page.

## Headings

Include section headings where possible. They help the reader to follow your structure and arguments.

## Tables and figures

Not all reports will have tables and figures, but if these are to be included, they should be numbered, given a title and carefully checked before you send off your report for marking. (Tables are generally numerical presentations, in lists or columns, though there can be tables of names or other items. Figures are other types of presentation of data.)

## Quotations

All quotations must be acknowledged, Remember that your tutor has probably read the same books, so is likely to recognize the source. If you are quoting only a few words or one sentence, it will be sufficient to indicate this by using inverted commas in the main text, with the source in brackets. If words are missed out of the quotation, indicate by three full stops. For example, as Hopkins (1985, p. 78) says, 'Documents . . . can illuminate rationale and purpose in interesting ways.' If the quotation is longer, indent it and (if the report is typed), use single spacing.

As Hopkins says:

> Documents (memos, letters, position papers, examination papers, newspaper clippings, etc.) surrounding a curriculum or other educational concern can illuminate rationale and purpose in interesting ways. The use of such material can provide background information and understanding of issues that would not otherwise be available.
>
> (Hopkins, 1985, p. 78)

Some institutional guidelines ask you to put quotation marks at the beginning and end of each longer quotation; others do not, so follow the 'house' rules.

## Appendices

Copies of research instruments (questionnaires, interview schedules, etc.) that have been used should be included in an appendix, unless you have been instructed otherwise. Your tutor will not wish to receive all completed questionnaires and would no doubt be dismayed if weighty parcels arrived on the doorstep, but one copy of any data-collecting instrument that has been used is generally required.

## The abstract

In most cases, an abstract will be required, though again, practices vary so consult the 'house' rules. It is quite difficult to say in a few words what your investigation set out to do, the methods employed and what conclusions were reached. You may need several attempts before you achieve a sufficiently brief yet informative statement. The following example fulfils all the requirements of an abstract, and might serve as a model.

> This case study is an investigation into how the governing body of one comprehensive school defines its role in relation to the curriculum. It attempts to identify the influences and constraints which affect the way in which the role of the governing body is conducted in practice. Data were gathered through non-participant observation, an analysis of minutes of governors' meetings, LEA documents and a questionnaire which also acted as an interview schedule. The report concludes that there is scope for developing the partnership between the school and the governing body in relation to the curriculum and proposes ways in which this might be approached.

## Presentation

It is desirable, though not always essential for small-scale studies, that reports should be typed (check institutional rules). Typed copy should be in double spacing, with quotations (other than very short ones) indented and in single spacing. Pages should be numbered. Type or write on one side of the page only, leaving a left-hand margin of one and a half inches. Incidentally, whether you are sending your report to be typed or are submitting a handwritten copy, make sure your writing is legible. It is not fair to a typist, and it is not wise to annoy the examiner by handing in an illegible scrawl. Do not expect the typist to interpret your abbreviations or to make corrections. It is your job to hand in good copy.

## The need for revision

Barzun and Graff (1977, p. 31) remind us that 'NO ONE, HOWEVER GIFTED, CAN PRODUCE A PASSABLE FIRST DRAFT. WRITING MEANS REWRITING.' You may find you need two, three or even more drafts before you are satisfied with the final result, so time must be set aside for this writing and refining process.

One problem about spending so much time on the original draft (the most difficult part of the writing stage) is that parts of it may seem right simply because they have been read so often. Another is that you may be so familiar with the subject that you assume something is understandable to the reader when it is not. Time will give you a better perspective on your writing, so you should put the script aside – for several days if you can – so that you can return to it with a more critical eye. This will help you to identify repetitive passages, errors of expression and lack of clarity.

Work through your first draft section by section to ensure its sense, accuracy, logical sequencing and soundness of expression. [. . .]. In particular, check spelling (always have a dictionary to hand), quotations, punctuation, referencing, the overuse of certain terms (a *Roget's Thesaurus* can help you to find alternative forms of expression), and grammar (particularly consistency of tense).

Remind yourself as you read that whatever structure has been selected, your readers will wish to be quite clear why you carried out the investigation, how you conducted it, what methods you used to gather your evidence and what you found out. It is not enough to describe; you will be expected to analyse, to evaluate and if the evidence merits it, to make recommendations.

If research findings are to be put into practice, they have to be presented in a way in which practitioners and policy-makers can understand them. Please bear this in mind when you present your projects. There is no special academic language that should be used in academic papers. Good, clear English remains good, clear English, whatever the context. Technical language may well save time when you are talking to colleagues with a similar background to your own, but it rarely translates well on to paper, and your readers (and your examiner) may become irritated by too much jargon or obscure language.

The need for revision and rewriting was emphasized in a recent radio interview, when a world-famous economist who had many scholarly books to his credit, was complimented by the interviewer on his style of writing. 'It must be a great advantage to you', said the interviewer, 'to be able to write so freely and so easily. How do you do it?' The economist revealed his secret as follows:

> First I produce a draft and then I leave it alone for a day or two. Then I go back to it and decide that it has been written by an ignoramus, so I throw it away. Then I produce a second draft and leave it alone for a few days. I read it and decide there are the germs of a few good ideas there, but it is so badly written that it is not worth keeping, so I throw it away. After a few days, I write a third draft. I leave it alone for a while and when I read it again I discover that the ideas are developing, that there is some coherence to my arguments and that the grammar is not too bad. I correct this draft, change paragraphs around, insert new thoughts, remove overlapping passages and begin to feel quite pleased with myself. After a few days, I read this fourth draft, make final corrections and hand over the fifth draft to the typist. At that stage, I find I have usually achieved the degree of spontaneity for which I have been striving.

You may not need five drafts. Three may be enough if you write easily, but rest assured that no one gets away with one or two – and most of us take four or five.

When you have completed the writing to the best of your ability, try to enlist the help of someone who will read over the manuscript to look for remaining errors. Failing that, you could read your report out loud, though make sure you are alone or your family may feel the strain has been too much for you! Reading aloud is particularly useful for detecting the need for better linking passages.

Depending on what 'house' rules require, either write out a fair copy or give the final draft to the typist. If the report is to be typed, give clear instructions about layout, punctuation, headings and so on. It is your job to hand in good copy and to make it quite clear what is to be done. Check the final, typed copy. Even expert typists can make mistakes, and if your writing is bad, it is inevitable that mistakes will be made. Finally, congratulate yourself on an excellent job completed on time. Hand in the report and give yourself an evening off!

## WRITING THE REPORT: GENERAL CHECKLIST

(1) *Set deadlines:* Allocate dates for sections, subsections and the whole report. Keep an eye on your schedule.
(2) *Write regularly.*
(3) *Create a rhythm of work:* Don't stop to check references. Make a note of what has to be checked, but don't stop.
(4) *Write up a section as soon as it is ready:* Try particularly to produce a draft of the literature review as soon as the bulk of your reading is completed.
(5) *Stop at a point from which it is easy to resume writing.*
[. . .]
(6) *Publicize your plans:* You may need a little help from your friends to meet the deadlines.
(7) *Check that all essential sections have been covered:* Outline of the research, review of previous work, statement of the scope and aims of the investigation, description of procedures, statement of results, discussion, summary and conclusions, references, abstract.
(8) *Check length is according to institutional requirements:* You don't want to be failed on a technicality.
(9) *Don't forget the title page.*
(10) *Any acknowledgements and thanks?*
(11) *Include headings where possible:* Anything to make it easier for readers to follow the structure will help.
(12) *Number tables and figures and provide titles:* Check tables and figures for accuracy, particularly after typing.
(13) *Make sure all quotations are acknowledged:* Check that quotations are presented in a consistent format.
(14) *Provide a list of references:* Unless instructed otherwise, include only items to which reference is made in the report. Check that a consistent system is used and that there are no omissions.
(15) *Appendices should only include items that are required for reference purposes. Do not clutter the report with irrelevant items:* Unless instructed otherwise, one copy of each data-collecting instrument should be included.
(16) *Remember to leave sufficient time for revision and rewriting:* Check that you have written in plain English. Check that your writing is legible.
(17) *Try to get someone to read the report:* Fresh eyes will often see the errors you have overlooked.

## WRITING THE REPORT: CHECKLIST BEFORE HANDING OVER TO THE TYPIST

If you were writing a critique of a piece of research done by someone else, you might ask the following questions. Before handing over what you hope will be your final draft for typing, subject your own report to the same sort of examination. Ask yourself:

(1) Is the meaning clear? Are there any obscure passages?
(2) Is the report well written? Check tenses, grammar, spelling, overlapping passages, punctuation, jargon.
(3) Is the referencing well done? Are there any omissions?
(4) Does the abstract give the reader a clear idea of what is in the report?
(5) Does the title indicate the nature of the study?
(6) Are the objectives of the study stated clearly?
(7) Are the objectives fulfilled?
(8) If hypotheses were postulated, were they testable? Are they proved or not proved?
(9) Has a sufficient amount of literature relating to the topic been studied?
(10) Does the literature review, if any, provide an indication of the state of knowledge in the subject? Is your topic placed in the context of the area of study as a whole?
(11) Are all terms clearly defined?
(12) Are the selected methods of data collection accurately described? Are they suitable for the task? Why were they chosen?
(13) Are any limitations of the study clearly presented?
(14) Have any statistical techniques been used? If so, are they appropriate for the task?
(15) Are the data analysed and interpreted or merely described?
(16) Are the results clearly presented? Are tables, diagrams and figures well drawn?
(17) Are conclusions based on evidence? Have any claims been made that cannot be substantiated?
(18) Is there any evidence of bias? Any emotive terms or intemperate language?
(19) Are the data likely to be reliable? Could another researcher repeat the methods used and have a reasonable chance of getting the same or similar results?
(20) Are recommendations (if any) feasible?
(21) Are there any unnecessary items in the appendix?
(22) Would you give the report a passing grade if you were the examiner? If not, perhaps an overhaul is necessary.

## REFERENCES

Barzun, J. and Graff, H. E. (1977) *The modern researcher* (3rd edn). New York: Harcourt Brace Jovanovich.

Bogdan, R. C. and Biklen, S. K. (1982) *Qualitative research for education: an introduction to theory and methods.* Boston, Mass: Allyn & Bacon.

Haywood, P. and Wragg, E. C. (1982) *Evaluating the literature.* Rediguide 2, University of Nottingham School of Education.

Hopkins, D. (1985) *A teacher's guide to classroom research.* Milton Keynes: Open University Press.

Nisbet, J. D. and Entwistle, N. J. (1970) *Educational research methods*. London: University of London Press.

Travers, R. M. W. (1964) *An introduction to educational research* (2nd edn). New York: Macmillan.

Turney, B. and Robb, G. (1971) *Research in education: an introduction*. Hinsdale, Ill: Dryden Press.

# Index

abstract conceptualization, 47–8, 70–1
access, research, 174–5, 178
accountability, 101–2, 103
action research, 3, 5, 28, 41–5, 84–5, 156–66,
        300
    critique of, 44
    implementation, 43
    moments, 42
    observation, 43–4
    plan of action, 42–3
    reflection, 44
    theory from practice, 163–5
active experimentation, 47–8, 70–1
aims, 106, 109
analysis, units of, 137–8
arithmetic mean, 339
auditing, 4, 108, 117–26
    data–processing, 119
    ethnographic, 121–5
    fiscal, 117–18
    investigative, 119–20
    management consulting, 120–1
    operational, 118–19

bar charts, 336, 342, 358, 360–1
behavioural accounting, 91
behavioural change, 52–7, 61–3, 73
bibliographies, 358, 368
brainstorming, 193, 294, 317
breakdown, 88

case studies, 5, 44, 122–5, 135–54, 246, 300,
        304, 326–9
    design, 146–54
        embedded, 147–9, 153–4
        holistic, 147–9, 153–4
        multiple-case, 147–54
        single-case, 147–50, 152
    generalizing from, 141–3
    interpretation, 138–9
    pilot, 154
Central Limit Theory, 133–4
change (see also organizational change)
    behavioural, 52–7, 61–3, 73
    cultural, 28, 45
    political, 27–8, 45
    strategies for, 3
    technological, 27, 28, 45
change agents, 34–5, 40, 41, 45

cognition, 57
collaborative school management, 28–34, 38,
        45
    budgeting, 32
    critique of, 33–4
    evaluation, 33, 34
    goal setting, 30–1, 34
    implementation, 32–3, 34
    needs identification, 30–1
    planning, 32
    policy groups, 29–30, 34
    policy-making, 31
    project teams, 29–30, 34
communication, 314–17
computers, 6, 235, 260, 330, 335–6, 340,
        341, 343, 353–63
concrete experience, 48–9, 69–71
confidentiality, 44, 65, 95–6, 116, 172, 175,
        180, 244, 265, 268, 279, 288, 333, 351
conscious awareness, 46–7
consent, 93–4
construct categories, 241–2
consultancy, 4, 38, 44, 58–75, 120–5, 187–208
    client-centred, 59–63, 66, 67, 68, 74
    clients, 63–4
        real, 64, 65, 74
    contracting, 65, 66, 188–90, 197, 199–200,
        203, 207
    cycle, 65–9, 74, 200–1
    data analysis, 196–7
    data gathering, 191–6
    diagnosis, 187–20
        dilemmas, 197–200
        independent, 189
        joint, 189
        self, 189
    feedback, 200–5
        meetings, 203–5
    implementation dilemmas, 207–8
    internal consultants, 64–5, 68, 196
    intervention styles, 72–4, 75
    learning styles, 69–72
    skills, 59, 60, 74
    support, 205
content analysis, 237–46, 277–8, 345–7
co-operative inquiry, 85
copyright, 97–8
co-researchers, 161–3, 165–6
cost – see finance

counselling, 58, 73, 74
critical event, 280, 324
critical friends, 44
critical subjectivity, 89
cross-tabulation, 341–2
culture, 53–4, 56, 79–81, 82, 121–5, 195,
　　200, 237

data
　　analysis, 5, 176, 179, 196–7, 213–14, 330–43
　　　　qualitative, 344–52, 355–9
　　　　quantitative, 330–43
　　coding, 334, 345–7, 349
　　collection, 5–6, 73, 177, 213–14
　　fabrication of, 97
　　measurement, 331–2
　　presentation, 330–43
deception, 96–7
decision-making processes, 317
development, 101–2, 103
　　plans, 107, 110–12
dialectic learning, 55–6
diaries, 301–10
　　design, 302–9
　　issues, 309–10
　　reflective practice, 301–2, 310
didacticism, 55
disconformity, 88–9
documentary research – *see* literature reviews
documents – *see* records
double-loop learning, 50
drawing, 194

Education Reform Act 1988, 101
emotions, 53, 73
ethics, 4, 93–8, 116, 158–66, 178, 244, 273,
　　279, 305, 308, 310, 351
　　statement, 116
ethnography, 87–8, 157–8, 300, 328
evaluation, 4
　　data, 209–22
　　definitions, 106–8
　　instruments, 107–8, 109–10, 214–15
　　in the management cycle, 101–16
　　planned approach, 102–4
　　planning triangle, 108–11
experiential learning, 47–52, 75
　　abstract reconceptualization, 47–8, 50–1, 52
　　analysis, 49–50, 51, 52
　　experience, 47
　　experimentation, 47–8, 51–2
　　observation, 47–8, 49–51
　　problem identification, 48–51
　　reflection, 47
experimental design, 87–8
explanation-building, 145

factor analysis, 242
falsification, 88–9 (*see also* honesty)
feedback, 200–5

content, 201–2
　　meetings, 203–5
fieldwork, 87–8, 174, 176–9
files – *see* records
finance, 34, 130, 198, 297
focus group interviews, 290–8
　　analysis of results, 296
　　benefits and drawbacks, 296–7
　　conducting, 294–6
　　moderators, 292–4, 295
　　planning, 291–4, 297–8
　　service providers, 295
formal theory, 86

generalizability, 89–90
gentrification, 145, 153
grounded theory, 86–7, 345, 347–50
group exercises, 194

harm, 95
histograms, 338
honesty, 98, 350 (*see also* fabrication)

index cards, 193–4
interactive videos, 308–9
interpretism, 4
interviews, 176–8, 191–4, 197, 239, 267–82,
　　290–2, 300, 309–10
　　analysis, 277–8, 350–1
　　checklist, 281–2
　　conducting, 278–9
　　difficult topics, 279–80
　　focus group, 290–8
　　group, 193–4, 197, 268, 274
　　pilots, 271, 274, 276
　　pitfalls, 267
　　sampling, 269–70, 272, 274
　　schedule, 275–6
　　stereotypes (interviewer), 280
　　telephone, 283–8
　　timing, 270–7
　　types, 271–5
　　　　more than one interviewer, 274
　　　　semi-structured, 272–3
　　　　structured, 272
　　　　unstructured, 273
　　validity and reliability, 278

journals, 300–1 (*see also* diaries)

knowledge, 54–7, 77–9

laddering, 349
leadership, 11–25, 124–5, 161–2
　　definitions, 17
　　skills, 20–6
　　tasks, 18–20
learning
　　cycles, 344
　　styles, 69–72

libraries, 233–5
Likert scale, 253–4
literature reviews, 173, 183, 223–35, 249, 366
  computer searches, 229–3
  libraries, 223–5
  planning, 225–7
  records of, 223, 233–5
LMS, 102
logs, 300–1 (*see also* diaries)

management information systems, 244–6
managers, 81–3
market research, 290–9
meetings, 176, 196, 312–24
  checklists, 313–14
  content, 312–14
  direction, 319
  feedback, 203–5
  functional roles, 319–20, 321
  norms, 322–4
  observing, 312–24
  process, 312–19
  rate of progress, 319
  recording, 312–24
  self-oriented behaviour, 320–2
  types of, 312–13
monitoring, 4, 101–2, 111, 221
mutual adaptation, 28

non-verbal communication, 316–17

objectives, 106, 108–11
observation, 81–2, 177, 195–7, 238–9, 268,
    296, 300, 310, 312–24, 325–9
  recording, 327–9
organizational change, 11–26
  models, 14–16
  operational, 14
  strategic, 14
organizational culture, 198–9
organizational structure, 79–81, 82

paradigm, 77–81, 83, 84, 86–7, 89, 91
participant observation, 125, 182–3, 300,
    325–9
pattern-matching, 138–9, 145, 152
people-centred action, 3, 28, 34–41, 45
  assessment, 38–9
  critique of, 41
  establishing, 38
  goal-setting, 38–9
  implementation, 39–40
  institutionalization, 41
  levels of use, 37–8, 40
  reviewing, 40–1
  solution identification, 39
  stages of concern, 35–7, 40
performance
  areas, 210, 213, 216–17
  assessment, 216

indicators, 107–11, 209–22
  managing, 220–1
  responses to, 218–20
permissions, 97–8
personal reflection, 3
phenomenology, 4, 76–91, 290, 291, 292
pie charts, 336–7, 358
pilot studies, 154, 176, 251, 254, 255, 262–3,
    271, 274, 276, 288
plagiarism, 97
positivism, 4, 76–91, 182–3, 344, 347
power, 321–2
practice, 56–7
problem-solving, 317–19
professional development, 46–57
projection, 280
provision, 213

quality statements, 211–12, 214–15
questionnaires, 174, 176–7, 184, 195, 197,
    239, 248–66, 268, 272, 285–8, 350–1
  design, 259–62, 359–60
  distribution and return, 263–6
  planning, 248
  question specification, 249–59
  question structure, 251–5
    difficulty, 255–8
    suggestion, 258
  question types, 249–59
    categories, 252–3
    checklist, 252
    descriptions, 252
    lists, 252
    open, 250–1
    partial agreement, 253–4
    ranking, 255
    rating, 254–5
    semantic differential, 254
    statement/questions, 251
    structured, 250–1
    yes/no, 249–50, 251, 253, 272
quotations, 369

randomness, 87
rank ordering, 280, 331
rating scales, 254–5, 318–19, 323–4
recording units, 240–1
records, 176, 183–4, 223, 233–5
  administrative, 244–6
  analysing, 195, 237–46
  archives, 243–6
  and computers, 242–3, 245
reductionism, 350
references, 234–5, 358, 368
reflection, 46, 158, 160, 163, 165, 348
reflective
  conversation, 56
  observation, 47–8, 49–51, 69–71
  practice, 46–57, 301–2, 310
relativism, 182

reliability, 89–90, 144, 146, 219, 237, 241–3, 255, 258, 263, 278
replication, 152, 165, 218, 243, 278, 367
report writing, 6, 364–73
  checklists, 372–3
  mechanics of, 368–72
  starting, 364–5
  structure, 365–8
research design, 171, 182, 219, 239–40, 249, 291, 302–3, 309, 329, 330, 344, 345, 351, 366, 367
  choice of, 84–9
  components, 136–9
  definitions, 135–6
  in management studies, 90–1
  philosophy of, 76–91
  test of, 143–6
  theory-building, 140–3
research findings, negative, 98
research, small scale, 171–84, 274, 286–8, 330, 334, 353, 366, 370
  access, 174–5
  data analysis, 176, 179, 358–62
  data collection, 177
  dissemination, 180–1
  finishing, 178
  identifying objectives, 173–4
  instrument, 175–7
  method, 174
  planning, 171–2
  stages, 172–81
  study focus, 172–3
  writing up, 179–80, 355
researcher involvement, 84–5
reviews, 101–2, 108, 110–11, 113–15, 221
  in consultancy, 190–1, 205–6
  in schools, 114–15
rituals, 121–5
role playing, 97
rounds, 193

sampling, 85–6, 127–34, 142–3, 145, 150–3, 240, 242, 245, 263, 269–70, 272, 274, 283, 285–6, 288, 295–6
  analysis, 332–43
  error, 133–4
  non-probability, 131–2
  populations, 129–34, 142–3, 151, 286, 292–4
  probability, 130–1
  size, 132–3
scattergrams, 342–3, 358, 361–2
school improvement strategies, 3, 27–46
sculpting, 194
self-awareness, 51, 53, 60
self-evaluation, 110
self-managing school, 3
shifting goal-post syndrome, 102
single-loop learning, 50
situated cognition, 47

social constructionism, 78–9, 81, 84, 89–91, 344
social research, 171, 177, 178, 184
soft systems, 91
sponsors, 182, 351
spreadsheets, 358–62
stability, 11–12
standard deviation, 340–1
statistical techniques, 330–43, 358–62
  bivariate analysis, 341–2
  charts, 335–42
  frequency distribution, 334–9
  tables, 335–42
strategic planning, 114
strategies, 107
stress, 78
study propositions, 136 (*see also* research design)
study questions, 136
substantive theory, 86
success criteria, 209–22
  design and use, 209–18
  managing, 220–1
  responses to, 218–20
surveys, 5, 127–34, 142, 145, 151, 183–4, 246, 248, 283–4

tables, 335–42
talking walls, 193
tape-recorders, 175
target-setting, 209
tests, 268
theory, 54–6, 67–8, 86–7, 141–2, 154
  building, 140–3, 150
  development, 140–1, 151–2
  testing, 147
time, 35, 37–8, 44, 103–7, 113, 130, 172, 175, 177–9, 181, 183, 198, 277, 284, 286, 301, 305, 309, 364–5, 370
time-series analysis, 145, 245
total quality management, 157, 159
transcribing, 354
triangulation, 119, 122–3, 165, 218, 239, 241, 243

validation, 165–6
  meetings, 165–6
validity, 89–90, 218–19, 237, 243, 263, 264
  construct, 143–4, 278
  external, 144, 145–6, 153, 327
  internal, 143–5, 327
variables, 242, 331–42, 348
  central tendency, 339–41
  measures of dispersion, 340–1
verification, 88–9
video-recording, 294

word processing, 354–8, 362–3
written diagnostic tools, 195